# Knowledge as Power

## CRIMINAL REGISTRATION AND COMMUNITY
## NOTIFICATION LAWS IN AMERICA

Wayne A. Logan

Stanford Law Books
An Imprint of Stanford University Press
Stanford, California

Stanford University Press
Stanford, California

Printed in the United States of America on acid-free, archival-quality paper

Library of Congress Cataloging-in-Publication Data

Logan, Wayne A., 1960–
    Knowledge as power : criminal registration and community notification laws in America
/ Wayne A. Logan.
        p.   cm. — (Critical perspectives on crime and law)
    Includes bibliographical references and index.
    ISBN 978-0-8047-5710-2 (cloth : alk. paper)
    ISBN 978-0-8047-6136-9 (pbk. : alk. paper)
        1. Criminal registers—United States.   I. Title.   II. Series: Critical perspectives on
crime and law.
KF9751.L645   2009
345.73'077—dc22

                                                                            2008055252

# CONTENTS

To Meg, Anna, and Charlotte

# ACKNOWLEDGMENTS

THIS BOOK, LIKE MOST, benefited from the significant help of many others. I owe a special debt of gratitude to Eric Janus, Roxanne Lieb, David Logan, Daniel Solove, and Kevin Washburn, as well as outside reviewers retained by Stanford University Press, for their insights and suggestions, all of which improved the book. I also thank the many wonderful research assistants and library staff who have shared their talents over time. In particular, I thank Christopher Ewbank, Florida State University Law class of 2009, for his tireless high-caliber research support, and Margaret Clark, Marin Dell, Elizabeth Farrell, Robin Gault, Faye Jones, Mary McCormick, and Trisha Simonds, of the Florida State University College of Law Library, for their wonderful help and expertise. Finally, I am grateful for the institutional support provided me by the deans and administrators of William Mitchell College of Law and the Florida State University College of Law.

Portions of this book were adapted from the following articles: "Constitutional Collectivism and Ex-Offender Residence Exclusion Laws," *Iowa Law Review* 92 (2006): 1; "Crime, Criminals and Competitive Crime Control," *Michigan Law Review* 104 (2006): 1733; "Horizontal Federalism in an Age of Criminal Justice Interconnectedness," *University of Pennsylvania Law Review* 154 (2005): 257; "Federal Habeas in the Information Age," *Minnesota Law Review* 85 (2000): 147; "Liberty Interests in the Preventive State: Procedural Due Process and Sex Offender Community Notification Laws," *Journal of Criminal Law and Criminology* 89 (1999): 1167; "Criminal Justice Federalism and National Sex Offender Policy," *Ohio State Journal of Criminal Law* 6 (2008): 51; "Jacob's

Legacy: Sex Offender Registration and Community Notification Laws, Practice and Procedure in Minnesota," *William Mitchell Law Review* 29 (2003): 1287; and "Sex Offender Registration and Community Notification: Emerging Legal and Research Issues," in *Sexually Coercive Behavior: Understanding and Management* (Annals of the New York Academy of Sciences) (2003): 337.

# INTRODUCTION

HUMAN SOCIETIES have long felt a powerful need to identify potentially dangerous individuals in their midst, a need vividly evoked in philosopher Jeremy
Bentham's 1843 plaintive query: "Who are you, with whom I have to deal?"[1]
*Knowledge as Power* examines this phenomenon, focusing in particular on
American laws that require criminal offenders to provide authorities with
identifying information, allowing for their continued surveillance after incarceration.

While to most Americans criminal registration laws are a modern phenomenon, originating in the 1990s and eponymously associated with child
victims such as Jacob Wetterling and Megan Kanka, in reality the motivating
force behind the laws is ancient, and their direct historical antecedents lie in
the nineteenth century. One can, for instance, see clear links with predecessor
strategies such as "spotting" by police in the 1820s, whereby officers sought
to memorize the faces of convicted criminals; use of daguerreotype images
in the 1840s, later used to create the first "rogues' galleries" in police stations;
Alphonse Bertillon's "signalment" system that measured and stored data on
offenders' physical traits starting in the 1880s; and shortly thereafter (and still
today), fingerprint analysis. Unquestionably as well, American registration
laws share a lineage with prior European efforts to register criminals, indeed
entire populations (as in nineteenth-century Germany), and laws in northern and southern states alike in antebellum America requiring that African
American freedmen register with authorities.

American criminal registration laws, however, have evolved in a manner
distinctly in keeping with developments in the nation as a whole over the past

century. Originating in counties and cities in the 1930s, amid acute public concern over "gangsters" who anonymously traveled within the nation's increasingly mobile population, the registries had decided advantages over previous strategies, which merely passively collected and stored identifying information on offenders. Registration did this and more; it afforded knowledge of the actual whereabouts of individuals and required that they themselves provide and update such information, threatening criminal punishment if they did not. Registration, as a result, compelled individuals to be complicit in their own ongoing surveillance, perhaps for their lifetimes.

In addition, and critically important, sixty years after their origin, American registration laws in the mid-1990s were complemented by a historically unprecedented strategy: community notification, which rather than providing registrants' identifying information to police alone, as before, disseminated it to the public at large, to guard against recidivist criminality. With the advent of community notification, there has thus arisen, as Michel Foucault once said of empiricist techniques first taking root in the mid-eighteenth century, "a whole domain of knowledge, a whole type of power."[2]

*Knowledge as Power* explores this empowerment premise through the lens of American criminal registration and community notification laws. Despite being in existence for over seventy years, and today subjecting hundreds of thousands of individuals to ongoing public scrutiny after they have "done their time" and costing millions of dollars to effectuate, registration and notification laws have eluded sustained scholarly attention.

This book seeks to fill the void, providing the first in-depth history and analysis of registration and community notification laws, highlighting their relationship to past efforts to monitor offenders, as well as their distinct motivations, characteristics, and impact on U.S. law, society, and government. With registration, the nation has empowered police with information, creating a universal, location-based identification system—a development vigorously resisted in the past. With community notification, the nation has gone one step further, empowering communities with information, reconfiguring notions of informational privacy and radically transforming traditional understandings of state-citizen relations and social control. Moreover, while distinct because they single out a disdained subpopulation, principally convicted sex offenders, the current nationwide network of registration and notification laws reflects a sea-change in American social and political sensibility, which while highly significant in itself, lays the foundation for potential future expansion.

The discussion begins with an overview of early intellectual and techno-logical developments giving rise to modern registration and notification laws. While the roots of the anxiety bred by anonymous harm doers are ancient, the laws owe their existence to the more recent recognition that criminal risk is not random; that one-time criminal offenders are prone to commit additional crimes. As Chapter 1 relates, this recognition, combined with rapid popula-tion growth and ever-increasing mobility, motivated government efforts to render criminal risk more knowable. While over time fingerprint technology emerged as the worldwide identification method of choice, being prized for its accuracy and superior organizational capacity, registration predated fin-gerprinting by several decades and its instrumental appeal has persisted over the years. Rather than merely providing a biological basis to assess a criminal match after a criminal event, registries maintained location-related and other identifying information on *potential* recidivists, increasing the investigative and preventive capacity of police. They also, ideally, instilled in registrants a sense that they were being watched, thereby promoting deterrence.

Chapter 2 chronicles the genesis and growth of the first wave of Ameri-can criminal registration laws, starting in the 1930s when cities and counties rushed to enact laws. While motivated by fear of an increasingly mobile and anonymous breed of professional "gangsters," the laws in actuality targeted persons with offending histories belying hardened criminal status (a single conviction typically triggered eligibility) and otherwise focused on crimes not typically thought worthy of public safety concern (such as miscegena-tion). Moreover, the laws swept up newcomer and resident ex-offenders alike, contrary to the ostensible motivating concern over itinerant anonymity. Only later did state governments enact registration laws, with California adopting the nation's first statewide law in 1947; state interest in registration, however, remained limited and sporadic up through the 1980s.

During the first fifty years of their existence, registration laws scarcely fig-ured in American public life. While press accounts of the day made clear that authorities often favored registration as a get-tough strategy signaling intoler-ance for potential lawbreakers, providing a basis to jettison ex-offenders to other jurisdictions, registration in reality seemingly had little practical im-pact. Moreover, the laws themselves were the frequent subject of principled criticism. To critics, including members of the political establishment and law enforcement community, registration unfairly targeted ex-offenders who had served their time, serving to open "psychic sores," and was "un-American." In addition, over time it became clear, as it had to earlier users of registration in Europe, that registries were riddled with errors and that the individuals most inclined to comply were those most likely to remain law-abiding.

This decades-long disinterest, however, quickly evaporated in the early 1990s when registration seized the imagination of Americans anew, with states (not local governments, as before) adopting laws in rapid-fire succession. As Chapter 3 discusses, a key triggering event occurred in Washington State, which in 1990 enacted its first registration law and introduced the concept of community notification. The law was adopted in response to the May 1989 sexual mutilation of a young boy by a convicted sex offender who, despite inspiring great recidivist concern among state officials, was released from prison without the knowledge of community members. Similar tragedies soon prompted other states to enact registration and notification laws targeting persons convicted of sex and child-related offenses in particular. However, unlike Washington (where the child victim's name was not made publicly known), such laws typically came to be denominated by the names of child victims. New Jersey's Megan's Law, enacted in 1994 after the rape and murder of 7-year-old Megan Kanka by a twice-convicted sex offender who anonymously lived nearby, served as the nation's most significant catalyst, inspiring a torrent of other state registration and notification provisions, quickly enacted often without meaningful debate or consideration. By the late 1990s, registration and notification laws were in effect nationwide, resulting from initiative by individual states or pressure from the U.S. Congress, which starting in 1994 required that states either adopt laws or lose allocated federal funds.

Modern laws, as Chapter 3 makes clear, differ not merely because of their nationwide effect, but also because of their far more onerous quality. Registration today targets a considerably greater expanse of offenses and offenders (including juveniles), requires far more identifying information, mandates frequent verification, and threatens felony-level punishment for noncompliance. In turn, community notification singles out individuals for public scrutiny and disdain, with manifold negative effects for registrants and those with whom they associate, perhaps for their lifetimes. Finally, while modern laws have mainly singled out sex and child offenders, of late the appeal of registration and notification has inspired state expansions, focusing on such criminal subpopulations as drug offenders and arsonists.

The rapid nationwide embrace of registration and community notification laws is a remarkable story, made all the more so when one realizes that by the late 1980s criminal registration itself was moribund. By the early to mid-1990s, something had changed in American social and political life, creating a fertile environment for its modern proliferation. Not only were criticisms of the unfairness and oppressiveness of registration largely absent, but so too were objections to the far more significant negative personal effects of community notification, which with the advent of the Internet has permitted worldwide "rogues' galleries." The shift was also evidenced in the judiciary. In the 1970s and 1980s courts had, upon the rare occasion of entertaining constitutional challenges, tended to find fault with registration alone, even in its then-muted form. In the late 1990s, however, the vast majority of courts condoned not only registration but notification as well, and in 2003 the U.S. Supreme Court agreed, clearing away the limited doubt created by the handful of courts that earlier cast critical judgment.

Chapter 4 examines the chief reasons behind the rapid nationwide resurgence of registration and the genesis of community notification. The foundation for this evolution was laid by "panics" over sex offenders felt in prior decades as well as heightened public concern over child abductions in the 1980s. In the 1990s, however, a variety of other influences converged to account for the how and why of modern laws, including the public taste for punitiveness, which remains with us today.

These foundational elements, however, were augmented by a constellation of other forces that propelled both the quick passage of the laws and their onerous quality. One force in particular concerned the overt personalization of the politics driving the laws, focusing on the innocent victims of abuse and their demonic perpetrators. The personal profiles, backed by vastly overstated assertions of sex offender recidivist tendencies, instilled a sense of exigency (much as with 1930s-era registration laws targeting gangsters) and served to neutralize possible concern over the scope of registration and its ever-expanding array of requirements.

The political success of community notification, coming somewhat later, derived from an even more potent and visceral motivation. Politicians readily acquiesced to their constituents' sense of informational entitlement, predicated on the idea that the public was morally entitled to registrants' information in order to self-protect, and that the failure of government to ensure public safety made public dissemination a practical necessity. Finally, not to be overlooked, Congress also played a key role. As a result of federal threats to withhold funds in 1994 (the Jacob Wetterling Act) and 1996 (Megan's Law), not only were registration and notification adopted nationwide by the late 1990s, but the state laws themselves bore the indelible imprint of congressional policy preferences.

Chapter 5 examines the effects and consequences of registration and notification. Remarkably, despite being in effect nationwide for over a decade, the laws have been subject to little empirical assessment. Although premised on empirical certitudes of recidivism, and the expectations that they assist police, deter recidivism, and empower communities with information to self-protect, it remains unclear whether registration and notification actually work as intended. What is known is that modern registries, like their historic forebears, are rife with errors, undercutting their knowledge-based premise. Moreover, there is growing reason to believe that the laws, especially relating to notification, actually might make communities less safe and contribute to recidivism.

The final two chapters attempt to take stock of the broader effects of registration and notification and where they might be headed in coming years. Chapter 6 begins with an examination of the important ways in which the nation's constitutional jurisprudence has been affected, especially as a result of the two 2003 U.S. Supreme Court decisions mentioned above. In both decisions the Court upheld registration and notification against constitutional attack, exhibiting an uncritical judicial blitheness that warrants both precedential concern and worry that the judiciary has abdicated its oversight role in the nation's tripartite separation of powers system.

Attention then shifts to the important ways in which the laws have affected notions of informational privacy. The data contained in registries—such as home and work addresses, conviction histories, and vehicle descriptions—are of course "public" in the strictest sense. Registration and notification, however, compel the collection and updating of such information from individuals, when it otherwise would remain disaggregated, and disseminate it to the public at large. The process and its effects irreducibly impact traditional notions of privacy and figure centrally in an important ongoing national debate over the appropriate contours and limits of disclosure.

This shift in privacy understanding has given rise to a corollary shift in public safety governance, one based on a new triangular relationship. The linchpin of the relationship is registrants themselves, who under pain of punishment are required to provide identifying information to government authorities, making them complicit in their own surveillance, after they have discharged their penal debt to society. The second component part concerns community members, who rather than being passive beneficiaries of police public safety efforts, as in the past, are expected to be active consumers and users of registry information. Armed with such information, they, rather than police, have shouldered paramount responsibility for defending against recidivist criminality and the apprehension of perpetrators. Lastly, government, while still expected to arrest and imprison recidivists, has assumed the principal role of information broker—a role, courts have held, is lacking in causal responsibility for the vigilantism and other negative consequences of community notification because the information conveyed is "public."

Chapter 6 closes with a discussion of the way in which registration and notification have transformed traditional notions of state-federal relations. As a result of sustained federal pressure, a matter squarely within state police power authority, the community control of ex-offenders, has been driven and defined by Congress and the White House, with major ramifications for the nation's federalist system of governance.

Chapter 7 considers the likely future evolution of registration and notification. Given the considerable resources required to operate the laws, and the increasing sense that they are either ineffective or even counterproductive, one would expect to soon witness either their sharp limitation or demise. For a variety of reasons, however, neither outcome is likely. Backing limitation or abolition of the laws would carry the political risk of appearing weak on crime or, worse yet, mounting a personal assault on the legacies of victims after whom laws have been named. Similarly, the critical research findings amassed to date, and any published in the future, can be expected to be rebuffed by the intuitive certitude that has always insulated the laws from question, or the common refrain that the laws are justified "if one child is saved."

Furthermore, until such time as registration and notification adversely affect the politically empowered, indulging them will remain, as Cass Sunstein observed in another context, "costless."[3] And while it is possible that ever-harsher incarnations of registration and notification might result in reassessment of their constitutionality, on the margin, the firm backing of the U.S. Supreme Court makes it unlikely that the judiciary will intercede and curb state efforts in a fundamental way. Finally, the central role registration and notification have come to play in the modern corrections system make retrenchment even less likely. Along with global positioning system (GPS) technology and similar strategies, they promise community and information-based public safety, at substantial cost savings relative to prison or jail.

Indeed, strong reason exists to conclude that future years will witness expansion of registration and notification. Already, other criminal subpopulations have been targeted, and the political dynamic driving the laws makes it likely that this growth will continue. Whether the line of inclusion will be drawn at persons convicted of crime also remains to be seen; other information, such as civil judgments, is also "public," presumably warranting similar indulgence. In coming years, this growth might also extend to the international arena, which to date has resisted American-style registration and community notification.

In sum, the effort here will be part genealogical, part sociological, and part legal in orientation. Together, it is hoped, the approaches will afford a comprehensive understanding of the past, present, and perhaps future of registration and community notification laws in America.

Knowledge as Power

# 1 HISTORICAL ANTECEDENTS

MODERN-DAY CRIMINAL REGISTRATION and community notification laws owe an unmistakable intellectual and technological debt to predecessor efforts. As governments and individuals over time recognized the reality of individualized criminal risk, techniques were devised to render it more knowable, and hence possibly more susceptible to control. This chapter traces the several major developments that laid the foundation for contemporary registration and community notification laws, providing the necessary background for an understanding of the forces propelling their modern proliferation in America.

## MEASURING MISCONDUCT

Governments have long valued gathering and storing information on their subjects. Dating back to efforts by ecclesiastics in mid-1500s Finland and Sweden,[1] and later public authorities in seventeenth-century England and Prussia,[2] governments have recognized the importance of population data. By recording events such as births, deaths, and marriages, a "legible people"[3] could be created, and this legibility served the important instrumental purpose of evincing state power itself.[4]

Over time, however, statistical knowledge came to be valued for more particularized reasons, including its capacity to reflect the incidence of criminal deviance, an issue of increasing governmental concern. With improvements in data collection methods, statistical inferences were possible, allowing, as Belgian statistician Adolphe Quetlet put it in 1829, knowledge of the "terrifying exactitude with which crimes reproduce themselves."[5] Governments could "know in advance how many individuals will dirty their hands with the blood of others, how many will be forgers, how many prisoners, nearly as well as one can enumerate in advance the births and deaths that must take place."[6] With such information, one could develop a "kind of budget for the scaffold, the galley and the prisons."[7]

Criminal deviance, nascent social science instructed, was not random. Rather, just as the aggregate occurrence of crime was a social fact, so too was the propensity of certain individuals to repeatedly engage in criminal misconduct. This recognition fueled efforts to amass and maintain records on individual wrongdoers. As early as the late thirteenth century, local governments exchanged names and primitive physical descriptions of wanted outlaws,[8] and over the years such efforts became increasingly routinized. In England, London's court at Bow Street in 1753 initiated a registry containing names and descriptions of all persons suspected of having committed fraud or a felony.[9] In 1844, the French ascribed semantic distinction to the phenomenon, coining the term *recidiviste*,[10] which itself coincided with a change in governmental perspective. European governments shifted from a preoccupation over dangerous *classes* to concern over dangerous *individuals*. Criminal danger, as historian John Pratt has written, became "a quality no longer . . . possessed by a class but [rather] by individuals or small groups of criminals." The danger no longer threatened to "tear down the portals of the state in an orgy of blood and destruction," but was instead "targeted at the quality of life of its individual subjects."[11]

## PROCESSING THE CRIMINAL ELEMENT

Developing awareness of the individualized nature of criminality had a critically important impact on the administration of justice, which during the late eighteenth and early nineteenth centuries increasingly sought to individualize sanctions. This was especially so in the early American Republic, where two policies, both contingent on the ability to distinguish individual criminal actors, were taking hold. The first was sentence enhancements, which Americans since colonial times imposed on repeat offenders.[12] If such individuals were to be held accountable and singled out for heightened punishment, they had to be reliably identified.

A second policy concerned the goal of offender rehabilitation, which in Jacksonian America emerged as the dominant penal goal and rationale. Under the model, not all convicts were seen as similarly predisposed to recidivism. If prison was to avoid serving as a "school for crime," prior offenders needed to be identified and isolated from perhaps less crime-prone peers. In addition, for reform to be successful, punishments needed to be tailored to the offending histories and backgrounds of individual offenders, which presupposed accurate identification.

Procedures employed in the early 1800s at Philadelphia's Walnut Street Jail highlighted this effort.[13] Upon arrival, officials collected information on each inmate, including name, age, crime of conviction, sentence imposed and date, and adjudicating court. This information was then used to classify individuals in the name of optimizing prospects for rehabilitation, and was augmented by physical descriptions at their time of departure. As a result, future newcomers to Walnut Street could be compared against institutional records, and in the event of a match punishment and reform-related decisions could be made accordingly. Under this regime, "neither change of name or [sic] disguise" would allow reoffenders to escape detection.[14]

Such efforts at individuation, however, were often less than successful. This was so for two chief reasons. First, clerks failed to consistently and comprehensively record available data on convicts (for example, one clerk might note the height of a convict, while another would not). Furthermore, the data points recorded often included vague or relative assessments or descriptors (such as "quick" speech, "sallow" complexion) and focused on too few unalterable features (such as eye color); worse yet, records reflected matters capable of fabrication (such as place or date of birth).[15]

Second, almost as important, the information gathered was not capable of being readily retrieved. Records were typically stored according to sentencing date, with no capacity for cross-referencing, requiring officials to review the entirety of jail records.[16] Although by the mid-1820s the information gathered increased in complexity, and utility was enhanced by storing convict names by means of alphabetization, jail records remained of limited practical use in detecting recidivists.[17]

## MONITORING THE CRIMINAL ELEMENT

Concern over recidivists, however, was not limited to government actors; it surely extended to society at large, which in the late eighteenth and early nineteenth centuries was buffeted by broader destabilizing influences. American society in particular experienced massive social and economic change, prompted by rapid industrialization and increases in mobility, urbanization, population growth, and immigration. No longer did neighbors necessarily know one another; America became, in the words of historian Michael Ignatieff, a "society of strangers."[18] In 1829, Alexis de Tocqueville, visiting the country under the auspices of the French government to study American penal reforms, observed that in America "[n]othing is easier than to pass from one state to another, and it is in the criminal's interest to do so."[19]

Available methods of identifying potential criminal offenders, however, provided only modest basis to assuage public anxiety. While in the past offenders could be identified because they had been branded or mutilated, by the early 1800s disfigurement had passed from social acceptability[20] and a new means of identifying at-large criminally risky individuals was needed.

The job of filling this need fell to an emerging institutional entity: the police, which by the mid-1800s had become better organized and more professional and had assumed a more proactive role in public safety.[21] During the time, as Peter Becker observed, "stigma was no longer directly inscribed on the body of the perpetrator, but rather was administered in collections of data by the police."[22] With this information, police could single out risky individuals for monitoring and possible intervention, and in the event a crime was committed, more effectively secure their custody.

Effective identification methods, however, were slow in coming. In Europe, police had used standardized forms to identify suspected perpetrators since the early 1700s, and Prussian police were required to do so by decree in 1828.[23] U.S. police, for the first time assigned to specific geographic zones or "beats" in cities, were encouraged and trained to recall the faces and body types of dangerous individuals prone to be in their areas. Officers also adopted the technique of "spotting," whereby they would record suspects' features in their diaries, for subsequent possible identification.[24]

Police soon took advantage of emerging photographic technology, which was more objective and reliable than human memory and descriptions. Initially used by British and French authorities in the 1840s to record images of prisoners and criminal suspects,[25] the New York City Police Department in 1858 staged the first-known police station "rogues' gallery," containing images of 450 arrestees.[26] While initially the galleries solely focused on local offenders, in time duplicate images from other cities were arrayed, and the public was invited to view the displays.[27] Despite being an improvement over prose descriptions, the images suffered from an age-old shortcoming: they could not be assembled in such a way as to ensure their ready retrieval. In addition, the utility of the identification technology was significantly undercut by the protean nature of individuals' physical appearances, which could change either as a result of time and circumstance or overt efforts to deceive.[28]

Meanwhile, European governments were experimenting with more systematic methods. In 1850, the French instituted *casiers judiciares,* the brainchild of penal reformer Arnould Bonneville de Marsangy, which revolutionized criminal record keeping in France and later much of the Continent. Instead of storing convict records solely in courts where convictions took place, Bonneville's strategy required that a copy of each conviction and sentence be sent to the court in the district of the offender's place of birth, or if such place was not known or the offender was foreign born, to a central repository in Paris. With such information consolidated, a "criminal register" could hold repeat offenders to proper account, and first-time offenders could benefit from lenience. In a speech to the Prison Association of New York in 1868, Bonneville noted that Italy and Portugal had begun using registers and predicted the bright future that lay ahead with further adoptions:

> [T]here will be no more frontiers for the administration of justice. Every country regarding it as a duty to transmit to foreign governments the certificates of conviction of those born on their soil, no criminal, however nomadic his life, will be able, on returning to his own country, to shield himself under a false assumption of virtue . . . All his antecedents will be revealed; and then, at length, like the Divine justice of which it is the reflection, human justice will, thanks to the registers, have its eyes everywhere.[29]

Bonneville added that the "many signal services" afforded by registries in France would yield "incomparably more" in the United States, which he described as

> a vast confederation, composed of a large number of different States, all having their own proper autonomy, their legislatures, their administrative and judicial authority, and only connected together, with a view to their general and political interests, by the guarantee of a compact of national union. In a country so constituted, in the midst of the perpetual movement of mutual immigration caused by the necessities of commerce and industry, in the midst of this incessant coming and going, incapable of exact measurement among the inhabitants of so vast a territory, different for the most part in origin, race, language and habits.[30]

Registries, Bonneville urged, would allow a judge to know the "moral character and antecedents of a criminal, who has pursued his adventurous career successively in the different States of the confederation" and determine the "exact measure of punishment necessary to his reformation."[31]

Yet Bonneville touted the French registration system for more than its adjudication and punishment benefits—the system could actually prevent crime, in two ways. First, he posited, individuals with a prior conviction would be less likely to recidivate because they would be aware that the courts had access to their entire criminal history, permitting enhanced punishment. Second, situating a centralized criminal registry in an offender's place of birth would serve to deter crime in the first instance. Criminal history information, Bonneville wrote in 1870, "instead of remaining hidden in the archives of the government, would be engraved in characters of infamy on the registry of their native village." As a result, "criminals themselves would be restrained by the dread of this local publicity of their misdeeds." The "terrifying certainty" that convictions would be recorded and thus "stain the name and honor of their family" and their "desire of general esteem" would have significant deterrent value.[32]

Germany, by 1867, had an even more advanced registration method—its *Meldewesen*, which required *all citizens* (not merely offenders) to register with the police and to report all travel and changes of residence. Whereas the French system was static in its content, reflecting only name and conviction-related information, the German registry contained individuals' names and addresses in each locality they lived or visited. The registry served a broad variety of purposes, including identifying children subject to compulsory vaccination, monitoring satisfaction of military service requirements, and allowing police to apprehend criminal suspects. Moreover, because it contained criminal conviction information, the registry allowed governments to exclude individuals from a jurisdiction.[33] Writing in his seminal book *European Police Systems* (1915), American penal reformer Raymond Fosdick observed that "[n]o laws are more rigidly enforced than those relating to the *Meldewesen*. Evasion is difficult and when detected is severely punished."[34]

At the time, in Berlin, which had its own registration system since 1836, twelve million cards were on file, containing data on all persons who had at any time been in the city, and the registration bureau itself had two hundred employees and occupied 130 rooms.[35] Data on file included an individual's place and date of birth, parents' names, current and prior residence (and moving date), children's names and dates of birth or death, religious affiliation, and criminal record. Fosdick wrote that in Germany, as well as in Austria, the *Meldewesen* constituted the "core of the detective department. Through its agency the police can put their hands on any citizen when they want him."[36] The *Meldewesen* was also used to check the identities of "suspicious persons or persons inhabiting disorderly houses" to determine if they were wanted for crimes.[37] With the system, Mathieu Deflem recently wrote, "German police squads would raid hotels, lodging houses and public places, and check apprehended persons with information collected in the registration system."[38]

The system was complemented by the *Steckbrief*, a daily or weekly notice containing the names or descriptions of criminal suspects being sought in Germany and elsewhere. Police used the notice to both apprehend fugitives and, upon arrest, check their identities against the registry to learn if they were wanted.

Fosdick had high praise for the *Meldewesen* and the *Steckbrief*, writing that they "together form[ed] an intricate network."[39] Police were trained to know the inhabitants of their beat and unknown individuals immediately attracted attention. Providing a false name was the only way for the system to be defeated, and even this was of little avail in the case of German citizens, "who must satisfy the police as to their identity by means of military papers or their employment and insurance cards. In cases of doubt, men are held pending further investigation."[40]

Around the same time, the British were experimenting with registration systems of their own. No longer able to banish their criminal lawbreakers to faraway lands, the crown by the mid-1800s was acutely aware of the need to monitor and control them domestically. As legal historian Sir Leon Radzinowicz observed, "[t]he perception of a mass of offenders at home, moving about and yet anonymous, fostered an escalating fear of a criminal or dangerous class and a resolve to do something drastic about it."[41] In response, the government enacted a series of laws allowing for the registration and monitoring of criminal offenders, as well as newly heightened sentences for recidivists. The first such law targeted individuals released before the expiration of their sentences, subject to terms and conditions ("tickets-of-leave" men). Despite initial resistance to the idea, based on the belief that continued community monitoring would stigmatize such persons and thus predispose them to further crime, in 1864 the government, borrowing from the Irish, required that individuals released on ticket-of-leave report to police on a monthly basis and provide notice of any change of address.[42]

In 1869, the Habitual Criminals Bill required that all felons and certain misdemeanants register with police and provide a photo, and subjected such persons to a one-year prison term upon proof that they acted suspiciously or derived their livelihood by dishonest means.[43] The government, however, having dispelled concerns that the practice was unduly "vexatious" to those intending to be law-abiding, soon recognized practical problems with registration. In particular, released offenders often failed to report residence changes to authorities and the sheer number of registrants overwhelmed police.[44] Over time, other problems arose, including allegations that police used registry information to harass registrants.[45] In all, according to Sir James Frazer, London's chief of police, the law creating the registry "was the most absurd measure that ever was passed; that only those who chose to report themselves did so, and . . . they were the men who wanted to live honestly, but that those who would not report themselves disappeared."[46]

Mindful of these deficiencies, during the 1870s the British experimented with other identification methods. For instance, the "Alphabetical Register of Habitual Criminals," first published in 1877, contained information on 22,115 individuals (excluding aliases, 12,164 individuals).[47] Each entry was accompanied by the individual's physical description, offense history, and intended place of residence after prison. The registry, however, was of little use for a number of reasons, not the least of which was that it was published almost a year after individuals had been released, and arrayed information by year rather than in comprehensive aggregated fashion. More problematic, the descriptions it contained were vague and the index itself was of no use if individuals provided false names or aliases.[48] This latter flaw was exemplified by the stratagems of one Lacenaire, described as a "professional criminal" who "adopted false names, multiplied forgeries and disguises, and preyed actively on society."[49]

Difficulty remained even when identification efforts were combined with the "Register of Distinctive Marks," which contained photos and information on bodily marks, as well as criminal modus operandi. Its chief benefit was of an organizational nature.[50] The Register apportioned the body into nine parts, and what was deemed the most distinctive permanent mark, such as a scar or tattoo, determined where the individual's name was placed in the register.

While again an improvement, the technique was problematic because savvy registrants could alter the location and appearance of their marks; moreover, the register proved too cumbersome and labor intensive to enjoy continued use, resulting in its eventual demise in the 1890s.[51]

Finally, no discussion of nineteenth-century British registration efforts would be complete without mention of the effort, in 1871 colonial India, to register "criminal tribes." Enacted at the urging of eminent British legal authority James Fitzjames Stephen, the "Criminal Tribes Act" authorized local government officials to designate "any tribe, gang, or class of persons" a "criminal tribe" if its members were "addicted to the systematic commission of non-bailable offenses."[52] Persons or groups so designated[53] were subject to residence and travel limits, forced to periodically report to specified officials, and faced "rigorous punishment" for violations.[54]

In sum, by the late nineteenth century, European governments were acutely aware of the criminal risk posed by individuals and possessed ample data on convicted offenders. The challenge, however, lay in organizing such information, keeping it accurate and current, and making it accessible for use. U.S. officials, in turn, were aware of European criminal registration efforts, especially the French system touted by Bonneville. In St. Louis, in 1871, attendees at the first National Police Conference urged, without success, creation of a national criminal identification system.[55] Later, in 1887, the Wardens' Association for the Registration of Criminals was formed, the purpose of which was to secure "the registration in a central office, of the criminal records of prisoners . . . and the mutual interchange, between prisons, of such information, with a view to distinguishing between habitual and occasional offenders, and as an aid to reformatory work in prisons."[56] To this end, member institutions were expected to submit to a central office photos, physical descriptions, and life histories of recent prison arrivals.[57] The system, however, was never implemented, as members were alerted to the availability of a new identification system, one that was thought to be cheaper, more effective, and easier to implement.[58]

## BERTILLONISM

The heralded innovation was a regimen of bodily (anthropometric) identification created by a French police official, Alphonse Bertillon. Originating in late nineteenth-century France, an anxious time as elsewhere marked by rapid industrial growth, increasing urbanization, and concern over criminal recidivists, Bertillonism afforded governments a new criminal identification method. The ornate approach depended on three data points: (1) body part dimensions, such as the head, finger, and ear; (2) descriptions of facial features; and (3) notations of "peculiar marks," such as scars, birthmarks, and tattoos.[59] Measurements were taken with calipers and other tools by specially trained clerks and complemented by full-face and profile photographs, as well as more subjective entries such as complexion, demeanor, voice, and hair color, described pursuant to Bertillon's specific "morphological vocabulary."[60]

The recordings consisted of the signalment phase; Bertillonism's appeal, however, also stemmed from its classification system. Measurements taken by clerks were inscribed on index cards and assembled in large specially built cabinets with multiple rows and columns, each concerning a distinct body part. Cards were first separated by gender, then by head length (small, medium or large), each subject to quantitative definition. Cards were then subclassified by head breadth, divided again by middle finger length and other bodily measures, and divided yet again by eye color. Each group was then placed in a separate file drawer and arrayed by ear length.[61] With each new suspect in custody, operators would endeavor to match information taken from the suspect with the anthropometric information filed.[62]

With Bertillonism, officials could link individuals by means of quantified biologic data on replicable, systematically collected measures that were far more objective than those used in the past. In addition, rather than having to rely on the personal knowledge or recollection of officials, the records were readily accessible.

Bertillon's system derived from ongoing advances in the fields of criminology and criminal anthropology, which had long been engaged in an effort to refute dominant determinist explanations of criminality. In conjunction with evolutionary theorists Charles Darwin and Herbert Spencer, eugenic theorist Sir Francis Galton, and phrenologists, who posited that propensity for crime was manifest in the shape of individuals' skulls,[63] Bertillon emphasized the importance of individualized assessment. Bertillon's overtly scientific orientation received a ready welcome from Americans anxious over "criminal types" in their midst.[64]

Bertillonism was first adopted in the United States in 1887 under the auspices of Major R. W. McClaughry, warden of the Illinois State Penitentiary, and by 1888 roughly a dozen large U.S. prisons used the system.[65] In 1889, the federal government urged public support for creation of a centralized anthropometric identification bureau in the nation's capital.[66] Singing the praises of Bertillonism, an 1896 editorial in Indiana's *Ft. Wayne News* urged that the system was essential to the development of a "general system of criminal registration . . . Properly used [the system] will be as nearly infallible as a system designed by man can be."[67] A week later, the same paper published a follow-up, noting that the law-abiding had nothing to fear from "scientific registration":

> To the reclaimed man, who goes out from prison to a life of honest industry, the Bertillon registry works no hardship or injustice. Unless he commits a new crime and is arrested and sentenced, it will not be known that he was ever registered . . . Indeed, the knowledge that a man is on the record and that a new crime may not only bring a new punishment, but may revive the almost forgotten story of his past, may be a powerful deterrent under temptation.[68]

In 1898, a New York State prison official informed attendees at a national gathering of police chiefs that over twenty thousand individuals had been measured, and "many" had been determined to be recidivists. Moreover, since New York had adopted Bertillonism, "the number of criminals in Connecticut [where the system is not in operation] has increased twenty percent."[69] In 1896, Warden McClaughry touted the system as a method to achieve broader social control aims, permitting identification of the entire world populace, with signalment becoming the universal means of human identification:

> It would then be possible to find any person at once whenever desired, whether for his own good or that of society at large, in whatever place he might be and however he might alter his appearance or name. Crime could thus be rooted out, elections purified, immigration laws effectively enforced, innumerable misunderstandings and much injustice prevented and all business relations greatly facilitated.[70]

Nationwide adoption of Bertillon's regime, however, never came to fruition. The accuracy of measurements remained a foremost concern. This was because they had to be consistently taken, with painstaking care, which was difficult because training was uneven, in part due to the unavailability of skilled personnel and imperfections in translating Bertillon's work from French. Relatedly, despite the apparent quantitative objectivity of the biologic measures themselves, anthropometry depended on humans to carry out and record the measures, which could be transcribed improperly and subject to rounding inconsistencies.[71]

Other critics raised principled concern, including some who viewed anthropometry not as a tool of reform but rather oppression. They viewed the record keeping as violative of privacy and feared that information would be released to the police or the media and would unfairly shadow convicts for the remainder of their lives, impeding rehabilitation.[72] As one Pennsylvania warden stated, "I will not persecute a man for his natural life."[73]

Anthropometry received a warmer reception among police. In 1893, the year of the World Columbian Exposition, which would attract hundreds of thousands of visitors, police in host city Chicago applied Bertillon's system.[74] That same year, the National Chiefs of Police Union, later to be renamed the International Association of Chiefs of Police (IACP), unanimously endorsed its use.[75] The group soon created a National Bureau for Criminal Identification (NBCI), in the hope of spawning a nationwide network of offices that would collect anthropometric information on criminal offenders and store it in a centralized office in Washington, DC.

Although the NBCI never achieved universal voluntary acceptance among the nation's police departments, within a few years it had received and stored three thousand index cards annually. Moreover, during the 1890s several large urban police departments, including those of New York City and Washington, DC, as well as the Pinkerton Detective Agency, instituted stand-alone anthropometric departments.[76]

Why, precisely, anthropometry was better received by police, compared to corrections officials, remains an open question, but likely can be explained by the varied responsibilities of police. First, the method held promise as a deterrent to ex-convicts, who perhaps would be fearful of being more readily detected due to law enforcement's ready access to identification information. Second, police would have the capacity to intervene earlier, before criminal misconduct was even contemplated: they could identify and prosecute the criminally culpable and otherwise banish undesirable individuals from their jurisdictions.[77] Finally, the approach itself jibed with the increasing recognition that police needed to join forces in order to effectively combat crime. Bertillonism, one police chief observed, "would not only furnish information to each detective of a city, but [also] it might form a connecting link as evidence as to crime committed elsewhere."[78]

## FINGERPRINTING

Bertillon's calipers held sway until around 1910, when they faced competition from yet another criminal identification tool—the recording and analysis of fingerprints. Originating in seventh-century China, the first Western use of fingerprints within the criminal justice system is variously attributed to Englishmen William Herschel in the 1870s[79] or Henry Faulds in 1880.[80] The idea, however, did not achieve public notice until Sir Francis Galton refined and championed the idea at the turn of the century. In 1904, dazzling feats of fingerprint matches at the World's Fair in St. Louis captivated huge crowds.[81]

The system eventually developed by Galton and others, consisting of fingerprint pattern types containing "arches," "loops," and "whorls," with distinct subclassifications within each, was well received in America.[82] While for many years anthropometry and dactyloscopy (as fingerprint analysis came to be called) shared popularity, with police departments using them in tandem,[83] the latter soon emerged as the preferred identification method. In 1911, the IACP endorsed fingerprinting and encouraged its use by members,[84] and by the 1930s fingerprinting was the nation's criminal identification method of choice.[85]

Several reasons accounted for the speedy embrace of fingerprinting at the expense of anthropometry. First, like the early photographic technology that preceded it, anthropometry failed to accommodate humans' physical changes. Because the body continued its physical growth into adulthood, anthropometry could not, for instance, accurately record juvenile offenders. Fingerprints, available in immutable form since birth, were not so limited. Second, anthropometry continued to be plagued by accuracy concerns. Justifying its switch from anthropometry to fingerprinting in 1910, for instance, the Boston Police Department asserted that "as the digits *record themselves* there are no inaccuracies."[86] Compounding this, anthropometry was difficult to master, and despite Bertillon's exhortations, individual police departments took it upon themselves to add to, modify, and at times ignore bodily measurements prescribed by the system.[87] Fingerprinting, on the other hand, could be readily mastered and was cheaper and less time consuming for clerks to administer. Finally, fingerprints themselves could be more easily stored and organized than the data in Bertillon's complex system.

State and local adoption of fingerprint analysis soon inspired interest by the federal government. While for many years it rebuffed state requests to store fingerprints, deeming crime control a local not federal responsibility, in time Washington assumed the institutional role with zeal. Under the leadership of J. Edgar Hoover, the U.S. Department of Justice's Bureau of Investigation, predecessor of the Federal Bureau of Investigation, had over three million fingerprints of criminal suspects on file in 1932, with prints provided by almost five thousand law enforcement agencies nationwide.[88]

Fingerprint technology was soon applied to noncriminal populations. The movement first took shape with the nation's entry into World War I, when in early 1918 the federal government required German American aliens to provide identifying information, photographs, and fingerprints to authorities. Individuals were provided an identification card that featured their name, address, photograph, and thumbprint, which they were obliged to possess at all times. They were also required to inform authorities of address changes and to seek permission to enter or reside in specified security-sensitive areas.[89] The law was administered by Hoover's Bureau of Investigation, and violations resulted in imprisonment up to five years and a $2,000 fine.[90] The effort ultimately secured registration records on nearly a half-million German Americans[91] yet ended (as projected) at the war's end.

During the era interest in broader use of registration continued. In 1919, Henry P. DeForest, Chief Medical Examiner of the New York City Civil Commission,[92] founded the International Society for Personal Identification, which advocated "universal identification" of all "law abiding citizens."[93] Proponents identified the numerous advantages of a national fingerprint-based identification system, which would commence with prints from school-age children,[94] including allowing for identification in the event of amnesia, suicide, kidnapping, severe injury, or death.[95] Universal identification was also urged as a general crime-fighting strategy. In Chicago, city officials in 1921 considered universal identification in the wake of a reported record-breaking increase in crime the year before, with advocates attributing the increase to "ignorance of who the criminals are."[96]

Proponents could also point to national identification systems used in other countries. Britain, during World War I, adopted a National Register of all persons between the ages of 15 and 65, excluding convicts, the certified mentally ill, and prisoners of war (subpopulations already subject to specialized registers).[97] Other nations, such as Mexico, Chile, and Argentina, had compulsory national fingerprinting systems even when not subject to the exigencies of war.[98]

The movement experienced a major surge in support with the Lindbergh baby kidnapping in 1932, and in 1934 the Executive Committee of the New York State Chamber of Commerce urged compulsory fingerprint identification of the entire population.[99] That same year, Berkeley, California, police chief August Vollmer, identified twenty-three principal benefits of a universal system, including its capacity to

> allow businesses to assess credit worthiness; guard against fraud and establish identities of job applicants; aid census enumeration and provide more accurate vital statistics; ensure against unworthy persons (e.g., "criminals and dope fiends") [obtaining] vehicle and chauffeur licenses; trace income tax evaders; prevent illegal voting; verify the identity of persons seeking all manner of permits; allow "communists and anarchists" to be "followed from place to place and their activities noted"; and permit the backgrounds of civil service applicants to be checked.[100]

During the time, voluntary fingerprinting was urged as a matter of civic duty. As one police chief put it, "[n]o decent man would object to having his prints taken or his picture taken. It is only the man who may do something wrong who objects . . . That is the man we want to get a record on.[101]

Advocates were leery of obvious police involvement in fingerprint drives, fearing associated taint with criminal populations, and emphasized that police were not involved in the effort.[102] FBI Director Hoover opined that "[t]he old prejudice held by the honest man against fingerprinting is fast disappearing," emphasizing that fingerprints were "of course maintained separate and apart from criminal records."[103] Evidence that this shift in sentiment was in fact occurring was found in the 1932 *Encyclopedia of the Social Sciences*, which highlighted the variety of non–law enforcement benefits accruing to citizens, suggesting that identification was an important means of guarding against fraudulent confusion and safeguarding individual rights.[104] Testament to this more secular appeal, according to a Gallup opinion survey published in 1939, 71% of respondents stated that "everybody in the country should be fingerprinted by the federal government."[105]

The effort to secure universal identification, however, soon stalled. Ultimately, many recoiled at the idea that law-abiding citizens would have personal information collected and stored, just like criminal offenders.[106] The American Civil Liberties Union, in turn, questioned the ostensibly benign motives for the push. The actual goal of universal registration, the ACLU maintained, was "intimidation, control, restriction upon freedom of movement," amounting to "an early—and effective—move in the direction of general regimentation of the population that subjects the whole populace to police surveillance" and violated "the freedom of the individual's anonymity."[107]

Skepticism was also manifest in Congress. In 1935, federal lawmakers passed up a chance to associate fingerprints with the issuance of social security cards, each with a unique personal identification number. In 1940 a bill calling for universal fingerprinting failed in Congress, and in 1943 the Citizens Identification Act, which would require identification cards and fingerprinting of all persons 16 years of age and older, was defeated.[108] Despite the increasing use of driver's licenses, voter and draft eligibility cards, as well as other new documentary forms of government regulation, Americans simply were not ready to be subject to universal monitoring by the national government.

Short of universal identification, the federal government succeeded in requiring fingerprints of select subpopulations having direct involvement with the government: federal employees (1929),[109] enlistees in branches of the military (1930s),[110] noncitizen aliens (1939),[111] and persons involved in the Work Progress Administration (1939) and the Civilian Conservation Corps (1937).[112] Later, in the 1950s, Communists[113] and gamblers[114] were also required to provide prints.

During the 1930s and 1940s, states and municipalities also targeted subgroups.[115] Bootblacks and sellers of newspapers and magazines on the street,[116] taxicab drivers,[117] dealers in secondhand items,[118] and workers in cities such as Miami Beach, Las Vegas, and Atlantic City engaged in the saloon and entertainment industry work (such as bartenders and casino workers)[119] were required to provide fingerprints and other identifying information to local authorities.

### MONITORING "OTHERS"

Before concluding this survey of early identification efforts, attention must be paid to their use in the monitoring of distinct racial and ethnic subpopulations. In the face of war, as mentioned above, the United States and other nations targeted residents whose national origin was that of a belligerent. Mention was also made of the British effort to register "criminal tribes" in 1870s colonial India. The same proclivity, however, also has been manifest in other times and contexts.

Notably, in the United States from the late 1700s until after the Civil War, emancipated African Americans were often required to register. In numerous northern and southern states, freedmen were required to provide identifying information to authorities and to obtain certification of their manumitted status. An 1804 Tennessee law, for instance, required that freedmen register with local county clerks and specify their "age, name, color, and stature . . . together with any apparent mark or scar . . . and in what court, and by what authority he she was emancipated, or [to specify] that such negro . . . was born free."[120]

In 1785, North Carolina passed an act applicable to several towns (specified because they contained sufficient numbers of freedmen to pose a threat of insurrection),[121] intended to "discriminate between free negroes, mulattoes, and other persons of mixed blood and slaves." Under the law, all freedmen were to register within three days, pay a registration fee, and obtain a "badge of cloth . . . to be fixed on the left shoulder, and to have wrought thereon in legible capital letters the word FREE." The registration requirement was to remain in effect for their stay in the town and was enforced by a fine, resulting in forced servitude in the event of nonpayment.[122] In the District of Columbia, an 1827 law required collection of not only names and physical description data, but also residence, and made it a criminal offense for any resident to harbor an unregistered freedman.[123] Later, in 1848, the District required annual reregistration and payment of a sum of fifty dollars, threatening expulsion upon nonpayment.[124] In Virginia, employers faced a fine if they employed unregistered freedmen, and any African American claiming to be free but who lacked a registration certificate could be jailed.[125] In the north and south alike, such laws not only sought to monitor freedmen, but were also intended to discourage their entry and encourage their exit.[126]

Another notorious use of registration arose in France, where government authorities in the early 1900s targeted "Gypsies," whose nomadic lifestyle threatened the established order and who were thought to engage in such barbarities as child theft. In 1907, newly organized mobile police squads photographed and recorded via Bertillon's methods the physical descriptions of all Gypsies they encountered. "Itinerance itself," as Martine Kaluszynski has noted, thus "became a 'pre-offense.'" Five years later, French politicians, responding to public concern over roaming bands of Gypsies, mandated use of the "anthropometric nomad passbook," which all Gypsies of at least 13 years of age were required to show upon police demand. Failures to comply with the law or efforts at falsification were punished by severe fines complemented by the threat to seize Gypsies' personal possessions and sell them in the event of nonpayment.[127]

During this time, Gypsies were actually treated more harshly than convicted criminals, who were also required to carry anthropometric passes. Just as state and local governments today use registrant status to prohibit individuals from living in prescribed areas (near schools, for example), as discussed in Chapter 3, local mayors in France banished Gypsy pass holders from their towns and posted signs at town boundaries prohibiting entry. Also, like the laws targeting freedman just discussed, and again like criminal registration laws later to be enacted in the United States, the 1912 French law sought to at once monitor worrisome individuals and provide them incentive to depart. According to French officials:

> [The law] should reduce the number of nomads and especially of foreign nomads by forbidding them access to French territory [or] by requiring them either to take up a permanent abode or to leave France . . . The provisions of the law can only be fully effective if all individuals . . . are made the objects of constant control and continual supervision.[128]

The foregoing examples, of course, do not exhaust the instances of oppressive government deployment of registration. Indeed, they figure as only two in a history of abuses, including the Nazis' use of identification cards and other insignia to round up, oppress, and kill Jews and others during the World War II era.[129] In their effort, the Nazis were greatly aided by Germany's preexisting national *Meldewesen* registration system, noted earlier, the comprehensive and highly organized nature of which provided ready access to the whereabouts and backgrounds of residents, including persons with criminal records.[130] This infrastructure was augmented by the more particularized indices administered by the Gestapo, targeting inter alia "highly dangerous persons," "dangerous persons," Jews, "part-Jews," and political enemies.[131] In addition, the Reich Criminal Police kept separate card indices of "professional criminals," Gypsies, and wanted criminals, allowing for their ready identification and detention.[132]

Finally, similar identification methods have played a critical role in oppressive governmental regimes in more recent times. One need only recall the use of internal passports by the U.S.S.R. for much of the twentieth century,[133] and by apartheid South Africa during the 1950–1980s,[134] which proved highly valuable in the monitoring and mistreatment of inhabitants.

## CONCLUSION

As the preceding discussion suggests, the strong desire to identify criminally risky persons has endured for centuries, and over time numerous technologies have sought to satisfy it. With the passing acceptability of physical branding and mutilation, governments were obliged to devise noncorporeal methods of identification. Early on, unsystematic technologies, such as "spotting" by police, were employed, yet such efforts were soon found wanting due both to their impermanence and subjectivity and to their inability to accommodate the transitoriness of the criminal element. After all, the keen memory and perceptiveness of, say, a Boston police officer was of scant help to an officer in New Orleans, when a Boston-bred perpetrator was arrested in the Crescent City.

The need for a more systematic method to distinguish individuals gave rise to important innovations, each designed to render the criminal element more knowable: daguerreotype "rogues' galleries," Bertillonism, and fingerprint analysis in particular. In addition, in Germany, France, Britain, and antebellum America, governments engaged in early registration efforts, requiring that individuals themselves, including noncriminal offenders, provide identifying information. With registration, governments secured a powerful new way to identify and monitor individuals on an ongoing basis, facilitated, importantly, by the compelled extraction of information from the individuals themselves, adding a unique plank to the platform of government surveillance capability and authority.

# 2 EARLY LAWS: 1930–1990

CHAPTER 1 SURVEYED the evolving array of methods used to identify and monitor criminal offenders. While initially chiefly retrospective in orientation, and first used by penal officials to sort first-time from repeat criminal offenders, the methods were soon deployed in the name of preventing and detecting crime beyond prison walls. Nineteenth-century efforts in Germany, France, and England to register criminals, in particular, exemplified this orientation and significantly enhanced the knowledge base and surveillance capacity of governments. In the United States, registration was only haltingly embraced—targeting particular noncriminal subpopulations: emancipated African Americans in antebellum times, German Americans during World War I, and other select subgroups. With increasing anxiety over crime during the 1920s and 1930s, however, came growing interest in registering criminal offenders. This chapter traces the evolution of U.S. criminal registration laws during the first sixty years of their use.

## PRELUDE

The desire to reliably identify criminal types assumed new importance in the late 1920s and early 1930s, when national anxiety over crime was at a fever pitch. Crime commissions, headed by such legal giants as Dean Roscoe Pound of Harvard Law School and Supreme Court Justice Felix Frankfurter, offered extensive analyses and critiques of state and local criminal justice systems.[1] Similar efforts were undertaken by the federal government under the auspices of the Wickersham Commission[2] and the National Crime Commission.[3] In

1933, the Senate held hearings in Chicago, Detroit, and New York on criminal "rackets,"[4] and Senator Royal Ferguson direly proclaimed on the Senate floor that "[t]here are places in America where orderly government has disappeared, where the underworld is in control . . . I am here to say that unless America shall be aroused the underworld gangster will come more and more into control in the United States."[5] Increasingly influential media outlets, in turn, fed public alarm over "professional criminals" and "hoodlums" who extended their geographic reach by means of newly available transportation methods.[6]

In retrospect, it remains unclear whether crime rates in the early to mid-1930s were actually surging[7]; indeed, social scientists of the time acknowledged that the available crime data were woefully inadequate.[8] Americans, however, were convinced that they in fact faced unique criminal peril.

Given these anxieties, it should come as no surprise that criminal convicts would be singled out for particular scrutiny. While the nation as a whole bridled against the prospect of universal fingerprinting and being required to carry identification cards, ex-offenders (like emancipated African Americans decades before) were a far easier target. August Vollmer, police chief of Berkeley, California, part-time professor at UC Berkeley, and as noted in Chapter 1, a proponent of universal fingerprinting, was among the first to advocate registration of ex-offenders. In 1925, Vollmer urged registration of "all known criminals coming to California so that police can check their movements."[9] The practice, Vollmer later asserted, would have manifold benefits, including "putting beggars out of business"; "positively preventing bigamy"; "keeping track of migratory criminals"; "locating persons wanted for crime"; "tracing family deserters"; "locating escaped prisoners, probation and parole violators"; "furnishing the opportunity for the officer to identify suspects"; "preventing prostitutes from engaging quarters without [lessors'] knowledge of their identity"; "cataloging sex inverts and perverts"; "preventing criminals from roaming about and concealing their identity"; and "establishing the identity" of "poison purchasers," "automobile prostitutes," "pimps and panderers," "professional gamblers," "drug peddlers and users," and "confidence men."[10]

Echoing Vollmer's enthusiasm, one police chief asserted in 1930 that registration would permit "police officers throughout the cities and throughout the rural districts . . . to say to a suspected person, 'Who are you? Where do you belong? Where is your card?'"[11] The official predicted that the strategy "would cut down crime by fifty percent or more, because [criminal actors would] know they must have an identification card with them."[12]

The appeal of registration was compounded because other laws targeting recidivists at the time were not up to the task. One strategy involved singling out recidivists for enhanced prison terms.[13] The progeny of recidivist enhancement laws dating back to the colonial era (see Chapter 1), and predecessors of the modern habitual offender and "three strikes" provisions (see Chapter 3), the laws were predicated on the idea that repeat lawbreakers were more culpable, could possibly be deterred by the threat of heightened punishment, and if not, should be segregated from society for a greater period of time. Then as now, however, the laws failed to provide any psychic benefit to a society feeling itself under siege from a population of transient, anonymous potential criminal recidivists.

A second strategy gaining popularity in the early 1930s held greater preemptive promise. Rather than waiting for the criminally predisposed to offend, governments sought to nip crime in the bud by targeting persons thought to be criminally predisposed. Like vagrancy laws, which since the Elizabethan era had allowed governments to in effect criminalize status and condition,[14] new laws in the 1930s allowed for the arrest of individuals branded a "public enemy" (New York), a "habitual criminal" (Michigan), or a "gangster" (Illinois). The efforts, however, soon came under constitutional attack on a variety of grounds, including due process (due to vagueness), equal protection, and freedom of association.[15]

Around the same time, courts were also showing increasing disdain for the practice of banishing criminal offenders, a time-honored means for American state and local governments to rid themselves of unwanted individuals.[16] With physical branding and mutilation no longer permissible, and static information technologies such as Bertillonism and fingerprinting of little practical use in the continued monitoring of offenders, the time was ripe for registration.

## LOCAL CRIMINAL REGISTRATION LAWS

The first American criminal registration laws originated in the Los Angeles area in the early 1930s, when the rapidly growing region was beset by fear over gangsters invading from Chicago and eastern cities. Testament to this concern, the *Los Angeles Times* in January 1931 published on its front page the views of local judges and experts on how to handle what the paper called the "gravest problem now confronting the metropolitan area of Los Angeles." In response, a former federal judge offered that "[i]n the curbing of professional crime there may be some merit in the continental method of individual registration," adding that such an undertaking "of course should be considered in the proper manner."[17]

In late September 1931, Los Angeles District Attorney Burton Fitts presented for consideration to the County Board of Supervisors the nation's first criminal registration law. Fitts's statement accompanying the proposed ordinance provided as follows:

> While the registration system is in vogue generally throughout the world outside the United States and has proved a great deterrent to criminals changing their location with facility to avoid detection or to carry on their operations, such registration has not been initiated in the United States.
>
> The class of persons whose criminal convictions are the basis for the requirement of their reporting to the Sheriff [constitutes persons] who are moving from one large center to another and enjoying the immunity that their residence in new locations affords them. They are able to become installed in this community under aliases, and to operate directly or through their associates with comparative freedom . . .
>
> It is not too much to say that this ordinance, if passed, will do as much as any one thing can possibly do to make safe this community from this menacing class of social outlaws; nor is it believed that opposition to the ordinance will come from any source except those who to seek to carry on their several "rackets" in Los Angeles [C]ounty without interference from the authorities.

A new tool was needed, the statement continued, to fight the emerging menace: "former convicts, who are well supplied with money and all the luxuries of life . . . [and] able, through the technicalities of the present laws to make it impossible to proceed against them under any existing statute or ordinance."[18] While chiefly targeting "culprits en route to Los Angeles or harboring expectancy of visiting the area," the *Los Angeles Times* reported, the proposed law "nevertheless provides means for the indexing of all persons convicted" of the crimes specified who already resided in the area.[19]

Despite initial optimism over its quick passage, what the *Times* called "scores of letters" poured into the County Board's offices voicing criticism and support for the proposed ordinance, resulting in delay.[20] On September

29, the *Times* reported that local attorney S. S. Hahn, representing a "delegation of citizens," appeared before the Board in opposition to the ordinance.
Hahn argued:

> Not only is the measure vicious, but it places in the hands of ignorant police
> officers too much power. It will create a tremendous amount of suffering for
> ex-convicts who are trying to rehabilitate themselves, especially those who
> are in good positions of trust. It appears to be a harmless law, but we have too
> many harmless laws that appeared to be harmless until adopted, when they
> became dangerous weapons in the hands of certain interests.[21]

By mid-October, opinion on the ordinance was "hopelessly divided" and
votes were again delayed pending further study.[22]

In late October, public debate resumed, and District Attorney Fitts stressed
to the Board that "[s]omething has got to be done, something drastic. A number of eastern gangsters are already here or headed this way," and Fitts identified several by name. Fitts added that "only this week 'Bugs' Moran at Chicago
issued orders that the price of alcohol here be raised $1 a gallon."[23]

Again, however, opponents raised concerns. Some, the *Times* reported,
reiterated that registration would "work a hardship on the man at one time
convicted but who is now attempting to go straight." Such hardships, a Reverend Gustav Brieglieb contended, would include loss of work, and the reverend
cited several instances of men he personally knew who would lose jobs if their
pasts were disclosed. A representative of the State Department of Welfare,
Reba Spilva, worried about the effects on dependent members of households
who "had never committed a crime but who would have to suffer if the man
in the house had to expose his past."[24]

Practical concerns over the law's implementation were also expressed.
The supervisor of probation within the State Department of Welfare, echoing
concern over registration voiced by London's chief of police in the 1870s (see
Chapter 1), worried that individuals trying to remain law-abiding would be
penalized by the law, while "the man who is breaking the law now will keep
on breaking it and will evade registering." A spokesperson for the Los Angeles
County sheriff similarly offered that "the criminal not intending to live right
will evade the law. It will be a law that will be very difficult to enforce."[25]

In the face of this opposition, interest in the ordinance waned at the county
level, yet soon attracted the attention of municipalities. On December 1, 1931,
city prosecutors in Long Beach persuaded the City Council to adopt on voice

vote a registration law similar to that proposed to the county,[26] and the City of Alhambra adopted a registration ordinance around the same time.[27]

Not until September 11, 1933, did the Los Angeles County Board of Supervisors, by a unanimous vote, finally approve a criminal registration ordinance, endorsing what the *New York Times* called a "quick move" to rid the area "of organized crime and a possible reign of gangsterism," and an "ace card" in the campaign to rid itself of organized crime.[28] A day later, on September 12, 1933, at the urging of its Board of Police Commissioners,[29] the City of Los Angeles, adopted the ordinance in substantially identical form, also by unanimous vote.[30]

The findings made by the County Board in support of the emergency measure reflect the anxious tenor of the times and the felt need for registration, stating:

> WHEREAS, it is established by undisputed proof and by recent daily criminal acts of major character in this county that a wave of crime is sweeping through this nation and is occurring with menacing frequency in the County of Los Angeles and that throughout this nation there is a commendable accord of all good citizens in endeavoring to stop the activities of modern criminals, and
>
> WHEREAS, experience has shown that most of the crimes herein enumerated and which are fraught with the greatest danger to this community, have been and are being committed by habitual and dangerous criminals traveling from place to place throughout this nation and state, and
>
> WHEREAS, the Board of Supervisors has information of greatly increased numbers of such criminals to remove to said county for the purpose of pursuing therein their criminal operation, and
>
> WHEREAS, many of such criminals are known and reputed to be "gangsters," and it is their intention to engage in unlawful gangster operations within said county, and
>
> WHEREAS, most of such gangsters have criminal records within or without the State of California, and
>
> WHEREAS, there is no means provided by law whereby the law enforcement officers of said county may be apprised of the arrival into, or the presence in, said county of such criminals until a crime or act of violence shall have been committed by them, and

WHEREAS, the undisclosed presence of such criminals within said county will constitute a serious menace to the peace and safety of the community and will seriously endanger the life and limb and property of the people of said county,

NOW, THEREFORE, this ordinance is necessary for the immediate preservation of the public peace, health and safety, and shall take effect immediately.[31]

The list of enumerated crimes warranting registration reflected the breadth of the perceived threat. Unlike modern criminal registration laws, originating in the 1990s amid marked concern over sex crimes and child victimizations (see Chapter 3), the Los Angeles ordinance focused on a diversity of offenses, exclusive of sex crimes. Registration was required of all persons convicted in state or federal court within the past ten years of

counterfeiting, grand theft, grand larceny, embezzlement, forgery, obtaining money or property by false pretenses, burglary, felonious assault, robbery, arson, murder, kidnapping, extortion, carrying a deadly weapon, taking or enticing a person for purposes of obtaining ransom, or violation of any state or federal criminal law relating to the possession, sale or transportation of narcotics.[32]

The law exempted from coverage persons who received a full pardon, as well as those on probation or parole under California law and whose probation or parole "expired without any revocation."[33]

Individuals subject to registration had to do so within 48 hours of arrival in Los Angeles or, if already a resident, within 48 hours of the law's enactment. In addition to being fingerprinted and photographed, registrants were required to provide the following information to law enforcement:

their name and any alias(es); a complete physical description; the name of each registration-eligible conviction, where the crime was committed, the name under which the person was convicted, the date of the conviction, the name of the penal institution where incarcerated; address of each residence or stopping place in Los Angeles; a description of each such place (e.g., a hotel); and the length of time the person expected to remain in Los Angeles.[34]

While not required to verify the aforementioned information at specified intervals, registrants were obliged to notify authorities of any change of address or living location within 24 hours of making the change.[35] Any violation of the ordinance was punishable by a maximum $500 fine, imprisonment of up to six months, or both.[36]

The idea of registering ex-convicts quickly caught on elsewhere. Perhaps heeding humorist Will Rogers's recommendation in a *New York Times* letter to the editor that Los Angeles' registration ordinance "look[ed] like one of the best measures to help offset this crime racket," and was worth "looking into,"[37] registration was soon embraced by other Sun Belt localities. Later in 1933, two other southern California communities—South Gate and Arcadia— and two Florida communities—the City of Miami Beach and Coral Gables— enacted registration ordinances.

The ordinances of the era shared an obvious lineage with the seminal Los Angeles effort yet varied in certain respects. Miami Beach, for instance, provided findings that virtually copied those contained in the Los Angeles ordinance;[38] imposed identical limits regarding registration timeliness and updates; and also targeted persons convicted of specified crimes within the past ten years. However, the list of registration-eligible crimes in Miami Beach varied, and included those of a sexual nature: grand larceny; burglary; coun-terfeiting; obtaining money by false pretenses; robbery; arson; murder; kid-napping; taking or enticing any person for the purpose of obtaining ransom; extortion; forgery; violation of any law prohibiting the carrying of deadly weapons; possession, sale, or transportation of narcotics; felonious or aggra-vated assault; crime against nature; mayhem; transporting a female across state lines for immoral purposes; and rape. Miami Beach also singled out for registration the crimes of miscegenation and keeping a brothel or house of ill fame, crimes not typically regarded as foremost public safety threats. Like Los Angeles, Miami Beach designated registration violations as misdemeanors, punished by a fine of up to $500, yet prescribed only a jail term of up to ninety days, or both.[39]

As they do today, however, early-era registration evolved in response to crime concerns. By November 1936, for instance, the City of Los Angeles' registration ordinance was recast, differing in several important ways from the original law adopted just over three years before, including specifying a broader range of registerable offenses. Instead of targeting individuals con-victed of specified crimes, the law broadly required registration of persons convicted of "an offense punishable as a felony in the State of California" or an offense committed elsewhere that would be punishable as a felony in California. The amended ordinance also specified other, possibly misdemeanor offenses that warranted registration: possession, distribution or use of illegal drugs; carrying, possessing or owning a concealed or deadly weapon or silencer; use, possession or manufacture of tear gas; any attempt or conspiracy to commit any of the aforementioned offenses; and conviction or adjudication as a "drug addict."[40]

The new provision also specified that persons who "enter[ed] and remain[ed]" in the city for twenty-four hours had to register more quickly (within three hours), and inform police of when they entered California and of any address they anticipated for the ensuing three months. Nonresidents who visited the city five times during a thirty-day period were also required to register.[41] Furthermore, the new ordinance rescinded the prior exemption for persons who satisfied probation or parole terms.[42]

Finally, the 1936 version specified that the information contained in the registry was not "open to inspection by the public," except when necessary for assisting in the apprehension of criminal suspects. Any police officer or department employee who disclosed registrant information "otherwise in the regular course of his duties" could be subject to misdemeanor liability.[43]

The spurt of interest in registration in the 1930s soon tapered off, with the nation in the 1940s seemingly otherwise absorbed in wartime efforts. In the 1950s, however, interest was rekindled when the public imagination was captured anew by crime—this time by a new breed of professional criminals: the Mafia.[44] With little apparent political resistance to the new laws,[45] registration grew in popularity. By 1969, 52 U.S. localities had registration laws.[46] Of these, 47 specified felony-level offenders for inclusion; 14, sex offenders; 20, narcotics law violators; 2, persons convicted of "any crime," and 1, persons convicted of any crime involving "moral turpitude." While 28 localities targeted only one of these subpopulations, the balance required registration of some combination thereof.[47]

While a number of major U.S. cities lacked registration provisions, including Boston, Chicago, Detroit, New Orleans, New York,[48] and St. Louis, and the laws in existence were scattered throughout the nation (except the northeast), localities with registration laws tended to clump together[49] with the laws assuming identical substantive form.[50] While it is impossible to say with certainty why this occurred, one might venture that localities were motivated by something more than a desire to adopt a perceived good policy. They may well have been motivated by a desire to avoid being perceived as adjacent havens for persons wishing to avoid the burdens of registration.[51]

Viewed en masse, early-generation laws were not altogether true to their avowed animating purpose, in several respects. First, rather than targeting solely itinerant offenders, the laws required that current residents and new arrivals alike register. Moreover, while ostensibly concerned with "professional criminals," the laws typically did not condition registration eligibility on more than one prior conviction. Rather than inferring criminal propensity on the basis of two or more convictions, as did recidivist offender sentence enhancement laws, or assessing individuals for recidivist risk,[52] local registration laws typically were triggered upon a single conviction.[53] More fundamentally, although organized crime interests were allegedly of paramount concern, those with ties to organized crime stood a good chance of evading registration because they often lacked criminal records or their records involved nonregisterable offenses (such as tax-evasion or gambling).

The breadth of early-era registration eligibility criteria similarly betrayed their avowed intent. Persons convicted of a "felony" or "any crime" often had to register, sweeping up a wide range of offenses not associated with recidivist risk. Similarly, registration was required in Los Angeles for the crime of abducting a woman for marriage and, as noted, in Miami Beach (as well as Pensacola and St. Petersburg), Florida, for miscegenation.[54] Then as now, singling out sex offenders, a group known to have lower recidivism rates than other offender groups,[55] highlighted a similar inconsistency.

The laws also exhibited significant variation in their procedural requirements. The time within which persons had to register varied considerably, including "immediately" or "promptly" (St. Paul, Minnesota); 2 hours (Wilmington, Delaware, where a sign at the city limits warned entrants of the registration requirement)[56]; 6 hours (Philadelphia); 24 hours (Evansville, Indiana); 48 hours (Seattle, Washington); and 30 days (Long Beach, California). Over time, several though not all localities required registrants to report their place of employment and its location, and to inform police of any related changes.[57] A few localities (such as Camden, New Jersey; Montgomery, Alabama; Wilmington, Delaware; and Zanesville, Ohio) also required registrants to carry identification cards,[58] imposing penalties for failure to present them upon demand.[59]

The extent of retroactive application of the laws likewise varied among localities. Although many did not specify how many years back into an offender's criminal history the registration requirement extended, those that did imposed limits of varied length. As a result, in Birmingham, Alabama, one would have to register when a conviction had occurred within the past thirty years, whereas in Philadelphia, Pennsylvania (as in most places), only when a conviction dated back ten years.

Registration of juvenile offenders, a matter of significant controversy today (see Chapter 3), did not appear to be much of an issue during the early era. Like today, many jurisdictions left it unclear whether youths adjudicated delinquent in juvenile court (as opposed to being waived and convicted in adult court) were required to register. However, because jurisdictions customarily required that a "conviction" occur, a term typically reserved for adult offenders, juveniles were presumably exempted. One exception was Jersey City, New Jersey, which expressly required that juveniles register.[60]

Early-era registration laws typically failed to specify the duration of registration. As a result, individuals once subject to registration presumably were required to comply with registration requirements while they remained in the jurisdiction. This was so even if the individual remained crime free and otherwise satisfied all registration-related requirements.[61]

Finally, while local laws at most made violation of registration a misdemeanor (likely due in part to their limited sovereign authority to punish), they also refrained from requiring that violations be willful or based on a knowing refusal or failure to comply. Only a failure to comply with the ordinance apparently needed to be shown.

## STATE CRIMINAL REGISTRATION LAWS

State legislatures gravitated to registration somewhat later. That registration provisions first appeared in localities should perhaps come as no surprise, given that it is at the local level that crime is felt most directly and concern over anonymous (potentially criminal) neighbors is likely most acute. Florida, in 1937, became the first state to concern itself with criminal registration but did so sparingly, requiring registration only of those persons residing in counties with a population over 150,000 (Dade, Duval, and Hillsborough).[62] In 1947, California enacted the nation's first registration law of statewide applicability (retroactive to 1944),[63] and over the next several years three other states enacted laws: Arizona (1951),[64] New Jersey (1952),[65] and Illinois (1953).[66] By 1967, the number of states with registration laws had grown to eight, including Nevada (1961),[67] Ohio (1963),[68] and Alabama (1967).[69] By 1989, with the addition of Arkansas (1987),[70] Utah (1987),[71] Montana (1989),[72] and Oklahoma (1989),[73] twelve states at some point had criminal registration laws on the books.

Unlike local governments, which often focused on broad categories of crimes, such as felonies, or enumerated a litany of specific registerable offenses, early state laws were more prone to focus on particular offender subgroups. With the exception of Florida, which initially required that persons convicted of felonies "involving moral turpitude" register, a category it saw fit to define quite broadly,[74] and later targeted felons more generally,[75] other states targeted specific subgroups with registration.

Sex offenders, as today, were a main target of state government concern. Of the early-era state registration laws singling out a subgroup, all except two (New Jersey and Illinois, which had "drug addict" registration laws) targeted sex offenders. Notably, the first statewide law, California's 1947 registration law, was sex offender specific. The law, introduced at the behest of the California State Peace Officers' Association, was patterned after the Los Angeles "convicted persons" ordinance[76] and passed with unanimous support in both houses of the state legislature.[77] (Proponents originally sought to require that a broader swath of offenders register, as in Los Angeles, but because all legislative proposals targeted only sex offenders, lobbying efforts were eventually directed to that end.[78])

Four years later, in 1951, Arizona became the second state to target sex offenders for registration,[79] followed by three others: Nevada (1961), Ohio (1963), and Alabama (1967). Illinois enacted a sex offender registration law in 1986 (complementing its 1953 drug offender registration law),[80] followed by Arkansas and Utah in 1987, and Montana and Oklahoma in 1989. Altogether, as of 1989, every state with at least one registration law targeted sex offenders.

Compared to the mainly sex offender–related registries of today, discussed in Chapter 3, sex offender registry laws of the early era were of modest scope. California's law, for instance, specified that persons convicted since 1944 of the following offenses were required to register:

- rape (felony)
- enticement of a female (felony or misdemeanor)
- abduction of underage female to practice prostitution (felony)
- seduction of a female (felony)
- incest (felony)
- crime against nature (felony)
- lewd or lascivious act on a child under age 14 (felony)

- oral copulation (felony)
- indecent exposure (misdemeanor)
- annoying or molesting a child or loitering near a school (misdemeanor)
- lewd or lascivious conduct contributing to the delinquency of a child (misdemeanor).[81]

The law afforded a thirty-day period to register with either the local county sheriff or chief of police, and individuals were required to provide a photograph, fingerprints, and a signed written statement containing "such information as may be required by the State Bureau of Criminal Identification." Authorities were to be "promptly" notified in writing of any address changes. Failure to comply was punished as a misdemeanor. The law further specified that registration information was not to be "open to inspection by the public or by any persons other than a regularly employed peace or other law enforcement officer."[82]

Like their municipal counterparts, state registration laws generally did not target recidivist offenders; a single conviction for an enumerated offense sufficed. The sole exceptions were laws in Arkansas, Illinois, and Ohio, which were triggered only upon a second or subsequent conviction for an enumerated offense. (In each state, however, the law was subsequently amended to require registration for first-time convictions.)

States, like municipalities, also evinced a desire to single out drug offenders for attention. New Jersey's law, enacted in 1952 and in effect until 1971,[83] specified that all persons who intended to remain in the state for more than twenty-four hours must register if they had been convicted of a drug offense within the past ten years.[84] In addition to being fingerprinted and photographed, individuals were required to carry an identification card containing a "registry number" and other identifying information.[85] They were also required to inform local police of any change in address within a day of its occurrence. Registrants wishing to visit another locality had to report to local police, show their identification card, and "furnish such information relating to his intended residence or whereabouts within such municipality and such other information" as local police demanded.[86] Violation of the statute resulted in being punished as a "disorderly person."[87]

Illinois enacted a law in 1953 requiring registration of "drug addicts," defined as "any person who repeatedly uses narcotic drugs."[88] The law, repealed in 1957, required individuals to register with the Department of Registration and Education and carry a card containing their name, address, and occupation, the length of time they had "been an addict and the type of narcotic drugs used." Each registrant was required to carry the card at all times. Any failure to register resulted in imprisonment for between six months and one year, and a failure to carry a card resulted in a fine from $1 to $100, a prison term not to exceed one year, or both.

In 1961, California began registering drug offenders, requiring that registration take place within thirty days of conviction or arrival in the state.[89] Address changes had to be reported within ten days and violations were punished as a misdemeanor. The registration requirement terminated five years after release into the community.[90] Before being repealed in 1972,[91] the provision was complemented by a limited form of community notification, which as discussed in Chapter 3 today complements each state's registration law. If "any school employee" was arrested (not convicted) for any of the drug offenses specified, police were required to notify education authorities in the community where the individual was employed.[92]

Finally, state registration laws in the early era at times singled out additional offenses—other than sex and narcotic crimes—for registration. In 1984, for instance, California enacted its criminal registry for persons convicted of arson.[93]

## REGISTRATION'S GOALS

Early-era registration provisions had several ostensible goals. Like prior identification methods, the information collected was thought to be helpful in facilitating police apprehension of recidivists and possibly in deterring criminal activity inasmuch as registrants knew themselves to be under police scrutiny. However, unlike Bertillonism and other predecessor strategies, registration provided data on the whereabouts of individuals. In addition, and critically important, registration required that subjects themselves affirmatively provide identifying information and update authorities on their whereabouts, obliging their active involvement in their own surveillance and likely enhancing its psychic force.

Although empirical evidence on whether registration actually fulfilled these goals is lacking, some anecdotal support was found for such a surveillance effect. A study conducted by the *University of Pennsylvania Law Review* in 1954, for instance, reported that a "Negro woman" registrant took the initiative to visit local police to inform them that she was leaving the city for four days to attend her mother's funeral, doing so in order "that she would not be in trouble when she returned." Another individual immediately went to police to report loss of his criminal registration card, in order to avoid punishment (despite the fact that the local law did not require that a card be carried).[94]

Governments also hoped that the mere requirement of informing police of one's presence might motivate criminally prone individuals to leave town in search of another jurisdiction lacking a registration law. In Los Angeles, for instance, on the day its law was enacted the police chief predicted that it would "drive out of the city 95 per cent of the ex-convicts."[95] Within a week of registration being imposed, the *Los Angeles Times* reported a "speedy exodus of suspected gangsters and racketeers from Los Angeles to other cities . . . due to their fear of arrest under the new felon registration law."[96] On the East Coast, the *New York Times* reported that in Camden, New Jersey, where a new ordinance required registration within twenty-four hours of arrival:

> Police officials confidently expect to see the crime curve for Camden to turn sharply downward immediately. The city is determined that it shall no longer be known as a haven for criminals who . . . find living conditions too uncomfortable in Philadelphia and flee across the Delaware. The new criminal registration ordinance . . . is anything but a "Welcome to Camden" sign for the habitual lawbreaker.[97]

Birmingham, Alabama, police embraced registration not only because it would give them "an accurate check upon the criminal element," but also because it likely would "result in an exodus of a great many known criminals."[98] It was reported that in Los Angeles registration fostered the view in the "underworld" that the city was "hot," and caused "Eastern gangsters" to flee the city.[99] A Philadelphia detective favored his city's ordinance based on his personal experience of several "undesirables" being discouraged from entering the city.[100] In St. Paul, Minnesota, a town renowned in the 1930s for being a haven for gangsters such as John Dillinger, Ma Barker, and Alvin "Creepy" Karpis, city officials reported "several cases" of ex-felons electing to live elsewhere. In 1955, almost twenty years after the law's enactment, one official confidently stated that "[w]e have no racketeers or gangsters in our town—and hardly any prostitutes."[101]

Registration also had appeal as a street-level patrol tool for police, enhancing their capacity to monitor and detain potential recidivists in their midst. In St. Paul, for instance, the mayor lauded registration "not as an offensive weapon but as a defensive one." According to a newspaper account, police would not engage in

> spectacular roundups of unregistered criminals . . . But when a St. Paul detective recognizes a known felon on the street or gets a tip that he is in town (perhaps to case a job), the detective either knows where the man can be reached—if he has registered—or has grounds on which to pick him up and hold him—if he hasn't.[102]

Registration was also lauded as a means to actually make life easier for ex-convicts. According to an advocate of a bill before the North Carolina Legislature, with registration in place police would have no reason to detain ex-offenders who were compliant and "known to be cooperating with officers."[103]

The enhanced power to arrest, in particular, held promise as a new and welcome option. Unlike vagrancy and "gangster" laws, which required proof that the suspect lacked a visible means of support or had a criminal reputation, registration merely required proof of presence in the jurisdiction, a prior conviction, and a failure to satisfy registration requirements.[104]

Moreover, individuals arrested under suspicion for unrelated crimes could, with a registration law in place, be convicted of a registration violation in the event sufficient evidence in support of such other crimes did not surface.[105] In Los Angeles, the chief of police offered the following optimistic appraisal in the immediate wake of the enactment of the city's law:

> In the past after every major crime we have picked up many suspects with criminal records. In some of these cases we have been sure that we had in custody the guilty men, but we often lacked legal proof to convict. Under the new registration law, each of these men can now be dealt with not for the crime suspected, but for failing to register.[106]

This discretionary authority to detain and arrest, in turn, enhanced another related police power: the capacity to selectively target individuals.[107] In one particularly high-profile instance, Philadelphia police in 1958 broke down the door of a hotel room inhabited by "pint sized" Los Angeles "gangster" Mickey Cohen and arrested him (while shaving) for failing to register within twenty-four hours of his arrival in the city. Cohen was in town to confer with his lawyer, former district attorney Samuel Dash, on a libel case Cohen had filed against a local magazine. His Los Angeles attorney, Samuel Brody, who was also swept up in the hotel room raid, had reportedly received assurances from the police commissioner and district attorney that it was "all right" for Cohen to visit the city.

At the trial for the registration violation, an officer testified that Cohen was arrested because "he is marked for a rub-out and we don't want that happening here." The officer elaborated that "I have no apologies for arresting the nation's No. 1 gangster. I would do it again today, tomorrow and the next day if I had to." With tempers in the courtroom high, Dash branded the arrest an "outrage" and a "crying shame" given the prior assurance of officials. Ultimately, the charge was dismissed and the judge apologized to Brody for his having been mistaken for a "hood."[108] According to Dash, Cohen was not subject to registration because he had never been convicted of gambling or a felony—only a violation of income tax laws.[109]

Less newsworthy, a Philadelphia police officer reportedly invoked the city's registration law to arrest a suspected vagrant who "answered back" when told to "move on," and another officer deployed the law to arrest a confederate of a suspected gangster who was "arrogant, obnoxious, and a self-admitted 'cop-hater,'" which the officer asserted was "enough reason to get this guy on something."[110] Other Philadelphia officers used registration selectively to "make it rough on a fellow" known to be "wrong," or to detain individuals until details regarding criminal activity in which they might possibly be involved could be obtained.[111] In California, where registration targeted a broad range of consensual homosexual activity, Los Angeles police regarded the state registration law as being "effective as a deterrent to homosexual activity" and useful because "homosexuals are prone to commit violent crimes and crimes against children."[112]

As is the case today, by providing a basis to arrest, registration also afforded police the attendant authority to search, and to use any evidence discovered in a subsequent criminal case against the arrestee. Because the evidence need not be factually related to the basis for arrest, the discretionary arrest authority provided by registration laws provided police considerable potential advantage.[113]

Finally, registration laws provided police and prosecutors welcome discretionary authority in charging decisions. In California, for instance, the same facts could allow an arrest or charge to be for a registerable offense such as sodomy or indecent exposure, or, in the alternative, a nonregisterable offense such as disorderly conduct or outraging public decency.[114] This authority enhanced the plea bargaining power of prosecutors, allowing them to extract better deals from defendants wishing to avoid registration by pleading to a nonregisterable offense.[115] Such flexibility also allowed judges a measure of latitude to reduce charges to nonregisterable offenses (such as for heterosexuals caught in a public sexual act).[116]

## REGISTRATION'S OUTCOMES

Despite the high praise for registration from authorities and anecdotal supporting evidence provided above, it appears that in actuality the laws had little practical effect. The authors of the aforementioned 1954 *University of Pennsylvania Law Review* study, for instance, reported that while Philadelphia reported 4,100 registrants, other localities had unrealistically few, belying its actual use: Canton, Ohio, 0; Gadsen, Alabama, 17; Harrisburg, Pennsylvania, 35; Rochester, Minnesota, 2.[117]

But even experience in Philadelphia, with its comparatively high number of registrants, indicated limited use. Most officers and detectives were aware that a registration law existed but "did not seem to know the specific content of the ordinance" and mistakenly believed (and told registrants) that registration identification cards had to be carried at all times, when no such requirement existed.[118] More significant, the study reported that there appeared to be no arrests in the city (or in nearby Camden, New Jersey) based solely on a registration violation[119] and that registration information was not used in a proactive manner by police.[120] Rather, violations were detected when individuals were arrested for other crimes and police learned that they were not properly registered.[121] According to the study, "[r]egistration information may get lost in the mass of police records and no attempt is made to advise [police] . . . who will come into contact with the registrant that they are to keep a particularly close watch on him."[122] In short, "the practices observed lead to the conclusion that the registration data [are] rarely used by the police."[123]

Prosecution data painted a no more robust picture. Louisville, Kentucky, for instance, reported only two prosecutions for registration violations, with both cases being resolved by asking the defendants to register and leave town.[124] Los Angeles had a total of 74 prosecutions (53 for "sex criminals"); Cincinnati, 3; Ft. Lauderdale, 6; Reno, 21; Trenton, 38; and Seattle, 12.[125] In Philadelphia, during the first nine months of 1953, there were a total of 69 registration prosecutions, with 21 convictions resulting.[126] All alleged violations related to a failure to register or carry a card (itself, again, not actually an offense); it was thought unlikely that any violations stemmed from a failure to update address information or from supplying false information.[127] Of the 48 cases not resulting in conviction, over half (28) actually constituted violations of the city's registration provision, yet they were dismissed.[128] On this basis the study discerned a judicial bias against enforcement of registration laws,[129] about which local law enforcement were seemingly well aware and contributed to the view that the laws had little utility.[130]

Other sources during the period revealed similar disinterest. In Los Angeles in 1956, for instance, the city attorney issued 39 complaints for violations of the "convicted persons" registration law, with 32 resulting in convictions (and 21 of these receiving straight probation). In addition, as elsewhere, individuals were rarely booked solely on a registration violation. Most frequently, when a patrol officer discovered that a registration-eligible individual was violating the law, the violator was forced to register and then released. The policy was "to allow the subject to register and then release him, except in those cases where a subject is uncooperative or is frequenting high crime areas of the city."[131]

## CRITICAL CONCERNS

Meanwhile, although broadly popular, early registration laws were not free of controversy, as the public debates surrounding consideration of Los Angeles's registration ordinance attested. In 1949, journalist Howard Whitman condemned what he saw as the stigmatizing effects of registration:

> It was the old idea of the brand all over again, though it took the form of this blacklist file instead of the old scarlet letter of New England. There was little thought of doing anything to rehabilitate these people—or even to protect society from them. The emphasis was merely on having them branded and filed, Gestapo style, so that they could be hounded and cracked down upon when the public mood so demanded . . . Why not burn them at the stake? Saves transportation.[132]

Still more noteworthy were the reservations voiced by justice officials, who expressed concerns that would never be voiced by their contemporary peers. A remarkable example is contained in a memorandum written by California Director of Corrections Richard McGee to Governor Earl Warren outlining McGee's concerns over the wisdom of the proposed statewide sex offender registration law that Warren was considering (and eventually signed) in July 1947.[133] McGee wrote that while the offenses committed by registrants were "revolting," there was a "principle involved which should not be disregarded.

It has never been the practice in America to require citizens to register with the police, except while actually serving a sentence under the Probation or Parole Laws." McGee also worried that subjecting sex offenders to registration would establish a problematic precedent, warning that "[b]efore embarking upon this new practice with a particularly offensive group of individuals, we should not overlook the fact that we may be opening the door to similar practices for other groups as time goes on."

McGee also noted practical concerns over effectiveness that resonate to this day (see Chapter 5), and indeed were voiced in the 1930s (see above) and before that in 1870s England (see Chapter 1), predicting that individuals would likely fail to comply, thereby undercutting the very knowledge-based premise of registration itself. To McGee, it was

> questionable whether those cases most in need of careful supervision would continue to register and hence submit to questioning every time a sex crime is committed in the community. It is probable that a large percentage of these individuals would change their residence without registering and run the risk of being convicted of a misdemeanor for failing to do so.

McGee closed his memo by stating that while he was "entirely in sympathy" with the purposes of the bill, he felt "the problem was far too complex to attempt to control it by such a simple expedient as registration with the police."

Similar dissent was expressed by the Utah attorney general in 1956.[134] With the state embroiled in public debate over whether Utah should enact a registration law, the state's chief law enforcement officer expressed uncertainty over the constitutionality of registration:

> The imposition of the registration requirements upon persons merely because they have been convicted of a single crime, the fact that persons in some cases are subject to the registration requirement for the rest of their lives, and especially the manner in which these laws are often used, leads to the conclusion that these ordinances are of questionable constitutionality.

Criticism was also often heard from personnel engaged in enforcing registration laws, including prosecutors. For instance, in November 1953 the city solicitor of Canton, Ohio, stated that he was "not in sympathy [with] the ordinance as it is impossible to administer and it has only been used in isolated cases to eliminate an undesirable individual coming into the community."[135]

He also expressed concern over the stigmatizing effect of registration, offering that even though registration "may be of value in checking hardened criminals, it works a definite hardship on an individual who has paid his debt to society and is attempting to rehabilitate himself."

Among police, it was reported that "the vast majority" of Philadelphia detectives were "apathetic" to the city's registration ordinance, considering it ineffective for a variety of reasons. These reasons included the belief that registration was superfluous because individuals were usually arrested for other crimes, often rendering the registration violation of no practical use; the inability to arrest as an initial matter because it was not possible to visually detect violations; and, as noted above, the tendency of trial courts to dismiss registration charges.[136] Philadelphia police also expressed concern over the constitutionality of registration, considering it indistinguishable from New Jersey's anti-"gangster" law, recently invalidated by the U.S. Supreme Court.[137] A police officer in an unspecified jurisdiction believed "this was not the kind of control that the police should have" and that individuals should not be subject to continued police scrutiny after they have served their time.[138]

Similar concern was manifest among corrections personnel. For instance, in 1958 a nationwide survey of administrators charged with overseeing the interstate transfer of probationers and parolees reflected that 63% of respondents opposed registration.[139] One anonymous respondent related that registration "would be evaded by the very ones we would like to have recorded," and believed that "the philosophy is wrong and smacks of a Communistic or Nazi police state."[140] In Utah, the Board of Corrections in the 1950s unanimously opposed a proposed law on the ground that registration would stigmatize ex-convicts.[141] An editorial in the *Prison Journal*, published by the Pennsylvania Prison Society, expressed concern over the surveillance effects of registration. Even though registry information was not authorized for public release, registration itself was problematic because of

> the psychic effect which it has on every man who has committed a crime. It opens up old sores. It re-affirms the conviction which exists in the minds of too many of these people that the police are anxious to get something on them. The fact that this is not so does not matter. The important thing is that this group of individuals feels that it is so . . . Moreover, it is extremely doubtful that the law accomplishes anything. The men who want to be law-abiding and forget their past criminal record will register, while those engaging in criminal activities of course will not.[142]

## REGISTRATION IN THE COURTS

During the first two decades of their existence, criminal registration laws failed to attract the attention of appellate courts. However, the judiciary— including the U.S. Supreme Court—did address the validity of a variety of registration laws targeting noncriminal offenders shortly before and during the era. In *Bryant v. Zimmerman* (1928),[143] for instance, the Court upheld the constitutionality of a New York State law mandating registration of organizations (such as the Ku Klux Klan) that were comprised of at least twenty persons and required an oath. Later, in *Hines v. Davidowitz* (1941),[144] the Court invalidated a Pennsylvania law that required resident aliens to register and carry an identification card, not because it objected to registration in principle, but rather because the state law conflicted with the Federal Alien Registration Act of 1940, which did not require that cards be carried.[145]

In subsequent years, the Supreme Court upheld other registration laws targeting individuals engaged in various endeavors, such as lobbyists and gamblers.[146] Lower federal courts similarly upheld occupation-specific registration laws, such as those targeting taxi and bus drivers, bootblacks and persons selling newspapers on the streets, and foreign agents.[147] In the early 1950s federal courts also upheld the growing number of state and local laws requiring that Communists register with authorities.[148]

By the mid-1900s, state courts had also addressed a variety of requirements with close similarity to criminal registration. The photographing and fingerprinting of criminal offenders, in particular, was the subject of frequent challenge, especially by persons never convicted of a crime. While courts typically found no fault with local police retaining prints and photos, even of mere arrestees, finding that any diminution of privacy was justified by the needs of an increasingly mobile and complex society,[149] the courts expressed concern when photos were disseminated as part of "rogues' galleries," and not "filed away from public gaze."[150] At least with respect to mere arrestees, posting their images next to convicted criminals, as the Supreme Court of Louisiana put it in 1906, would improperly amount to a "permanent proof of dishonesty."[151]

Not until 1957, almost twenty-five years after enactment of the nation's first criminal registration provision, a time when dozens of localities and six states had laws,[152] did the U.S. Supreme Court consider their constitutionality. In *Lambert v. California*,[153] the Court addressed a claim brought by Virginia Lambert, who in 1951 had been convicted of felony forgery in Los Angeles and eventually served six months in the county jail. In February 1955, Lambert was approached by two Los Angeles police officers, who without telling her why she was under suspicion, proceeded to roll up her sleeves, inspect her arms, and search her purse, in an apparent effort to detect illegal drug use or possession. Unsuccessful, the officers, without telling Lambert the basis for her detention, handcuffed and transported her to the police station, where she was questioned for two hours and subject to a more thorough bodily search, which again failed to reveal evidence of any contraband.[154]

Lambert was thereafter charged with violating the Los Angeles registration law, which as noted above required registration of persons previously convicted "of an offense punishable as a felony in the State of California." At trial, Lambert stipulated to the fact that she had resided in Los Angeles during the preceding seven years, that her prior conviction had not been set aside or nullified, and that she had not registered with police.[155] She contended, however, that she was never informed of a duty of felons to register and that she had no reason to know of such a duty, given that she had served only jail and not prison time (the latter typically reserved for felons).[156]

For its part, the City of Los Angeles disputed Lambert's claim that notice was lacking, asserting that if the Court were to endorse the position advanced by the defense, "it would be necessary to continually publish all ordinances and statutes each day."[157] Moreover, the ordinance constituted a reasonable exercise of police power in the face of an increasingly mobile, anonymous, and crime-prone population. Without registration, it was not "possible to be aware of the presence of all persons deemed to be a potential threat to the community."[158] The law was no more burdensome than other laws requiring registration of lobbyists, bootblacks, or other similar groups and was a necessary protective measure directed against "the evil of professionalism in crime, providing a convenient method of ascertaining the number and whereabouts of persons who have previously been convicted, generally of crime of the felony class."[159]

By a 5-4 vote, the Court invalidated the provision, concluding that it violated the Due Process Clause of the Fourteenth Amendment because it imposed a criminal sanction upon persons who lacked actual or constructive notice of their duty to register. Before getting to the merits of the case the majority acknowledged that registration laws were "common" with respect to regulation of businesses and other activities and "their range wide." Registration in principle passed muster: the ordinance was at most . . . a law enforcement technique designed for the convenience of law enforcement agencies through which a list of the names and addresses of felons then residing in a given community is compiled. The disclosure is merely a compilation of former convictions already publicly recorded in the jurisdiction where obtained.[160]

The majority, however, emphasized that the law was unique insofar as it imposed criminal liability solely on "wholly passive" behavior. Unlike registration laws previously condoned by the Court, which were "akin to licensing statutes in that they pertain to the regulation of business activities," the Los Angeles ordinance was not "accompanied by any activity whatsoever, mere presence in the city being the test."[161] This distinction was problematic because "circumstances which might move one to inquire as to the necessity of registration were completely lacking" and actual knowledge of the registration requirement was also absent.[162] According to the majority, "[w]here a person did not know of the duty to register and where there was no proof of the probability of such knowledge, he may not be convicted consistently with due process. Were it otherwise, the evil would be as great as it is when the law is written in print too fine to read or in a language foreign to the community."[163]

In the wake of *Lambert*, state courts addressed state and local criminal registration laws, entertaining a new basis for challenge: preemption. In *Abbott v. Los Angeles* (1960),[164] the defendant, a conscientious objector previously convicted of a federal felony for draft evasion, and who admitted knowledge of both the Los Angeles and California registration laws, was convicted of violating the former. The California Supreme Court reversed the conviction, finding that the State's sex offender-specific registration requirement had "occupied the field," barring application of the Los Angeles law of more general scope.

Similarly, in 1969, the New Jersey Supreme Court invalidated a local law requiring that all persons convicted of a crime or a narcotics violation register, when state law only singled out narcotics offenders for registration. Before getting to the merits of the preemption claim, the court in *State v. Ulesky*[165] first emphasized that registration in principle was not objectionable, and that the State could if it wished delegate to local government legislative authority over registration: "The objective of the ordinance is to alert local police of the presence of persons convicted of crime. The premise is that recidivism is a reality, and hence law enforcement will be aided by an awareness of individuals whose prior offenses reveal an added risk."[166]

At the same time, however, the *Ulesky* court recognized that registration "imposes a burden upon persons convicted of crime . . . The ordinance touches all who have transgressed and does so in far reaching terms."[167] To the court, in the absence of an express legislative delegation, which might for instance specify "the particular crimes which it believes to be so suggestive of recidivism as to warrant the burden of registration,"[168] the aggregate impact of such local laws was simply too great: "If every municipality required registration for no reason other than being within its borders, the cumulative burden would be intense. It could crush a man if he had to reveal a past error wherever he abides or whenever he sojourns in another place."[169] Because the State had seen fit to require registration of narcotics offenders alone, the local law betrayed the inference that the "Legislature was unwilling to say that other convictions warranted such restraint upon the right of the individual merely to be or to move about."[170]

California's sex offender registration law attracted additional judicial scrutiny during the 1970s and 1980s. In *In re Birch* (1973),[171] the state supreme court addressed whether a guilty plea was entered with requisite knowledge when the defendant, who pled guilty to misdemeanor lewd and dissolute conduct for urinating in public, without being told that the conviction would trigger lifelong registration. The court unanimously held that Birch's lack of knowledge of "the unusual and onerous nature" of registration rendered the plea invalid. Registration would make Birch "the subject of continual police surveillance. . . . Although the stigma of a short jail sentence should eventually fade, the ignominious badge carried by the convicted sex offender can remain for a lifetime."[172]

In *In re Reed* (1983),[173] the state supreme court held that requiring registration as a result of being convicted of soliciting "lewd or dissolute conduct" from an undercover officer, a misdemeanor, violated the California Constitution's prohibition of "cruel or unusual" punishment. The court again focused on the lifetime ignominy associated, entailing "command performances" before police, and concluded that in light of the law's uncertain efficacy as a police investigative tool, it appeared "out of all proportion to the crime of which petitioner was convicted."[174]

While significant, *Birch* and *Reed*, along with *In re King*, which deemed

California's registration requirement for indecent exposure cruel and unusual punishment,[175] did not undercut registration in principle. In 1968, for instance, the Nevada Supreme Court unanimously rejected a claim that Nevada's registration law violated the Fifth Amendment privilege against compelled self-incrimination. According to the court, "[t]he disclosure required by the act is merely a compilation of former convictions already publicly recorded in the jurisdiction where obtained."[176] While the law could be used "for 'rousting' purposes by the police," and it might "be desirable and wise" to exempt certain ex-convicts (such as those who had remained crime free for many years), such concerns were for the legislature to consider.[177] Registration itself was permissible. According to the court, registration was "no doubt a valuable tool in the hands of the police, because it gives them a current record of the identity and location of ex-felons."[178] (Indeed, a few years later, in 1977, newspaper heiress Patty Hearst, free on bond in connection with her recent federal bank robbery conviction while allegedly a captive of the Symbionese Liberation Army, dutifully registered with Las Vegas authorities when visiting Frank Sinatra.[179])

Similarly, in 1978, in *People v. Mills*,[180] the California Court of Appeals rejected a variety of claims, including that registration violates the constitutional rights to privacy and equal protection. With respect to privacy, the court reasoned, Mills "waived" any such right when he was convicted of child molestation, and to the extent the right endured, it was trumped by the state's right to collect and maintain information on convicted sex offenders.[181] With respect to equal protection, California's decision to subject some sex offenders to registration, but not others, was a legislative determination that it refused to second-guess. All that was needed to uphold the decision was a rational basis, which the court had no hesitance in finding, concluding that California had "a legitimate state interest in controlling crime and preventing recidivism by sex offenders."[182]

The preceding survey permits several conclusions to be drawn with respect to the tenability, so far as the courts were concerned, of criminal registration. *Lambert, Abbott,* and *Ulesky* together effectively sounded the death knell for local registration laws. Absent some effective method of notifying potentially eligible individuals of their duty to register, perhaps such as in Wilmington, Delaware, where a sign at the city's borders served notice, or a defendant himself did not claim lack of knowledge,[183] *Lambert* rendered local-level registration laws problematic. *Abbott* and *Ulesky,* in turn, precluded localities from enacting registration laws that conflicted with any state registration law in effect.

*Lambert* and the decisions noted, however, did not condemn registration in principle,[184] and indeed often expressly endorsed registration laws and lauded their potential benefit.[185] Registration, in short, remained a viable policy option for states.

## DESUETUDE

States, however, showed meager interest in registration during the latter half of the twentieth century. No new state registration laws were enacted between 1968 and 1984,[186] and thereafter only Illinois (1985)[187] and Arkansas (1987)[188] adopted laws. Arizona repealed its law (enacted in 1951) in 1978 and reinstated it in 1983.[189]

In addition, the handful of state laws in existence came in for heavy criticism and eventual disuse, with the most sustained criticism coming in California.[190] In 1949, over two years after statewide sex offender registration was required, a mere 550 individuals were registered, prompting the state attorney general to issue a bulletin urging more vigorous enforcement of the law.[191] In 1983, the Los Angeles city attorney branded the state registry "dysfunctional" because it included a superabundance of nonserious sex offenders and was of no use in the effort to locate the "Hillside Strangler" that terrorized the community.[192] And in 1986, the *Los Angeles Times* published a lengthy exposé on problems with the state registry, focusing on the widespread failure of eligible individuals to register and chronic informational inaccuracies.[193] Noting that accuracy and enforcement concerns had plagued the state's effort from the start, the *Times* reported that the current attorney general questioned the utility of the law. A spokesperson had "no idea" of the extent of wrong address information in the registry, adding that the fundamental problem was that "we have a people-tracking system of people that don't want to be tracked." Consistent with this view, 90% of the address information concerning registrants in San Bernardino County in 1984 was believed to be erroneous.

The *Times* also reported that some authorities felt that any effort to construct and maintain a comprehensive and accurate registry was impossible due to resource and personnel limits. The captain in charge of records for the Los Angeles County Sherriff's Office, a jurisdiction that at the time had over 26,000 registrants on file, offered that it is "totally impractical to follow up to the degree that we'd be able to know where they are. It's a matter of workload and numbers." In light of this, the Sherriff's Office had ceased mailing notices to newly released offenders who did not voluntarily present themselves for registration because the office was receiving a less than a 1% response rate.[194]

Finally, the *Times* noted that uncertainty remained over whether, in light of the effort involved, the law was worthwhile. According to the Sacramento County Sherriff:

> And the question is, how much is gained? Suppose we had a file that was 100% accurate. What use is that file? How effective is that file in combating the sex crime problem? I'm not sure that anyone has really done that kind of analysis. We don't know how many crimes we would solve, or prevent.[195]

Nor, for that matter, was the record clear that sex offenders in particular warranted being singled out for registration. While an effort had been proposed to comprehensively assess comparative recidivism rates in the state, the study never came to fruition; a more limited study conducted in 1983, however, indicated that sex offender recidivism rates were lower than those of other offender subpopulations.[196]

Similarly ambivalent results were reflected in research findings contained in a 1988 California Department of Justice study. For instance, only 63% of law enforcement felt that registration was effective in "following the whereabouts (residence address) of sex registrants." More damning, and reflecting prior empiric concerns, the study concluded that

> lack of up-to-date address information was considered a major problem of the system . . . Sex offenders, like other types of offenders[,] are a mobile group and, given the inconsistent approach to offender registration, it is unlikely that offenders more likely to offend are those keeping their residence address information up-to-date with law enforcement.[197]

The report also identified seven major problems with registration in California, including the lack of resources to devote to enforcement of registration requirements and the lack of punishment for violators.[198]

## CONCLUSION

The foregoing account of first-generation American criminal registration laws highlights their evolutionary debt owed to prior information-based social control technologies. Early-era registration laws, like prior efforts, derived from an awareness of individual-level criminal risk and endeavored to render the risk more knowable. Yet state and local registration laws afforded unique advantages, especially compared to Bertillonism and fingerprint analysis. They did more than merely store identification information: they provided knowledge of the physical whereabouts of individuals, enhancing government capacity to monitor and detain. Moreover, in theory, registration fostered a belief among registrants that they were being watched, a psychic sensibility augmented by the requirement that registrants themselves provide identifying information and keep it updated. Finally, so far as the historical record reveals, during the period of 1930–1980s American criminal registration was free of the systematic racist and ethnocentric tendencies of Bertillonism and fingerprint technology, whereby offenders were arrayed by crude racial classification.[199]

Nevertheless, by the end of the 1980s registration seemed doomed as a social control method. Although civil liberties and fairness concerns had largely abated, and principled judicial opposition remained a nonissue, registration laws scarcely figured in American life. More important, the basic utility of registration itself was very much in doubt, echoing fundamental concern over the accuracy and completeness of registries dating back to nineteenth-century Europe. As the next chapter demonstrates, however, while these core concerns persisted as the 1990s dawned, the nation's disinterest in criminal registration laws would soon experience a radical reversal.

# 3 MODERN LAWS: 1990–TODAY

IN THE 1990S, INTEREST IN CRIMINAL registration laws experienced a dramatic resurgence. While in 1990 only a handful of states had registration laws, by the middle part of the decade registration was in effect nationwide and was the subject of ubiquitous public attention. In addition, modern-day registration was complemented by community notification, a new social control strategy designed to expand the premise of knowledge empowerment beyond law enforcement to communities as a whole. This chapter chronicles the reemergence of registration and the genesis of community notification, as well as the content of the registration and notification laws themselves. The chapter concludes with a comparison of new- and old-generation laws that, while sharing many similarities, nonetheless differ radically in their reach and requirements.

## EARLY STATE ACTIVITY

The modern revitalization of registration laws has been highly personalized. Today, the images of Jacob Wetterling, Megan Kanka, and other child victims that spurred the nationwide embrace of registration in the 1990s are indelibly linked with registration, and indeed the names of child victims themselves have very often been contained in the titles of laws passed by legislatures.

As history would have it, however, the event that inspired modern registration had an anonymous cast. On May 20, 1989, in Tacoma, Washington, a 7-year-old boy, whose identity remains publicly unknown, was kidnapped, raped, sexually mutilated, and left to die in the woods. Found by a local family that had ventured into the woods to bury a pet cat, the boy, partially clothed, mumbling incoherently and in a state of shock, managed to identify his assailant, Earl Shriner. Shriner, who had been released from prison five months earlier and had a long record of convictions involving physical and sexual victimization of children, was well known to authorities. Indeed, state prison officials had been aware that Shriner intended to sexually abuse children upon his release and had tried to have him involuntarily committed to a state psychiatric institution.[1] The effort failed, however, because the presiding judge concluded that the commitment criteria were not satisfied.

Upon learning of Shriner's alleged involvement, and that authorities were aware of his proclivities, an outraged group of citizens calling itself the "Tennis Shoe Brigade" demanded that Washington Governor Booth Gardner initiate a special session to revamp Washington's sex offender laws.[2] The organization, created by the boy's mother (Jean Harlow)[3] and others,[4] urged citizens to send a single child's tennis shoe to the governor—intended to symbolize the feet of those entitled to walk without fear—along with a note stating "please protect us, have a special session." The governor's office soon received fifteen thousand shoes, and a private fund was established for the boy with over $335,000 in contributions.

Three weeks after the assault, Governor Booth Gardner issued an executive order creating the Governor's Task Force on Community Protection. The Task Force, consisting of criminal justice and treatment professionals, legislators, academics, and victims' advocates (including Ms. Harlow), was asked to undertake a comprehensive reexamination of the state's efforts to combat sexual violence.[5] In late November 1989, the Task Force issued its report, which contained an expansive array of suggested reforms, unanimously adopted by the legislature as the Community Protection Act of 1990. According to Task Force member David Boerner, the problem lay not so much in a discrete error of judgment but rather a systemic incapacity to handle individuals such as Shriner:

> The core of this problem was not the exercise of governmental power but the absence of that power. The boy's story was different not only because of the horrific violence that was inflicted, but also because so many government officials knew so much about Earl Shriner, had predicted that he would do what he did, had sought to use the legal system to prevent him from doing what he did, and had failed. Apparently, the law was powerless to protect.[6]

The new law contained provisions designed to maintain custodial and non-

custodial control over convicted sex offenders, including a controversial provision designed to broaden involuntary civil commitment of "sexual psychopaths." In contrast to prior commitment laws also targeting sex offenders, in
effect in several states since the 1930s,[7] Washington's new law did not commit
individuals in lieu of criminal confinement. Rather, it permitted potentially
indefinite institutionalization in addition to—and after—prison terms served
by individuals deemed "sexual predators," a new phrase destined to become a
staple of the American lexicon.[8]

Although the commitment provision dominated public attention, the Act
also contained the State's first registration requirement, which came with a
new wrinkle. In contrast to early registration laws, which expressly prohibited
public disclosure of registrants' identifying information,[9] the Act allowed law
enforcement to make such information publicly known.[10] While the strategy,
today known as community notification, had been considered by California
in the mid-1980s,[11] and information "leakage" on registrants (whether intentional or not) had occurred since the 1930s, Washington became the first
jurisdiction to officially authorize dissemination of registrants' identifying
information.

The Washington Legislature backed its new regime with legislative findings. With respect to registration, the Act provided:

> The legislature finds that sex offenders often pose a high risk of reoffense,
> and that law enforcement's efforts to protect their communities, conduct
> investigations, and quickly apprehend offenders who commit sex offenses,
> are impaired by the lack of information available to law enforcement agencies
> about convicted sex offenders who live within the law enforcement agency's
> jurisdiction. Therefore, this state's policy is to assist local law enforcement
> agencies' efforts to protect their communities by regulating sex offenders by
> requiring sex offenders to register with local law enforcement agencies.[12]

With respect to community notification, the legislature reiterated that persons
convicted of sex offenses posed a "high risk" of recidivism and concluded:

> Persons found to have committed a sex offense have a reduced expectation
> of privacy because of the public's interest in public safety and in the effective
> operation of government. Release of information about sexual predators to
> public agencies and under limited circumstances, the general public, will
> further the governmental interests of public safety and public scrutiny of

the criminal and mental health systems so long as the information released is rationally related to the furtherance of those goals. Therefore, this state's policy ... is to require the exchange of relevant information about sexual predators among public agencies and officials and to authorize the release of necessary and relevant information about sexual predators to members of the general public.[13]

The law was sex offender specific in scope, requiring registration of a juvenile or adult convicted of an array of offenses, including: rape (fist–third degree), rape of a child (first–third degree), child molestation (first–third degree), sexual misconduct with a minor (first and second degrees), indecent liberties, and any felony "with a finding of sexual motivation."[14] It applied to all persons who committed their offense on or after the date of the law's enactment in 1990 or were then in custody or under supervision. Individuals newly released from prison had to provide registration information within thirty days of release and newcomers to the state had forty-five days to comply.[15] While the law did not prescribe the periodic verification of registrants' information, it did specify that any change of residence was to be reported to the sheriff within ten days.

Duration of registration was tied to the seriousness of the crime triggering registration: lifetime for class A felonies, fifteen years for class B, and ten years for class C. Juveniles who were 15 years of age or older at the time of offense were subject to the same registration requirements; younger juveniles had to register for two years. Registration violators were subject to a sliding scale of punishment. If registration was triggered by a class A felony, a knowing registration violation was treated as a class C felony; if the conviction triggering registration was other than a class A felony, the violation was a gross misdemeanor.

Local law enforcement was responsible for handling community notification and was authorized to "release relevant and necessary information" on registrants when "necessary for public protection." Such necessity was determined in part on the basis of information provided by an End of Sentence Review Committee that evaluated each ex-offender prior to release from prison, yet notification decisions were primarily made by local police, most often pursuant to a policy proposed by the Washington Association of Sheriffs and Police Chiefs. Under the policy, local police determined recidivist risk level, which in turn determined who would receive information: for level I offenders, only local police; for level II, community groups, school districts, and registrants' neighbors; for level III, the most serious registrants, all of the above as well as members of the media.[16] Other departments opted for a more liberal policy and made information on all registrants (including photographs, and home and work addresses) available to the public upon request. Still others made case-by-case decisions on notification in a less category-specific manner.[17]

In terms of the history of criminal registration laws, Washington's 1990 provision was hugely significant. It drew the nation's attention to registration, and public sentiment and policy quickly awakened to the perceived benefits of empowering police with readily accessible information on criminally risky individuals. As a result of the law's community notification provision, moreover, such information was not to be monopolized by police. Rather, like the "rogues' galleries" of the mid-nineteenth century, information was made available to the public as well. Unlike the galleries, however, the information would be provided directly to communities, by means of affirmative government effort, rather than being passively reposed in police stations. Finally, Washington's law underscored the political power of an outraged community, galvanized by the belief that crucial information was being withheld by government officials, information that could be used to defend against the likes of Earl Shriner.

Washington's 1990 law, however, was not the sole catalyst behind the modern proliferation of registration and community notification. Events and legislative developments elsewhere also played a key role. Chief among these was the October 1989 abduction of 11-year-old Jacob Wetterling, who while riding his bike in rural Minnesota was seized by a masked man brandishing a gun. Although Jacob was never found, and no arrests were made in the case, the tragedy proved a potent catalyst for change. His mother, Patty Wetterling, in February 1990, created the Jacob Wetterling Foundation, which soon became a highly influential national force on matters relating to child victims of violence and sexual abuse.

The group's influence was felt in Minnesota with creation of the Task Force on Missing Children, the findings of which resulted in the state's June 1991 adoption of a registration law. With passage of the law, entitled the "Predatory Offender Registration Act," Minnesota became the fifteenth state to have a registration provision. In contrast to Washington's law, the Minnesota law set a flat registration term of ten years, and only targeted individuals convicted of offenses involving child victims, including kidnapping and those of a sexual nature.[18] Like Washington, however, Minnesota's law was retroactive, requiring that persons register if released into the community after the law's effective date, regardless of the date of offense or conviction. Registrants had ten days to inform state authorities of any address changes and violators of the requirement faced prosecution at the misdemeanor level and an additional five years of registration.[19]

In June 1992, after the murder of a 6-year-old boy by a recidivist sex offender,[20] Louisiana became the second state to adopt a registration law with a community notification feature, adopting in almost verbatim form legislative findings contained in Washington's law.[21] While Louisiana limited community notification to probationers and parolees,[22] it was far more onerous than Washington's seminal law because it required registrants themselves to notify community members by means of mailings and newspaper advertisements (at their own expense).[23]

In 1993, interest among states was further fed by a series of highly publicized child victimizations by recidivist sex offenders. In July, 10-year-old Zachary Snider of Indiana was molested and murdered by a neighbor who, unbeknownst to community members, was a convicted sex offender.[24] In September, 7-year-old Ashley Estell was abducted from a Texas playground and killed, resulting in the arrest of a previously convicted child molester.[25] A month later, 12-year-old Polly Klaas was kidnapped at knifepoint from a slumber party in her California home, while her mother slept in an adjacent room. Her body was found two months later and Richard Allen Davis, who had a history of kidnapping and other offenses, was arrested, convicted, and eventually executed for the crime.[26]

Of even greater national influence, however, was the July 1994 rape and murder of 7-year-old Megan Kanka, in Hamilton Township, New Jersey. Police soon arrested Jesse Timmendequas, a twice-convicted sex offender who lived across the street from the Kankas along with two other sex offenders he had met in a facility for "compulsive and repetitive sex offenders." Timmendequas lured the young girl into his home by promising to show her a puppy, and proceeded to sexually abuse and kill her. While local police were aware of Timmendequas's history, his neighbors in Hamilton Township reportedly were not. Voicing a sentiment that would come to define modern registration and notification laws, Megan's outraged and grieving mother, Maureen Kanka, asserted that if she and her family "had known there was a pedophile living on our street, [Megan] would be alive today."[27] The sentiment had immediate resonance with the public. As a story in the *Philadelphia Inquirer* noted, "the public outcry last week . . . said: let us know. Tell us when dangerous sex criminals are living next door."[28]

In the wake of Timmendequas's arrest, the Kanka family initiated a petition drive to urge adoption of community notification, gathering more than 200,000 signatures in three weeks.[29] In response, Speaker of the Assembly Garabed "Chuck" Haytaian, running for the U.S. Senate, declared a legislative emergency, bypassing customary committee debate and forcing proposals to move directly to the floor for consideration.[30] After winning unanimous support in both the state houses, on October 31, 1994, three months and two days after Megan Kanka was murdered, Governor Christine Todd Whitman (with Maureen Kanka at her side) signed Megan's Law.[31] With its passage, New Jersey became the fifth state to allow for some form of community notification (Tennessee and Alaska adopted notification laws earlier in 1994).[32]

Like Washington's law, New Jersey's Megan's Law contained a variety of initiatives, including a provision intended to reinvigorate the state's extant involuntary civil commitment law, which like similar provisions in other states had fallen into disuse.[33] In New Jersey, however, registration and community notification—not involuntary commitment—garnered most public attention. And unlike laws in Washington and other states, New Jersey required, rather than only permitted, that information on particular registrants (those deemed most likely to reoffend) be disseminated to community members.[34] The goal, as the New Jersey Supreme Court observed in a 1995 constitutional challenge to the law, was "to give people a chance to protect themselves and their children."[35]

### FEDERAL INVOLVEMENT

The aforementioned state developments did not escape the attention of Congress. Indeed, Jacob Wetterling's October 1989 disappearance in Minnesota prompted U.S. Senator David Durenberger (R-MN) in May 1991 to push for adoption of the "Crimes Against Children Registration Act."[36] As Durenberger told his Senate colleagues:

> The reasons for enacting this legislation on the national level are clear: sexual crimes against children are widespread; the people who commit these offenses repeat their crimes again and again; and local law enforcement officials need

access to an interstate system of information to prevent and respond to these horrible crimes against children.[37]

Even though Jacob's abductor's was never identified and there was no evidence that he had been sexually abused (his body was never found), Durenberger stressed that if law enforcement "had been aware of the presence of any convicted sex offenders in the community, it would have been of invaluable assistance during those first critical hours of investigation." Consistent with this presumption, Durenberger urged adoption of a registration regime like that recently enacted in Minnesota.[38] Later that summer, Representative Jim Ramstad (R-MN), introduced a similar registration bill in the House.[39] Despite the backing of the Wetterling Foundation, and bipartisan support in both houses of Congress, registration failed to gain Senate approval after conference.[40]

Undaunted, Durenberger continued his push for legislation, which soon was renamed in memory of Jacob Wetterling.[41] In November 1993, the campaign was advanced in the House by Ramstad, who, along with many supporters, emphasized the need for a registration law in light of the purported high recidivism risk of sex offenders.[42] Again, registration was touted by Ramstad and others for its capacity to provide law enforcement with access to information on convicted offenders in the immediate wake of a child being abducted or harmed.[43] Registration was also lauded for its perceived value as a deterrent to criminal activity. According to Ramstad, registration would put an individual "on notice that when subsequent sexual crimes are committed in the area where he lives, he may well be subject to investigation. This may well have a prophylactic effect, deterring him from future sexual crimes."[44]

Although twenty-four states at the time had registration laws, a federal "stick"[45] was needed "to prod all States to enact similar laws and to provide for a national registration system to handle offenders who move from one State to another."[46] Federal law would do so by threatening to withhold crime-fighting funds from states that failed to adopt registration requirements prescribed by Congress.

In its original incarnations, starting in 1991, what was to become the Jacob Wetterling Act, treated registrants' information as "private data," available only to law enforcement for investigative purposes and government agencies for confidential background checks on persons working with children.[47] A provision authorizing notification and also requiring registration of "sexually violent predators" who victimized adults was eventually advanced by Senator

Slade Gorton (R-WA) and Representative Jennifer Dunn (R-WA), based on
Washington State's 1990 law.[48] Because the House and Senate bills differed,
with the House version omitting community notification,[49] a conference
committee was convened. Advocating adoption of notification Dunn urged
on the House floor in the summer of 1994:

> What is the point of registering and tracking these convicted predators if we
> are not going to share that information with the very citizens who are at risk?
> How can we justify knowing where a sexual predator has located, and not
> notify the women and families in that neighborhood? The rate of recidivism
> for these crimes is astronomical. We know that. And that is why it is incumbent
> upon us to ensure that community notification is encouraged. Without the
> community notification, the effort is reduced simply to the collection of
> data.[50]

Dunn's motion urging the conference committee to include a notification
provision prevailed by a 409-10 vote, yet the committee report, likely as a result of concern over potential vigilantism associated with making registrant
information available,[51] ultimately omitted notification.[52]

As history would have it, however, the report was released on same day in
late July that the media was dominated by reports of Megan Kanka's victimization in New Jersey. Shortly thereafter, Gorton and Dunn took to the floor
to castigate the conferees for omitting the community notification provision.
Gorton stated:

> [T]he conferees just do not get it. [Only providing information to police] is
> meaningless. It would not have helped Megan Kanka . . . It would not have
> helped Polly Klaas . . .
>
>  The families in these communities and these innocent victims had a right
> to know that dangerous sexual predators were in their midst . . .
>
>  I offer this bipartisan bill today in memory of Megan Kanka, Polly Klaas,
> and the thousands of innocent victims of brutal rapists, molesters, and
> murderers, that deserve to know when sexually violent predators were released
> into their community.[53]

A week later, Dunn rose to speak in the House "with a deep sense of
outrage":

Seven-year-old Megan Kanka of New Jersey is dead, Mr. Speaker. Sexual predators were released into her community and they lured that precious little girl to a grisly death.

Conferees who worked to protect the rights of sexual predators should understand this: The next little girl killed by a released predator will haunt them.

Mr. Speaker[,] it is outrageous that a few conferees have supplanted their will for the will of the House. It is outrageous that this bill effectively denies notification to the next Megan Kanka or the next Polly Klaas, or to your mother or sister or daughter. And it is outrageous that we would place the rights of criminals over the rights of victims.[54]

Representative Dick Zimmer (R-NJ) made the absence of notification a key rallying point, and Chris Smith (R-NJ), representing the township in which Megan Kanka lived, condemned the "arrogance" of the conferees and demanded that notification be permitted. Smith stated:

No one in the community knew the killer's sordid past, Mr. Speaker. Had Megan's grieving parents known that their neighbor was a dangerous person, they would have taken steps to protect their precious child. Megan's parents had a right to know.[55]

The redoubled effort to include a notification provision proved a success, in part as a result of lobbying efforts by President Bill Clinton,[56] who signed the legislation into law (with Maureen Kanka at his side)[57] as part of the massive $30 billion omnibus anticrime crime bill on September 13, 1994.[58]

Intended to encourage states to adopt registration minima,[59] the resulting law, the Jacob Wetterling Crimes Against Children and Sexually Violent Offender Registration Act, required states to adopt its provisions if they wished to avoid losing 10% of their Byrne Formula Grant Program criminal justice funds, the main general federal founding source for state criminal justice programs.[60] States had to do so within three years of the law's enactment, subject to a two-year extension for states making "good faith efforts," and any undistributed funds resulting from a state's failure to comply were to be reallocated to compliant states.[61]

In its final form, Wetterling affected more offenders than originally envisioned. In its initial form, in May 1991, the legislation only targeted persons "convicted of a criminal offense against a victim who is a minor."[62] When enacted in September 1994, this requirement persisted,[63] but the law also targeted persons (1) convicted of "a sexually violent offense"[64] and (2) designated by the sentencing court as a "sexually violent predator."[65] Registration was required of persons released from prison or placed on probation, parole, or supervised release after the Act's implementation, providing them ten days to comply.

Sexually violent predators were subject to lifetime registration (with possible judicial relief) and were required to verify their residential addresses every ninety days; the other two categories of registrants had to register for ten years and annually verify their addresses. Individuals who knowingly violated the law were "subject to criminal penalties in any State" in which the violation occurred.

Congress, tracking the Washington State provision, elected to make community notification permissive, not mandatory. Wetterling specified that law enforcement "may release relevant information that is necessary to protect the public" regarding a registrant, and like state laws then in effect provided officials immunity from civil liability for actions taken in "good faith" pursuant to the law.

Wetterling further provided that the Attorney General was to issue implementing guidelines, and in April 1996, final guidelines were released,[66] emphasizing that federal law specified only minimum requirements for states (constituting a "floor . . . not a ceiling").[67] According to the Attorney General, "[t]he general objective of the Act is to protect people from child molesters and violent sex offenders through registration requirements. It is not intended, and does not have the effect, of making states *less* free than they were under prior law to impose registration requirements for this purpose."

The states enjoyed similar upward latitude with respect to community notification. Federal law imposed no limits on the "standards and procedures that states may adopt for determining when public safety necessitates community notification." With respect to which registrants should be subject to community notification, states were free to (1) engage in "particularized determinations that individual offenders are sufficiently dangerous to require community notification" or (2) make "categorical judgments that protection of the public necessitates community notification with respect to all offenders with certain characteristics or in certain offense categories." Finally, the guidelines acknowledged that community notification was permitted but not required. States could authorize agencies "to release information as neces-sary" and to allow the public to access registrants' information.

Wetterling was not the federal government's last word on registration and notification—far from it. Indeed, federal interest manifested itself anew in July 1995, less than a year after Wetterling became law, when Representative Zimmer introduced H.R. 2137, mandating that states utilize community no-tification, again under threat of losing federal funds.[68] Prompted by concern that states were "reluctant" to release information on registrants,[69] and that a lack of community notification in some twenty states might leave communi-ties vulnerable and encourage sex offenders to migrate in search of anonym-ity,[70] the bill won unanimous support in both Houses of Congress.[71] In May 1996, President Clinton signed the federal Megan's Law.[72] With Richard and Maureen Kanka, Patty Wetterling, and Marc Klaas (father of Polly) at his side at the White House Rose Garden signing ceremony, Clinton remarked:

> From now on, every State in the country will be required by law to tell a community when a dangerous sexual predator enters its midst. We respect people's rights, but today America proclaims there is no greater right than a parent's right to raise a child in safety and love. Today America warns: If you dare prey on our children, the law will follow you wherever you go. State to State, town to town. Today, America circles the wagon[s] around our children.[73]

Later, in a radio address to the nation, President Clinton invoked Megan Kanka and emphasized the informational empowerment premise of the new federal mandate:

> We have taken decisive steps to help families protect their children, especially from sex offenders, people who according to study after study are likely to commit their crimes again and again . . . That's why in the [1994] crime bill we required every state in the country to compile a registry of sex offenders, and gave states the power to notify communities about child sex offenders and violent sex offenders that move into their neighborhoods.
>
> But that wasn't enough, and last month I signed Megan's [L]aw. That insists that states tell a community whenever a dangerous sexual predator enters its midst. Too many children and their families have paid a terrible price because parents didn't know about the dangers hidden in their own neighborhood. Megan's [L]aw, named after a seven-year-old girl taken so wrongly at the beginning of her life, will help to prevent more of these terrible crimes.[74]

With Megan's Law, the federal government did not now merely permit community notification. Rather, renouncing the permissive approach of Washington State, on which Wetterling was based,[75] the new federal law adopted the mandatory approach used in New Jersey's namesake law: states were instructed that they "*shall* release relevant information that is necessary to protect the public concerning a specific person required to register."[76] Again, guidelines elaborated on the new law, this time specifying how states would not satisfy federal community notification expectations. States wishing to receive Byrne Grant funds could not merely provide registrants' information to police, government agencies, victims, or potential employers. Nor could they comply by affording "purely permissive or discretionary authority" to officials to conduct notification. Rather, "[i]nformation must be released to members of the public as necessary to protect the public from registered offenders."[77]

The guidelines emphasized, however, that states retained discretion over which registrants in particular would be subject to community notification and how registry information would be disseminated. The guidelines identified several ways that states could satisfy the federal mandate, including:

1. Conducting risk assessments of all registrants and releasing information in accord with assessed risk levels (as in Washington and New Jersey)

2. Releasing information only on registrants convicted of certain offenses

3. Making registrant information available to members of the public for inspection upon their request, and making judgments about which individual registrants or registrant classes would be covered and what information would be disclosed concerning these registrants.[78]

The guidelines did not address how information was to be disseminated, such as by means of mailings or community meetings. Nor did they specify what qualified as the "relevant information" that must be disclosed.

Since the enactment of Megan's Law, the federal government has imposed an ongoing series of registration and notification requirements, backed by federal funding threats. In October 1996, less than five months after Megan's Law was signed, came the Pam Lychner Sexual Offender Tracking and Identification Act of 1996,[79] named after a Houston real estate agent who was sexually assaulted by a twice-convicted felon.[80] Lychner retained the baseline ten-year registration requirement but expanded the lifetime registration requirement beyond designated sexually violent predators to also include offenders (1) twice convicted of committing a criminal offense against a minor, (2) twice convicted of committing a sexually violent offense, or (3) convicted of aggravated sexual abuse.[81] Lychner also greatly enhanced federal involvement in the monitoring of registrants, creating a national database at the FBI consisting of registrant information provided by states (address, photograph, and fingerprints).

Over the next decade came other laws, each modifying or in some way broadening registration and notification: in 1997,[82] 1998 (two laws),[83] 2000,[84] 2003,[85] and 2005.[86] The most significant change to date, however, came in 2006, when by voice votes in both the House and Senate, and with more than three dozen cosponsors, Congress adopted the Adam Walsh Child Protection and Safety Act of 2006 (AWA).[87] The bill was signed by President Bush on July 27, 2006, twenty-five years to the day after 6-year-old Adam Walsh disappeared from a Florida shopping mall.

While named after Adam Walsh and enacted in recognition of the advocacy work of his parents John and Reve Walsh (the former became host of the popular television show "America's Most Wanted"),[88] the AWA formally established the Jacob Wetterling, Megan Nicole Kanka, and Pam Lychner Sex Offender Registration and Notification Program[89] and named several of its constituent programs after other victims.[90] The AWA substantially overhauled federal registration and notification policy, expressly repealing Wetterling, Megan's Law, and Lychner.[91] It seeks, in the words of Congress, to establish a "comprehensive national system for the registration [of] sex offenders and offenders against children."[92]

Like Megan's Law in 1996,[93] the AWA was motivated by concern over the diversity of state registration provisions, which advocates asserted created "loopholes" and "deficiencies," allowing thousands of registrants to become "lost."[94] As Utah Republican Senator Orrin Hatch, a cosponsor of the AWA, explained:

> Laws regarding registration for sex offenders have not been consistent from State to State[;] now all states will lock arms and present a unified front in the battle to protect children. Web sites that have been weak in the past, due to weak laws and haphazard updating and based on inaccurate information, will now be accurate, updated and useful for finding sex offenders.[95]

Almost three years in the making, the AWA heightened requirements across the board, including the range of registerable offenses. All persons convicted of a "sex offense" were required to register, a category encompassing several expansive subcategories,[96] including criminal offenses having "an element involving a sexual act or sexual contact with another,"[97] "video voyeurism"; the possession, production, or distribution of child pornography; and any "conduct that by its nature is a sex offense against a minor."[98]

The AWA also contains several significant policy changes. First, registration is to be retroactive in scope, requiring that all eligible "sex offenders," irrespective of date of conviction or release, register and comply with its terms.[99] Second, juveniles must register. While juveniles convicted as adults were previously required to register, the AWA requires registration of individuals 14 years of age or over who are adjudicated delinquent for committing (or attempting or conspiring to commit) (1) a sexual act with another involving force or threat of force and (2) a sexual act with another done by rendering unconscious or drugging the victim.[100] Third, no longer can registrants verify their identifying information by responding to a mailed inquiry; they must do so in person.

In addition, the AWA broadens the jurisdictional scope of registration. Equivalent qualifying offenses can now arise in state, local, tribal, foreign,[101] federal, military, District of Columbia, and U.S. Territory courts. In addition, Indian tribes are expected to effectuate registration on their lands (or delegate a state to do so),[102] and the AWA also requires participation of U.S. Territories and Puerto Rico.

Eligible individuals now must register, keep their registration current, and provide a new photo, in each place they live, go to school, and work, and they must do so before completing a sentence of imprisonment or not later than three business days after entering the community. Those with older convictions must register if they reenter the criminal justice system as a result of a conviction for any crime—whether or not a sex offense. When they register, far more information is to be collected for inclusion in state registries, including social security number, employment and school location information, finger and palm prints, a DNA sample, and vehicle license plate number and description. Finally, if they intend to leave their jurisdiction of residence for seven days or more, registrants must inform their home jurisdiction as well as the jurisdiction they intend to visit.

The centerpiece of the AWA is its tier classification system. Whereas in the past federal law left to states how individuals were to be distinguished for purposes of registration and community notification, the AWA specifies that a conviction-based regime must be employed. Unlike the risk-based tier systems, such as employed in Washington State and New Jersey, the AWA expressly eschews individualized risk assessments. Individuals are relegated to Tier I through III (the latter being the most serious),[103] with the tier determining the duration of registration and the intervals at which registration information must be updated (on an in-person basis). Tier I offenders must register for a minimum of fifteen years and verify their registration annually; Tier II offenders must register for twenty-five years and verify information twice a year; and Tier III offenders must register for their lifetimes and verify information on a quarterly basis.[104] When verifying information, registrants must also submit a new photograph. Any changes to one's registration information (such as home or work address) must be reported in person within three business days to at least one jurisdiction in which the registrant resides, works, or attends school.[105] All statutorily eligible registrants must register, and no basis exists to challenge the registration requirement for the specified duration.

Under the AWA, all registrants are automatically subject to community notification by means of Internet websites that states are required to create and maintain.[106] "[A]ll information about each sex offender in the registry" is to be made available, except for certain specified information (such as the victim's name and the registrant's social security number). In turn, registrants' information will be included in and made available for public view on the Dru Sjodin National Sex Offender Public Website maintained by the attorney general. Information must also be provided to community entities such as schools, public housing agencies, and child social service organizations.[107]

The AWA also adds new and harsher penalties for registration violations. For the first time, federal law specifies a minimum penalty that states must impose—a term of imprisonment in excess of one year. The AWA also imposes federal (not state) criminal liability when an individual required to register knowingly fails to satisfy registration requirements and "travels in interstate or foreign commerce, or enters or leaves, or resides, in, Indian country." Violators are subject to a $250,000 fine and a maximum ten years in federal prison.[108] Furthermore, the AWA specifies that federal law enforcement, including the U.S. Marshals Service (USMS), shall "assist jurisdictions in locating and apprehending sex offenders who violate sex offender registration requirements."[109] Pursuant to this authority, the USMS has since launched

Operation FALCON, resulting in the arrest of hundreds of individuals for alleged registration violations.[110]

Finally, the AWA significantly expands the federal bureaucratic role in registration and notification. It authorizes a grant program to help jurisdictions implement and satisfy new requirements, with bonus payments for early implementation[111] and creates a Sex Offender Sentencing, Monitoring, Apprehending, Registering and Tracking (SMART) Office within the Department of Justice to administer and enforce standards and issue grants.[112] The attorney general and the National Institute of Justice, the research arm of the Department of Justice, are expressly directed to play an ongoing role in the evaluation of registration and community notification efforts.[113] The attorney general must obtain and maintain state registry information that will constitute the basis of the National Sex Offender Registry to be operated by the FBI, which is to make such information available to jurisdictions (yet not the public). The attorney general must also maintain the Dru Sjodin National Sex Offender Public Website, which makes registrants' information publicly accessible.

As with prior federal demands, Congress afforded states a period of time to comply with new federal mandates. The AWA specifies that jurisdictions have until July 27, 2009, subject to extension, to comply and thus avoid losing 10% of Byrne Grant funds.[114] If past experience can serve as a guide, federal pressure will prove effective in satisfying fundamental U.S. will. With financial pressure imposed by Wetterling in 1994, all states had registration laws by 1996 (when Massachusetts passed its law).[115] Likewise, nationwide compliance with the community notification requirement contained in Megan's Law in 1996 was achieved in 1999 (when New Mexico passed its law).[116]

The AWA, however, compels massive changes to existing state registration and notification systems, crafted and maintained for over a decade, and might prove an exception to the federal government's record of success. Indeed, as this book goes to press, states are showing considerable resistance to compliance, citing either principled objection (for instance, over registration of juveniles) or the belief that instituting the massive changes will entail costs far greater than the Byrne Grant money jeopardized.[117]

If AWA compliance occurs, state laws will become broader and more onerous in numerous respects, including the scope of offenses covered; duration of registration; frequency and methods that registration and updates must occur (in person); and extent of registrants subject to community notification (based on conviction, not individual risk). In addition, Indian tribes will, for the first time, be expected to create and maintain registries and make registrants' information available to the public. As a result, tribal registries will augment those already existing in all fifty states, the District of Columbia, and the territories of American Samoa, Guam, Northern Mariana Islands, Puerto Rico, and the U.S. Virgin Islands.

## MODERN-DAY STATE LAWS

While hugely significant, federal directives have never had definitive effect. Indeed, as Chapter 2 established, registration itself originated in municipalities in the early 1930s, and later was embraced by the states (albeit sporadically). The federal government remained uninvolved until 1994, with the Wetterling Act—when thirty-eight states had laws.[118] Moreover, community notification originated in the State of Washington in 1990 and was thrust onto the national stage as a result of New Jersey's Megan's Law, enacted in 1994.

Nor have federal directives always been warmly received by states, a fact that often escapes attention. This resistance has been reflected in several ways, including passively with states acknowledging that conforming legislation was motivated by a concern over losing grant money, rather than endorsement of the federal policies themselves.[119] At other times, state officials have publicly criticized federal strictures and expressed resentment over being subject to perceived unfunded federal mandates.[120]

More notably, state prerogative has been manifest in the nature and content of state laws. Because federal law since 1994 has prescribed only minima, states have been free to indulge their sovereign prerogative to adopt independent policies. States have, in the words of Justice Louis Brandeis, acted as "laborator[ies]" of experimentation.[121] Federal law is thus only part of modern registration and notification's story, with the states playing a foremost role.

### Qualifying Offenses

One area in which states have charted their own course concerns the scope of registerable offenses.[122] While states as a rule have required that persons convicted of serious sexual and child-victim offenses register, and registries are dominated by such registrants,[123] it is also the case that registration criteria can be quite expansive. Like earlier municipal registration laws (such as Pensacola, Florida's targeting of miscegenation), states have specified a broad array of less serious offenses. Since the early 1990s, states have at various times specified the following as warranting registration:

- adult prostitution involving solicitation of sodomy (Louisiana)
- adultery (if one party is under the age of 18) (Kansas)
- posting an obscene bumper sticker or writing (Alabama)
- bigamy and abetting bigamy (Louisiana)
- seduction, if the person seduced "is of previously-chaste character" (Mississippi)
- public urination (numerous states)
- possession of child pornography (numerous states)
- sale, purchase, or distribution of obscene materials (Oklahoma)
- indecent exposure (Alabama, California, Oklahoma, and South Carolina)
- peeping (South Carolina).

"Romeo and Juliet" sexual encounters between juveniles have also been the frequent target of state registration.[124]

State laws have also had some highly unusual applications. In 2006, for instance, Michigan required Jeffrey Haynes to register after being convicted of sodomizing a sheep. The prosecutor successfully urged registration out of her belief that once Haynes was released from prison he might prey on children or vulnerable adults.[125] The outcome was later overturned on appeal.[126] However, in Kansas, in 2008, Joshua Coman, on probation for an unspecified similar offense, was successfully required to register after being convicted of having sex with a female Rottweiler dog, based on a judicial finding that the crime was "sexually motivated."[127] Finally, an Oklahoma judge was required to register as a result of his indecent exposure convictions based on his use of a "penis pump" to masturbate in court during trials.[128]

Adults convicted of consensual homosexual sodomy have been subject to registration over the years as well. Until the U.S. Supreme Court's landmark 2003 decision *Lawrence v. Texas*, invalidating laws criminalizing the behavior, such convictions triggered registration in at least six states.[129]

State registration laws have also often extended beyond the gamut of offenses specified by legislatures. Several states, concerned that offenders will plead to nonregisterable offenses, have criteria that permit courts to exercise judgment on registration. Kansas, as noted above, allows registration if a conviction is based on a "sexually motivated" crime,[130] which one court used to require registration of an offender who pled guilty to burglary and misdemeanor theft in relation to his taking several items of female underwear.[131] Other state laws contain similar provisions, requiring registration when an offense is committed "for the purpose of sexual gratification" (California and Washington)[132] or "vicarious sexual gratification" (Indiana).[133] In South Carolina, courts are free to impose registration upon a showing of good cause by the state.[134]

In Minnesota, registration is warranted if a conviction "arise[s] out of the same set of circumstances" as a charged offense that statutory law specifies as requiring registration.[135] Construing the provision, and upholding the registration of a defendant based on a guilty plea to a nonenumerated crime, the state court of appeals commented on "the enormity of the potential unchecked power" the provision bestowed upon prosecutors: "This is one of the few times in American jurisprudence where the 'charge is the conviction,' meaning that once you are charged with an enumerated felony under the statute, you are 'convicted of having to register' even if the ultimate result is a low-ranking misdemeanor."[136]

Expansiveness has manifested in several other ways as well. First, one sees it in the increasing tendency of state laws to sweep up inchoate offenses (attempts, conspiracies, solicitations, and instances of aiding or abetting) and various dispositional outcomes. Today, as with early-era registration laws, all states regard lawful convictions as a basis for registration. But they now also typically include other dispositions, requiring registration of persons found not guilty by reason of insanity, found guilty but mentally ill, or when subject to state involuntary civil commitment provisions.

Second, in practical effect, the scope of registration has expanded as a result of the increasing tendency of states to defer to one another's registration criteria. Concerned about possible travel-evasion—that is, moving from a state requiring registration for an offense to another that does not—many states now require that one's registration status will carry over into a new state residence.[137] Thus, for example, an individual required to register in South Carolina because of a "peeping" conviction can be required to register in another state, even if the latter does not specify peeping as worthy of registration.[138] As a result, registration criteria have assumed a self-replicating nature, with state registration eligibility preferences being transported from state to state.

Finally, a recent development in Ohio indicates that registration might be headed in a new direction. In 2006, Ohio initiated a Sexual Civil Child Abuse

Registry, targeting individuals never actually charged with a crime.[139] Registration results when a declaratory judgment action is brought in civil court by the government or the victim, and the court finds by a preponderance of the evidence (not beyond a reasonable doubt, as in a criminal trial) that "the defendant would be liable for assault or battery based on childhood sexual abuse but for the expiration of the limitation period."[140] Registrants' information remains posted on the State's Internet registry for six years, and they must comply with the same requirements imposed on individuals subject to Ohio's conventional sex offender registry regime.[141]

### Registration Requirements and Penalties

As in the past, registration is typically required as a matter of law, occurring without exception or opportunity for appeal. However, in the pre-AWA era, in some instances states afforded a modest right to avoid registration. In Massachusetts, for instance, a subpopulation of less serious offenders can be excused by the agency that administers the registry if found to not pose a risk of reoffense or a danger to the public.[142] Likewise, in Idaho, persons convicted of rapes who are 19 or 20 years old at the time of the offense, and not more than three years older than the victim, can be exempted if it is determined by clear and convincing evidence that they do not pose a risk and their case did not involve allegations of more serious misconduct.[143] In addition, in states that use a risk-based classification scheme, a right of appeal can exist as to classification.[144]

Duration of registration has also varied among jurisdictions. In the early to mid-1990s most states set a flat, ten-year registration period, although lifetime registration was also possible.[145] Several state laws (like the original Washington State law and the AWA today) conditioned length of registration on the severity of the offense triggering registration.[146] As of 1996, four states (Alabama, Arizona, Florida, and Missouri) did not specify registration duration.[147] Fifteen states required lifetime registration for some or all offenders.[148] One-third of the states allowed registrants to petition for relief from registration, generally after a period of ten to twenty years.[149] In 2006, eight jurisdictions required lifetime registration, regardless of predicate crime, while six set the minimum registraion term at fifteen years, one at twenty years, one at twenty-five years, and the reminaing thirty-five at ten years.[150]

The time period allotted for initial registration has shown less variation. Unlike in the early to mid-1990s (as in prior decades), when it was not unusual for states to allow considerable time for compliance,[151] today all states require registration on, before, or shortly after an individual's release into the community or arrival in the state.

The intervals at which registrants must verify information and the methods by which this occurs have become more exacting over time. As of 1996, roughly thirty states did not specifically require verification. The balance required some form of verification: for instance, four required verification but failed to specify when it had to occur; nine required annual verification; two (New Jersey and Vermont) required verification every ninety days for all registrants; and two others (New York and Pennsylvania ) required that designated sexually violent predators verify every ninety days.[152] In states requiring verification, registrants were asked to mail back address confirmation forms, on either an annual or quarterly basis.[153] By 2006, all states required at least annual verification, with several requiring it on a quarterly basis, and eight by means of in-person visits by registrants with authorities (as the AWA mandates).[154]

States have also varied over time with respect to the mental state sufficient to be convicted of failing to comply with registration. It has not been unusual to distinguish between failing to register (or reregister) when required, deemed a strict liability offense not requiring any intent to violate the law, and violations based on the provision of false information, which require that the violation be "knowing."[155] In late 2007, at least eighteen jurisdictions either did not specify a mental state or required knowing registration violations in only limited instances.[156]

Finally, variation has existed over available punishments for registration violations. While since the 1990s violations have usually been treated as felonies, some states imposed misdemeanor liability,[157] but this latter tendency has decreased over time. In 1996, for instance, thirty-eight states punished registration violations in some form as misdemeanors,[158] but by 2008 the number decreased to twenty-five.[159] Registration violations also figure in recidivist sentence enhancements—with potential major effect: in California, for instance, a conviction can serve as a "third strike" justifying a life sentence.[160] Less dire, Alaska recently augmented punishment of registration failures by withholding payments from the State Permanent Fund,[161] and New Hampshire suspended the driver's licenses of noncompliant registrants.[162]

## Retroactivity

Whether registration should apply to persons convicted of crimes before the effective date of the laws has been another matter on which states have disagreed over the years. Initially, in the 1990s, states most often required that laws only apply to persons who were convicted, imprisoned, or under some form of community supervision when or after the law was enacted. This limited temporal coverage was not only motivated by concern that registration (and/or community notification) constituted punishment, and thus retroactive application possibly violated the constitutional prohibition of ex post facto laws. The conservative approach also made pragmatic sense. Retroactivity exponentially expanded registration, requiring greater resources to maintain registries and effectuate community notification. This impact would be felt especially in states with laws requiring risk assessments (such as Minnesota, New Jersey, and Washington), a complex process requiring significant time and resources. Finally, retroactivity presents potential fairness concerns, reviving criminal convictions, sometimes from the distant past, possibly subjecting individuals who have been law-abiding for years to renewed state attention (and, with notification, attention of fellow community members).[163]

Even before the Supreme Court held in *Smith v. Doe* (2003) (discussed below) that registration and notification did not constitute punishment for constitutional purposes, and hence could be imposed retroactively, states were inclined toward retroactivity. In 1999, for instance, only five state laws were solely prospective, and the remaining laws were retrospective to some extent. Fourteen laws were fully retroactive, tying registration eligibility to conviction prior to the effective date of laws, often from the distant past: for instance, 1944 in California and 1979 in Missouri. In over thirty states (including New Jersey and Washington), laws remained partially retroactive, requiring registration of persons convicted of crimes before the law's effective date but either imprisoned or under community supervision when the law went into effect.[164]

Increasingly, as the effective dates of 1990s-era registration provisions have receded further into the past, retroactivity has assumed less practical importance. Nevertheless, as of 2008 at least twenty-five jurisdictions had fully retroactive provisions, with several more tying eligibility to pre-1990 convictions. In addition, if states wish to receive full Byrne Grant funding from the federal government, under the terms of the Adam Walsh Act, their laws must be retroactive in coverage.

## Juvenile Offenders

Another area in which states have shown a willingness to expand registration concerns juveniles. While early registration laws swept up young offenders prosecuted in adult criminal courts, juveniles adjudicated in the juvenile system were not targeted. The exemption was consistent with the view that youths were less culpable, deserved a second chance, and should be shielded from the harsh consequences of the adult system. In the 1990s, this philosophy went into disfavor. Americans, alarmed by stories of youthful "superpredators," backed a wave of legislative efforts to allow serious juvenile offenders to be prosecuted as adults.[165]

This same sensibility has resulted in states applying registration to juvenile offenders. In 1996, thirteen states required that at least some juveniles register,[166] with New Jersey at one point targeting a 12-year-old boy (registered for life for having sexually experimented with his younger brother with a douche bottle).[167] In January 2007, thirty-six states did so,[168] and laws in others were unclear on the issue, leaving it open to judicial interpretation.[169] While the federal government historically did not take a stand on registering juveniles, the AWA affirmatively requires that states register (and subject to community notification) all juveniles 14 years of age or older who are adjudicated of particular forms of sexual misconduct. Such juveniles must register for a minimum period of twenty-five years and perhaps for life and verify in person their registration information with authorities every three months.

Current state juvenile registration laws vary considerably in their nature and scope and will likely continue to do so even after the AWA. While many states use eligibility criteria identical to that of adults, states often consider the nature or number of prior juvenile offenses before requiring registration, at times affording courts discretion on the question.[170] States also vary in terms of allowing juveniles relief from registration and at times exempt juveniles from notification or delay notification until they turn a certain age (such as 18). Finally, some states are taking steps to exclude from registration so-called "Romeo and Juliet" offenders—teenagers who have consensual (although not legal) sex with peers.[171] Overall, however, there is no mistaking that states have become far less tolerant of juvenile sexual misconduct. Whereas in the past such misconduct was often dealt with informally, especially when it involved peers, today it very likely triggers registration and notification.[172]

## STATE STAND-ALONE REGISTRIES

Although not the focus of frequent public attention, several states maintain stand-alone registries, operating in tandem with registries targeting sex offenders and persons victimizing children. Florida's system is perhaps most ambitious. Since 1957, the state has required that felons register,[173] and since 2002 it has imposed lifetime registration on any person designated a "habitual violent offender," a "violent career criminal," a "three-time violent felony offender," or a "prison releasee reoffender."[174] Both laws expressly exclude individuals required to register under Florida's sex offender registry (enacted in 1993), which contains "sexual offenders"[175] and "sexual predators."[176]

Similar felon-related registries exist in several other states. Mississippi requires that all felons register;[177] Nevada requires registration of persons convicted of two or more felonies in any state and persons convicted of a crime warranting "category A" felony status in Nevada;[178] and Alabama requires registration of persons convicted of three or more felonies.[179]

States have also singled out nonsexual victimizers of children for stand-alone registries. In 2006, for instance, Illinois, in response to public concern that including non–sex offenders in its registry with sex offenders might mislead the public and unduly subject such persons to the unique stigma attached to sex offenders,[180] disaggregated its registry by means of the Child Murderer and Violent Offender Against Youth Registration Act[181] and the Sex Offender Registration Act.[182] Hawaii, similarly, has a Sex Offender Registry and an Offender Against Minors Registry.[183]

Other states, such as Connecticut, Indiana, Kansas, Montana, and Oklahoma, have targeted violent offenders. In Oklahoma, the Mary Rippy Violent Crime Offenders Registration Act specifies the following offenses for registration: murder (first and second degree); first-degree manslaughter; shooting with intent to kill; assault and battery with a deadly weapon; use of a vehicle to facilitate use of a firearm, crossbow or other weapon; assault with intent to kill; and bombing and explosives violations.[184] Hawaii has a publicly accessible registry for persons convicted of murder.[185]

Drug offenders, as with earlier registration laws, have also sparked state legislative interest. Persons convicted of selling or producing methamphetamine in particular have been targeted,[186] with Tennessee initiating the nation's first meth registry in 2005.[187] The federal government operates a National Clandestine Laboratory Register, which provides county-by-county address listings (with no individual names) of locations in states where police have found indicia of drug laboratories or dumpsites. Moreover, in 2007 both New Mexico and New York considered drug offender registries. In New Mexico, the legislation was entitled the CLEAN TOWN Act of 2006—"Communities Leading Everyone Away from Narcotics Through Online Warning Notification."[188]

States have also seen fit to create registries for a wide array of other, more specific nonsexual offenses. Arsonists are required to register in California[189] and Illinois;[190] gang-related offenders in California;[191] persons convicted of abusing a youth or vulnerable adult in Tennessee;[192] and persons convicted of violent offenses against peace officers in Louisiana.[193] Pennsylvania recently considered "Robin's Law,"[194] a domestic violence registry named after a woman killed by an estranged boyfriend who, unbeknownst to her, had been previously convicted of violently assaulting a spouse.[195] Moreover, in the recent past registries have been proposed for persons convicted of hate crimes (Maryland),[196] animal abuse (Tennessee),[197] and owning a dangerous dog (Illinois).[198] In addition, a nonprofit private organization operates Through Their Eyes: the National Animal Abuse Registry, a website with fifteen thousand entries in its database.[199]

Finally, individual cities (as in the 1930s) have also created registries. Recently, for instance, New York City and Baltimore enacted ordinances requiring that persons convicted of gun-related offenses register with authorities.[200]

Such registries often differ from sex offender registries in important ways, including less onerous registration requirements (regarding registration deadlines and verification intervals, for example); punishments for violation (typically at misdemeanor level or less); and shorter registration durations (such as five years). Moreover, the registries are often not complemented by community notification,[201] and if they are, they provide less in the way of information (for example, no home addresses, places of employment, or registrant photos).[202] Like child abuse registries now operative in all states,[203] registrants' identifying information is regarded as private data, not for public consumption.

## COMMUNITY NOTIFICATION

As noted above, a critically important, complementary component of modern registration is community notification. Here, again, modern laws have differed on a key matter: whether all registrants should be subject to community notification and, if not, how such eligibility distinctions should be made. New Jersey's Megan's Law (1994), while containing the nation's fifth community notification provision, was the first to require that some form of notification occur.[204] Adopting New Jersey's mandatory approach, the federal Megan's Law (1996) required notification but left to states how notification decisions were to be made and how notification itself was to occur.

## Classification Approaches

Over time, states have employed two basic approaches to registrant classification: a risk-based and a conviction-based method. With the risk-based approach, only registrants thought most likely to recidivate are subject to community notification, on the basis of individualized risk assessments. As of mid-2007, roughly a dozen jurisdictions used a risk-based approach, including Massachusetts, Minnesota, New Jersey, New York, and Washington State, with state appellate courts often mandating that procedural rights and protections be afforded registrants as a precondition to being subject to community notification.

With the conviction-based approach, all registrants are subject to community notification, without consideration of individual risk. Examples of this approach are found in Connecticut, Florida, and Illinois. Other states adopt an intermediate approach. In California, for instance, identifying information on registrants is made available on the state's website in accord with offense seriousness. Individuals convicted of the specified serious offenses have their home addresses posted, while less serious offenders have only their residence zip codes or city and/or county in which they reside posted. In addition, the state has a "No Post" classification, consisting of persons required to register but not convicted of sex offenses specified in the two aforementioned categories. Michigan maintains both a Sex Offender Registry, which contains juveniles and less serious offenders who have completed a special probation process, and a Public Sex Offender Registry, with only the latter being accessible to the public.

The federal Adam Walsh Act, if implemented by states, promises to inspire significant change on this front. Under the AWA's conviction-based regime, all statutorily eligible registrants are subject to community notification, at least by means of the Internet. The duration of registration and hence exposure to community notification, however, depends on the nature of the offense triggering registration. Congress, mindful of the federalism-related ramifications of imposing its will on states relative to the traditionally state-centric realm of criminal justice, provided that states using a risk approach can be exempted from "substantially implement[ing]" the AWA, upon proof of a "good faith effort" to reconcile conflicts based on state constitutional stricture.[205] (Such a conflict might arise, as in several states noted above, when the state's supreme court concludes that due process requires that a registrant be afforded a hearing before being subject to community notification.[206])

### Notification Methods: Passive and Active

Methods used by jurisdictions to effectuate community notification have also varied over time. As a general matter, approaches have been passive or active in nature; the former requires that community members make affirmative efforts to obtain registrant information, while with the latter the government disseminates the information.[207]

*Passive methods* have shown the greatest variation over time. In the mid-late 1990s, states employed a variety of passive methods, including making registrants' information accessible via telephone hotlines, by means of CD-ROMs, or on lists made available by law enforcement.[208] To monitor access, jurisdictions would often ask that individuals requesting registry information identify themselves and at times required that the request be motivated by a particular safety concern.[209] For instance, California's "900" phone-in system, in operation until October 2005, required callers to supply personal information (name, date of birth, social security number, and address), the reason for the inquiry, and "the number of persons who may be at risk."[210] Callers were also assessed a $10 fee and could obtain information on a maximum of two individuals, based on identifying information they provided (registrant's name, date of birth, and so forth). If a "hit" occurred, the caller would be provided with the registrant's physical description, community of residence (not specific address), and the offense(s) triggering registration.

In recent years, the Internet has quickly become the passive notification method of choice.[211] In 1994, Indiana, as part of "Zachary's Law," named after a 10-year-old boy who was molested and murdered by a recidivist sex offender, created perhaps the nation's first Internet sex offender registry. The idea quickly caught on; by 2001 half the states had such websites, and today all do so.[212]

The websites have enjoyed staggering popularity. During 2006 alone, for instance, California's sex offender website (available in thirteen languages) had almost eight million users[213] (by comparison, its "900 line" received 3,710 telephone inquiries in 2000[214]). In Louisiana, the state website had over two million visitors within two weeks of appearing online in 2000,[215] and the federal government's website received twenty-two million visits—a rate of almost one thousand per second—within the first twelve hours of being unveiled in 2006.[216]

The remarkable surge in the popularity of Web registries has several explanations. First, states scrambled to create sites as a result of pressure from the federal government, which in 2003 threatened to withhold funds from states that lacked such sites. Second, the Internet has great appeal from a resource perspective: websites are far cheaper than community notification meetings, door-to-door visits, or postings of flyers and other active methods of notification (discussed below). Third, to those enamored of the idea, websites—replete with registrants' identifying information and designations like "sex predator"—have superior shaming benefit. Unlike nineteenth-century "rogues' galleries," reposed in police stations, Web registries are continuously, conveniently, and anonymously available for view on the computers of concerned community members and distant voyeurs alike.[217]

Finally, pressure for the shift has come from below. With society becoming increasingly sophisticated in the use of the Internet and aware of its capacity to store and permit access to data, less user-friendly technology such as hotlines and CD-ROMs fell into disfavor.[218] Users can now search by area (by locality or zip code) or name, and maps that pinpoint the location of registrants are common. In Florida, where the state website in the late 1990s featured photos of offenders framed by flashing lights and boldface lettering denoting a "Sex Offender,"[219] the website now allows searches of "predators" and "offenders" by name or home address, and the registry provides a pinpoint map of the registrant's residential location, physical description, offense history, date of birth, and a photo. In Oklahoma, searches can be based on registrants' physical description and type of offense, and in Texas, in a strategy that would make Alphonse Bertillon proud, the shoe size of registrants is provided.

State websites vary in the extent of the registry populations that they publicize and the extent and nature of risk-related information provided. According to a September 2007 report issued by the group Human Rights Watch,[220] 32 states include on their websites every registrant convicted as an adult, while 18 states and the District of Columbia exclude low- and sometimes moderate-risk individuals from public display. Thirty-two states required at least some juveniles to be posted. The report also noted that in only a slight majority of jurisdictions (28) is any effort made to indicate registrants' level of dangerousness, for instance by noting how long they are required to register (9), expressly stating that only high-risk offenders are listed (2), or using terms such as "aggravated" or "habitual" in association with particular offenders (7).

Websites customarily also specify the avowed public safety purpose of disseminating the information and warn against use of the information to harass or otherwise engage in unlawful misconduct against registrants. Ten states, however, failed to provide any warning about misuse of registry information, and only fourteen states and the District of Columbia have laws specifically proscribing misuse.[221]

The websites often contain disclaimers, stating that the information provided might not be accurate, up to date,[222] or relevant to the individual for whom information is sought.[223] In states using conviction-based classification, websites frequently contain disclaimers indicating that no determination of current dangerousness has been undertaken and that the posted information is merely being provided for public educational use.[224]

*Active methods* of community notification have shown less variation over time. One common method, used in risk-based regimes, has been to host meetings in communities where the registrant (typically high risk) is to reside. At such meetings, police provide information on the registrant, answer questions, and offer advice on self-protective measures. Another active method entails police issuing leaflets and visiting residences. In Alabama, for instance, police disseminate a "community notification flyer" containing information on registrants.[225] They hand deliver or mail flyers to all legal residences, hotels, and motels, with the radius of distribution determined by the population size of the community, but inclusive of all schools within a three-mile radius of the registrant's address.[226] In Texas, police mail a postcard containing information on high-risk registrants to all addresses within a one-mile radius. Notice can also be effectuated by "any manner determined appropriate by local law enforcement authority," including newspaper notices, community meetings, or notices posted in the area where the registrant resides.[227]

Louisiana—the second state to adopt notification—has employed the nation's most aggressive active notification strategy, requiring since 1995 that registrants themselves conduct community notification. Within three days of establishing residence in an area, registrants must among other things "[p]ersonally notify at least one person in every residence or business within a one-mile radius in a rural area and at least three-tenths of a mile radius in an urban or suburban area" and publish notice in the local newspaper on two separate days. In addition, they must (also at their own expense) "[g]ive any other notice deemed appropriate by the court including but not limited to "signs, handbills, bumper stickers, or clothing."[228]

Technology has also influenced active notification methods. For instance, community members can now receive e-mail alerts, informing them when a registrant moves into their area or relating that one has relocated.[229] In addition, for fees, private vendors now provide community members with a sophisticated array of notification and tracking technology, including e-mail alerts and mapping capability.[230] In New York, Parents for Megan's Law, a nongovernmental nonprofit organization, contracts with the state to disseminate information on recently released registrants.[231]

## ANCILLARY CONSEQUENCES

The consequences attending registration and notification are not, however, solely direct in nature. The laws have a broad array of ancillary consequences, imposed as a result of registration eligibility.

One consequence relates to the requirement that registrants carry special identification. Like several jurisdictions in the 1950s, a number of states now require that registrants carry special driver's licenses or identification cards indicating their registrant status.[232] In Louisiana, the cards, which must be renewed annually, are orange, and emblazoned with "sexual offender."[233] States have also considered requiring registrants to affix special color-coded license plates to their vehicles.[234]

Registration can also affect the physical space that registrants can lawfully inhabit. Over twenty states and hundreds of localities, reminiscent of early twentieth-century French treatment of Gypsies (see Chapter 1), now prohibit registrants from living within specified distances (for example, one thousand feet) of schools, day care centers, and other places where minors congregate.[235] The laws can apply even though registrants lack offending history relating to minors and even if they established residence within the area prior to the provision taking effect. In addition, some private homeowner associations have banned registrants,[236] and some jurisdictions have enacted laws requiring separate housing of registrants in the event of natural disasters such as hurricanes.[237] Spatial limits also curtail the capacity of registrants to visit and work in certain areas, such as parks and playgrounds,[238] and local school boards often bar registrants from visiting and volunteering at schools where their children are enrolled.[239]

Many states also preclude registrants from working particular jobs, such as in day care or recreation centers, again even if they were not convicted of child-related offenses.[240] Owners or operators of such facilities can face criminal liability[241] or a civil fine[242] if they employ or accept volunteer services from a registrant.

Other consequences are more personal in nature. For example, states often prohibit or severely restrict the ability of registrants to change their legal names[243] and can require that they inform authorities of any intent to change their facial features (such as growing a beard) or borrow a car.[244] Moreover, in keeping with a federal directive, states are now collecting information on registrants' e-mail addresses and Web identities.[245] In Florida, individuals communicating online with a registrant will receive a message indicating that the person they have contacted is a registered sex offender.[246]

## A STORY OF GROWTH AND CHANGE

As the preceding suggests, registration and notification have enjoyed enormous political success since the early 1990s. Congress, for its part, since 1994 has regarded registration and notification as the equivalent of legislative catnip, perennially (often in tandem with election cycles) revising federal mandates. In states, registration and notification laws have been quickly and often unanimously adopted,[247] and laws have been regularly revisited. In California, for instance, since 1986 the state's registration law has been amended on over fifty different occasions.[248]

Almost always legislative involvement has resulted in expansion.[249] There have, however, been a few instances of retrenchment worthy of mention. In March 1995, for instance, a bill proposed in Montana to expand eligibility to include adult consensual sodomy was derailed. Protesters compared the proposal to the Nazi practice of registering homosexuals, and the governor received a flurry of negative calls, including from tourists who threatened to boycott the state if the bill passed.[250] In 1996, a similar effort in Kansas was defeated.[251]

Likewise, in 1994, California, in conjunction with its decision to permit community notification and public access, removed several misdemeanor offenses from its list of registration-eligible offenses.[252] Later, in 1997, the state rescinded its consensual sodomy registration requirement and allowed persons with prior convictions to be removed from the registry.[253] More recently, as noted above, several states have backed away from registration requirements for "Romeo and Juliet" convictions involving minors who engaged in consensual underage sex.

Viewed in the broader recent history, however, such limits have been aberrations. For evidence of this one need only consider the growth in registry rolls. From April 1998 to February 2001, the number of registrants nationwide grew from 277,000 to 386,000,[254] and from 2001 to 2007, to over 614,000[255]—a 221% increase in less than a decade. With the AWA's retroactivity and expanded eligibility requirements as a floor, and states continuing to add their own sex offender eligibility criteria, combined with interest in stand-alone registries, the number of registrants should soon easily pass the one-million mark. With increased registration, in turn, will come corresponding increases in community notification, especially if the AWA's conviction-based approach becomes the national norm.

## REGISTRATION AND NOTIFICATION IN THE COURTS

Modern laws, like those of the early era, have not been significantly affected by judicial intervention. This stasis, however, has not been attributable to judicial inattention, as was the case from the 1930s to the 1980s (Chapter 2). In the 1990s, registration laws—combined with community notification laws—were the subject of frequent judicial challenge,[256] with two constitutional challenges figuring most centrally.

First, registrants contended that registration and notification qualified as "punishment" and hence violated the Ex Post Facto Clause of the Constitution (Article I), and the Double Jeopardy (Fifth Amendment) and Cruel and Unusual Punishment (Eighth Amendment) Clauses of the Bill of Rights. Second, it was argued that the laws deprived registrants of a constitutionally protectable "liberty interest" under the Fourteenth Amendment, requiring that they first be provided with procedural rights, such as an opportunity to contest registration eligibility and community notification. While the vast majority of state and federal courts rejected such challenges, a few granted relief, leaving the issues ripe for intervention by the U.S. Supreme Court.

This intervention came in 2003 with two Supreme Court decisions, which while omitting any reference to the Court's 1957 *Lambert* decision (see Chapter 2), marked the Court's continued principled support of registration. In *Smith v. Doe*,[257] the Court held that Alaska's Sex Offender Registration Act (SORA), entailing Internet notification, mail-in verification on an annual or quarterly basis, and other common requirements, did not impose punishment and hence did not violate the Ex Post Facto Clause. SORA, the Court concluded, was regulatory, not punitive, in both its legislative intent and effect on registrants, allowing it to be retroactively applied, consistent with the Ex Post Facto Clause.

On the same day *Smith* was decided, the Court issued *Connecticut Department of Public Safety v. Doe (CDPS)*,[258] which addressed whether individuals are entitled to procedural due process protection before being subjected to registration and community notification. *CDPS* involved a challenge to Connecticut's conviction-based regime, requiring that individuals convicted of statutorily specified offenses register and undergo community notification via the Internet, without first being evaluated for risk. The State's website specified that individuals were included on the registry "solely by virtue of their conviction record and state law" and that the State had made no "determination that any individual included in the registry is currently dangerous."[259] Registrants asserted that the regime jeopardized their right to be free of stigma and related burdens (qualifying as a protectable liberty interest), requiring that, at a minimum, they have a right to be meaningfully heard at a hearing on whether they should be targeted.

The Supreme Court rejected the challenge. The Court found no need to address whether Connecticut jeopardized any liberty interest of registrants, attaching particular importance to the website's disclaimer. By explicitly proclaiming that "officials have not determined that any registrant is currently dangerous," the Court concluded, the State rendered moot any due process obligation that it might otherwise have: "due process does not require the opportunity to prove a fact that is not material to the State's statutory scheme."[260] Registration and notification via the Internet were permissible because they were based "on an offender's conviction alone," and conviction was "a fact" that registrants had already had a "procedurally safeguarded opportunity to contest."[261] It was thus permissible for Connecticut to decide, the Court concluded, "that the registry information of *all* sex offenders—currently dangerous or not—must be publicly disclosed."[262]

The upshot of the Court's decision in *CDPS* is that conviction-based regimes do not violate procedural due process—at least when accompanied by a disclaimer, such as in Connecticut. As a result, the conviction-based approach, widely condemned for its overinclusiveness (see Chapter 5), yet soon possibly the national norm as a result of being mandated by the Adam Walsh Act, is constitutionally permissible. As courts have found in the wake of *CDPS*,[263] a prior conviction is both a necessary and sufficient condition for registration and community notification, at least when the government posts a dangerousness disclaimer.

## CONCLUSION: BACK TO THE FUTURE (AND THEN SOME)

With remarkable speed, registration and notification laws have come to play a central role in U.S. social control efforts. The reasons for this resurgence, and the particular content and tenor of modern laws, will be examined in the next chapter. Before proceeding, however, it is worthwhile to reflect upon how modern laws compare to predecessor efforts.

In fundamental terms, both generations of laws seek to empower police by providing them with information on criminally risky individuals, and to discourage recidivism in such individuals by instilling a sense that they are being watched. The kinds of individuals targeted have varied over time: in the early 1930s, "gangsters," followed by increasingly broader swaths of specified criminal subgroups; in the 1990s to today, mainly sex offenders and child kidnappers, augmented by registries for other specified criminal subgroups. While registration has varied over time in those it targets, its central appeal of rendering the criminal element more knowable has remained constant.

Early and modern laws also share substantive traits. While modern laws are far more detailed and expansive, they parallel earlier efforts in important ways. Perhaps most significantly, like early laws, most modern laws are conviction based: despite major advances in actuarial and clinical assessments since the 1930s, today in most jurisdictions a criminal conviction alone drives registration. And, as with the early-generation laws, a single conviction typically triggers registration and eligibility criteria very often do not jibe with the reality of recidivist risk or dangerousness (for example, registering miscagenationists in prior times and public urinators today).

Importantly, moreover, unlike nineteenth-century strategies such as Bertillonism and fingerprinting, both early-generation and contemporary registration laws function as more than mere passive information technologies. They require, under threat of criminal sanction, individuals to be complicit in their own ongoing surveillance and, if not complied with, the laws purge communities of individuals (by imprisonment).

Despite these similarities, modern laws differ in critically important ways. Most notably, they are complemented by community notification. While early registration laws had some informational "leakage," modern laws affirmatively allow governments to make such information available to communities. Knowledge empowerment, as a result, no longer solely benefits police. Community members are now privy to registry information, opening up new avenues of social control, the consequences of which are more fully explored in later chapters.

A second critically important difference relates to coverage. Modern laws not only target juveniles and a vastly greater expanse of offender subgroups, they are also in effect nationwide. Whereas in earlier times individuals could travel-evade registration, such a possibility has been largely foreclosed today. This, again, is attributable mainly (if not exclusively) to federal pressure imposed on states to enact laws. The goal, as President Clinton intoned when signing federal legislation authorizing a national registry, has been an all-encompassing surveillance: "If you dare to prey on our children, the law will follow you wherever you go. State to State, town to town."[264] With Wetterling (1994), Megan's Law (1996), the Adam Walsh Act (2006), and other federal mandates along the way, this goal has been largely achieved. Creation by Congress of a national Internet registry, complementing state Web registries, has in effect permitted an enormous "rogues' gallery" for the entire world to view whenever it wishes, with a few computer keystrokes.

Third and finally, modern laws are far more onerous than earlier incarnations. Unlike earlier laws, which required individuals to inform police only of address changes, today's laws require periodic verification and updating of information (in person, pursuant to the Adam Walsh Act) at frequent specified intervals, which further personalizes and heightens the psychic impact of the laws. Modern laws are also accompanied by an array of ancillary consequences—ranging from limits on where registrants can live, visit, and work, to requirements that they provide DNA samples, to limits on registrants' capacity to change their names.

In sum, modern and early-generation laws share fundamental similarities and derive from an enduring need to render the criminal element more knowable. Yet modern laws differ in fundamental ways, with their substance and reach manifesting the distinct social and political era in which they took shape. The next chapter examines how and why this is so.

# 4 SOCIAL AND POLITICAL CATALYSTS

ON THE DAY MEGAN'S LAW was unanimously approved by the New Jersey Senate, with each voting member wearing a pink ribbon emblazoned with Megan's name,[1] Maureen Kanka confidently proclaimed that the bill "was just the beginning of a nationwide effort to pass similar laws."[2] As Chapter 3 showed, her words proved prescient. Over the course of only a few years, in the mid-late 1990s, registration and notification laws swept the nation,[3] and today the phrase "Megan's Law" is a fixture in the American lexicon.[4]

The dramatic resurgence of registration in particular is especially striking given its near-moribund status as of the late 1980s, when beset by chronic concerns over the accuracy and completeness of registries, the social control method scarcely figured in American life. Such concerns, however, were rarely if ever voiced in the 1990s as legislatures rushed to adopt laws. Similarly, while the appeal of earlier laws was hindered by widespread civil liberties concerns, such concerns from 1990 onward were largely absent. Seemingly, as public sensitivity to the association of registration with Nazi Germany and other repressive governments faded, so too did resistance. In its place, a complex array of social, political, and historical forces came to the fore, driving renewed interest in registration and the genesis of community notification. This chapter examines the causal forces and mechanisms accounting for the proliferation of modern laws and their content.

## PANIC REDUX

A common framework for conceiving of the current wave of harsh provisions targeting sex offenders, including registration and notification laws, is that of a "panic." In his study of state laws enacted in the late 1930s permitting the involuntary commitment of "sexual psychopaths" to psychiatric institutions, sociologist Edwin Sutherland identified the following process at work: first, the community is thrown into a panic by a few serious sex crimes, which are given nationwide publicity; next, the community acts in an agitated manner, and all sorts of proposals are made; finally, a committee is appointed to study the facts and to make recommendations.[5] In 1972, another sociologist, Stanley Cohen, studied the exaggerated response in England to "Mods and Rockers," teenage groups who in the mid-1960s engaged in a series of minor disturbances. Cohen observed that "societies appear to be subject, every now and then, to periods of moral panic," resulting in the "moral barricades [being] manned by editors, bishops, politicians and other right-thinking people," and drastic solutions proffered.[6] That the actual extent and nature of the disturbances was distorted, and the images of the nefarious youth gangs largely invented, was of no moment; what mattered was that the particular social threat was perceived.

Applying the work of Sutherland and Cohen, Phillip Jenkins more recently focused on the broader cyclical nature of panics concerning sexual abuse. To Jenkins, the nation's fixation on sex offenders has manifested in three periods: 1910–1930 ("defective delinquent" laws), 1930–1960 ("sexual psychopath" commitment laws), and 1980–present ("sexually violent predator" commitment, registration, and notification laws).[7] In each period, widely reported sex crimes triggered rampant fear resulting in harsh governmental responses. While Jenkins comprehensively explores the initial period, a time when serial sexual criminal misconduct, including against children, was first identified and perpetrators were prosecuted, his primary focus is on parallels between the latter two periods.

Jenkins chronicles the panics, highlighting how the public imagination has been seized and fueled by particular events. Chief among them was the capture of Albert Fish, who in 1934 was arrested in upstate New York for the murder, mutilation, and cannibalism of 12-year-old Grace Budd. Fish, despite several stints in prison, had murdered and molested children for almost thirty years and was thought responsible for as many as fifteen killings. In the wake of his capture, other gruesome episodes from across the nation attracted widespread attention, feeding public alarm that innocents were being targeted at will.

Newspapers and magazines of the time ran lengthy, often lurid exposés on the rampant rape, molestation, and murder of women and children by compulsive sex fiends and psychopaths, who often had lengthy criminal records. Consistent with the tenor of the times, FBI head J. Edgar Hoover in 1937 urged a "war on the sex criminal," stressing that the "sex fiend, most loathsome of all the vast army of crime, has become a sinister threat to the safety of American childhood and womanhood."[8] Ten years later, in a magazine article titled "How Safe Is Your Daughter?" Hoover warned that "the most rapidly increasing type of crime is that perpetrated by degenerate sex offenders." Hoover urged "an aroused public opinion" so that "something may be done to correct a situation that leaves maimed and murdered women lying in isolated areas, which leaves violated children in a sense of hysteria, and which is a perpetual nightmare to the loved ones and friends of the victims."[9] In 1955, a time when the phrase "child molesting" first emerged, Hoover reprised his earlier article with another entitled "How Safe Is Your Youngster?"[10] Jenkins writes that as of 1957 "[s]elf-help and community child-protection schemes became a flourishing subgenre" among magazines such as *Ladies' Home Journal*, *Good Housekeeping*, and *Better Homes and Gardens*.[11]

Pressured to respond, states enacted laws that permitted the indefinite involuntary commitment of sex offenders in psychiatric institutions, allowing release only when they were deemed safe to walk the streets. Michigan enacted the nation's first "sexual psychopath" law in 1937, and by 1957 thirty states and the District of Columbia had laws.[12] The provisions were predicated on the idea that sex offenders as a subgroup were not worthy of differentiation[13] and that those committing minor misdeeds would in time engage in extreme violence. As a result, many nonviolent offenders were subject to potentially indefinite deprivations of liberty in mental hospitals,[14] including homosexuals and others who engaged in behaviors deemed deviant or degenerate.[15]

The laws continued to grow in popularity despite increasing evidence of their shortcomings. Other than Edwin Sutherland, perhaps the most influential critic was Paul Tappan, who in 1950 served as technical consultant for the New Jersey Commission on the Habitual Sex Offender. Tappan's research showed that "the vast majority of the sex deviates are minor offenders," and that at most 5% of offenders used force or inflicted injury.[16] Tappan also rejected the accepted wisdom of chronic recidivism, concluding that "sex offenders have one of the lowest rates as 'repeaters' of all types of crime . . . Among serious crimes homicide alone has a lower rate of recidivism."[17] Tappan's findings found support in a report from a New York City Commission conducted some seven years earlier:

> [F]irst offenders commit most sex crimes...Where sex offenders do have prior criminal records, it is usually for non-sexual crimes...Police department fingerprint records disclose that only 7% of the persons convicted of sex crimes in 1930 were arrested on charges of sex crime during the period 1930–1941.[18]

Tappan's report resulted in changes to the law proposed in New Jersey,[19] which like many bills then being considered nationwide, ultimately won support. Amid the desperate public mood of the time, Jenkins observes, "it would have taken suicidal courage to oppose or even question a bill ostensibly intended to protect the innocent from sex fiends, even if a legislator knew perfectly well that the measure would be worse than useless." Given the option of adopting legislation in the name of protecting women and children, "the possibility of injustice against minor offenders was scarcely worth considering."[20]

While symbolically important for manifesting fear and disdain of their targets, however, commitment laws, like early registration laws, fell into gradual disuse. Concerns over the vague "psychopath" category, over- and underinclusiveness, statistically unfounded assertions of high sex offender recidivism, and the fallibility of predictive expertise resulted in the laws being ignored or repealed by the 1970s.[21] The commitment laws, Jenkins observes, came to be viewed "[f]or many years as a model example of failed legislation called forth by politicians pandering to ill-focused public fears but that had done nothing to reduce crime or detain the truly dangerous."[22]

The following years, 1958–1976, a period Jenkins refers to as the "liberal era," were marked by a cooler political temperament over the perils and extent of sexual victimization of children and adults alike. In the early 1980s, however, panic set in again, this time because of child abductions, laying the groundwork for the unprecedented panic taking root in the 1990s and still resonating today.

A main catalyst was the July 1981 disappearance of 6-year-old Adam Walsh in Hollywood, Florida, which prompted a massive two-week rescue effort that captivated the nation's attention. After the boy's severed head was discovered in a canal, his parents, John and Reve Walsh, initiated a national crusade to "make the country safe for these little people."[23] In October 1982, President

Reagan signed the federal Missing Children Act, which required the FBI to gather information on missing children, and later designated May 25, 1983, as national "Missing Children's Day."

Meanwhile, John Walsh established four Adam Walsh Resource Centers, dedicated to locating missing children, and the Adam Walsh tragedy inspired a network television movie in October 1983, "Adam," which proved hugely popular. Immediately after the movie, NBC aired photos of missing children and informed viewers that fifty thousand children were abducted annually in the United States. NBC rebroadcast the movie a year later, and Congress allocated $57 million to establish the National Resource Center on Missing Children. In testimony before Congress, John Walsh related that "[m]ore than 1.5 million children are reported missing every year" and "we don't have clues to what happened to over 50,000 of them."[24] In conjunction with widely reported serial killings, such as by the notorious John Wayne Gacy in suburban Chicago in the late 1970s, and Wayne Williams in Atlanta in the early 1980s, child homicide added mortal urgency to the public debate.[25]

Congress responded by creating the National Center for Missing and Exploited Children, which John Walsh, an hotelier, was appointed to head. By 1985, over one hundred agencies, with annual combined funding in excess of $15 million, were engaged in the campaign against child abductions, increasing public awareness by such efforts as emblazoning milk cartons and cereal boxes with the faces of missing children. Parents, as they had in the 1930s in the wake of the Lindbergh baby kidnapping, responded proactively, by having their children fingerprinted, and some even had radio transponders inserted in their children's teeth.[26]

The child abduction and murder panic, however, soon lost steam, undercut by claims that abduction rates had been exaggerated. In a 1985 exposé that won a Pulitzer Prize, the *Denver Post* reported that 330,000, not 1.5 million, children were reported missing annually, and that most of the children were runaways. Moreover, fewer than one thousand children were the victims of homicide, most often at the hands of acquaintances or relatives—not trench-coated strangers.[27] The finding was soon backed by a 1989 study indicating that only 52 to 158 children annually were killed or abducted by strangers[28] and a 1990 U.S. Department of Justice study[29] concluding that in 1988 of the estimated 3,200–4,600 nonfamily abductions, only 200–300 were "stereotypical kidnappings"; and that from 1976 to 1987, an estimated 43–147 "stranger abduction homicides" occurred annually. Furthermore, missing children fell into five categories, with at least four of the categories containing children who were not "literally missing." Rather, their location was known; "the problem was recovering them." The report further stated that "it was not possible to develop a meaningful and useful global figure for the 'number of missing children,'" and the authors discouraged efforts "to create or use such a global number."

In the face of these data, focus soon shifted from child abduction and abuse to child sexual victimization. The groundwork for this transition was laid with trials stemming from reported mass child sexual abuse at the McMartin preschool in Southern California (1983) and a day care center in rural Jordan, Minnesota (1984), which received major sustained media attention and prompted congressional hearings. By 1990, when the National Center for Missing and Exploited Children merged with the Adam Walsh Child Resource Center, child sexual molestation had become a major focus of national concern.[30]

In the early 1990s, as Jenkins notes, the nation had thus come "full circle," revisiting its earlier obsession over sexual abuse, especially of the young. While the 1989 abduction of Minnesotan Jacob Wetterling never provably involved sexual abuse and his assailant was never arrested, the disappearance seamlessly combined with fears of child sexual predations, resulting in state and federal legislative responses targeting sex offenders.

The panic framework, while broadly helpful as a basis to contextualize the modern proliferation of registration and notification laws, however, accounts for only part of the story.[31] Sex crime panics, as the framework instructs, have beset the nation before. Their net outcome, however, pales when compared to the uniquely severe, comprehensive, and sustained legislative response of the 1990s resulting in today's nationwide network of registration and notification laws. American jurisdictions targeted sex offenders with registration starting in the 1930s, a time when crime risks were first becoming "sexualized,"[32] and from the late 1930s through the 1960s laws permitting the commitment of "sexual psychopaths" were widely adopted. Registration in general, and of sex offenders in particular, however, inspired comparatively little interest. Only in the 1990s did registration—with its predominant focus on sex offenders— combined with notification, fully blossom.

In short, while there is no mistaking that today's registration and notification laws derive in significant part from a sustained panic, full explanation lies in the additive force of several other factors.

## PUNITIVENESS

One such factor involved a discernible shift in sensibility. While as late as the 1970s the American response to crime was marked mainly by a desire to rehabilitate rather than punish offenders, starting in the 1980s American criminal justice became unabashedly punitive.[33] This shift was readily apparent in huge increases in incarceration rates. Whereas in 1972 the rate of imprisonment per 100,000 residents was 93 inmates, by 1990 the rate was 297, and by 2000 it was 478—an increase of over 400% in less than thirty years.[34] From 1980 to 2000, the number of individuals in jail, in prison, or under community supervision grew from 1.8 million to 6.4 million.[35] By the end of 2005, more than 7 million adults were ensnared in the U.S. criminal justice system, roughly 3.2% of the U.S. adult population.[36]

These increases, however, fail to convey the actual human impact of the nation's surge in punitiveness. An alternate method is what Kevin Reitz has called "person-years." Using 1990–1999 as his frame of reference, Reitz observes: "The human impact of changing confinement policy during the 1990s . . . measures in several millions of years over and above the incarceration terms that would have been served if there had been zero incarceration growth after 1990." Moreover, even though rates have slowed since 2000, they have not significantly diminished, meaning that 2000–2009 will be the "most punitive decade in U.S. history by far."[37]

Other indicia further highlight the punitive shift. In addition to standing alone among Western nations in the use of the death penalty,[38] America since the 1990s has effectively renounced the *parens patriae* goals of the juvenile justice system[39] and embraced such anachronistic penal strategies as public "shame sanctions" on offenders[40] and prison chain gangs.[41] The era also witnessed a spike in support of habitual offender laws,[42] which first gained popularity concurrently with registration in the 1930s and prompted similar crime-fighting plaudits,[43] but thereafter experienced a similar decline in interest.[44]

The 1990s were also marked by an unprecedented desire to get tough on sex offenders especially, the principal targets of registration and notification and a subpopulation inspiring special hatred and disdain.[45] During the 1990s prison terms increased dramatically,[46] triggering massive increases in sex offender prison populations,[47] and several states adopted laws permitting chemical and surgical castration of sex offenders.[48]

States also gravitated anew to laws permitting the involuntary commitment of sex offenders, as noted, a strategy that had gone into decline by the

1970s, only to arise in harsher form as "sexually violent predator" laws that committed individuals to state psychiatric institutions in addition to (not in lieu of) prison.[49]

In sum, the proliferation of registration and notification was part of a much broader shift toward harsh crime control responses. Why the era proved so hospitable to draconian criminal justice policies has been a matter of ongoing interest to scholars. One school of thought, most prominently advanced by Jonathan Simon[50] and David Garland,[51] is that the shift stemmed from a need to quell postmodernist anxiety and disillusionment with neoliberal government. To Anthony Bottoms, the laws derived from a "populist punitiveness,"[52] with major attendant gains for political leaders; Katherine Beckett and others have similarly tied the shift to a potent synergy of media and politically induced pressures.[53]

A fair assessment, however, lies in any number of these and doubtless other explanations, with none standing alone. Nor should it be inferred that modern American punitiveness is unprecedented. As Franklin Zimring and his coauthors observe, "public hostility toward criminals is a historical constant in stable democracies."[54] Indeed, crackdowns, triggered by widely reported criminal events within an increasingly interconnected society,[55] were common in the 1930s, when registration and a host of other get-tough provisions were enacted.[56] Relative harshness in American criminal justice, as James Whitman recently observed,[57] is thus a constant, differing only in degree and particulars. However, there is no mistaking that the sensibility played a major role in the resurgence of registration and adoption of notification laws in the 1990s, with policies being driven by what David Garland has called "the sense of a fearful, angry public."[58] Registration, a social control strategy that essentially lay dormant for decades, despite myriad criminal depravations in the intervening years, enjoyed new life in the early 1990s, assuming far more onerous form over time. And with it came community notification, as well, with harsh personal consequences for those it targeted.

## POLITICS OF PERSONALIZATION AND DEHUMANIZATION

Changes in the legislative process, in particular the unprecedented political use and influence of individual victims and defendants, also played a key role. Like prior harsh laws originating amid panics, registration and notification laws in the 1990s were triggered by gruesome events. Modern registration and notification, however, differed not only in degree but also in kind, drawing political strength from intense focus upon particular victims and their survivors (typically parents). At the same time, the political atmosphere giving rise to the modern proliferation of registration and notification was unique for its unprecedented tendency to depersonalize and dehumanize the principal targets of the laws—sex offenders.

The foundation for the this victim-centrism was laid in the 1970s when victims' advocates, building on the successes of the women's rights movement,[59] succeeded not only in increasing the role of victims in the criminal justice process,[60] but also in emphasizing the harms suffered by victims.[61] Registration and notification advocates also learned from the successes of child abuse advocates in the 1980s who skillfully used victim narrative and imagery, especially concerning female and child victims of physical and sexual abuse, to great political effect.[62]

The emphasis was very evident in Congress. From 1991, when Minnesota Senator David Durenberger invoked the plight of Jacob Wetterling to underscore the need for registration, to 2006, when the federal Adam Walsh Child Protection and Safety Act was enacted, stories of individual victims dominated the legislative process. Just one example among many occurred in 1994 when efforts were redoubled in the U.S. House of Representatives to augment registration with notification after Megan Kanka's sexual abuse and murder. Representative Dick Zimmer (R-NJ), a chief advocate, recounted that "on July 29, 1994, a beautiful little girl named Megan Kanka was lured into the home of a man who literally lived across the street from her. He said that he had a puppy he wanted to show her. He then proceeded to brutally rape and murder this little girl."[63] Representative Shirley Jackson Lee (D-TX) invoked the memory of "Megan Kanka, who was raped and strangled and murdered by a twice-convicted pedophile who lived across the street from her."[64] In myriad other instances, legislators nationwide recounted in detail the Megan Kanka tragedy, along with other less publicized victimizations,[65] demanding that laws be enacted.

Aptly called "advocacy through storytelling" by one commentator,[66] the political strategy proved highly successful. Putting victims' faces on initiatives humanized and rendered more understandable the perceived urgent need for policy change. As Senator Durenberger stated in 1991 during early consideration of the Wetterling Act, if imposing a registration requirement "will assist law enforcement authorities in one criminal apprehension, or if it will deter a single kidnapping, I believe it is worth implementing."[67]

Personalization also inoculated proposed legislation against challenge. Opponents risked being portrayed as being "soft on criminals," potentially leaving them responsible for any subsequent victimization, a highly effective and at times overtly personal political strategy.[68] Worse yet, they could be branded "anti-victim," or, even more fearsome, "anti–this victim." As Representative William Martini (R-NJ) stressed in urging adoption of the federal Megan's Law in 1996: "We must not allow this little girl's life to be taken in vain."[69] Representative Zimmer urged that the law was Megan's "legacy . . . her gift to all children whose lives will be saved."[70] Under such circumstances, as Professor Daniel Filler has observed, any attack "was a political impossibility,"[71] much as opposition to the "sexual psychopath" laws was fifty years before.[72]

The ultimate success of this personalization is manifest in the names of the laws themselves—Megan's Law (U.S. and New Jersey), Zachary's Law (Indiana), Ashley's Law (Texas), or any of the litany of other state laws. Moreover, as noted in Chapter 3, the desire to name registration laws has not been limited to those mainly targeting sex offenders, but also extends to stand-alone registries (for example, Oklahoma's Mary Rippy Violent Crime Offenders Registration Act).

The zenith in this personalization was perhaps recently reached with the federal Adam Walsh Act (AWA) in 2006, which enshrined the law's namesake as well as the names of seventeen other victims in the law's "declaration of purpose," along with brief personal descriptions and how they were victimized. The law was enacted "to protect the public from sex offenders and offenders against children, and *in response to the vicious attacks by violent predators against the victims*" specified.[73] Wary of in any way besmirching the memory of prior namesakes, Congress established within the broader AWA "the Jacob Wetterling, Megan Nicole Kanka, and Pam Lychner Sex Offender Registration and Community Notification Program," victims already named in the list of seventeen.[74]

That a complex and major piece of federal legislation, affecting all U.S. states, territories, and Indian tribal areas, would expressly single out particular victims manifests the tenor of the times. Even more telling, perhaps, is that despite the scores of individuals victimized by sex crimes since the 1980s, hailing from all racial and ethnic backgrounds, all eighteen victims memorialized by name by Congress in its AWA "roll call" are white[75] and, with the exception of Pam Lychner, children.

Political personalization of victims, however, only partly accounts for the massive widespread appeal of registration and notification. Of perhaps equal importance has been the way assailants have been portrayed. Just as Albert Fish served as the prototype repeat deviant offender in the 1930s and 1940s, in the 1990s Jesse Timmendequas and other modern predator prototypes served as focal points justifying the laws. What changed in the 1990s was the manner in which the victimizers were portrayed. Whereas Fish and others of his generation were often referenced in laws in clinical terms, such as "sexual psychopath" or "sexually dangerous person,"[76] Timmendequas and his cohort were portrayed in far more evocative and pejorative ways, such as "predatory sex offenders."[77] Even more graphic terms were used in legislative debates leading to enactment of the laws. To Senate Majority Leader Bob Dole (R-KS), Timmendequas was a "beast,"[78] and to Representative Susan Molinari (R-NY) he was a "wolf among lambs."[79] To Senator Kay Hutchison (R-TX), sex offenders were "monsters,"[80] to Representative Mark Foley (R-FL) they were "animals."[81] To one New York State legislator, sex offenders were the "human equivalent of toxic waste."[82]

Just as referring to juvenile offenders as "superpredators" facilitated renunciation in the 1990s of the historic benign *parens patriae* orientation,[83] framing sex offenders as less than human paved the way for the nationwide embrace of registration and notification. The political logic behind this rhetorical shift is explained by a large academic literature. Mary Douglas, writing in 1966, recognized the appeal of recognizing pollutants, human and otherwise, as warranting remedies to preserve the social order.[84] William Ian Miller, similarly, identifies disgust as having "intensely political significance," naturally prompting self-defensive efforts to guard against pollution.[85] Joseph Kennedy, applying the teachings of sociologist Emile Durkheim, has reasoned that the "severity revolution" of the 1990s stemmed from a deep, collectively felt anxiety over rapidly changing social and economic structures, serving as a way for the law-abiding "us" to condemn and express solidarity against the lawbreaking "them."[86]

More recently, Cass Sunstein has applied the model to explain the imperative behind the nation's post-9/11 responses. As Sunstein points out, recent antiterrorism laws and military campaigns benefited from having concrete antagonists—Osama bin Laden and Saddam Hussein, in particular—upon whom to affix outrage and scorn. "If a wrongdoer has a clear identity—a face and a narrative—the public is far more likely to support an aggressive response." Like the character Emmanuel Goldstein in George Orwell's novel *Nineteen Eighty-Four*, a despised enemy of the state inspiring public fear and disdain, Sunstein sees Osama and Saddam as fueling the nation's willingness to back harsh measures.[87]

A similar "Goldstein Effect" has informed the nation's ongoing effort to single out antagonists such as Jesse Timmendequas for harsh treatment and public scorn, lending credence to Jeremy Bentham's observation that social policies informed by antipathy for "individuals represented as dangerous and vile pushes them onward to an undue severity."[88] As Representative Randall "Duke" Cunningham (R-CA) vividly framed the issue in 1996: "perhaps a sexual predator's life should be just a little more toxic than someone [else's] in the American citizenry."[89]

## RISK AVERSION AND SCIENTISM

A fourth factor concerns a shift in modern sensibility: the increasing tendency to conceive of and respond to modern social challenges and problems in terms of risk. The shift was identified in 1991 by Anthony Giddens, who in an important work wrote that modern society is a "risk culture" marked by "a calculative attitude."[90] From the 1990s through the present, as Cass Sunstein has noted, the reigning view has been that "regulators should take steps to protect against potential harms, even if causal chains are unclear and even if we do not know that those harms will come to fruition."[91]

This broader sensibility paralleled a shift in criminal justice orientation. While positivism had dominated penal policy since at least the mid-nineteenth century (Chapter 1), the 1990s marked a zenith in this orientation—but with a twist. Whereas in the past the focus was individualized, seeking to identify and monitor dangerous individuals, modern policy conceived of danger in aggregate terms: what Malcolm Feeley and Jonathan Simon in 1992 called a "new penology." Criminal risk came to be understood in aggregate statistical terms and seen as a constant, not an aberration, a social fact to be managed. The new penology, Feeley and Simon wrote, "seeks to regulate levels of deviance, not intervene or respond to *individual* deviants or social malformation."[92]

The proliferation of registration and notification laws was driven by and reflected this orientation. While personal tragedies and names of victims and offenders might have differed among jurisdictions, from the outset policy discourse was dominated by assertions that sex offenders as a group were intractably compulsive, predatory, and unusually prone to recidivism. For instance, in 1991, U.S. Senator David Durenberger (R-MN), a sponsor of what came to be the Wetterling Act, stated on the Senate floor that "the people who commit these offenses repeat their crimes again and again and again; and local law enforcement officials need access to an interstate system of information to prevent and respond to these horrible crimes against our children."[93] Through the years, similar pronouncements on the recidivist certainties of child sex offenders dominated federal[94] and state legislative debates and findings.[95]

Much as the nation's first registration laws were prompted by an "emergency" over the perceived threat of an influx of "gangsters," modern laws have been motivated by a sustained sense of exigency concerning sex offenders. Alarming statistics adduced by political leaders have, in turn, been absorbed by the media[96] and the public,[97] leading to a self-perpetuating legislative process resulting in today's nationwide network of registration and notification laws.[98] And, much as in the early 1930s, when the nation was convinced that it was in the grip of a "crime wave," compelling immediate action, the statistical record belied this perception: child[99] and adult[100] sexual abuse has actually declined since the 1990s.[101]

Perceived statistical risk, however, not only played a motivational role with registration and notification laws; it also has infused their nature. As was the case with early registration laws, a single static factor—a conviction—has triggered use of the laws. Today, under the Adam Walsh Act and most state regimes, conviction of an enumerated crime determines the duration of registration and the intervals at which registry information must be updated. And, as with earlier laws, the triggering criterion of conviction often sweeps up broad offender groups without consideration of particular circumstances, and singles out crimes not known to pose particular recidivist risk (such as murder) and nonassaultive crimes (such as peeping).

The advent of community notification, in turn, has introduced a new actuarial component. As discussed in Chapter 3, jurisdictions today differ in how they go about implementing community notification, and these policies reflect varied faith in actuarialism. In a majority of jurisdictions, laws require that individuals convicted of specified offenses register and, without regard for individual risk, be subject to notification based on legislative understandings of aggregate risk. This approach, earlier referred to as "conviction based," is the method required by the Adam Walsh Act, and because of congressional threats to withhold federal funds from noncompliant states, the approach might soon be the national norm. To date, however, many jurisdictions have used a "risk-based" approach, which tempers legislative concerns for aggregate risk by subjecting registrants to individual risk assessments. Only registrants deemed to pose the relative higher risk are subject to broad community notification. Yet, even this apparent embrace of clinical individualized assessment is less than it seems. This is because the risk assessment tools used by experts to conduct evaluations rely on broad statistically based actuarial factors.[102]

Registration and notification are thus very much part of the ongoing effort to make crime control more actuarial and scientific. The impulse first manifested itself in early efforts to "know the criminal" in order to predict and control individual deviance, leading to concern over "dangerous classes" in the early to mid-1800s. From the late 1800s through the 1970s, the focus shifted back to the individual, and today we again witness a focus on classes of individuals.[103]

Ironically, however, despite their overtly empiric orientation, registration and notification are decidedly unempiric in several important respects. First, and most fundamentally, it is now clear that the recidivism-related premise of sex offender registration, in particular, is well off the mark. Just as the extent of child abductions was exaggerated in the 1980s, statements by political leaders in the 1990s suggesting extremely high rates of sex offender recidivism lack empirical support. Recidivism among sex offenders in general (defined to include recommitting a sex offense) has been shown to range from 5% to 14% over three- to six-year follow-up periods,[104] and 24% over a fifteen-year follow-up period.[105] Contrary to legislative pronouncements, sex offenders have among the lowest criminal recidivism rates, with robbers, burglars, and persons committing nonsexual assault all recommitting similar crimes at considerably higher rates.[106] In short, even though sexual victimization without question remains a significant concern, and the full extent of victimizations is known to be underreported,[107] it is also clear that the drive for registration and notification has been fueled by vastly overstated understandings of recidivist risk.

Second, sex offenders are a markedly heterogeneous criminal subpopulation with respect to recidivist risk. Some sex offenders—such as male pedophiles who victimize nonfamilial boys, and male rapists targeting women[108]— do recidivate at alarmingly high rates. Registration laws, however, manifest a marked tendency to indulge in what social scientists refer to as "overinclusive labeling."[109] Like early-era registration laws, modern registration is triggered not only by convictions for a broad array of nondangerous crimes, but also by crimes not associated with recidivist risk.[110] Likewise, stand-alone registries often cover offenders not known for their high recidivism rates—such as murderers.

Finally, contrary to the "stranger danger" predicate of the laws, most sex offenses are not committed by strangers. Rather, while offender profiles differ depending on the nature of the sex offense, the overwhelming majority of child sexual victimizations are committed by someone known by the victim. For instance, from 1991 to 1996 only 7% of reported instances of child sexual victimizations (age 0–17) involved strangers—34% were victimized by family and 59% by acquaintances.[111] Among adults aged 18–24, only 24% of sexual victimizations are committed by strangers, while the rate among older adults is 30%.[112] Moreover, of the estimated 260,000 children kidnapped annually, only approximately 115 are taken by strangers.[113] Even more problematic, the overwhelming majority of strangers committing sex crimes are first-time offenders,[114] with no recorded offending history, a statistic that belies the very premise of the laws.[115]

Registration and notification, in short, have been based on a mere verisimilitude of empirical justfication,[116] which served to insulate them from attack.[117] While the inconsistencies were reported by the mainstream media from the outset,[118] the reports—unlike in the 1980s when, as noted, critical analysis of child abduction rates put the breaks on policy changes—had no effect. Likewise, unlike the 1950s, when expert opinion on the shortcomings of "sexual psychopath" involuntary commitment laws exercised some influence on the content of laws, such reservations got no traction in the 1990s with registration and notification.[119]

Modern laws are unempiric in yet another sense. As noted above, particular child victimizations played a crucial role in the political discourse driving registration and notification. However, often the tragedies invoked as representative of the need for registration were, in actuality, inapt factual catalysts. We do not know, for instance, whether Jacob Wetterling was the victim of sexual abuse, or whether his abductor(s) had a history of sexual offending, or lived anywhere nearby.[120] Moreover, although disputed by the Kanka family, media sources reported that a number of people in the neighborhood (perhaps including Maureen Kanka herself) were aware that a convicted sex offender lived at Timmendequas's address.[121]

It also escaped attention that particular victimizations figuring so centrally in advocacy actually at times resulted from specific failures in the preexisting criminal justice system, capable of specific remedy, rather than evidencing a need for a major nationwide programmatic shift like registration and notification. For instance, Jesse Timmendequas was free to live near Megan Kanka only because local prosecutors agreed to a ten-year sentence and not the thirty-year sentence legally prescribed for recidivist offenders such as he.[122]

Jonathan Simon, after surveying the empirically based criminal justice efforts mind-set dominant for much of the twentieth century, recently inquired: "What might a post-positivist criminology look like, and how might it influence American crime control?"[123] With registration and notification laws we have the answer—a regime that merely has the appearance of being empirically based, but in actuality is driven by an implacable desire to achieve individualized safety without regard for rational risk. As recognized by Washington State Representative Jim Clements, "[p]eople don't necessarily want statistical analysis . . . They want security for their children—real or imagined."[124]

The reasons for this state of affairs are without question complex and numerous. Two partial explanations, however, perhaps lie in the teachings of social psychology—in particular, what is called the "psychometric paradigm" of risk perception and management.[125] Under this view, statistics tend to lack persuasive influence on the public, which interprets life situations in a "richer" manner, assigning importance to such considerations as whether a risk is involuntarily suffered or especially dreaded.[126] On this account, sexual victimizations of women and children qualify as particularly compelling catalysts. This is so despite the reality that the prototypical "stranger danger" circumstances informing public understanding of the threats posed do not statistically warrant equivalent concern. Just as the nation has ignored or discounted the actual low statistical threat of terrorism and waged a "war on terror" based on the events of September 11, 2001,[127] so too has it obsessed over sexual "stranger danger," despite the actual remoteness of the risk.

The laws also bear the earmarks of a related construct known as an "availability heuristic," whereby a focal point serves as a "mental shortcut for a more deliberative or analytic assessment of underlying issues"[128] and drives public perception of risk out of proportion to empirical reality.[129] As Cass Sunstein has summarized the literature, when people use the availability heuristic, they assess the magnitude of risks by

> asking whether examples can readily come to mind. For example, a class whose instances are easily retrieved will appear more numerous than a class of equal frequency whose instances are less retrievable. If people can think of relevant examples, they are far more likely to be frightened and concerned than if they cannot.[130]

The victimizations of Megan Kanka and others by strangers, while not statistically representative, have served as highly potent availability heuristics. And like other heuristics, they have exercised a skewing effect on policy, resulting from the ancillary influence of "probability neglect." "The availability heuristic and probability neglect," Professor Sunstein observes, "often lead people to treat risks as much greater than they are in fact and hence to accept risk-reduction strategies that do considerable harm and little good."[131] Such has been the case with registration and notification. By focusing on "stranger danger," harsh laws have been adopted[132] and Americans, while optimistically comforted by the notion that danger emanates from unfamiliar others, have been distracted from the troubling reality that the people they should fear most are relatives, friends, and acquaintances.[133] This in turn has fed the pervasive tendency to downplay the harms attending victimization by familiars, making it even less likely to become a public safety priority.[134]

## INFORMATION ENTITLEMENT

Another factor explaining the modern proliferation centers on the appeal of community notification itself. As discussed in Chapter 2, early-generation registration laws reserved information on registrants to law enforcement. From the time of Bertillon through the 1980s, even the prospect that identifying information on ex-offenders would become public was strongly condemned.

By 1990, however, when Washington State first permitted registrants' identifying information to be made publicly known, sensibilities had quite clearly changed, and community notification suited the times. The public demanded that government release information on registrants, and government readily complied. This transformation chiefly stemmed from a newfound sense of community entitlement. Outraged that government had information on potentially dangerous individuals, yet failed to make it available, communities insisted on a right to access. As Maureen Kanka stated in a 1996 letter to the House Judiciary Committee during its consideration of what came to be Megan's Law, if pedophiles are going to be out on the street where they can accost children, then

> parents have the right to know if they live on our streets. My daughter Megan would be alive today if I had known that my neighbor was a twice convicted pedophile. I had the responsibility to protect my daughter. I have always told my children that I would never let anything happen to them. But I guess I lied. I could not protect my Megan as she was being brutally raped and murdered across the street from my home. I have to live with the fact that she screamed out my name as she was being murdered.[135]

In keeping with this sentiment, the Megan Nicole Kanka Foundation website proclaims that "every parent should have the right to know if a dangerous sexual predator moves into their neighborhood."[136] The community, as the title of Idaho's law proclaims, has a "Right to Know."[137]

This asserted moral entitlement, typically made by parents suffering grievous loss, in itself would likely have accounted for the political success of community notification. The claim, however, also benefited from a broader shift in public sensibility over the role of government commencing in the 1990s. As Margaret Canovan has observed, the era witnessed emergence of the "service station state," marked by an emergent sense that citizens were consumers with desires that the state must identify and satisfy.[138] This sentiment assumed especially potent form with respect to public safety, based on a growing sense of state failure. Before 1990, communities privileged and trusted government to protect them against recidivist criminal risk. The damage wrought by Earl Shriner, Jesse Timmendequas, and others shattered this faith. While Washington's community notification law itself was ostensibly motivated by a neutral goal of achieving greater governmental transparency and accountability,[139] there was no mistaking that it—like every community notification law enacted since 1990—was driven by this sense of betrayal and lack of trust.[140]

The public, in short, came to feel that it was entitled to registrant information not only as a moral matter but also due to practical necessity. Government had shown that its historic monopoly on information was unjustified; community members needed access to such information so that they could take self-protective measures. As discussed next in Chapter 5, whether public disclosure of registrants' information in fact secures personal safety remains unclear. However, from the outset the assumption that it does affect personal safety has driven legislative efforts, as evidenced in arguments made by political leaders,[141] and assertions in numerous state laws,[142] and on websites.[143] As the Alabama website stated in 2008: "an informed public is a safer public."[144]

This sense of entitlement, moreover, significantly affected political discourse. To the extent that the benefits associated with notification would unfairly impact convicted criminals, the apparent choice faced by political leaders was really no choice at all. The community's right to information readily trumped any possible registrant concerns. Politicians defiantly cast their lot with communities, with numerous state laws containing "findings" explicitly stating that communities' right to have access to information superseded registrants' putative right to privacy in particular.[145]

Moreover, political appeal was augmented by a secondary benefit: shaming. Community notification at once served to satisfy the asserted public entitlement to information and cast opprobrium on registrants. With community notification, as David Garland has observed, society can "simultaneously punish the offender for his crime and alert the community to his danger."[146] Indeed, use of pejorative terms such as "predator" suggests that community notification is about something more than mere record keeping and informational empowerment; so, too, does the staggering number of "hits" to state and federal Internet registries (see Chapter 3) that disseminate information on registrants far beyond their communities, which is the geographic region of avowed concern.

## FEDERAL GOVERNMENT

A final and quite important factor accounting for modern registration and notification laws stems from the policy involvement of the federal government. Historically, criminal justice was regarded as principally a matter of state government concern,[147] both out of tradition, stemming from historic fears over a too-powerful national police authority,[148] and constitutional structure, federal enumerated powers being "few and defined."[149] Starting in the late nineteenth century, however, what Lawrence Friedman has termed the "culture of mobility," fostered by the increasing availability of automobiles and railroads, made state boundaries "increasingly porous" for criminal offenders. Believing the states ill-equipped to address this shift,[150] Congress during the first decades of the twentieth century gradually expanded the reach of federal criminal law.

Registration and countless other criminal justice undertakings nevertheless remained the focus of state and local governments, and the federal impact on criminal justice matters remained limited and episodic. Indeed, while President Herbert Hoover is generally credited with first characterizing crime as a national political issue in his 1929 inaugural address,[151] Hoover himself—consistent with the age—conceived of the federal crime-control role as being highly circumscribed, preferring that the states take the lead on criminal justice.[152] Even the hugely popular Lindbergh Kidnapping Act, enacted in the wake of the notorious abduction and murder of aviator Charles Lindbergh's child, and dubbed by one newspaper "a challenge to the whole order of the nation,"[153] was initially resisted out of concern that the federal government would unduly intrude upon the criminal law bailiwick of states.[154]

In the wake of the 1964 presidential campaign of Barry Goldwater, "law and order" and crime became national issues, and federal reluctance to pass laws on criminal justice matters dissolved.[155] Crime control became a matter of major salience to federal legislators, with neither liberals nor conservatives defending the states' rights ramparts.[156] Today, it is estimated that there are over four thousand federal criminal laws, and the rate of congressional activity has increased dramatically. According to an American Bar Association task force, over 40% of the federal criminal provisions enacted after the Civil War were passed from 1970 to 1998. Another study noted a 30% increase in federal criminal offenses between 1980 and 2004.[157]

This surge in federal police power has been enabled on two chief bases. First, Congress has relied on authority afforded by Article I of the Constitution to "regulate Commerce . . . among the several states,"[158] asserting that its power to define and punish particular crimes, even those traditionally addressed by states, affects interstate commerce. The judiciary, for its part, has largely refused to limit the effort. While the U.S. Supreme Court held on two occasions (*United States v. Lopez* (1995), *United States v. Morrison* (2000)) that Congress had overstepped its Commerce Clause authority, the holdings were soon recognized as aberrations in what otherwise has been a steady increase in federal criminal law empowerment.[159] This conclusion was underscored by the Court's more recent decision in *Gonzales v. Raich* (2005), which upheld a federal law criminalizing the use and production of marijuana, rejecting a claim by California that its contrary law allowing for a medical use exception warranted deference.

The upshot of this exercise of authority has been that Congress has to a very significant extent duplicated state criminal codes. As a result, in effect concurrent or dual jurisdiction now exists over many crimes, allowing a criminal case to be brought in state or federal court. To critics, Congress's unconstrained use of its Commerce Clause authority has amounted to a federal power grab, contrary to constitutional text and tradition.[160] Critics also point to disparity created by the dual system. While state and federal law might define crimes similarly, federal sentences, especially relative to drug crimes, are often much harsher than those imposed by states, giving rise to fairness concerns.[161]

The second source of congressional power is less direct. Rather than creating new criminal laws, Congress has used its Spending Power authority to pressure states to adopt laws of their own consistent with federal will. Based on power bestowed by Article I of the Constitution to "provide for the . . . general Welfare of the United States,"[162] Congress conditions receipt of federal funds on the willingness of states to adopt federally prescribed policies. Congress, as the Supreme Court put it, essentially enters into a quasi-contract with states: "in return for federal funds, the states agree to comply with federally imposed conditions."[163] With this arrangement, Congress can achieve indirectly what it often cannot achieve directly, due to either the absence of Commerce Clause or other lawmaking authority. Meanwhile, federal courts have imposed few limits on such federal "encouragement."[164] Congressional Spending Power authority, as one commentator has noted, "continues to provide practically limitless opportunities for the national government indirectly to shape policy at the state and local levels of society and government."[165]

Spending Power authority has been the main, albeit not exclusive,[166] modus operandi of Congress with respect to registration and notification. Since 1994, with enactment of the Wetterling Act, itself part of a massive bill containing numerous new federal crimes based on congressional Commerce Clause authority, Congress has told states that if they wish to avoid losing their full allocation of Byrne Grant funding, they must adopt federal registration and notification directives. This "contracting" with states has, as a general proposition, proved less controversial than federal Commerce Clause–based jurisdiction. After all, states are merely agreeing to adhere to federal policy in exchange for federal dollars.

This view, however, understates the true effect of Congress's exercise of its Spending Power authority, compared to its Commerce Clause authority. With the latter, what the Supreme Court has called the "sensitive relation between federal and state criminal jurisdiction"[167] is altered; by creating federal crimes, Congress has extended its legal authority beyond its traditional circumscribed realm, creating prosecutorial and punishment authority concurrent with that of states. In reality, however, the federal government never has and never will serve as the main criminal justice authority; the states continue to process the lion's share of criminal cases. As a result, the true significance of federal exercise of Commerce Clause authority lies more in doctrinal and principled terms than real-world effect.[168]

Congressional use of Spending Power authority, on the other hand, has a very real effect; it actually hastens changes in state laws and regulations, requiring states to conform to federal policy. As noted by Justice Anthony Kennedy, resorting to Spending Power authority "has the potential to obliterate distinctions between national and local spheres of interest and power by permitting the Federal Government to set policy in the most sensitive areas of traditional state concern, areas which would otherwise lie outside its reach."[169]

The broader federalism consequences of this incursion will be discussed in Chapter 6; for present purposes, however, it is sufficient to note that federal involvement has been essential in the history of registration and notification. While registration was certainly of interest to the states by 1994, when Congress compelled states to create registries, and notification was popular in the states by 1996, when Congress mandated it, there is no mistaking that federal pressure drove the current nationwide network of laws[170] and that it was especially instrumental in overcoming initial state ambivalence over notification.[171] On at least a semiannual basis Congress has legislated on registration and notification, and federal legislators, including those otherwise reflexively prone to defend state sovereignty, have remained silent. Perhaps most emblematic of this inconsistency is that 1994, the year Congress first imposed its will on states with respect to registration, was also the time of the Republican Party's "Contract With America," a central premise of which was that the federal government had become too powerful at the expense of the states.

Federal intrusiveness with respect to registration has had two main consequences. First, by conditioning receipt of federal funds on state compliance with its requirements, the federal government compelled those states perhaps not otherwise inclined to adopt registration and notification laws to do so. Second, by tying receipt of federal funds to adoption of federal requirements, the U.S. modified the substantive content of state laws, requiring them to adopt federal minima with respect to such matters as the offenses triggering registration, registration of juveniles, duration of registration, retroactivity, and use of a "conviction-based" classification system. While states have often exceeded the federal "floor," the impact of federal involvement overall has been to make state laws not only more uniform, but also often more demanding—to in effect "level up" registration and notification policy.[172]

Importantly, the federal policy preferences bear the earmarks of having originated in a national legislative body that is fundamentally distinct from its state legislative counterparts, especially on cost and practicality concerns. While states very often must balance budgets and temper criminal justice desires with fiscal and real-world constraints, federal policy is developed in an environment largely inured to such concerns,[173] and federal politicians secure major political benefits from their support of harsh laws. State legislatures, in turn, do not relish being accused of failing to secure "free" federal funds and do not wish to look "soft" by renouncing federal minimum requirements relative to the disdained targets of registration and notification. With the door open to amendments, states have added to the minima with ardor.

Finally, federal influence has been manifest in a more subtle but quite important respect. Congress has fostered and sustained a political climate conducive to the growth of state registration and notification laws. State legislators, themselves in the C-SPAN audience and acutely aware of the political salience of toughened requirements, have seized the opportunity, enacting provisions with impressive speed. And, as with criminal justice policy more generally,[174] registration has typically been a one-way ratchet, with provisions getting tougher by the year, backed by overwhelming bipartisan political support, with any possible slackening deterred by the dreaded threat noted earlier—being tagged as "soft on crime" (or even worse, sex offenders), "anti-victim," or, most daunting of all, "anti–this victim."

## CONCLUSION

The modern resurgence of registration, and concomitant adoption of community notification, has been both rapid and dramatic. As the preceding discussion suggests, the proliferation of laws stemmed from a complex array of social and political forces converging in the 1990s that are still with us today. That the transformation began in the 1990s, a period of not only relative economic prosperity and optimism but also decreasing crime, remains a paradox. Draconian in nature, and enjoying rapid nationwide popularity, the laws represent stark exceptions to the historic understanding that harsh and reactionary measures flourish only in times of economic uncertainty and social adversity.[175]

# 5 EFFECTS AND CONSEQUENCES

THE PRECEDING TWO CHAPTERS chronicled the rapid nationwide proliferation of registration and community notification laws, which today directly affect hundreds of thousands of individuals and impose significant burdens on state and local governments. In addition to enjoying enormous political appeal, registries—especially when complemented by community notification—are very popular with the public. Two studies of Washington State residents, for instance, found that roughly 80% thought community notification "very important."[1] In Georgia, a poll indicated that 79% of respondents believed that "the public has a right to know of a convicted sex offender's past, and that right is more important than the sex offender's privacy rights."[2] Additional testament of the popularity of the laws is found in the massive number of "hits" to government-run website registries, with some sites boasting hundreds of thousands a month.[3]

The proliferation of registration and notification laws is based on the expectations that they make communities safer by (1) providing police with information to facilitate the surveillance and apprehension of registrant-recidivists; (2) giving community members information on registrants so that they can take self-protective steps to monitor and possibly help capture recidivists; and (3) deterring recidivism among registrants themselves, by enhancing consciousness that they are being watched. Today, however, almost two decades after the renaissance of registration, and the genesis of community notification, these expectations remain largely untested and unproven. Equally problematic, we know little about their negative effects, including whether the social control strategies actually diminish public safety.

The absence of such basic, critically important information on a policy that directly affects hundreds of thousands of individuals, and requires significant government resources, is itself remarkable. One would be hard-pressed to identify a national social policy, ambitiously expanded upon for many years, which has similarly failed to command empirical assessment. This deficit itself, however, represents an important piece of the history of criminal registration and community notification laws. The effectiveness of registration has always been accepted as an article of faith—common sense has dictated that it would enhance public safety; so too, in the modern context, notification. Augmenting this self-assurance is the sentiment, noted in Chapter 4, that communities are entitled to information on registrants, and even if not efficacious, that the strategies are justified if "only one child is saved."

Only today is comprehensive research on registration and notification being pursued. This chapter examines the empirical work done to date, focusing on several basic areas: the reliability of information contained in registries; crime reduction effects; empowerment of police; community self-protection; adverse effects on registrants; and other considerations, including costs.

## RELIABILITY OF REGISTRIES

A fundamental prerequisite to the knowledge-as-power predicate of registration and community notification is, of course, the availability of complete and accurate identifying information on registrants. As noted in Chapters 1 and 2, securing and maintaining such identifying information has been the Achilles' heel of registration and other government-sponsored methods of identification from the outset. Expecting that ex-offenders, individuals with a proven capacity for antisocial conduct, will cooperate with the government in their ongoing surveillance and stigmatization would appear contrary to both logic and human experience. As noted by a commentator in 1936, individuals "who want to be law-abiding and forget their past criminal record will register, while those engaging in criminal activities of course will not."[4] Registration, as a local sheriff observed more recently, "just keeps honest offenders honest."[5] Moreover, as the burdens associated with the laws have increased over time, the prospects for success would appear even more attenuated.

Current research amply demonstrates the data deficiencies of modern laws. Complete and accurate registries face two distinct challenges: (1) obtaining information on registrants at the time of initial eligibility and (2) maintaining accurate identifying information on registrants thereafter. With respect to both challenges, studies have revealed that registries are rife with shortcomings.

On the national level, the National Center for Missing or Exploited Children estimates that over 100,000 registrants cannot be accounted for.[6] While the accuracy of this number (much like estimates of victimized children used in the 1980s) has been disputed,[7] there is no disputing that registries are deeply flawed. According to Parents for Megan's Law, an advocacy group that monitors state registration efforts, on average, in 2003 state officials could not account for 24% of registrants, with rates in several states (California and Massachusetts, 44%; Oklahoma, 50%) being especially high. Moreover, 17 states were unable to offer even an estimate of how many registrants were noncompliant.[8] In addition to containing erroneous or inaccurate information on persons required to register,[9] registries also often contain information on individuals who are deceased, deported, or no longer residing in the state.[10]

Such dismal findings, however, stand in sharp contrast to reports from some states indicating very high compliance rates. Florida, for instance, in 2003 reported only 4.7% of its registrants as noncompliant,[11] and North Dakota in 2007 reported a 3% noncompliance rate.[12] While encouraging, such reports must be interpreted with caution, not only given the vastly greater rates in other states, but also because of the meager information-verification measures in use. For instance, an analysis of Florida's registry, ranked by one organization as the nation's third-best Web registry, in part because of "daily" updates,[13] revealed that of the over thirty thousand individuals registered in November 2005, nearly 50% were not residing at their stated address or were dead, incarcerated, or living outside the state.[14]

Yet concern remains even when registry information is reputedly accurate and complete. As noted in Chapter 3, governments have traditionally verified registrants' information by means of mailing nonreturnable letters to their last-known address. As authorities have come to learn, however, this method is far from perfect. Not only can registrants ignore letters, but they can also deceive authorities by having a confederate at their putative residence supply them with the letter, which they can then return (and appear compliant, despite living elsewhere). In an effort to redress such problems, the federal Adam Walsh Act requires that states conduct in-person verification on a periodic basis. This strategy, however, not only requires considerably more in the way of government resources, especially at the local level where compliance typically occurs. It also fails to ensure that registrants actually live where they say they do: if an "in-person" verification does not entail a home visit by police (itself very costly), but rather only that registrants visit a police station, deception remains possible.

Given these difficulties, some states (such as Minnesota and Oklahoma) have attempted to harness community input by listing noncompliant individuals on the Internet and asking that website viewers with information on noncompliant registrants alert authorities. This strategy, while perhaps encouraging compliance by threatening public stigmatization, can ultimately provide only piecemeal benefit inasmuch as it is merely directed at registrants known to be noncompliant.

Recently, authorities have contemplated use of increasingly sophisticated technologies as aids in ensuring greater compliance. In particular, global positioning satellite (GPS) technology and subdermal "chipping" of registrants have been considered. Both promise the tantalizing benefit of permitting real-time location of registrants, helpful for instance in determining where a registrant might be during bedtime hours. Again, however, both strategies have downsides. Neither ensures the accuracy of the litany of non–location based information contained in registries (such as facial images and vehicle identification information). Moreover, GPS, in particular, is very expensive[15] and chipping technology as yet is helpful only if the "reader" is located within several feet of the subject.[16]

Data mining represents another possible technique. For instance, the federal National Directory of New Hires is a massive repository of personal information. Yet consulting the Directory for data quality checks is costly and poses significant practical challenges (for example, "matches" would be difficult because many registrants lack social security numbers).[17] The private sector, not surprisingly, is trying to fill the void. Lexis/Nexis, for instance, has created a search program that fuses numerous publicly available data sources, yet it too is expensive (up to several million dollars a year) and only allows for individualized searches.[18]

The aforementioned difficulties, again, should come as no surprise given that registration is fundamentally an honor system–based regime.[19] Even among individuals inclined to cooperate and sensitive to the threat of criminal punishment for failing to comply, the bureaucratic demands of registration— imposed on a subpopulation already prone to problems organizing their lives, and who often change work and living locations with frequency—can prove insurmountable. Moreover, in some instances, it might be the case that such individuals cannot afford the administrative fees that state and local govern-ments are now imposing.

These challenges, moreover, are compounded by the collateral effects of the laws, which make an already stigmatized and marginalized subpopulation even less prone to cooperate. Registering and updating personal information is itself burdensome and will become increasingly so as a result of the changes possibly wrought by the Adam Walsh Act. The many negative consequences of community notification (discussed below) can be avoided altogether if one does not register, or neutralized if one fails to provide accurate identifying information.[20] Failing to register, or registering a false address, can avoid per-haps the harshest of all collateral consequences: laws limiting where regis-trants can live. Today, as discussed in Chapter 3, almost half of the states and hundreds of localities prohibit registrants from living near schools, recreation centers, and other places where children congregate. In Iowa, the number of "lost" registrants doubled in the wake of a statewide law sharply limiting where registrants could live.[21]

Finally, as with prior information-based criminal identification efforts, technological and infrastructural difficulties limit the efficacy of registration. While computers have exponentially expanded the capacity of governments to store, update, and make information available, difficulties remain. Most notably, the information stored is only as good as that collected; "garbage in, garbage out" is as true with data collection, storage, and evaluation more generally as it is with registration. Evidence of this is found in a 2006 study conducted by the U.S. Government Accountability Office, which discov-ered chronic data irregularities in the FBI's National Sex Offender Registry (NSOR), accessible only to law enforcement. According to the report, NSOR, which in theory is a compilation of all state sex offender registries, in fact did not track their content: a random comparison sample of the NSOR and several states revealed that the NSOR included only about 57% of state regis-trants.[22] A subsequent more comprehensive study, conducted in 2008 by the U.S. Department of Justice's Office of the Inspector General, identified wide-spread omissions, inconsistencies, and inaccuracies in state registry informa-tion contained in the NSOR as well as the publicly accessible national website (the National Sex Offender Public Registry).[23]

Second, state registries themselves can lag in reporting information. Whether due to expense, limited personnel, or the sheer logistical challenge resulting from the ever-increasing volume of registrants, state registries can fail to reflect information that is actually provided by local authorities. In Alabama, for instance, the state online registry in 2007 had an estimated six-month delay in posting information provided by local law enforcement.[24] As a result of this backlog, once information is posted, it can quickly become outdated, leading to discrepancies between state and locally managed registries.

In sum, despite state and federal laws making it a felony to violate registration requirements, research makes clear that today's registries—like those in the past—are rife with errors, both with respect to completeness and accuracy. And despite disclaimers often provided on registries cautioning that reported information might be inaccurate, the data remain integral. Without accurate information on registrants, the police cannot readily observe and apprehend recidivist registrants; the public cannot assist police and take self-protective measures; and registries lack the deterrent influence thought associated with police and community surveillance. Furthermore, to the extent registries contain information on individuals not properly the subject of attention, such as deceased or deported registrants, public safety is diminished because police and the public alike are distracted from the intended target of registration—individuals who actually reside in their community. Finally, perversely, registry inaccuracies can mislead community members into mistakenly thinking that a registry-specified address contains a registrant, as a result not only possibly fostering undue hypervigilance, but also possibly triggering harassment or violence toward nonregistrants (discussed below).

## CRIME REDUCTION

Crime reduction has always been a primary goal of registration and notification. Early on, as discussed in Chapter 2, when registration enjoyed only sporadic use, mainly at the local level, it was embraced not only because it ideally fostered among registrants a sense of being watched by police, and hence made them potentially less prone to recidivate, but also because it would have a purgative effect, encouraging potential recidivists to flee jurisdictions to avoid registration. Today, with registration laws in place nationwide, this latter purpose is no longer explicitly in play,[25] yet registration continues to be justified for its desired surveillance influence. With the advent of community notification, it is further hoped, recidivism will be reduced because communities can self-protect and help police monitor registrants. Finally, registration and notification have been justified by the hope that individuals will refrain from committing a registerable offense in order to avoid the increasingly onerous consequences of registration and notification.

To date, however, it is unclear whether registration and notification actually reduce crime. Studies conducted in Washington State in 1995,[26] 1996,[27] and 1998[28] and Iowa in 2000[29] found no statistically significant recidivism differences in offenders who were subject to the laws and those who were not. Similarly, a 2006 study of Wisconsin's highest-risk sex offenders, subject to the state's most aggressive community notification methods, were compared against a similarly high-risk cohort not subject to community notification.[30] Over a four-and-half-year period, the study found no statistically significant differences between the high-risk group subject to community notification (19% recidivism for a sex offense) and the high-risk group not subject to it (12% recidivism for a sex offense). Another study (2008), of ten states, found that registration and community notification had no effect on the incidence of reported rapes.[31] Six states showed no statistically significant change in the monthly number of rapes; of the four states indicating statistically significant results, three had decreases, while a fourth, California, actually experienced a steep increase. Finally, a 2008 New Jersey study, examining sex offense arrest rates in the decade before and after Megan's Law was enacted in 1994, concluded that registration and notification had no demonstrable effect.[32]

Two other recent studies reached somewhat more promising yet still mixed results. In 2008, J. J. Prescott and Jonah Rockoff examined the effects of registration and notification on the incidence of sex crimes in the nation as a whole.[33] They concluded that the threat of registration had no deterrent effect on first-time offenders (that is, nonregistrants), but did reduce recidivism among registrants, presumably because it "increase[ed] monitoring and the likelihood of punishment for potential recidivists." Community notification, however, had the opposite effect. While it appeared that notification possibly reduced sex crimes among nonregistrants, it actually *increased criminal activity* among registrants. According to the study, increases in the size of registries led to sex crime increases, suggesting that "the punitive aspects of notification laws may create perverse effects." In summarizing their results, Prescott and Rockoff recommended that states adopt a "narrow notification regime, in which all or most sex offenders are required to register, but only a small subset of those offenders are subject to community notification."

Grant Duwe and William Donnay, in a 2008 study, assessed whether community notification had a crime-reducing effect in Minnesota, a state with a risk-based individual assessment regime permitting broad community notification only relative to high-risk (level 3) offenders.[34] Duwe and Donnay compared the recidivism rates of three registrant populations: a study group of high-risk offenders, subject to level 3 notification (via community meetings and the Internet), and two control groups—high risk, not subject to notification at all (registrants who were released before the law went into effect), and lower risk (levels 1 and 2), not subject to broad notification.

The researchers found that notification decreased the timing of sexual reoffense. No positive deterrent effect was discerned, however, relative to nonsexual recidivism, which is significant because such offenses comprised roughly three-quarters of new offenses committed by registrants. Duwe and Donnay also qualified that the study group alone was subject to intensive supervision, entailing continuous supervision, and that they lacked data on the impact of community-based treatment. On a more general level, the researchers cautioned that their results did not necessarily support broadened use of notification, given the substantial resources associated with targeting the vastly greater number of non–level 3 registrants, and the population's already quite low recidivism rates. Finally, Duwe and Donnay emphasized that it was unclear what aspect of notification was responsible for the apparent deterrent effect achieved and expressed uncertainty over whether use of Internet notification alone would have the same effect.

While the foregoing studies are most welcome, and indispensable to public policy analysis, the research continues to face major challenges. Because such empirical work is typically of a longitudinal nature, tracking groups of individuals and crimes over extended periods of time, it can be distorted by a variety of influences. Perhaps most perplexing is that the number of sexual offenses against children and adults, as well as nonsexual crimes of violence against children, has plummeted nationwide since the early 1990s when registration and notification came into nationwide effect.[35] In New Jersey, for instance, the state's steady decline in sex offenses against children began in 1991, three years before Megan's Law was enacted.[36] As a result, researchers cannot definitively say whether, or to what extent, the laws have enhanced public safety. Indeed, it might be the case that the onerous personal consequences of the laws—experienced by registrants and those with whom they associate—might contribute to decreased reporting of crimes, especially in the context in which sexual offending most commonly occurs: among family, friends, and acquaintances (discussed below).

Likewise, changes in public policy very often complicate research design efforts. For instance, a 2005 Washington State study reported a 70% drop in recidivism among violent sex offender and felony sex offender registrants after registration and notification approaches were standardized across the state in 1997.[37] However, while concluding that registration and notification "should not be ruled out as a factor," the study was unable to conclude that the laws caused the drop, in light of other possible contemporaneous causal factors such as more severe sentencing laws that removed more high-risk offenders from the sample population and intensified community supervision practices. Consistent with this view, in 2007 researchers seeking explanations for the recent drop in sex crimes in Minnesota concluded that the increasing intensity and duration of postrelease supervision were mainly responsible, but that other factors such as community notification (for the state's most risky offenders) also might have played a role.[38]

Additional cause for confusion derives from the fact that the sustained drop in sexual offending has been nationwide, without regard to the varied registration and notification regimes used by states. To date, little work has sought to examine comparative state drops in crime relative to distinct state approaches, such as use of a conviction versus risk-based registrant classification approach. The limited research conducted to date has mainly concentrated on only a few jurisdictions—Florida, Kentucky, Minnesota, Washington State, and Wisconsin, in particular—each with unique registration and community notification systems. While registrant populations might be broadly similar, the varied approaches sharply limit the capacity to generalize research results. Comparative work in this area is very much needed if the public safety benefits or detriments of registration and notification are to be known.[39]

## EMPOWERING POLICE

Closely related to the goal of crime reduction is the long-held expectation that registration allows police to monitor ex-offenders and, in the event a registrant recidivates, use registry information to investigate and arrest.[40] With the advent of community notification, in turn, police empowerment is theoretically augmented by the input of watchful communities. Whether in fact these expectations hold true, of course, depends on the completeness and accuracy of registries, which as discussed above remain in doubt. Nevertheless, because police empowerment figures so centrally in the asserted public purpose of registration, the claim warrants scrutiny.

Surveys conducted to date suggest that police are rather ambivalent about the value of registration and notification. A survey of Arkansas law enforcement (1999), for instance, indicated that 30% of individual respondents "somewhat agreed" that registration enhanced their ability to monitor registrants and 21% "agreed," while only 11% "strongly agreed."[41] When asked if their agency was able to track address changes by registrants, 28% stated they "strongly disagree" and only 3% said they "strongly agree." A survey of Wisconsin police agencies (2000) suggested that while most agencies saw registration as beneficial, views on community notification were decidedly mixed, with only 41% asserting that it "improved management and containment of sex offender behavior through greater visibility."[42]

Less research has assessed the actual utility of registration as a means for police to intervene and preempt crime. As discussed in Chapter 2, early registration laws were welcomed by police for their perceived preemptive benefit. Much like antivagrancy laws, popular since Elizabethan times, and "public enemy" laws also originating in the 1930s, registration was regarded as a tool to detain, question, and arrest identifiably risky individuals. During the early era, this authority prompted concern that that police were engaged in harassment, facilitating efforts, as the film *Casablanca* put it, to "round up the usual suspects." Today, while concern has arisen over harassment of registrants by community members, no evidence apparently exists of police using registry information to harass registrants.

Indeed, much as in the past when the data indicated that the laws were of little actual use, a more significant concern is that the laws are ignored by police. As before, while anecdotal evidence exists of police having intervened to prevent a registrant from reoffending, such instances have been sporadic and isolated, and to date have appeared only in news reports.[43] Moreover, it does not appear that compliance enforcement ranks as a high police priority. Despite the enormous number of noncompliant registrants and high-profile congressional attention to the issue of "lost" registrants (resulting in the Adam Walsh Act in 2006 creating the first federal felony for failure to register), arrest data indicate that enforcement today continues to play a nominal role in daily police work.[44] In California, for instance, with the nation's largest registry— in which thousands of individuals are known to be out of compliance—there were a mere 1,702 recorded arrests in 2006 for failure to register.[45]

Why this is so remains unclear. One likely explanation lies in the cost associated with monitoring compliance. Maintaining the accuracy of registries is extremely resource intensive, and local police, already hard-pressed to fulfill their customary public safety obligations, simply lack the requisite time and money (discussed below). Police might also be discouraged from aggressively enforcing registration compliance as a result of not-so-subtle signaling from other criminal justice actors, such as evidenced in the past (see Chapter 2). According to a June 2007 newspaper account, for instance, police in San Bernardino County, California, were instructed by the county district attorneys' office to first ask noncompliant registrants to register before executing arrests.[46] Pursuant to the office's policy, police were to then provide the violator a 30-day period to comply; if they did not, arrests would then be made. Police expressed concern that the "courtesy" extended to violators resulted in decreased compliance. It is also entirely possible that once being put on notice of noncompliance, scofflaw registrants simply disappeared, further reducing the chance of arrest or compliance.

Even when police execute arrests, however, the judicial system does not seem inclined to press for conviction. Data suggest that prosecutors and judges today—much as in the 1950s (see Chapter 2)—do not regard noncompliance with particular seriousness. In Massachusetts, for instance, the state auditor concluded in 2006 that of the 2,766 arraignments for registration violations, 1,206 cases were dismissed, 606 resulted in convictions, 127 were not prosecuted, and 23 were found not guilty (charges against others were still pending or missing).[47] The audit further reported that even when violators were convicted, courts often withheld punishment contingent on registration by individuals.

A Washington State study conducted in the mid-1990s highlights the potential negative consequence of this systemic indifference. Individuals convicted of failure to register had 50% higher subsequent recidivism rates than those who remained in compliance.[48] This finding might plausibly lead to the conclusion that registration itself plays a role in discouraging reoffending. Equally, if not more plausible, however, is the long-held suspicion that individuals inclined to remain law-abiding will also follow registration requirements, while persons inclined to recidivate (those the laws are most concerned about) will shun registration and commit new crimes.

Data on the postcrime investigative utility of registration to police has been no more promising. While the media over the years have reported instances of registration assisting police in apprehending offenders,[49] other reports have highlighted its lack of utility.[50] A 1995 Washington State study found that a group of registrants subject to community notification was arrested much more quickly than a comparison group released before use of notification, even though the overall recidivism rate of the two groups over a five-year period was almost the same.[51] The study, however, failed to illuminate how the arrests came about. The authors were only able to speculate that the greater alacrity in rearrest might stem from the fact that the latter group was "watched more closely" and that the "increased attention result[ed] in earlier detection of criminal behavior."[52] Another critically important uncertainty concerned how the reapprehended individuals came to the attention of the police. Did community members alert police upon seeing a registrant engage in misconduct? Did the police themselves learn of the misconduct? If the latter, the utility of registration alone would appear to have a public safety benefit, undercutting the need for notification. While such questions remain important, a more recent Wisconsin study (2006) cast doubt on the utility of notification. The study, which tracked registrants over a 4.5-year period, found no difference in the speed of rearrest relative to a high-risk registrant cohort subject to community notification and one that was not.[53]

Finally, the avowed informational empowerment benefit of registration to police, in the end, must reconcile a key reality of sexual offending: most sex crimes are committed by first-time offenders.[54] Because such individuals have not been convicted of a crime, they are not registered, and police thus lack information on them. As a result, for this major proportion of sexual victimization, registration does not even theoretically allow police to intervene before or during crimes or apprehend offenders after the fact. Furthermore, to the extent that individuals commit registerable offenses but plead guilty to or are otherwise convicted of nonregisterable offenses, a not uncommon occurrence, registries are similarly underinclusive.[55]

## COMMUNITY SELF-PROTECTION

A final justification for community notification, in particular, is the expectation that information on registrants, when made publicly available, can and will be used by community members to engage in self-protective measures. As with so many aspects of the laws, however, limited research has tested this assumption, and that which has been done calls into question current practices and raises concern that notification might actually diminish public safety and overall community well-being.

The community knowledge-empowerment premise depends on two key occurrences: first, residents learning of registrants' identifying information and, second, taking preventive measures to defend against victimization based on such information. To date, research has shown that significant gaps exist in this chain of occurrences.

With respect to the first, acquisition of knowledge, research has underscored the importance of community notification method. For instance, a 2006 comparative study of residents in Ohio, where residents are actively notified (via mailings sent by police to persons living near registrants), and Kentucky, where passive notification (via the Internet) is used, showed a dramatic variation. Ohio residents were significantly more likely to be aware that a registrant lived nearby: 77% of Hamilton County, Ohio, versus 26% of Jefferson County, Kentucky, residents.[56]

Active notification also appears to positively correlate with the second occurrence—the use of registrant information to take safety measures. According to a 2004 survey of two groups of residents in Hamilton County, Ohio, one receiving active notification (via police mailings) and the other receiving no notification, notified individuals were significantly more likely to undertake safety efforts, such as installing exterior lighting on their homes, warning household members that a dangerous individual lived nearby, and prohibiting strangers from entering their homes. They were also significantly more likely to report suspicious behavior to authorities, with 14.5% of respondents actually having reported on registrants to police.[57]

Other research on active notification, however, has been more ambiguous. A 2004 survey of Alabama residents, all of whom were actively notified about registrants, concluded that notification was not associated with protective measures.[58] Another study, from Washington State in 1998, noted that while most community members felt safer knowing the whereabouts of registrants, most parents reported no change in their behaviors with respect to supervision of their children as a result of having such knowledge.[59]

A 2008 study of Nebraska residents echoed this uncertainty.[60] Respondents there could receive information on high-risk, Tier III registrants by news media releases, a state website registry, community meetings, or visits from police. While an overwhelming majority (90%) was aware that their state had a registry, only 35% had actually obtained any registrants' information. Among those providing responses, most noted that they did so by means of the newspaper, with several specifically stating that they had not accessed information online. And even those who secured information indicated that they did so mainly for nonsafety reasons, such as to perform employment or residential leasing–related checks.

Of the Nebraska respondents who obtained information, a very high proportion (88%) reported feeling safer as a result. This sensibility, however, did not translate into preventive action being taken. Only a little more than a third undertook such measures, such as informing family or friends of the potential risk. The majority (62%) did not act on the information at all, and did not specify why, leaving the researchers to speculate that "[p]erhaps the enhanced feelings of safety reported by the majority of respondents precluded any further action." In summarizing their results, the researchers stated:

> To the degree that community notification laws were intended to make people feel safer, the [laws] . . . may have achieved this goal. If the laws were intended to have appreciable effects on actual public safety, however, it seems likely that these laws will fall short of that goal. It will be difficult for notification to inform the public if only about one third of the population accesses this information. Moreover, only about one third of people armed with sex offender information take any preventive measures, so it is likely that even if more people access this information, few will act on it.[61]

Additional empirical work assessing whether community notification induces preventive measures will be critically important. Yet positive findings, to the extent they accrue, must be evaluated against several key statistical realities that continue to undermine the very premise of registration and community notification. The first is that the vast majority of sexual offenses committed against children and adults alike are perpetrated by persons known to the victim or the victim's family—individuals such as family members, friends, and acquaintances and not the strangers presumably targeted by the laws.[62] The second statistic, noted earlier, is that sex offenses are most commonly committed by first-time offenders, who by definition are not on registries. And the third statistic is that sexual victimization is known to be vastly underreported,[63] meaning that the registries themselves are underinclusive. These realities, along with the chronic incompleteness and inaccuracy of registry information, are plausibly advanced by critics in support of the view that notification creates a dangerous false sense of security among community members.

Critics also contest another core premise of the laws—that one's neighbors pose most risk of sexual victimization and that information on such individuals is all that is needed to ensure protection. Both logic and research attest to the reality that social, not geographic, proximity influences offending and that criminally prone individuals can and will commit crimes in places other than their own neighborhoods.

A 1999 study of the offense characteristics of thirty-six incarcerated Massachusetts offenders, for instance, showed that the majority of registry-eligible individuals sexually victimized persons known to them, a family member, friend, or acquaintance.[64] To test the assumption that the laws empower communities, the researchers focused on the twelve offenders who were strangers and evaluated their residence and workplace locations relative to victimization sites. They also assessed the likelihood that information on registrants would reach the victim or the victim's guardian, and found that in only four of twelve (33%) of the cases there existed a "good probability" of potentially benefiting from advance warning that a stranger with an offending history lived nearby—for instance, the offender and victim lived in the same neighborhood or in the same building. In the remaining eight cases, the offender lived in another city or state or in a different part of the same city. Such results are consistent with numerous other studies finding that recidivist sex offenders typically reoffend outside their immediate living areas.[65]

The study hastened to add that registration and notification, if indeed effective at the neighborhood level in "target hardening"—that is, encouraging potential victims to take effective protective measures—risked shifting the predations of recidivist registrants to other areas. According to the authors, "[t]he crime or crimes might simply have been displaced toward other more vulnerable targets."[66] As noted in Chapter 2, such displacement was an explicit goal of early-generation registries, and research is only now considering this troublesome possibility. Two studies conducted by officials in Minnesota (in 2003 and 2007)[67] and Colorado (in 2004)[68] of recidivist sex offenders found that the offenders were more likely to travel to other neighborhoods to commit new crimes. On the other hand, the nationwide study of Prescott and Rockoff noted above,[69] found no evidence that registration and notification fostered crime displacement.

In short, much as recently enacted laws preventing registrants from living near schools have been justly criticized for their animating premise that pedophiles live in certain areas to better indulge their criminal propensities,[70] so too is it contestable that registrants predisposed to reoffend will not migrate in search of victims. If indeed registration and notification encourage crime displacement, from one knowledge-fortified area to another area ignorant of particular risk, the outcome would be quite perverse. Not only would registries significantly reduce residential property values for neighbors of registrants—as they do[71]—but they would also make other unsuspecting communities more dangerous.

Finally, on the community empowerment issue, the utility of the Internet—increasingly the notification medium of choice—remains questionable. As noted above, while websites are a comparatively cheap means of conveying registry information, research has shown that they are not very effective notification devices, certainly when compared to active notification methods (even a single mailing by police, as in Ohio).[72] According to a 2008 study of an unspecified county in the southeastern United States, which uses only website notifications, a mere 31% of residents who lived near a listed registrant were aware of the fact.[73] This figure is particularly notable given that 60% of residents who related that they were "very familiar" with their state's registration and notification regime did not know that a registrant lived nearby.

This study and others, unfortunately, did not examine whether the knowledge deficit stemmed from the "tech do nots" (persons with computer access but who do not customarily consult a registry website) or the "tech have nots" (persons lacking the desire or financial means to possess a computer). The former deficit, theoretically, can be cured by education and instruction. The latter deficit, unfortunately, is not so easily cured—meaning that the poor and socially disorganized communities that such individuals often inhabit, where registrants tend to cluster (due to limited housing options), and which constitute areas where children in particular are at increased risk of sexual victimization,[74] are left uninformed.

Registry websites have also been criticized for their substantive content. A 2007 Human Rights Watch report strongly criticized the failure of sites to provide helpful information on the nature of registrants' offending histories. According to the report, only five states (Alabama, Minnesota, New Jersey, and North and South Dakota) provided such descriptions:

> [These states] provide crime descriptions that the general public may be able to understand ("for example, when male was 41, raped a 14 year old female"). The other registries either cite the statute under which the offender was convicted or quote directly from it. The user is left to wonder what such terms as "lewd

and lascivious behavior," "indecent liberties with a child," or "crime against nature" actually mean and what the registrant actually did.[75]

The report emphasized two chief difficulties that stemmed from this deficiency. First, a viewer unfamiliar with a law (for example, the meaning of "criminal conduct in the fourth degree") might infer that the registrant committed a sexually violent offense, when in reality he had groped an adult female at a "clothing optional musical festival." Second, at the other extreme, by listing only the name of the offense, a viewer seeing "sexual battery of a child by an adult" would have no basis to know that the registrant had raped a 12-year-old boy on numerous occasions.[76]

## EFFECTS ON REGISTRANTS

A final core empirical question concerns how the laws affect the individuals targeted. A foremost criticism of early registration laws (Chapter 2) was that the stigmatization and sense of police surveillance would not only be unfair to those who had paid their penal debt to society, but would also lead to a self-fulfilling criminality. As one corrections official put it, the "psychic effect" of registration "opens up old sores . . . [and] tends only to stiffen resistance to police regulation of a large group of people in the community, most of whom are in the potential criminal class."[77]

If such concerns were warranted in the past, they would appear to be much more so today. Modern registration laws are far more demanding than predecessor laws, including: requiring more information from registrants, mandating information verification at specified intervals, and threatening felony-level prosecution for failures to comply. In addition, unlike in the early era, registration laws today are in effect nationwide, precluding any possibility of evasion. Finally, and most important, modern registration laws are complemented not only by a panoply of collateral effects (such as residence restrictions), but also by community notification, which magnifies the "psychic effect" of registration and carries numerous additional negative personal effects.

Extensive research shows that notification in particular makes it harder for registrants to find and maintain housing and work and to sustain social and family relationships, factors research has shown to positively correlate with crime desistance among sex offenders.[78] According to a 2000 study of Wisconsin registrants, "housing and employment have become nearly impossible."[79] Registrants have been forced to move as a result of public demonstrations or complaints to landlords[80] and have often been rendered homeless, forced to live in shelters or in public spaces.[81] Finding and keeping work, already a major challenge for ex-offenders, has also been made much more difficult. In Washington State, for instance, demonstrators staged a public protest during rush hour in front of a gas station to discourage motorists from patronizing the station because it employed a registrant.[82] In New Jersey, according to a 2008 study, 52% of Tier II and III registrants sampled reported having lost jobs as a result of notification.[83]

Registrants have also been the target of vigilantism. While most registries warn that registrants' information is to be used only for self-protective behavior, physical violence directed against registrants has been common,[84] including:

- two Maine registrants (one registered because when he was 20 he was convicted of having sex with his 15-year-old girlfriend) murdered by an assailant who found their addresses on the state Internet registry;[85]
- a New Hampshire registrant stabbed by an assailant, who also committed acts of arson against two other registrants and who left behind a printout of the state's Internet registry with checkmarks next to the names of his targets;[86]
- two Washington State registrants murdered by an individual who gained access to his victims' shared home by posing as a federal agent and explaining that the registrants were on an Internet "hit list."[87]

While killings have not been numerous, registrants have regularly suffered an array of nonlethal harms, such as repeated harassment,[88] including instances of registrants receiving death threats and having a pet dog decapitated,[89] or being targeted with gunfire.[90] Registrants have also suffered acts of arson and vandalism of their homes,[91] and several have committed suicide.[92]

Not surprisingly, registrants regularly convey feelings of isolation, stress, and feelings of hopelessness over their publicly identified status, prompting one Wisconsin registrant to offer that "No one believes I can change, so why even try?"[93] Surveys of registrants conducted in Kentucky and Indiana (2004),[94] Florida (2005),[95] Kentucky (2006),[96] and Connecticut and Indiana (2007)[97] reflect similar findings.

Nor are hardships suffered by registrants alone, as family and friends have been subject to harassment and disdain, serving to further isolate registrants and make their daily lives more difficult.[98] This spillover effect has even impacted the children of registrants, who have suffered hardships (including beatings) as a result of their parents' public designation.[99] Finally, community ire has been directed mistakenly at nonregistrants, a not unlikely prospect given registry address inaccuracies.[100]

While the vigilantism and opprobrium just described are troubling in their own right, the negative impact of community notification on the ability of registrants to find and maintain housing (a concern exacerbated by state and local laws limiting where they can live)[101] creates significant additional concern. Itinerancy and homelessness make it much harder for registries to remain accurate and complete, further undercutting the knowledge-as-power linchpin of the laws.[102] In addition, with fewer housing options, themselves typically situated in poorer, socially disorganized areas, registrants tend to cluster in and create "sex offender ghettoes,"[103] negatively affecting community life and further impeding social reintegration and possibly crime desistance.[104]

While the negative personal consequences of registration and notification on adults have been widely reported, only recently has the experience of juveniles received attention. Today, a majority of states require at least some adjudicated delinquents to register, and the federal Adam Walsh Act does as well. As a result, the issue—despite continuing to be controversial—will likely assume increasing practical importance.[105]

To critics, exposing juveniles to registration and the negative effects of notification, based on adjudications in juvenile court, is both unfair and counterproductive. It is unfair because such offenders are less culpable due to their age and because the juvenile system affords fewer procedural rights and protections. It is counterproductive, they assert, because juveniles, compared to adults, have substantially lower rates of recidivism, show a greater responsiveness to treatment, and are less likely to reoffend if given treatment.[106] Under this view, the policy risks imperiling low-risk juveniles not destined to become adult sex offenders, imposing harsh stigmatization and all it entails during a delicate transition life period,[107] making a crime-free life less likely.[108] Moreover, research has shown that few adult sex offenders were convicted of sex offenses as youths, suggesting that use of a juvenile sex crime adjudication as a predictor would miss 92–96% of all adult male sex offenders.[109]

Notwithstanding the foregoing, for juvenile and adult registrants alike, the negative personal effects of registration and notification continue to have mainly theoretical impact on recidivism. While studies such as that conducted by Prescott and Rockoff suggest a crime-enhancing influence of notification among registrants in particular, much more work must be done before this critically important aspect of the policy debate can be resolved.

As this knowledge base develops, policy makers should be mindful of an overlooked but growing literature on registrants' attitudes toward registration and notification. Because registries depend on their cooperation and seek to encourage law-abidingness, the perspectives of registrants are logically of considerable importance.

The few surveys conducted thus far have yielded some interesting and surprising results. Most notably, there appears to be some support among registrants for registration in principle[110] and evidence that registrants "understand" why it is something that the public would want.[111] More important, surveys show support, quite strong among particular registrants, for the sentiment that registration and notification deter reoffending. According to one survey of Connecticut and Indiana registrants, 74% agreed with the following statement: "[I am] more motivated to prevent reoffense to prove to others that I am not a bad person."[112] Another study, surveying female registrants in Kentucky, concluded that 61% agreed with the statement that "because my name and personal information is listed on the Sex Offender Registry I am less likely to commit another sexual offense in the future."[113]

Other surveys, working with other populations, have been less positive. A study of thirty Wisconsin registrants subject to community notification, for instance, found that only a "handful" identified therapeutic effects, including "acceptance of responsibility" and "minimization of denial."[114] Similarly, New Jersey Tier II and III registrants indicated that while they agreed that notification motivated them to prove to others that they were "not a bad person," they generally disagreed with the notion that they would desist from crime because they believed their neighbors were monitoring them.[115]

Echoing the view of treatment professionals,[116] large majorities of registrants in several surveys were highly critical of community notification in particular. To them, notification does not promote public safety, is "unfair,"[117] and results in them being "unfairly punished."[118] As one incarcerated child molester stated:

> I know I need help. I'm going to get out soon. If Megan's Law and monitoring meant that people could keep an eye on me, to help me help myself, then I'd be all for it. But instead, I feel like I'm going to have to hide, and in the end, that's not going to help anybody.[119]

The New Jersey study noted above found that registrants found it particularly "unfair" for employment-related identifying information to be the subject of notification.[120]

In addition, surveyed registrants in states not employing individualized risk assessments prior to community notification (Connecticut, Florida, Indiana, and Kentucky), were especially critical, urging that such assessments are necessary for the public to discern dangerous individuals,[121] and that incentives should be provided for the abatement of notification when individuals satisfy treatment or remain crime free for extended periods.[122] Such results would appear to be consistent with results from earlier research in Oregon, which limited community notification to persons posing the greatest recidivist risk, and where it was found that the specter of notification motivated prisoners (that is, future registrants) to complete treatment. According to the study:

> By cooperating with treatment and following supervision conditions, the offender can influence the level of notification by reducing the risk of re-offense. The ability to have some control over the level of notification by doing what is needed to lessen the risk to the community has motivated positive changes with long term effects. This ultimately creates a safer community. This incentive would be lost if notification was mandated on every offense.[123]

Such survey results, it is important to note, are quite tentative and exploratory in nature; they also suffer from significant methodological limits—self-report data typically warrant caution, and the populations surveyed were small and likely self-selected (for example, registrants taking the initiative to seek treatment at centers where surveys were administered). However, policy makers disregard the views of registrants at their peril. While complete "buy-in" by registrants is not to be expected, the studies suggest that it is occurring to some extent. Resistance appears to mainly stem from the ways in which community notification in particular is utilized. Other research has established that individuals are more prone to cooperate with laws perceived as just and fair,[124] and to the extent that registration and community notification can be modified to foster such sentiments, the laws themselves can have therapeutic—as opposed to possibly antitherapeutic—ends.[125]

## OTHER CONSIDERATIONS

Beyond the main considerations surveyed above, registration and community notification have a variety of other consequences that, while important, frequently escape attention.

The first consideration is resources. As jurisdictions have painfully become aware, registration and notification, whatever their benefits, are far from cost-free. Operation of registries—even suboptimally, with their numerous demonstrated inadequacies—entails considerable expense: governments must expend major amounts of money to pay police and administrative staff to secure and maintain registrants' information.[126] In 2003, for example, the San Jose, California, Police Department spent $600,000 annually for seven full-time staff members to operate its registry, and the state's attorney general, faced with a study indicating that 33,000 registrants were out of compliance estimated that a budget of $20 million would be needed for an effective registration system.[127] To date, however, such resources have not been forthcoming. As a consequence, in Tacoma, Washington, for instance, in late 2007 a single detective was responsible for monitoring compliance of the city's 1,200 registrants.[128]

Police, as one spokesperson in Washington State noted in 1991, simply do not "have the manpower to go chasing these people down."[129] Community notification, in turn, requires additional resources.[130] Jurisdictions employing active community notification, the most effective method of information dissemination—such as by means of community meetings or house visits by police—must shoulder particular expenses. In Wisconsin, where community notification meetings are employed, two-thirds of law enforcement surveyed expressed concern over having adequate resources to fulfill their duties.[131] Elsewhere, police have turned to citizen volunteers to help collect and verify registrants' information, and even to assist in individual risk assessments of registrants and notification of fellow community members.[132]

Resource burdens, moreover, are not merely fiscal. Registration and notification require considerable time and attention of authorities. Rather than processing the ever-expanding number of registrants, monitoring compliance with registration requirements, and conducting community notifications, police could pursue other perhaps more efficacious crime prevention, detection, and apprehension efforts. Moreover, registration and community notification, mainly predicated on "stranger danger," divert attention and resources from possible education and intervention applications within the network of

family, friends, and acquaintances where sexual abuse by far most often occurs. Finally, the laws can limit support for community-based treatment, a
proven means of reducing recidivism, on the theory that "well, they're being
watched, so why pay for therapy?"[133]

As registration rolls continue to grow, resource concerns will only increase, and as they do so it is likely that intergovernmental tensions will rise
as well. This is because registration and community notification laws have
been largely unfunded mandates from the outset. While enacted by state legislatures, they are principally implemented by local governments, and states
have failed to earmark adequate funds.[134] When criticized, however, states can
fairly blame the federal government, which since the Jacob Wetterling Act in
1994 has required states to adopt federal mandates without allocating adequate
funding. Given ongoing fiscal concerns, it is unlikely that these shortages will
be remedied any time soon, leading to continued tension among and between
levels of government.[135] Nor is the possibility of registries becoming self-
sustaining by fees imposed on registrants themselves, as now done in many
states, a realistic solution. The fees are little more than symbolic and provide
"gotcha" value to society, failing to meaningfully defray administrative costs,
and possibly serving to discourage registration compliance.[136]

The increasingly onerous nature of registration and notification also
threatens unanticipated burdens for the justice system. One area involves jury
trial rights. While the constitutional right to have one's case tried by a jury
belongs only to defendants charged with "serious" offenses (punishable by an
excess of six months imprisonment), the negative consequences of registration alone have been found by at least one state supreme court to trigger a jury
right.[137] Because juries require considerable resources, jurisdictions could be
faced with significant burdens if other courts follow suit.

Registration and notification can also impact the likelihood that defendants will plead guilty and avoid trial. Studies have shown that the prospect of
registration and notification discourages defendants from pleading to lesser
offenses, which while entailing less jail or prison time are nonetheless subject
to the increasingly broad coverage of registration laws.[138] If this continues, the
increased costs and burdens associated with more trials will be difficult for
the system to absorb. In addition, victims of sexual abuse, including children,
will face greater trauma as they will be expected to testify at trial.

Finally, concern remains over other several unintended and quite perverse
effects of registration and notification. The first relates to the possibility that

the laws might deter reporting of crimes, especially in the common context of intrafamilial offending, when states require incest offenders to register.[139] In Louisiana, for instance, two teenage girls molested by their stepfathers reported being "fearful of being identified when their stepfather's picture is published in the local newspaper."[140] In Oklahoma, as noted in Chapter 3, where the state's website in 2008 permitted registrants to be searched by type of crime, information on incest victims could be readily obtained by inference.

Alternatively, it is not difficult to imagine that sex crimes committed by a family member or friend will not be reported to authorities in order to avoid the onerous long-term burdens of registration and notification (including residence restrictions)—on the offender and persons associated with him/her. In such situations, not only is the chronic problem of underreported sex crimes exacerbated in precisely the context where the vast majority of sex crimes occur (among familiars),[141] but individual offenders also escape being held criminally responsible and avoid being legally compelled to undergo treatment (when available), leaving them free to commit other offenses.

The problem might prove especially common among juvenile offenders who sexually victimize family members or family friends, when reporting is deterred by the specter of placing juveniles on registries—potentially for their lifetimes.[142] If this occurs, such individuals again will go unsanctioned, and those in need of treatment will go without it, possibly resulting in continued misconduct. The specter of registration might also discourage prosecutors from aggressively prosecuting juveniles, as indicated by recent research,[143] with the same unfortunate results.

## CONCLUSION

As the foregoing suggests, registration and community notification laws stand on uncertain empirical grounds. Without complete and accurate information on registrants, police and communities cannot track their whereabouts, lessening the laws' avowed deterrent effect; police cannot locate recidivists; and community members lack information to take protective measures. The persistent problems on this front lend support to the long-held view that registration laws are ill-conceived from the outset: that the registries will be filled with ex-offenders who wish to remain law-abiding and flouted by those who do not, with the latter group posing the greatest recidivist risk. As registration and notification become more onerous, compliance and accuracy shortcomings can only be expected to grow. And in due course so will concern that registration and notification laws fuel a dangerous false sense of security among police and community members alike.

As significant, the actual effects of registration and notification remain very much in question. Empirical work done to date makes it unclear whether the laws enhance public safety. Perhaps even more troublesome, persistent concern exists over whether they might be counterproductive. Community members are often deluged with registry information—much of it either false or lacking in any basis to differentiate risk—impairing any tendency they might have to undertake self-protective measures. Meanwhile, the negative personal consequences of the laws very possibly foster recidivism and, even if not, unfairly relegate law-abiding ex-offenders (and their loved ones) to possibly lifelong hardships. Registration and notification are also quite costly to maintain, even at current suboptimal compliance levels, and their enforcement draws police away from other perhaps more useful law enforcement tasks. Finally, the empirically unfounded "stranger danger" emphasis of the laws distracts from initiatives of a more "bottom-up" nature, such as family interventions and education that might more effectively reduce the occurrence of sexual victimization.

The empirical landscape mapped here is of necessity incomplete, as research is only now belatedly being undertaken in earnest. As discussed in Chapter 7, whether such results will affect the continued use and substance of registration and notification remains uncertain. For present purposes, however, the persistence and even proliferation of the laws in the face of such empirical uncertainty, affords strong evidence of the public's abiding faith in their public safety benefit.

# 6 LAW, PRIVACY, AND GOVERNANCE

UP TO THIS POINT, DISCUSSION has focused on the history and form of registration and community notification laws, with emphasis on their content and the social and political forces inspiring their current nationwide use (Chapters 1–4), as well as the research thus far done on their effects and consequences (Chapter 5). Here, attention turns to several of the most significant influences the proliferation of registration and notification has had on U.S. society and its governing structure.

The chapter begins with an examination of the ways in which constitutional legal norms have been affected by the challenges lodged against registration and community notification laws since the 1990s. As will be evident, the resulting opinions, and two in particular from the U.S. Supreme Court in 2003, bear considerable jurisprudential significance, both relative to the particular constitutional provisions in question and the institutional role of the judiciary. Attention then turns to the laws' impact on understandings of informational privacy. In this context, too, registration and notification have had transformative effect: not only have they muted historic anxieties over government surveillance, they have redefined core understandings of what qualifies as "public." Finally, the chapter addresses the important ways in which registration and notification have altered American governance. In ways that have been both subtle and overt, registration and notification have recast traditional notions of public safety, with critically important consequences for individuals, communities, and governments. More broadly, as a result of ongoing pressure from Congress to adopt federally prescribed registration and notification policies, historic understandings of state-federal relations have been transformed.

## EFFECTS ON THE LAW

As noted in Chapter 2, registration spawned few legal challenges during its first sixty years of use in the United States, and the little attention it received was rather critical. In 1941, for instance, in a case challenging registration of immigrant aliens, the U.S. Supreme Court—while banning the practice by states but implicitly condoning federal efforts—emphasized that "champions of freedom for the individual have always vigorously opposed burdensome registration systems."[1] In 1957, in *Lambert v. California*,[2] while again refraining from condemning registration in principle, the Court invalidated a local registration law because it unfairly subjected individuals to criminal liability without adequate prior notice.

State courts as well faulted registration, either because local laws conflicted with state laws (New Jersey and California),[3] or because registration in connection with a particular conviction constituted cruel and unusual punishment (California).[4] Moreover, in 1973 the California Supreme Court held that a defendant must be advised of a registration requirement before pleading guilty, noting that the requirement amounted to "continual police surveillance . . . Although the stigma of a short jail sentence should eventually fade, the ignominious badge carried by the convicted sex offender can remain for a lifetime."[5] Subsequent California cases during the era echoed the view that the effects of registration—in its then comparatively mild form and without the harsher effects of community notification—raised constitutional concern.[6]

Constitutional challenges, however, remained infrequent through the 1980s, likely due to the fact that not all states had registration laws (permitting their avoidance) and their relative modest impact on the lives of registrants. As the laws proliferated and became harsher in the 1990s, and were augmented by community notification, challenges increased in number. By the mid-1990s state and federal courts were deluged with a broad range of arguments, with the vast majority of courts, unlike in times past, being unsympathetic. It was not until 2003, almost fifty years after *Lambert*, however, that the U.S. Supreme Court again weighed in, deciding two cases on the same day in March 2003: *Smith v. Doe*[7] and *Connecticut Department of Public Safety v. Smith*.[8]

## Registration and Notification as a Regulation

In *Smith*, discussed briefly in Chapter 3, the Supreme Court held that Alaska's registration and community notification law was regulatory in nature and did not qualify as punishment, allowing its retroactive use consistent with the Ex Post Facto Clause of the U.S. Constitution.[9] *Smith* has major jurisprudential significance. The determination that registration and community notification did not qualify as "punishment" implicitly also served to foreclose claims based on bill of attainder, double jeopardy, and cruel and unusual punishment, each of which requires that a punishment be involved. Indeed, relying on *Smith*, in 2004 the California Supreme Court reversed its 1983 decision invalidating registration as cruel and unusual punishment, concluding that "[d]evelopments since [1983] have persuaded us that [its] analysis is no longer viable."[10]

Categorization of registration and notification as nonpunitive also forecloses another avenue of potential constitutional relief—the Sixth Amendment right to a jury trial. As a result of the Supreme Court's decision *Apprendi v. New Jersey* (2000),[11] any fact that increases an offender's sentence beyond the statutory maximum must be established beyond a reasonable doubt by a jury. However, because registration and community notification have been found nonpunitive, the Sixth Amendment does not apply. As a result, in states where registration eligibility can turn on factual determinations (such as whether the nonenumerated crime was "sexually motivated"), the decision can be made by judges alone.[12]

The *Smith* Court's analysis of the "punishment question" also bears significant institutional importance, suggestive of a judiciary subject to a troublesomely uncritical analytic mode. Under reigning precedent, the Court was first required to answer whether Alaska's law was intended to be punitive, and if not, to then assess its effects on registrants to discern whether it qualified as punishment.[13] The Court blithely accepted the Alaska Legislature's avowed purpose—"protecting the public" by imposing "restrictive measures on sex offenders"—which Justice Souter (concurring in the majority's result yet not its analysis) fairly referred to as "naïve, given pervasive attitudes toward sex offenders." As Justice Souter noted:

> [t]he fact that the Act uses past crime as the touchstone, probably sweeping in a significant number of people who pose no real threat to the community, serves to feed suspicion that something more than regulation of safety is going on; when a legislature uses prior convictions to impose burdens that outpace

the law's stated civil aims, there is room for serious argument that the ulterior purpose is to revisit past crimes, not prevent future ones.[14]

Equally problematic, the Court manifested an obliviousness to broader shifts in penology, in which registration and notification have played a critical role. As discussed in Chapter 4, since the 1990s U.S. criminal justice has assumed an increasingly managerial and actuarial cast, seeking to exert ongoing control over potential recidivists in communities, without the enormous costs associated with "brick and mortar" incapacitation. As sociologist Gary Marx has observed, government has "diffuse[d] the surveillance of the prison to the community at large."[15] *Smith* failed to recognize that registration and notification function as a cornerstone effort in this broader shift in corrections modus operandi.

The *Smith* Court's analysis of the effects of Alaska's law was no more convincing. As Justice Ginsburg (joined by Justice Breyer) noted in dissent, registration and notification impose "onerous and intrusive obligations," similar to probation and parole conditions (which constitutionally qualify as punishment), and expose individuals, "through aggressive public notification of their crimes, to profound humiliation and community-wide ostracism."[16] Moreover, as Justice Stevens pointed out, also in dissent, merely because "recidivism is the statutory concern" did not justify a nonpunitive characterization: the same rationale supports enactment of "three strikes" sentence enhancement laws, which are unquestionably punitive.[17]

These observations, however, understate the actual effects of registration and community notification. The constant necessity to inform the government of one's whereabouts and identifying indicia under threat of criminal prosecution (likely at the felony level) represents a unique burden, which affects freedom of movement, including temporary visits to other jurisdictions and permanent moves (the latter possibly triggering a new round of disclosures in an "active" community notification system). As noted by one state appellate court judge: "It is inconceivable to think that one who must, as his first act, go to local law enforcement and announce that he is a felon convicted of a sex offense will not be deterred from moving in order to avoid divulging that ignominious event."[18]

Registrants must also apprise government of the personal decisions to change their name or appearance and, in over twenty states (not including Alaska) and hundreds of localities, suffer geographic limits on where they can live and work. In addition, the annual or quarterly mandate to verify one's registry information by mail (as in Alaska), and most certainly being required to verify in-person (as now required by the Adam Walsh Act), imposed only on those convicted of a crime, significantly belies the notion of regulation. Finally, the Court's decision to isolate particular effects of registration, and then to downplay them, ignored their aggregate impact.[19] Accurately viewed, the range of affirmative requirements and adverse consequences experienced as a result of registration well exceed those associated with customary probation and parole,[20] which as mentioned qualify as punishment.

The consequences of community notification are even more onerous. While minimized by the *Smith* majority, notification has resulted in significant hardships, including forced moves from homes, job losses, vandalism, harassment, physical violence (including murders), and suicides (Chapter 5). To the *Smith* Court, however, such outcomes were "conjecture" and otherwise lacked bearing on the punishment question, especially on whether the effects of the laws historically qualified as punishment and were an "affirmative disability or restraint." This was because the harms resulted only from "the dissemination of accurate information about a criminal record, most of which is already public." While the colonial-era shaming might qualify as punishment, the *Smith* Court held, its modern-day equivalent (community notification) did not because it was not "an integral part of the objective of the regulatory scheme." Negative consequences were but a "collateral consequence of a valid regulation," and despite having "a lasting and painful impact," merely flowed from dissemination of "accurate, nonprivate information" about registrants.

Again, the Court's position is questionable on a number of levels. First, while registries do disseminate "accurate information" otherwise available to the public, albeit in disaggregated form, the context in which the information is provided is far from neutral. The government's singling out of certain individuals, yet not others, combined with "legislative findings" that those targeted pose particular risk, and sobriquets such as "predatory sex offender," "sexually violent predator" or "habitual sex offender," contradict governmental neutrality. Even in jurisdictions that classify registrants in terms of risk, such as Washington State, each level carries a corresponding degree of disclosure and opprobrium, and hence community disdain. To conclude that registries only contain "accurate information" is to thus misstate the government's action; a wholly stigmatizing and unwelcome public status is being communicated, not mere neutral government-held information.[21] As one federal judge observed:

While it might seem that a convicted felon could have little left of his good name, community notification in this case will inflict a greater stigma than would result from conviction alone. Notification will clearly brand the plaintiff as a "criminal sex offender" . . . a "badge of infamy" that he will have to wear for at least 25 years—and strongly implies that he is a likely recidivist and a danger to his community.[22]

The formal government designation, as New York's highest court has observed, involves "[m]ore than name calling by public officials."[23] Individuals are adversely affected socially, economically, psychologically, and physically as a direct result of the exercise of state police power authority.

The negative personal effects of registration and notification also function to impose an "affirmative disability or restraint," one of the criteria courts use to determine whether a particular sanction qualifies as punishment. From the outset, registration has expressly sought to imbue its targets with a sense that they are being watched. That they inhabit the world of "the Other": the self-conscious existential realm identified by Jean-Paul Sartre hinging on "recognition of the fact that I am indeed that object which the Other is looking at and judging."[24] In 1950s Philadelphia, for instance, one local detective supported registration because "it led the 'criminals' to believe that they were under the constant surveillance of the police department. The registrant's feeling of constant surveillance and obligation to notify police of any change in address might impose some regimentation upon the criminals."[25] Today, with community notification and more intensive registration requirements, this sense of control is immeasurably expanded. As two Wisconsin registrants recently told an interviewer:

· I feared for the longest time going out on the street, that there might be some type of vigilante attitude . . . There were people in the building trying to get a petition together to have the [registrants] that were in the paper ousted from the building . . . It caused me to be more confined and I felt ostracized . . .

· Just wondering . . . do they know? It kind of induces paranoia, you get all worried every time you see someone looking at you like they read it. You think—they know. You wonder, if someone confronts me, what am I going to say?[26]

Registration and community notification have thus achieved an effect sought by eighteenth-century philosopher Jeremy Bentham's mythical Panopticon with its central tower and "inspector's lodge."[27] Like the Panopticon, the laws instill in their subjects the sense that they are constantly being watched by a few government actors, even when they are not: to induce, as Michel Foucault recognized, "a state of conscious and permanent visibility that assures the automatic functioning of power. So to arrange things that the surveillance is permanent in its effects, even if it is discontinuous in its action."[28] Indeed, with community notification, it is perhaps more accurate to say that government has instituted a synoptic surveillance regime whereby "the many [are] watching the few."[29]

As a result, registration and notification today achieve what sociologist Stanley Cohen years ago termed a "hidden custody,"[30] by means of a coalition of police, neighbors, and society at large, which, like panopticism, also depends on classification and observation.[31] As one state appellate judge put it: "One who is watched, investigated, questioned, and accused, albeit informally, lives in fear . . . People tend to think that if he did it once, he will do it again."[32] Or as President Clinton put it more bluntly in signing the federal Megan's Law legislation: "America warns—if you dare to prey on our children, the law will follow you wherever you go, state to state, town to town."[33]

The *Smith* majority's uncritical analysis and conclusion, while troubling in itself, was made all the more so given that it concerned the Ex Post Facto Clause. Compared to protections enshrined in the Bill of Rights, which typically seek to ensure individual rights, such as against compelled self-incrimination (Fifth Amendment), the Ex Post Facto Clause is a structural constraint found in Article I of the Constitution. The Framers' unmistakable purpose in imposing this constraint was to guard against hot-blooded retributive reactions of legislatures, targeting individuals retroactively. As Alexander Hamilton warned: "Nothing is more common than for a free people, in times of heat and violence, to gratify momentary passions, by letting into the government principles and precedents which afterwards prove fatal to themselves."[34] A few years later, in 1810, Chief Justice John Marshall noted: "Whatever respect might have been felt for the state sovereignties, it is not to be disguised that the framers of the constitution viewed, *with some apprehension, the violent acts which might grow out of the feelings of the moment,* . . . The restrictions on the legislative power of the states are obviously founded in this sentiment."[35]

Over the centuries, the Ex Post Facto Clause has been invoked by a veritable "who's who" of scorned Americans—from Confederate sympathizers in the late 1860s to Communist fellow travelers in the 1950s.[36] To this list we can now add sex offenders, and future legislatures will doubtless target other disdained subpopulations. In past cases the Court cautioned that ex post facto challenges should be analyzed in terms of the "evils" the Clause was "designed to eliminate"[37] and that the law under challenge should be "placed in the context of the structure and history of the legislation of which it is a part."[38] Under this standard, *Smith* fell well short of the mark. Already, it has served as precedent to turn back challenges to registration-based residence exclusion zones for sex offenders.[39] What *Smith* portends for other ex-offender groups, perhaps less feared and disdained than sex offenders, remains unclear. But given that the onerous consequences imposed on convicted sex offenders failed to raise concern that "something more than regulation of safety is going on,"[40] as Justice Souter put it, civil libertarians have little cause for optimism.

### "Liberty Interests" and Procedural Rights

The Court's decision in *Connecticut Department of Public Safety (CDPS)*, decided the same day as *Smith*, is significant both for what it did and did not resolve. As mentioned in Chapter 3, *CDPS* involved a challenge to Connecticut's "conviction-based" registration and community notification regime, under which a conviction for a statutorily eligible offense triggers application of the laws, without individualized risk assessment. The petitioners contended that the regime violated the Due Process Clause of the Fourteenth Amendment because it jeopardized a protectable liberty interest, requiring that they have a chance to challenge their eligibility (by notice and a hearing) before being subject to the laws. The Court held that Connecticut's approach did not violate procedural due process because its registry website contained a disclaimer indicating that individuals were listed solely as a result of conviction, and not according to any specific risk determination. With a disclaimer in place, the Court held, any hearing intended to assess whether a given registrant is dangerous would be a "bootless exercise."[41]

As a result, the conviction-based approach, widely condemned as being overinclusive (Chapter 5), is constitutionally permissible. If a disclaimer is used (itself a hollow exercise, given the registry context), a prior conviction is both a necessary and sufficient condition for registration and community notification. Moreover, there is room in *CDPS* to infer that a disclaimer is not even needed,[42] a position adopted by at least two courts.[43]

In addition to its practical effect, *CDPS* has significance because it dodged the important constitutional question before it: whether registration and notification implicate procedural due process concerns. The Court instead asked a quite distinct question: whether affording individuals risk-assessment hearings (that is, due process) would be material to their being subjected to registration and notification, when eligibility for both is based on the fact of a prior conviction alone. The answer to this question, as the Court rightly held, was "no"—such hearings would have no effect. But the relevant question was not whether offender differentiation was contemplated by the law being challenged. Rather, it was whether registration and notification jeopardized a liberty interest sufficient to warrant due process protection.

Fairly viewed, the answer to this question would be an unequivocal "yes." As the Second Circuit Court of Appeals earlier concluded in invalidating Connecticut's law, when the government singles out individuals in the interest of public safety, the message is clear: the individuals pose criminal risk and warrant fear. Under such circumstances, risk assessments are very material, notwithstanding any disclaimer. By placing its imprimatur on Connecticut's system, the Supreme Court disserved what it has long considered the two central concerns of procedural due process: "the prevention of unjustified or mistaken deprivations and the promotion of participation and dialogue by affected individuals in the decision-making process."[44]

Nor was it sufficient to conclude, as the Court did, that Connecticut's approach was justified because individuals were afforded procedural due process protections for the prior convictions that triggered registration. The government of course was constitutionally required to afford due process before depriving individuals of physical liberty in the first instance. This, however, failed to protect against the unjustified additional burdens of registration and notification. Nor was it enough to say, as the Court again did, that *all* convictions justify concern over future dangerousness. While a prior conviction surely signifies criminal predisposition, at the time and place of occurrence, its reliability as a crime predictor certainly varies.[45] Subjecting *all* individuals convicted of specified crimes to registration and notification, even though the great majority of them have remained law-abiding for years, raises precisely the kind of error that due process is intended to avoid.[46] The targeting of certain convicts yet not others obliges that those singled out receive an opportunity to contest their designation.

For better or worse, *CDPS* thus decided much while avoiding the core constitutional question that was before the Court. The avoidance has served to leave intact the view—held by a majority of courts—that registration and community notification do not affect a liberty interest sufficiently to require procedural due process protection. Courts refusing to find a liberty interest have done so by rejecting arguments that registration and notification (1) violate registrants' right to privacy and/or (2) violate the "stigma-plus" test.

Courts rejecting the privacy-related claim conclude that publicly disseminating identifying information on registrants is permissible because the information—name, conviction records, addresses, and the like—is already in the public domain. As the Ninth Circuit Court of Appeals concluded in one case, the information is "already fully available to the public and is not constitutionally protected."[47] Adopting a similar view, shared by numerous other courts, a federal district court in Michigan summarily found no privacy right implicated by the "compilation and dissemination of truthful information that is already, albeit less conveniently, a matter of public record."[48] Making pieces of public information more readily available,[49] and magnifying its scope of availability,[50] courts have held, does not change the constitutional analysis.

This view, however, is wrong for several reasons. Most fundamentally, the mere fact that the information is public in a technical sense in no way resolves the constitutional question. As the Supreme Court stated in 1989 with respect to the information contained in a criminal "rap sheet": "Plainly there is a vast difference between the public records that might be found after a diligent search of court house files . . . [and a] summary located in a single clearing-house of information."[51] In dismissing what it called a "cramped notion of personal privacy," the Court stated that "the fact that an event is not wholly private does not mean that an individual has no interest in limiting disclosure or dissemination of that information."[52] Registration and community notification, as the New Jersey Supreme Court has observed, similarly "link various bits of information—name, appearance, address and crime—that otherwise remain unconnected."[53] The Court continued:

> However public any of those individual pieces of information may be, were it not for the Notification Law, those connections might never be made . . . .Those convicted of crime may have no cognizable privacy interest in the fact of their conviction, but the Notification Law, given the compilation and dissemination of information, nonetheless implicates a privacy interest. The interests in privacy may fade when the information is a matter of public record, but they are not non-existent.[54]

In practical terms, as a federal district court in New Jersey concluded, registration and notification "ensure that, rather than lying potentially dormant in a courthouse record room, a sex offender's former mischief—whether habitual or once-off—shall remain with him for life, as long as he remains a resident of New Jersey."[55]

Registration and notification are also distinctive because the information involved—home addresses in particular—is of an especially sensitive nature. The Supreme Court itself has recognized a privacy interest in one's home address, stating that "[a]n individual's interest in controlling the dissemination of information regarding personal matters does not dissolve simply because that information may be available to the public in some form."[56] The Court emphasized that the disclosures (there, nonunion members' home addresses to union officials) were problematic because they threatened intrusions into the home (by means of unsolicited mailings, calls, or visits), a domain "accorded special consideration in our Constitution, laws, and traditions."[57]

If this concern warrants deference in the context just described, it should with registration and notification, where the risk of harassment and vigilantism has been amply demonstrated.[58] The troubling upshot of this judicial insouciance is evident in the decision by a federal trial court in Michigan denying a due process challenge brought by homeowners who had their address wrongly listed on the state website.[59] The court held that because the listing of the address did not jeopardize a protectable privacy interest, Michigan was not required to provide a mechanism by which the mistake could be corrected.

The reigning view of courts on the alternate method of finding a protectable liberty interest—the "stigma-plus" test—is equally problematic. The test originated in the Supreme Court's 1971 decision in *Wisconsin v. Constantineau*,[60] which addressed the constitutionality of a state law permitting local officials, without prior notice or hearing, to post in liquor stores the names of those engaged in "excessive drinking," and to prohibit liquor sales to such persons. By a 6-3 vote, the Court condemned the posting on due process grounds, holding that "where the State attaches a 'badge of infamy' to the citizen, due process comes into play. Where a person's good name, reputation, honor, or integrity is at stake because of what the government is doing to him, notice and an opportunity to be heard are essential."[61]

Five years later, in *Paul v. Davis*,[62] the Court again addressed whether individuals have a protectable interest in avoiding governmental stigmatization when it considered a case involving police distribution of flyers to local businesses containing the names and photographs of "active shoplifters." The plaintiff, who had been arrested for shoplifting (the charge was later dropped) sued, alleging that he was deprived of due process when he was so identified without first receiving notice and being provided an opportunity to be heard.

The Court denied relief, characterizing the claim as alleging damage to "mere reputation," which did not in itself implicate a protectable liberty interest. According to the majority, the plaintiff alleged only that "the State may not publicize a record of an official act such as an arrest," which is not actionable.[63] In so deciding, the majority distinguished *Constantineau*, which it characterized as involving more than "mere defamation"; according to the *Paul* majority, the posting in *Constantineau* deprived the plaintiff of a "right previously held under state law—the right to purchase or obtain liquor in common with the rest of the country."[64]

*Paul* has been fairly criticized as an unjustified departure from what appeared to be the unqualified recognition in *Constantineau* of a "reputational" interest against governmental stigmatization. As Professor Henry Paul Monaghan commented some twenty years ago, "it is an unsettling conception of 'liberty' that protects an individual against state interference with his access to liquor but not with his reputation in the community."[65] Nonetheless, *Paul's* "stigma-plus" test remains the law of the land, and courts have employed it to reject procedural due process claims of registrants.

These decisions have been based on one of two conclusions: either that registration and community notification do not stigmatize individuals, resulting in outright denial of a claim, or that if stigma is present, there is no additional harm to an established right sufficient to qualify as a "plus." Courts finding an absence of stigma have mainly based their conclusion on the view that stigma, if any, stemmed from the underlying conviction that triggered registration,[66] and that data in the registries is merely publicly available information.[67] However, as discussed, the laws do more than merely assemble and make available identifying information; they facilitate the active collection and dissemination of such information and require that it be verified and updated at regular intervals (as frequently as every three months). And, again, not just neutral information is provided; individuals are subject to a regime the very purpose of which carries the message that they merit fear as dangerous individuals, backed by designations such as "predator."[68]

While it is true that *Paul* approved of the plaintiff being branded an "active shoplifter," it is also the case that being branded a sex offender (along with accompanying epithets) is far more opprobrious, as evidenced in the vigilantism experienced by registrants. Indeed, even conceiving of the issue in terms of "reputation" understates the issue. When the government gathers and synthesizes information in order to label one of its citizens in a derogatory manner, as the Oregon Supreme Court observed, "[t]he interest of the person to be labeled goes beyond mere reputation . . . . It is an interest in knowing when the government is moving against you and why it has singled you out for special attention. It is an interest in avoiding the secret machinations of the Star Chamber."[69]

More commonly, courts have concluded that registration and notification stigmatize, but they do not find the requisite "plus." The Sixth Circuit Court of Appeals, for instance, presumed the existence of stigma, but rejected the proffered "plus" in the form of alleged loss of and right to pursue employment. The Tennessee law challenged merely made registrants "less attractive" to employers and did not "expressly infringe upon [the petitioner's] ability to seek, obtain and maintain a job."[70] Moreover, the court concluded, "plus" did not arise out of any privacy right, because none existed as to the information disseminated.[71] Another court, echoing *Smith*, concluded that while dissemination of the

> truthful, public information . . . may result in damage to plaintiff's reputation, or may destabilize their employment and other community relations, such effects are purely speculative on the present record and, in any event, would appear to flow most directly from plaintiff's own convicted misconduct and from private citizens' reactions thereto, and only tangentially from state action.[72]

A handful of courts, however, have found the "plus" criterion satisfied. A few have concluded that privacy loss stemming from notification qualifies,[73] while others have singled out loss or foreclosure of employment. One federal trial court in Alabama, after identifying several possible plus factors (including the requirement that registrants preadvise authorities of residence changes), noted that there could be "little doubt" that prospective employers "will think twice before doing business with an individual deemed to be a likely recidivist and a danger to the community, and because [of community notification] . . . it is likely that at least some of those prospective business partners will become aware of the State's warning."[74] Other "pluses" might include statutorily imposed limits on where registrants can live, limits on the capacity to change one's name, the imposition of fees, and prohibitions on the capacity to seek legal redress, based on legislative grants of immunity to government officials involved in implementing the laws.[75]

The Supreme Court's decision to sidestep the procedural due process challenge presented in *CDPS*, and its ultimate approval of Connecticut's conviction-based regime, will likely have greater long-term practical significance than *Smith*. The latter's rejection of an ex post facto claim affected only individuals convicted before the enactment of the laws; even if decided otherwise, it would not (as Justice Stevens noted in his concurrence) have limited application of the laws to persons convicted after enactment of a given law. Likewise, even if deemed punitive, the burdens of Alaska's law would not likely have been considered cruel and unusual punishment under the Court's current understanding of the Eighth Amendment.[76]

*CDPS*, on the other hand, affects the past, present, and future of registration and notification. So long as the government provides a disclaimer on registrants' dangerousness, public dissemination of their identifying information is permissible—despite the unsubtle message that listing itself conveys: that the persons singled out threaten public safety. Moreover, while the Connecticut law challenged in *CDPS* concerned individuals convicted of sex crimes, the logic implicit in the Court's decision and explicit in the majority of state and lower federal courts—that registry data is merely accumulated public information—is readily transferrable to other ex-offender subpopulations.

### Broader Consequences

Over fifty years ago, Justice Felix Frankfurter aptly summarized a key aspect of American constitutionalism, noting that "the safeguards of liberty have frequently been forged in controversies involving not very nice people."[77] The foregoing discussion makes clear that courts, by upholding the constitutionality of registration and notification, have the corollary power to insulate political preferences that negatively affect "not very nice people"—sex offenders in particular. It may be that future challenges, seeking to vindicate rights of other groups targeted, such as persons convicted of arson or drug offenses, will fare better. Nevertheless, for present purposes the decisional law surveyed above remains significant for several fundamental reasons.

First, the judiciary has decisively placed its imprimatur on what Professor Carol Steiker has called the "preventive state," wherein government acts not as a "punisher . . . but rather as a preventer of crime and disorder more generally," and seeks to "identify and neutralize dangerous individuals before they commit crimes by restricting their liberty in various ways."[78] Although writing mainly in response to the U.S. Supreme Court's decision in *Kansas v. Hendricks* (1997),[79] which rejected an ex post facto challenge to the postimprisonment involuntary commitment of "sexually violent predators" because the authorizing law was deemed regulatory, Steiker's observation rings true today, in the wake of judicial endorsement of registration and notification laws.

Indeed, the Court's approval of involuntary commitment, along with its subsequent backing of registration and community notification laws, can and should be viewed as complementary endorsements of a broader, ostensibly civil, risk-based social control regime. With *Hendricks*, the Court condoned a corporeal preventive strategy, serving as a gap filler for offenders seen as dangerous, yet who satisfied their period of criminal incarceration. With *Smith* and *CDPS*, the Court condoned a noncorporeal preventive strategy, based on information collection and disclosure, permitting (at far less cost) potentially indefinite control over the much larger population of convicts at large in communities.

*Hendricks*, *Smith*, and *CDPS*, along with the many lower court decisions rejecting challenges to registration and notification, also give rise to a troublesome jurisprudential possibility: creation of a subclass of individuals warranting diminished constitutional protection. Invoking the term "outsider jurisprudence," Professor Eric Janus has drawn parallels between *Hendricks* and a select few Supreme Court decisions, today justly condemned, that have in effect drawn a circle of exclusion around disfavored individuals. Most notably, he points to the Court's 1856 infamous decision in *Dred Scott v. Sandford*, in which Chief Justice Taney referred to enslaved African Americans "as a subordinate and inferior class of beings" who possessed "no rights or privileges but such as those who held the power and the Government might choose to grant them."[80] This degraded status, Janus reasons, which parallels reviled sex predators today, permitted "constraints on liberty to be seen as exceptional and allowed the larger society to sustain its belief that U.S. law protected individual liberty."[81] According to Janus, *Hendricks* provided "outsider jurisprudence with a renewed foothold in our national consciousness."[82]

While surely not to be equated with *Dred Scott* in terms of infamy, *Smith*, *CDPS*, and the other decisions surveyed above do suggest that a constitutional exceptionalism is at work. The obviously strained effort by courts to uphold registration and notification laws, by at once obfuscating their purposes and trivializing their consequences, and disavowing the causal role of government, provides compelling evidence of this reality.[83] Whereas in the past courts often vigorously resisted efforts to condemn in perpetuity ex-offenders as a group,[84] and the Supreme Court itself has intervened to protect disdained groups,[85] Chief Justice Rehnquist felt free in 2002 to aver that registrants "deserve stigmatization."[86] Meanwhile, state legislatures have enjoyed free rein to codify legislative "findings" expressly stating that the interests of registrants warrant reduced weight.[87] In New Jersey, the mind-set affected voters themselves, when they agreed to amend the state constitution to permit community notification by means of the Internet, "[n]otwithstanding any other provision of this constitution and irrespective of any right or interest in maintaining confidentiality."[88]

Finally, the case law prompts concern over whether the courts are fulfilling their institutional role of checking the potential overreaching of the executive and legislative branches. While statutes, as Justice Cardozo stated, are designed "to meet the fugitive exigencies of the hour,"[89] courts are charged with acting as a bulwark against excessive legislative zeal. As Chief Justice Warren wrote, the judiciary is "oath-bound to defend the Constitution . . . [and] has the duty of implementing the constitutional safeguards that protect individual rights . . . We cannot push back the limits of the Constitution merely to accommodate challenged legislation."[90] Without this judicial oversight, the other branches are afforded, as Chief Justice Marshall observed in the seminal 1803 decision *Marbury v. Madison*, a "practical and real omnipotence."[91] The job has fallen to courts to ensure that legislatures, in particular, do not succumb to what Justice Holmes called the "hydraulic pressures . . . which make what was previously clear seem doubtful, and before which even well-settled principles of law will bend."[92]

Remarkably, the judicial abdication described above has occurred in the face of constitutional concerns overtly expressed by the very political actors who pushed the laws. Advocates in the New York State General Assembly, for instance, publicly acknowledged concerns over the constitutionality of pending laws,[93] and New Jersey Assembly Speaker Chuck Haytain, who spearheaded the speedy enactment of Megan's Law, cavalierly told the press that he would "let the lawyers and the courts worry about" the law's constitutionality.[94] In other instances, legislatures have engaged in bold defiance. In Florida, the legislature insisted that reviewing courts had a "duty" to reject any constitutional challenge, adding that a court defying the directive "unlawfully encroaches on the Legislature's exclusive power to make laws and places at risk significant public interests of the state."[95] To date, however, the courts have failed to call the legislative bluff, leaving legislators free to expand registration and notification laws in accord with their political impulses. In so doing, the judiciary, as Justice Breyer condemned in his dissenting opinion in *Hendricks*, "cut corners," and compromised heretofore accepted constitutional limits on legislative authority.[96]

The broader effects of this abdication remain to be seen, but strong reason exists to expect that the resulting jurisprudence will be deployed to fend off challenges to the laws as they continue to evolve. Just as the "war on drugs" has recast the Fourth Amendment by easing government constraints on searches and seizures,[97] decisions on registration and notification have recast the important jurisprudential areas they implicate. Future challenges, brought against as yet unenacted provisions, will be assessed against the forgiving constitutional standards surveyed above.

## PRIVACY

Registration and community notification have also had critically important influence on privacy, doing so in two very fundamental ways.

The first concerns a shift in sensibility. Today, we are repeatedly reminded that we live in the "information age." Whereas in the past bits of person-specific data were reposed in isolated, disaggregated form, practically safe from the eyes of others, technological advances have permitted such information to be aggregated and accessed with relative ease. We have become, in the words of one commentator, a "Database Nation."[98]

Not surprisingly, the technological wherewithal driving this shift has been harnessed to satisfy the age-old goal of monitoring ex-offenders. One sees this in any number of recent government efforts, such as the national Combined DNA Index System known as CODIS, authorized by Congress in 1994 as part of the same omnibus anticrime bill containing the Jacob Wetterling Act. As of June 2006, the database contained the genetic profiles of 3.3 million individuals, with roughly eighty thousand being added every month.[99] Similarly, in late 2007, the FBI announced that it was working with other agencies to create the world's largest computer database of individuals' biometrics (face, fingerprint, and iris), which promises to provide unprecedented capacity for personal identification.[100]

Registration and notification laws, of course, are very much a part of this shift: they assemble a broad variety of information for use in the monitoring and identification of ex-offenders. Moreover, it is important to recognize, their history played a key role in the evolving national zeitgeist permitting the evolution itself to unfold, dating back to the Supreme Court's 1957 decision in *Lambert v. California*. In *Lambert*, as discussed, the Court endorsed registration in principle, expressing constitutional concern only over whether eligible individuals had adequate notice of the requirement. The collection of registrants' data in itself was not problematic. Registration, the majority held, was "[a]t most a law enforcement technique designed for the convenience of law enforcement agencies through which a list of names and addresses of felons then residing in a given community is compiled. Registration involves merely a compilation of former convictions already publicly recorded in the jurisdiction where obtained."[101]

While modern registries, CODIS, and other kindred database efforts surely radically differ from the comparatively modest Los Angles registration regime challenged in *Lambert*, they oblige the same judicial forbearance, which the courts have readily provided. Indeed, with the Court's 2003 decisions in *Smith* and *CDPS*, condoning not only use of a much more ambitious registration regime, but also worldwide dissemination of registry information via the Internet, the sensibility has significantly strengthened. As a result of these decisions and the coordinated effort of state, local, and federal governments, the nation now has an informational infrastructure of unprecedented scope, entailing data bits compelled on an ongoing basis from registrants themselves.

This shift in sensibility and the attendant proliferation of registration and notification laws account for the second major way in which the laws have affected privacy: understandings of informational privacy.[102]

When considering privacy, one first faces a definitional question. A common view is that offered by legal scholar Ruth Gavison in her influential 1980 article, "Privacy and the Limits of the Law." To Gavison, privacy is best understood in the negative sense of its loss. "A loss of privacy," she observed, "occurs as others obtain information about an individual, pay attention to him, or gain access to him." According to Gavison, three elements comprise the right to privacy: "secrecy, anonymity, and solitude."[103]

Registration and notification clearly implicate the first two elements. Secrecy is compromised because identifying information on registrants is made available to the police and public alike. Similarly, registration has always sought to remove the cloak of anonymity enjoyed by ex-offenders, by providing police with identifying information; since the 1990s, notification has sought to undercut anonymity by also empowering communities with such information. To the extent that registries contain complete and accurate information, and are consulted by police and community members, secrecy and anonymity are eroded.

The third element, solitude, is violated in a less obvious way. To Gavison, solitude suffers when another gains "physical access"; the invader enjoys sufficient physical proximity to "touch or observe" an individual. Narrowly defined, this interest can be thought unaffected by registration and notification, inasmuch as the laws do not facilitate physical or visual intrusion into registrants' homes. Surveillance, however, has always figured as a central animating purpose behind registration, which since the 1990s has been amplified by the watchful eyes of community members. While the laws do not invade the physical space of registrants, they surely achieve a broader surveillance effect that is every bit as intrusive as a window peeper, who might secretly view a surveillance subject on a single occasion. With registration and notification, police and fellow community members surveil targeted individuals overtly, very often for individuals' lifetimes.

A second common way to conceive of informational privacy is as a matter of personal autonomy. Under this model, as Professor Charles Fried has noted, privacy is "that aspect of social order by which persons control access to information about themselves,"[104] an essential trapping of personal liberty.[105] So conceived, registration and notification plainly intrude upon privacy, compelling disclosure of information that its subject would not willingly otherwise divulge. As a consequence, registrants lose the critically important capacity to manage their social identities,[106] experiencing a loss of "self-ownership," which Professor Jeffery Reiman notes flows from unlicensed informational disclosure: Privacy conveys to the individual his self-ownership precisely by the knowledge "that the individual gains of his ability and his authority to withdraw himself from the scrutiny of others. Those who lose this ability and authority are thereby told that they don't belong to themselves; they are specimens belonging to those who would investigate them."[107]

In 1971, the California Supreme Court made the same point, in a case allowing an individual to sue a media outlet for the publication of information concerning his aged criminal conviction:

The claim is not so much one of total secrecy as it is of the right to define . . . who shall see beneath the quotidian mask. Loss of control over which "face" one puts on may result in literal loss of self-identity, and is humiliating beneath the gaze of those whose curiosity treats a human being as an object.[108]

With registration and notification this deprivation is especially profound. In the eyes of society registrants become a data aggregate—a synecdoche[109]— defined by their state-certified status as a "predator." And with the advent of the Internet, the stunting effect of disclosure is dramatically expanded, not merely geographically, as a result of the worldwide reach of the Web, but also temporally, given its content durability.[110]

Registration and notification thus not only undermine privacy as other informational disclosures do. They also define and delimit personal identity, doing so in part by extracting information from registrants themselves, on a routinized basis, under threat of criminal prosecution. Registrants are thus forced to be complicit in their own surveillance and self-branding,[111] in an important sense implicating the range of interests guarded by the Fifth Amendment privilege against compelled self-incrimination. As Professor Fried has noted:

By according the privilege as fully as it does, our society affirms the extreme value of the individual's control over information about himself . . . .[I]t is the point of the privilege that a man cannot be forced to make public information about himself. Thereby his sense of control over what others know of him is significantly enhanced, even if other sources of the same information exist.[112]

The upshot is that registration and notification laws, now in effect nationwide and affecting hundreds of thousands of individuals, have significantly recast traditional understandings of informational privacy. Earlier privacy-related debates over whether police alone should have access to registry information seem remarkably quaint in modern times. Today, not only does the public at large feel itself entitled to freely access individuals' criminal history information,[113] it also feels entitled to know such things as where they live and work, their physical marks, and what cars they drive.

The ramifications of this shift figure centrally in the important debate over the tradeoffs associated with privacy. When the dissemination of truthful information is at issue, disclosure proponents assert, the benefits of transparency trump individual interest.[114] Any value in nondisclosure, as Professor Diane Zimmerman has asserted, is outweighed by society's "powerful countervailing interest in exchanges of accurate information about the private lives and characters of its citizenry."[115]

To adherents of law and economics theory, the value of transparency is especially salient when criminal records are involved. Making such records available, they contend, is socially efficient: it permits individuals to make informed decisions about one another, lessening the likelihood of interpersonal evasion and misperception, which can be tantamount to fraud.[116] For example, an employer who wishes to avoid hiring an ex-offender can, with accurate criminal history information in hand, make an informed hiring decision.[117] By analogy, with accurate information on a registrant, a neighbor is empowered to take protective measures. If the registrant is not identified, such self-help and the socially undesirable chilling effect associated with not knowing if a registrant lives nearby can be avoided. Under this view, "the problem [with dissemination practices] is not that they reveal too much, but that they reveal too little."[118]

The "more is better" argument, however defensible in principle, is problematic in its application, according to an opposing camp of privacy theorists. As Professor Daniel Solove has recognized, a central problem stems from the underlying premise that "more disclosure will generally yield more truth," and that more information ensures "more accurate judgments about others."[119] "[T]he 'truth' about a person is much more difficult to ascertain than the truth about a product or thing. People are far more complex than products."[120] Put another way, as Professor Jeffery Rosen has written, the free market mentality risks "mistaking information for knowledge."[121]

With registration and notification, this risk is very much in play. Even putting to one side the known inaccuracies of registries, their overinclusiveness, in tandem with the known relative lower recidivism rates of sex offenders more generally, make it very likely that a dangerousness inference is incorrect. The likelihood of mistake is especially high when, as is the case so often with current registries, little information is provided on the misconduct that triggered registration. Prospects for misperception are further enhanced under the dominant conviction-based system, such as the Connecticut regime upheld in 2003 by the Supreme Court in *CDPS* that posts information on all registrants—"currently dangerous or not."

Ultimately, the premise of informational empowerment is thus more complicated than might first appear. Even if it were possible to achieve full informational awareness—for example, a registry site that fully and accurately depicts the nature of the previous conviction, including offense modus operandi and description of the victim and relationship to the registrant, along with an assessment of risk of reoffense, and so forth—the social detriments can outweigh the benefits. This is because today, more than ever before, a criminal conviction—especially involving a sex offense—serves as a perpetual badge of dishonor.[122] Despite use of registry disclaimers, and government warnings against misuse of registry information, registries reflect and promote a vengeful public attitude, what one commentator has called a "fork and pitchfork mentality."[123] The huge volume of daily "hits" recorded by Internet website registries make abundantly clear that something more than neutral information is being supplied, and that the information is not being used by locals merely for self-protection.

This mentality, while troublesome in itself, has negative spillover effects. As discussed in Chapter 5, public disdain for registrants is often directed at innocents—the family, friends, and employers of registrants, as well as persons mistakenly believed to be registered—and is so potent as to result in significantly diminished property values in areas where registrants reside. Notification can also result in the identification of victims, especially in instances of intrafamilial abuse.

Another unintended consequence is that registries can serve as one-stop public directories for malefactors. Registries, for instance, can provide information on persons inclined toward child pornography, something quite useful to purveyors and consumers of such material; likewise, drug offender registries can serve as a veritable "Yellow Pages" for drug users and sellers. The perversity of public awareness was vividly evidenced in the recent episode of a 14-year-old-girl who was required to register as a result of fondling a 7-year-old boy when she was 11. As a result of being posted on her state's website registry, the girl received anonymous calls from men wanting to "hook up" with her.[124]

Further cause for concern stems from the expansive retroactive reach of the laws. Aged convictions, perhaps reflecting racial or homophobic animus, can be rejuvenated and brought back to life. For instance, before the Supreme Court's 2003 decision in *Lawrence v. Texas* invalidating on constitutional grounds laws criminalizing adult consensual sodomy, several states required registration for such offenses.[125] Even in the absence of such animus, retroactivity often forces registration and public exposure of individuals whose convictions date well into their past, making them subjects of public disdain despite having long since rejoined the ranks of law-abiding society.[126]

Such occurrences are regrettable not only because of fairness concerns.[127] They also have troubling implications for a society that continues to imprison unprecedented numbers of individuals and must eventually reintegrate them. As the California Supreme Court once noted with respect to an ex-offender whose aged conviction was made public by a magazine article: "Ideally, his neighbors should recognize his present worth and forget his past life of shame. But men are not so divine as to forgive the past trespasses of others."[128] Registration and notification create conditions that promote disdain for ex-offenders and cancel the possibility of this "divine" being achieved. Not only are the life prospects for ex-offenders reduced, perpetually setting them apart as the threatening "alien Other,"[129] but so are the prospects for achieving "social capital"—the network of human interrelations predicated on trust and cooperation thought necessary for successful civic and community life.[130]

Finally, the retroactive reach of registration undercuts the rational choice premise of law and economics theoreticians, noted above. Just as having information on a recently convicted person not likely to reoffend does not promote efficient social choices, for instance by inspiring unwarranted protective measures, providing information on those with aged convictions and years of law-abidingness multiplies the inefficiency.[131]

In short, even if an ex-offender has no "right" to keep his or her conviction record out of the public eye, and the public has a "right" to this and other identifying information, the crucial policy question of whether such information *should be* disseminated remains unresolved. The great popularity of registratin and notification has elided this question and indelibly changed the terms of the nation's debate over informational privacy.

## GOVERNANCE

Another way in which registration and notification have transformed modern America relates to the role of government in securing public safety. As discussed, the laws figure centrally in the modern shift toward the use of information to limit criminal risk, beyond prison walls, at far less cost. The upshot has been the creation of a triangle of relationships, involving registrants, government, and community members who serve as "coproducers" of public safety. Whether the strategy in fact achieves this goal, or actually has counter-productive effects, remains unclear (see Chapter 5). However, the shift itself is highly significant.

Requiring that ex-offenders assist government in their own continued monitoring marks a key governance development.[132] The shift itself dates back to 1957, with the Supreme Court's decision in *Lambert v. California*, which while invalidating on notice grounds a particular local application of criminal registration, implied principled support of its use. Ex-offenders thus joined the select ranks of other status-based registrant subpopulations, such as resident aliens, Communists, and members of the Ku Klux Klan.[133]

Of perhaps greater significance, however, is the manner in which the laws—especially relating to community notification—have reconfigured the governance role of communities. While for decades probation and parole entailed an element of community monitoring,[134] notification radically expanded this role, permitting a massive dispersion of surveillance and control. Unlike the case-specific surveillance of probation and parole (having a parolee's employer provide updates, for example), notification permits and encourages the active involvement of entire communities, well after offenders have satisfied the conditions of their period of formal community supervision.

Modern registration and notification are also important for what they signal: a willingness to have communities shoulder the responsibility—and risk—of criminal recidivism. As discussed in Chapters 3 and 4, modern laws were motivated by a complex constellation of social, political, and historical forces. From the outset, however, a chief motivation has been the desire to shift the onus of ensuring public safety from government to communities. Harshly ridiculed for failing to protect Tacoma residents from Earl Shriner, Washington State officials in 1990 initiated community notification amid public cries of a "right to know" about individuals such as Shriner. While this empowerment started out in modest terms, with Washington residents told only of registrants deemed especially risky, very soon states began disseminating identifying information on all registrants, massively expanding community informational empowerment. Today, just as Americans flood phone lines with tips on criminal fugitives in response to the popular television show "America's Most Wanted," hosted by John Walsh, who himself figured centrally in the modern push for notification, they are invited to police their fellow community members. Notification has thus pluralized public safety, creating a new relationship among citizens, registrants, and governments.[135]

By electing to empower communities, however, the government did not act solely out of benign deference to a populist assertion of informational entitlement. Rather, in implicit acknowledgement of its inability to protect citizens, government shifted its public safety responsibility. Community members are now expected to self-protect, and recidivist criminal harms are seen as community failures, not failures of government.[136] A double governmental impunity has thus materialized: not only does government enjoy statutory immunity from legal liability for flaws in the registration and notification processes, but it also lacks moral responsibility for any recidivist acts by registrants.[137]

This shift toward informational empowerment would appear a very positive development, at least from an antipaternalist perspective. Close examination of the shift, however, reveals that the empowerment ideal remains nothing more than that. The chronic inaccuracies and undue scope of registries (Chapter 5) mean that communities lack the basic informational wherewithal to self-protect. Moreover, research has shown that the public is often unaware of the content of registries, and even if aware, does not undertake protective measures (Chapter 5). Nor are families and communities equally predisposed to take action. As Professor Jonathan Simon has observed, the laws presume that a "family has the resources to protect itself by choosing a location in which the streets are safe and a family structure that allows the kind of surveillance that Maureen [Kanka] might have been able to provide Megan had she been alerted to that particular threat."[138] Sadly, of course, not all communities, families, or individuals are similarly predisposed or equipped to ensure their own safety. As a result, rather than promoting public safety, the laws can foster a dangerous false sense of security and liberate government from pressure to take more effective efforts to combat crime.

The government's attempt at disavowal has, at the same time, been paralleled by an effort to morally absolve itself of responsibility for its affirmatively created harms. With the blessing of the U.S. Supreme Court in *Smith*, government can now assemble and make publicly available highly stigmatizing information, without having imputed to it any causal role for resulting vigilante harms. This shift, it is important to note, has taken place despite the Court's repeated rejection of similar efforts by government in the past. In 1958, for instance, in granting a challenge to Alabama's forced disclosure of NAACP membership lists, a unanimous Court wrote:

> It is not sufficient to answer, as the State does here, that whatever repressive effect compulsory disclosures of names of petitioner's members may have on participation by Alabama citizens in petitioner's activities follows not from state action but from private [action]. The crucial factor is the interplay of government and private action, for it is only after the initial exertion of state power represented by the production order that private action takes hold.[139]

Similarly, in 1982, in invalidating an Ohio law requiring disclosure of contributors to the Socialist Workers' Party, the Court noted that there need only be a "reasonable possibility" that the compelled disclosure would subject individuals to "threats, harassment, or reprisals from either Government officials or private parties."[140]

While such cases arose in instances in which First Amendment–protected rights were threatened, *Smith*'s disregard of government responsibility remains problematic. Even if, as the Court has held in other cases, the government has no generalized duty to protect individuals from harm by third parties,[141] a duty does arise when the government creates the danger,[142] such as occurs when it informs a fearful and hateful community that a convicted criminal (especially a sex offender) is nearby, and provides identifying information on the individual.

Under such circumstances, the government does not serve as a passive conduit of information, but rather an active facilitator of possible vigilantism. To Professor James Whitman, government disclosure of stigmatizing information, including that contained in registries, involves an "ugly and politically dangerous complicity between the state and the crowd.[143] . . . Once the state stirs up public opprobrium against an offender it cannot really control the way the public treats that offender"; dissemination of such information marks a "dangerous willingness, on the part of government, to delegate part of its enforcement power to a fickle and uncontrolled general populace."[144] Government in effect deputizes the public to act in its own defense, based on information the government provides, and when the public reacts violently, abdicates any responsibility. Whereas with earlier-generation laws concern existed over occasional police harassment, today concern stems from the far more violent vigilante predisposition of community members.

Finally, community informational empowerment has resulted in a key change in social relations which, while more subtle than vigilantism, nonetheless colors the dynamic of governance. Although the research thus far has been mixed, community notification very possibly increases fear levels in unhealthy ways. One study of Wisconsin residents, for instance, reported a "heightened sense of vulnerability," a "lack of control over the environment in which they lived," and a sense of "helplessness" and "anxiety about what the future might hold for the neighborhood.[145] Such fears not only negatively affect the quality of life of individuals; they also threaten the social mucilage of community life by undercutting a shared sense of well-being and trust.

The conditions also create the risk of a psychologically harmful "bogeyman" effect. Children and parents especially, repeatedly told of dangerous individuals in their midst yet often lacking a sense of how safety can be better secured,[146] can possibly submit to a fear-based state of mind (one that is also misdirected against strangers, who statistically pose far less risk than nonstrangers). The dynamic further creates the perverse possibility that the fearsome "predator" imagery might discourage parents from broaching the issue of sexual abuse with their children altogether. Or, short of this, it can encourage a "binary" (yes/no) risk sensibility that contradicts reality—which is that abuse stems predominantly from ongoing "grooming" relationships rather than violent initial encounters.

## STATE-FEDERAL RELATIONS

A final influence of modern registration and notification laws concerns their impact on the nation's traditional federalist governing structure. Under this structure, governance responsibilities are shared by the federal government and the states, with sovereign lawmaking authority allocated to each. By constitutional design and tradition, the federal government, enjoys only the "enumerated powers" that are "few and defined" under the Constitution,[147] with the balance of authority "reserved" to the states under the Tenth Amendment.[148] The Framers hoped that this power-sharing arrangement would allow states to limit overreaching by the national government (and vice versa)[149] and permit power to remain localized, ideally allowing laws to be more responsive to local needs and sentiments.[150]

Historically, it has been accepted that policy regarding the police power— the "authority to provide for the public health, safety, and morals" of individuals—is primarily a matter of state, not federal, prerogative.[151] Through much of the nation's history, this demarcation was respected. As noted in Chapter 4, however, starting in the 1930s, and at an accelerated pace more recently, the federal government has assumed for itself ever greater police power authority. Federal efforts to pressure states to adopt registration and community notification laws represent a high-water mark in this regard.

Over time, Congress has used two primary means to influence state criminal justice policy. The first is the Commerce Clause, permitting federal laws that regulate "commerce among the states,"[152] which Congress has repeatedly used to enact criminal laws that replicate state criminal laws (for example, regarding drug offenses) and devise new bases for federal criminal liability (for example, carjacking). Such intrusions on the authority of states have been quite controversial and even prompted the Supreme Court, after several decades of judicial acquiescence, to invalidate (in 1995 and 2000) two federal provisions.[153]

The other, less common way in which Congress has exerted its influence is through the Spending Power Clause, which permits laws that "provide for the . . . general Welfare of the United States."[154] When it invokes this authority Congress imposes a quasi-contractual quid pro quo: if states wish to obtain federal money they must adopt the regulatory mandates of Congress.[155] With this arrangement, the federal government in effect uses honey (federal money) rather than vinegar (raw federal power, as under the Commerce Clause) to impose its will on the states. In doing so, Congress can avoid the controversy and difficulty typically associated with the exercise of its overt authority[156] and can dictate policy on matters well beyond its enumerated powers.[157]

The Spending Power has been the Congressional modus operandi of choice with respect to registration and notification. From the Wetterling Act in 1994, to the Adam Walsh Act in 2006, and mandates in between, Congress has threatened states with loss of federal money (10% of their allocated Byrne Program grants) if they do not enact laws satisfying federal will. Whereas before 1994, registration and notification provisions reflected state and local desires, they have since been recast in accord with federal desires. The results have been dramatic.

Congress has not only compelled states to enact registration and notification laws, when they might otherwise not have done so on their own. It has also micromanaged the scope and nature of the laws, dictating the duration of registration; the types of offenses requiring registration; the registration of juvenile offenders; use of the Internet to effectuate notification; how and the intervals at which registration information must be verified; and the use of a conviction-based system to effectuate registration duration and community notification. As a complement, in 2006 as part of the Adam Walsh Act, Congress invoked its Commerce Clause power to make it a federal crime for registrants to travel interstate and to knowingly violate registration requirements, and it authorized the U.S. Marshals to enforce the law.

These federal initiatives, carried out on an ongoing basis for well over a decade, have significantly affected state-federal relations. The aggregate impact has been the creation of a long-feared superstructure: a national crime-control apparatus with the power to locate lawbreakers and bring them to justice. While the FBI and other federal units have long assisted states with interstate crime control (such as in capturing fugitive felons) and facilitated the storage and collection of data (such as fingerprints and Bertillon measurements), the Wetterling Act and its progeny represent a radical growth in degree and kind. States have been compelled to help create a comprehensive national database to monitor registrants (the National Sex Offender Registry) and effectuate nationwide community notification (via the National Sex Offender Public Registry). Even more dramatic, a federal police force—the U.S. Marshals Service—has been deputized by Congress to enforce compliance with state registration laws, a task heretofore unreservedly the responsibility of states.

The threat of consolidated police powers typically prompts concern resonating in the hyperbolic or paranoid, and this is not the intent here. However, the federal intrusion associated with registration and notification warrants recognition for its historic significance. By combining authority previously divided among federal, state, and local authorities, the federal government has amassed a power greater than the sum of its parts. The federal government has achieved the ability to create and maintain a dossier on individuals and is using the information to enforce its will. While federalism has traditionally served to "split the atom of sovereignty"[158]—dispersing social control wherewithal among distinct sovereigns, theoretically to the benefit of individual liberty—federal efforts relative to registration and notification have reconstituted the atom.

A second, more direct way in which Congress has affected federalism concerns is by its impact on state autonomy. The "federalism revolution" mounted by conservative members of the Supreme Court in the 1990s, and the enormous scholarly literature condemning the "federalization of crime," both prompted by Congress's exercise of its Commerce Clause authority, highlight the political salience of federal intrusiveness. Such federal efforts, however, have in actuality had little practical effect on the nation's federalist structure. Not only have courts been loath to condemn federal criminal laws enacted under Commerce Clause authority,[159] but the laws themselves typically mirror criminal laws already existing in states, and bear chiefly symbolic effect because the states continue to handle the lion's share of criminal offenders.

Federal intrusion with registration and notification has been of a different order. Congress has not enacted discrete federal criminal laws redundant of state prohibitions. Rather, it has imposed a gamut of criminal justice *policies*, mandating changes in substantive laws and procedures in every state (as well as the District of Columbia, U.S territories, and Indian tribes). With each of these changes, federal policy prerogative has been imposed, with perhaps the high-water mark being reached with the Adam Walsh Act in 2006, which explicitly seeks "uniform standards,"[160] with the ultimate goal of securing a "comprehensive national system."[161]

A third and final way in which federalism values have been trammeled relates to the tenet that, by circumscribing federal authority, states will be free to enact laws reflective of local normative preferences, thereby allowing for a greater range of choices for the nation's residents. As the Supreme Court has stated, "the essence of federalism is that states must be free to develop a variety of solutions to problems and not be forced into a common, uniform mold."[162] With such autonomy, in turn, states ideally can serve as "laborator[ies]," enjoying the freedom, as Justice Brandeis long ago put it, to undertake "experiments without risk to the rest of the country."[163]

Imposition of federal will has diminished both of these possibilities. For instance, under the Adam Walsh Act states averse to requiring registration of juvenile offenders must do so, in the process quashing local preferences, precluding experimentation on the issue of the efficacy of the highly contested policy, and disallowing families to "vote with their feet" and express their policy preference by moving to a state without such a requirement.

Federal policy preferences, moreover, are in no sense prima facie preferable to those of states. Indeed, contrary to James Madison's presumptive favor of federal over state lawmakers,[164] federal policies typically originate in an impaired political atmosphere, one divorced from the fiscal and practical realities daily faced by state legislatures and distanced from where the effects of laws themselves are most directly felt. As a result, as Professor Rachel Barkow has observed, "the federal government is not only less likely to innovate, but also less likely to adopt cost-effective alternatives as quickly, if at all."[165] The efficacy and effects of registration remain uncertain in myriad respects (see Chapter 5), and the federal government's imposition of uniform requirements bespeaks a confidence far in excess of the factual record. That Congress should behave in this manner with respect to criminal justice policy is especially unfortunate, for it is in this realm that state innovations have been among the most creative and instructive to the nation as a whole.[166]

In short, since 1994 Congress has imposed its will on a policy matter clearly within the ambit of the states, and in the process has substantially impacted what the Supreme Court has referred to as the "sensitive relations" between the states and the federal government.[167] Remarkably, the intrusion has triggered precious little federalism-based concern. In Congress, the political actors who usually most ardently support states' rights—conservative Republicans—remained largely silent. To the extent federalism objections made it to the debate floor, concerns were raised by liberal Democrats.[168]

State actors, for their part, have been equally reticent. While there has been some state reluctance to follow federal prescriptions (see Chapter 3), such instances have been isolated, as manifest in the rapid nationwide adoption of registration and notification laws by the mid-1990s. Indeed, states have at times adopted federal strictures in advance of prescribed deadlines, in the hope of securing monetary bonuses offered by Congress.[169] Federal pressure, in short, has proved enormously successful, and state registration and notification policy, as one commentator stated with regard to exercises of Spending Power more generally, has "tag[ged] along after federal money like a hungry dog."[170]

## CONCLUSION

Modern registration and notification laws have had a variety of important consequences for American society. This chapter has singled out several in particular, examining how the laws have affected the nation's constitutional jurisprudence, understandings of privacy, and approaches to governance, including state-federal relations. These changes, important in themselves, promise to bear even greater significance in the years to come as registration and notification continue to evolve. The contours of this evolution will be taken up next.

# 7 PROSPECTS FOR THE FUTURE

GIVEN THE CONCERNS NOTED in the preceding two chapters, it would seem natural that policy makers would reconsider registration and community notification. Indeed, in the past it was not unusual for critical concerns to prompt changes in the implementation of crime-control policies, if not their outright discontinuance. For instance, "sexual psychopath" involuntary commitment laws enacted from the 1930s to the 1960s (Chapter 4) fell into disuse due to questions over their expansiveness and utility; before that, governments disavowed the physical branding of convicts, due to concern that it failed to deter crime and undermined offender reintegration (Chapter 2).[1] Of even greater relevance, by the late 1980s registration itself had all but disappeared, largely owing to its acknowledged shortcomings. For a variety of reasons, however, repeal or meaningful amendment of modern-day registration and community notification laws will not likely be forthcoming. If anything, we should expect the laws to expand. This chapter examines why this is so.

## POLITICAL RETRENCHMENT

One of the most striking aspects of the recent proliferation of registration and notification laws is the dearth of principled objection to their very use. While in the past concern over the negative "psychic effect" of registration, alone, prompted significant resistance and inspired comparisons to totalitarian and fascist regimes, registration today—even when combined with community notification—is readily accepted. The reasons and conditions accounting for this major shift were examined in Chapter 4. Still, a question remains: Was the political will animating and sustaining the wave of laws transitory, such that they will be rescinded in coming years?

The answer to the foregoing question is very likely no, for a variety of reasons. First, the associated political cost would simply be too great. For politicians, when it comes to crime control matters, as Michael Tonry has noted: "Leaving things as they are poses no electoral risks . . . No one loses elections for failing to lead or support a campaign for repeal of laws that are tough."[2] Indeed, any effort to soften crime policy risks not only sound-bite reprisals from political opponents, with dreaded consequences on election day,[3] but also the condemnation of advocacy groups. "Report cards," issued by watchdog groups, provide state-by-state assessments of the perceived vigor of registration and notification laws,[4] and popular media interests such as "The O'Reilly Factor" add to the political pressure.[5] This atmosphere, in turn, is only faintly tempered by critics of the laws. While criminal defense and civil liberties interests have over time sought to beat back the laws, their impact has been limited at best. Meanwhile, suffice it to say, registrants themselves, even if not subject to voter disenfranchisement,[6] enjoy scant political influence.[7]

Of equal if not greater importance, politicians are naturally reluctant to question the highly personalized laws. Any effort to dismantle a provision designated as "Megan's" or "Zachary's" Law, for instance, would be viewed as more than a mere policy shift. Rather, it would be seen as a personal assault on the victims' memories and legacies. Compelling proof of this tendency, as noted in Chapter 4, was the decision by Congress in the Adam Walsh Act (2006) to enshrine the law's namesake as well as the names of seventeen other victims in the law's "declaration of purpose," along with brief personal descriptions and how they were victimized. Wary of in any way besmirching the memory of prior namesakes, Congress established within the broader AWA "the Jacob Wetterling, Megan Nicole Kanka, and Pam Lychner Sex Offender Registration and Community Notification Program," victims already named in the list of seventeen.[8]

Interest in preserving the political status quo is further evidenced in the notable dearth of empirical scrutiny to which the laws have been subjected, discussed in Chapter 5. On this point it is important to note that agnosticism, if not aversion, for the actual impact of toughened crime control policy is not unusual today. For instance, in their book on the history of California's "three strikes" sentence-enhancement law, enacted in 1994, the same year as the federal Wetterling Act, Franklin Zimring and his coauthors tell of how the state legislature in 1999 heatedly debated and ultimately approved a bill for a publicly funded study of the law. Governor Gray Davis, however, vetoed the bill stating that "an additional study is unlikely to produce much, if any, useful information that is not already available." Analyzing the chain of events, Zimring et al. observe that empirical assessment of the policy was really beside the point; "belief in the effectiveness of a penal statute is rooted in the citizens' conviction that the law is appropriate. Since the penal measures feel right, they must be working well." Importantly, moreover, any attempt to evaluate the law's actual effectiveness was regarded as an insult to the believer and the belief. The doubts about "three strikes" were "not resented because they may have led to political difficulties; they are in and of themselves a denial of the normative beliefs that supporters hold. It is heresy itself rather than what further harm it might accomplish that provoke[d] the anger of Three Strikes supporters."[9]

A similar atmosphere has marked the modern history of registration and notification laws. While to date the evolution has been marked by disinterest in evaluative research, rather than an explicit effort to quell it, the end result is the same. Only very recently has empirical assessment become a priority. For instance, with the Adam Walsh Act in 2006 Congress directed the attorney general to assess the "efficiency," "effectiveness," and resource consequences of conviction and risk-based classification systems,[10] and asked the National Institute of Justice (the research bureau of the Department of Justice) to study other aspects of registration and notification.[11] Remarkably, this action was taken twelve years after Congress first required that states adopt registration (1994), ten years after mandating community notification (1996), and at the same time as the Walsh Act itself prescribed an array of fundamental changes for state registration and notification systems.

Although belated, this newfound interest in evaluative research is most welcome. Whatever the outcome of studies, however, there is reason to be pessimistic over the prospect that registration and notification policy will become more evidence based. Given the overt personalization of the laws, and the perceived stakes (sexual victimization, perhaps of one's child), the resistance noted by Zimring et al. would likely be at least as strong. As much as was evident in the remarks of national advocates after the recent release of two reports that were highly critical of registration and notification. In response to a September 2007 study by the group Human Rights Watch, which questioned the efficacy of the laws, Laura Ahearn, executive director of Parent's for Megan's

Law, retorted that "[y]ou can't prove a negative. You can't prove a child hasn't been sexually victimized because they haven't been."[12] Similarly, in response to a May 2007 preliminary study by the State of New Jersey indicating that Megan's Law had no effect on public safety, Maureen Kanka responded by simply reiterating that if she "had known there was a pedophile living across the street, Megan would be alive and well today," and added that she knew "the effectiveness of the law because I get e-mails about it all the time."[13]

Furthermore, it is not hard to imagine how the laws will survive continued criticism that they are based on the false premises of heightened risk of sex offender recidivism and the threat of "stranger danger." This impregnability stems in significant part from what behavioral economists refer to as an availability heuristic, which causes individuals to mispredict the likelihood of readily imagined events,[14] and probability neglect, which encourages individuals to focus on emotionally charged negative occurrences, rather than their empirical likelihood.[15] Resistance, as the above quote from Maureen Kanka makes clear, is also fueled by the common tendency to lend greater credence to information that confirms preexisting beliefs and to ignore conflicting information (confirmation bias).[16]

In a time when more Americans report being concerned about sex offenders than violent crime in general or even terrorism,[17] and registration and notification are thought justified "if one child is saved" (Chapter 4), continued support for such measures should come as no surprise.[18] This is especially so if, as has been the case to date (Chapter 5), empirical work is unable to disentangle recent drops in rates of sexual victimization from the contemporaneous proliferation of registration and community notification laws. Advocates, until data prove otherwise, can assert that despite growing research on the negative impact of the laws on registrants and others (such as their families), the laws still have possible public safety benefits.

It is also important to recognize that the laws, whatever their impact, will likely remain popular due to their harsh effects on the individuals they target—ex-criminal offenders. To a society increasingly unforgiving and scared of criminal malefactors, especially sex offenders, registration and notification are readily defensible: the fact of a prior conviction standing alone, however inaccurate a proxy of future dangerousness, justifies all personal hardships imposed. As Cass Sunstein recently observed in his book *Laws of Fear*, "if indulging fear is costless, because other people face the relevant burdens, then the mere fact of 'risk,' and the mere presence of fear, will seem to provide a justification."[19] When the "other people" are sex offenders the public policy choice will likely continue to be an easy one. This is especially so given that the choice carries the added expressive benefit of condemning targeted individuals with epithets such as "predator,"[20] a benefit so potent as to result in the continued public branding of registrants on websites even after their death (Chapter 5).

For similar reasons, the laws will likely continue to be inured to the persistent criticism that they are overinclusive and unjustly driven by worry over "false negatives," that is, individuals who recidivate but about whom the community and police are not warned. Under such a regime, the specter arises that, as Supreme Court Justice Potter Stewart observed in another context, "[w]hen everything is classified then nothing is classified, and the system becomes one to be disregarded by the cynical or the careless."[21] Yet, again, overinclusiveness today raises no principled concern; indeed, it is preferred, even at the likely expense of unhelpfully inundating the public with information (much of it inaccurate or incomplete) on registrants undifferentiated by risk.[22]

Given that access to criminal history information is now seen as a matter of consumerist entitlement (Chapter 4), the hundreds of thousands of "false positives" (persons required to register yet do not reoffend) are readily acceptable to the public. And with the Adam Walsh Act, with its blunderbuss conviction-based classification regime, the normative preference is now national policy. This despite the increasing consensus of experts (Chapter 5) and even Patty Wetterling (who played a foremost role in the genesis of modern laws)[23] that a more circumscribed regime based on individualized risk assessments has greater promise.

Along these same lines, advocates will have cause to resist claims that the laws wrongly focus on an overstated fear of "stranger danger." Even accepting the empirical reality that most sex crimes are committed by family members, friends, and acquaintances, registration and community notification could still be said to have value. Presuming that self-protective measures will be taken, notice of dangerous strangers is beneficial, but so is being told that someone familiar committed a registerable offense, when such prior misconduct was not previously known (an unlikely scenario among family, but quite possible regarding friends and acquaintances). Also, even though strangers commit a comparatively small percentage of registerable crimes, their involvement could be deemed more harmful and fearsome for individuals and communities,[24] justifying the collection and dissemination of information relative to them.

One final reason accounting for the likely persistence of registration and notification is that they have assumed an institutional life of their own, ensuring a measure of staying power. As discussed earlier, the laws play a linchpin role in the modern preference for "techno-corrections," providing an information-based technology for the ongoing community control of ex-offenders. This preference can be expected to continue given the ever-increasing number of ex-offenders and shrinking corrections budgets. In addition, as the infrastructure supporting registration and notification has grown over time, pressure from its constituent parts can be expected to exercise a self-perpetuating influence. Much as the increasingly large child-protection bureaucracy has been held safe from political challenge amid decreasing abuse rates,[25] the administrative structure of registration and notification can be expected to resist retrenchment efforts. Equally important, private industry—such as that providing data mining and notification services—also can be expected to press for maintenance of the political status quo, and with new technological innovations, even seek new money from government and private individuals.

In all, there is strong reason to believe that registration and notification are here to stay. Like the massive increases in imprisonment they accompanied in the 1990s, the laws are the product of a significant social and political transformation. While states have recently sought to curb their massive prison populations (due to cost concerns, not principle), a similar impulse will not likely impinge registration and notification. Indeed, the fact that the laws promise continued control of criminally risky individuals on the relative cheap—when prison populations can no longer be sustained—makes the likelihood of their sustainment all the greater.

Even more fundamentally, there is little reason to think that principled objection to the laws, pervasive up through the 1980s, will resurface. In 1941, in the shadow of totalitarian oppression abroad, the U.S. Supreme Court cautioned in *Hines v. Davidowitz* that "champions of freedom for the individual have always vigorously opposed burdensome registration systems," and noted historic opposition to requirements "at war with the fundamental principles of our free government, in that they would bring about unnecessary and irritating restrictions upon personal liberties of the individual."[26] Today, with onerous registration requirements and notification conditions politically accepted (including in some states the requirement that identification cards be carried, of particular concern in *Davidowitz*), the Court's words seem a quaint reminder of a distant past.

Perhaps some future use of registration and notification by a foreign government, an antagonist of the United States, will reawaken and stir political opposition.[27] If this were to come to pass, however, such a reaction very likely would not be directed against registration, which has become an accepted method of social control, endorsed by such mainstream institutions as the *New York Times*.[28] Whether some outgrowth or application of community notification, neither known nor imagined today, turns public sentiment against notification remains to be seen. However, given that the public has gone unperturbed by such tragic byproducts of community notification as vigilantism, including directed against the innocent children of registrants, makes such a reaction doubtful.

## JUDICIAL RETRENCHMENT

With political will lacking, registration and notification will continue to be contested in the courts. Even in the wake of the Supreme Court's twin 2003 decisions, *Connecticut Dept. of Public Safety* (*CDPS*) and *Smith* (Chapter 6), conceivable bases exist for challenge. Such claims might arise under federal or state constitutional law, as well as specific statutory provisions.

### Federal Constitutional Relief

The Supreme Court in *CDPS* and *Smith* rejected the two challenges most commonly advanced against registration and notification, relating to procedural due process and ex post facto principles. Because of the complexity of the laws, and their ever-changing nature, however, challenges continue to be mounted.

One area relates to whether the laws violate substantive due process under the Fourteenth Amendment. To date, a handful of such claims have succeeded, with courts deeming the legislative decision to target particular offender subgroups impermissibly arbitrary and irrational.

For instance, in 2004 the Alaska Supreme Court invalidated a state requirement that persons with set-aside convictions must register. The court found that the premise of Alaska's law—that persons convicted of sex offenses pose significant recidivism risk—was not served by the requirement. The "general assumption" of individual risk, the court reasoned, was "fundamentally

inconsistent with the individualized findings of fact a court makes before setting aside a particular offender's conviction."[29] Other courts have invalidated
state laws requiring registration of select subgroups, for instance child kidnappers, when no accompanying sexual offense or motivation was alleged.[30]

A greater number of courts, however, have rejected identical claims with
respect to child kidnappers, showing more characteristic deference to legislative discretion on the reasoning that child kidnappers have a propensity to
sexually assault or otherwise harm their victims.[31] A New York appellate court
shared this view and rejected the contention that the laws' stigmatizing effects were significant. After first concluding that the legislature "is free to use
statutory terms as it sees fit, even in an unexpected way," the court in *People
v. Taylor* stated that "[w]hether in common parlance the defendant is a sex offender, or his offense is a sex offense, is of no legal significance where, as here,
the Legislature has rationally chosen to categorize him or his offense as such.
We are not at liberty to depart from that determination."[32]

Courts have been only somewhat more amenable to second-guess the
rationality of registration and notification more generally. In one important
early case, the New Jersey Supreme Court in *Doe v. Poritz* (1995) found that
public dissemination of registrants' home addresses, along with other centralized identifying information that otherwise remained obscure and inacces-
sible without affirmative effort, implicated a constitutional right to privacy.[33]
This right, however, was outweighed by "a strong state interest in public disclosure" that was "clear and compelling": "The Legislature has determined
that there is a substantial danger of recidivism by sex offenders, and public
notification clearly advances the purpose of protecting the public from that
danger."[34]

More recently the New Mexico Court of Appeals freely acknowledged the
"harsh effects" of notification, and that "work and peaceable life in a community play an important role in our free society, and are generally not to
be burdened with government closely looking over our shoulder and tracing
our every step." Nonetheless, the state's decision to employ a conviction-based
regime was justified:

> The State, without question, has a legitimate and compelling interest in
> protecting the public from sex offenders, and the notification provisions are
> unquestionably rationally related to that goal. We think it proper to defer

to our Legislature's judgment as to a protective course of action in regard to persons convicted of notification-triggering offenses.[35]

In time, such conclusions of rationality may become less sustainable if research shows that registration and notification lack public safety benefit, or indeed are actually counterproductive. The legislative prescription of registration and notification, in turn, might prove less worthy of deference if courts recognize that the purported heightened recidivism rates of sex offenders, the main subpopulation targeted, lack empirical support.

However, both of these possibilities remain remote, because the judiciary will be as likely as the public and political leaders to shun empiricism. In the end, legislative choices, as the Supreme Court has emphasized, "may be based on rational speculation unsupported by evidence or empirical data,"[36] and the countervailing sentiments noted earlier in this chapter will likely justify rationality. And while courts have at times applied a "rational basis with teeth" in assessing laws,[37] current judicial favor of registration and notification, combined with disdain for their targets, give no cause to believe such a standard would afford relief.

Another constitutional question that has thus far evaded definitive resolution by the Supreme Court is whether the laws violate the Fourteenth Amendment's Equal Protection Clause.[38] State and lower federal courts, however, have addressed such claims. All courts have agreed that the ex-offenders targeted by the laws are not members of a suspect class and that the laws therefore warrant only rational basis scrutiny by courts.[39] The claims themselves have assumed several forms.

One type of equal protection claim has involved alleged "overinclusiveness." In such cases, petitioners assert that the laws sweep up individuals who do not pose public safety risk. Showing characteristic deference to legislative discretion with respect to such classifications, however, the courts have uniformly denied relief.

In *Does v. Munoz* (2007), for instance, the Sixth Circuit Court of Appeals—taking a view opposite to the Alaska Supreme Court above—denied a challenge to Michigan's decision to include on its website registry persons convicted of misdemeanors when their convictions had been set aside. The trial court "seriously question[ed]" whether the state's public safety goal was served by including in the registry persons that state court judges had found to pose no future threat, yet upheld the law. Classifications, the trial court stated, are permitted even if "imperfect" and "premised on the legislature's unfounded and irrational fear or belief that all classes of sex offenders must be publicly listed in order to protect citizens of th[e] State."[40] On appeal, the Sixth Circuit unanimously backed the approach, inferring—without apparent factual basis—that when a Michigan court sets aside a conviction

> it knows that the sex offender will continue to be subject to the registration requirements....Therefore, the state court determines that a sex offender does not pose a threat to the public only to the extent that the offender remains on the [public registry]. Furthermore, the state court's determination is not a guarantee that the offender poses no threat.[41]

Likewise, in *Aguirre v. State* (2004) the Texas Court of Appeals addressed whether the state could refuse to allow persons over age 19 convicted of consensual sexual activity with a minor to petition for exemption from lifetime registration yet allow petitions from younger individuals. The court rejected the claim, concluding that it was "plausible" that the two offender groups posed varied recidivism risk.[42]

Claims based on "underinclusiveness" have also regularly met defeat, with courts rejecting challenges based on the decision to exclude nonsexual offenders from registration and notification. As the Sixth Circuit Court of Appeals summarily concluded in rejecting a challenge against Tennessee's law, the State "has established legitimate concerns about law enforcement and public safety with respect to sex offenses. Given the indications that sex offenders pose a particular threat of reoffending, we cannot say that the Act is irrational."[43]

Hybrid claims—based on under- and overinclusiveness—also typically fail. For instance, in perhaps the broadest challenge to date, the Eleventh Circuit Court of Appeals in *Doe v. Moore* (2005) refused to substitute its judgment "on when and where to make" distinctions with respect to registration and notification for that of the Florida Legislature, and rejected challenges to a law that

> (1) subjected sex offenders to lifetime registration yet other felons to only five-year registration terms; (2) required registration of non-parents yet not parents convicted of kidnapping, false imprisonment and luring; (3) exempted persons found not guilty of sex offenses and those civilly committed; (4) subjected those eighteen and younger to only ten-year (not lifetime) registration; and (5) exempted from registration sex offenders who had been released from supervision prior to enactment of the registration law.[44]

In short, like substantive due process claims, equal protection claims have typically foundered on the shoals of judicial deference to legislative prerogative.[45] While the Supreme Court, in a 1985 case involving a challenge brought by mentally disabled individuals, opined that "mere negative attitudes, or fear, unsubstantiated by factors which are properly cognizable . . . are not permissible bases" to justify dissimilar treatment, the animus for ex-offenders—and sex offenders in particular—is such that this sentiment would not likely compel broad constitutional relief.

Finally, some hope exists that courts will be troubled by new or novel incarnations of registration and notification laws. This is perhaps especially so with respect to the increasing harshness of the laws. Notably, in 2006 the Maine Supreme Court signaled its concern over recent state changes, such as requiring that registrants verify their information in person (not required by the Alaska law upheld in *Smith*). While *Doe v. District Attorney* refrained from finding a constitutional violation per se, remanding the case to the trial court for further factual development, the court was concerned that the effects of the new provisions might qualify as punishment for ex post facto purposes, providing a basis to distinguish the Alaska regime condoned in *Smith* and rethink its own rejection of an ex post facto claim only five years earlier.[46] Other challenges to laws modeled on the more onerous requirements of the federal Adam Walsh Act, or initiated by states themselves, might similarly trouble courts.

Potential might also lie in a due process challenge to more unique state registration and notification provisions. As mentioned, courts have found in the wake of *CDPS* that a conviction for a statutorily enumerated offense is both a necessary and sufficient condition for registration and community notification,[47] at least when the government provides a dangerousness disclaimer.[48] Very recently, however, in *State v. Briggs* (2008), the Utah Supreme Court invalidated a conviction-based regime that employed a website disclaimer while also publishing identifying data on registrants and including information on their "primary and secondary targets," indicating for instance that the triggering conviction involved a minor female. The *Briggs* court held that posting registrants' identifying information in general was permissible, but that information on "targets" was "troubling in that it implies that the offender is *presently* focused on repeating past crimes with similar victims."[49] Under such circumstances the disclaimer failed to "effectively dispel the impression that the listed individuals are currently dangerous."[50] Because Briggs had a protectable liberty interest in not being branded currently dangerous (a finding the court unfortunately did not elaborate upon), and Briggs was not afforded a chance to contest the designation at a hearing, Utah's targeting provision violated procedural due process.[51]

Another specific claim could possibly lie in laws triggered without a conviction for an enumerated offense. Permitting registration based on a finding that a conviction for an unenumerated offense is "sexually motivated" (Kansas), was committed with the "purpose of sexual gratification" (California and Washington), or even involved a mere allegation of criminal misconduct (Ohio, of child sexual abuse) is potentially problematic. So, too, is the use of juvenile court adjudications, which trigger eligibility under the federal Adam Walsh Act, and most state laws, despite the fact that juveniles are typically not afforded procedural protections such as a right to trial by jury. Finally, while rare, not guilty by reason of insanity dispositions, which trigger registration in many states, might be said to raise procedural concern unlike that presented in *CDPS*.

The outcome of these cases, however, will again of course depend on the predisposition of courts, which if the Eighth Circuit's decision in *Gunderson v. Hvass* (2003)[52] is representative, bodes ill for registrants. In *Gunderson*, the court rejected a challenge to a Minnesota provision permitting registration (but at the time not notification)[53] based on a judicial conclusion that a defendant was convicted of any offense "arising out of the same set of circumstances" as an offense the legislature specified as warranting registration. The court concluded that Gunderson's substantive due process right to the presumption of innocence was not violated because registration was nonpunitive. In turn, a rational basis existed for the law, given the many "favorable" plea agreements in the system, and the valid governmental interest in having comprehensive registries. Likewise, Gunderson's lacked a right to procedural due process because the impact of registration was "minimal."[54]

More recently, in 2007, the Arkansas Supreme Court rejected a procedural due process claim brought by an insanity acquittee.[55] According to the court, requiring the defendant to register and labeling him a Tier III offender pursuant to a risk-classification proceeding was justified because his insanity acquittal was not tantamount to a failure of proof; the defendant admitted committing the act, and only successfully persuaded the justice system that his impaired mental state rendered him unworthy of punishment. Furthermore, substantive due process was not violated because the government's action was rationally related to its nonpunitive purpose of safeguarding Arkansas citizens.

Of course, one cannot reliably predict whether future federal constitutional challenges will prove any more successful than those mounted to date. As registration and notification laws continue to expand and grow more onerous, litigation will surely continue, and quite possibly succeed in some instances. However, given *CDPS* and *Smith* and the judiciary's ongoing marked unreceptivity to federal challenges more generally, broad-based success seems unlikely.

### State Constitutional Relief

Another basis for challenge possibly lies in state constitutional law. State constitutions—"a font of individual liberties," as Justice William Brennan once referred to them—can and often do provide more and different civil liberty protections to their citizens than that "required by the Supreme Court's interpretation of federal law."[56] Indeed, state constitutions often afford specific rights absent from the U.S. Constitution, such as expressly ensuring protection of "reputation"[57] and "privacy,"[58] or otherwise contain sweeping provisions that admit of broad interpretation.[59] This richness derives as much from the individual historical identities of states and their constitutions (which often predate the U.S. Bill of Rights), as from the animating ideal of U.S. federalism itself. Indeed, for a significant part of the nation's history, the Bill of Rights did not apply to the states, resulting in state courts being the primary guarantors of individual rights.[60]

Consistent with this perspective, a handful of state courts have invoked their state constitutions to find fault with registration and community notification laws enacted by their legislatures.[61] This has been especially evident with respect to whether registration and notification must be preconditioned on procedural due process. For instance, the New Jersey Supreme Court interpreted its state constitution to find that notification implicated a protectable liberty interest in reputation, irrespective of whether any other interest was adversely affected (such as the "plus" in the federal stigma-plus due process test, noted in Chapter 6), warranting procedural due process protection.[62] In 1997, the Massachusetts Supreme Judicial Court found a protectable liberty interest under the Commonwealth's Declaration of Rights, requiring that due process be afforded before registration and community notification, "without regard to whether such a person has an independent federally protected liberty or property interest."[63] In 2001, the Hawaii Supreme Court similarly held that notification implicates a protectable liberty interest,[64] and in 2004 concluded that lifetime registration did so as well, distinguishing *CDPS* by noting that Hawaii's Constitution "provided broader due process rights."[65]

State courts have also been willing to consider whether registration and notification qualify as punishment through the lens of their indigenous ex post facto prohibitions. In July 2008, the Alaska Supreme Court invoked the dissenting views expressed in *Smith* to conclude that the State's amended law constituted impermissible retroactive punishment under Alaska's Ex Post Facto Clause.[66]

Prospects for success on this front, however, must be tempered by the reality that state constitutional rights are typically interpreted in line with federal norms. Most often state courts interpret their similarly worded state constitutional provisions in "lockstep" with the way federal courts—including, of course, the U.S. Supreme Court—interpret kindred federal constitutional provisions.[67] This reticence also manifests in state judicial reluctance to broadly interpret rights expressly provided for in state constitutions (providing an express right to "privacy," for example), yet absent from the U.S. Constitution, a realm in which state courts enjoy free interpretative rein.[68]

## EXPANSION

Thus far discussion has focused on the prospects for legislative and judicial limits on registration and notification as it has come to be mainly known, affecting those convicted of child and sex offenses. Yet no discussion of the likely future of the laws would be complete without consideration of the prospects for future expansion to other subpopulations.

Evidence in favor of this evolution is already found in the increasing popularity of stand-alone registries (Chapter 3). These registries differ in important ways from those targeting child and sex offenders. Most obvious, the latter inspire unique fear and disdain, suggesting that the social, psychic, and other burdens experienced by other offender subpopulations (even murderers) would be diminished. Moreover, given the contrasting social circumstances under which the offenses occur (perhaps typically involving nonacquaintance victims, for example), the entire analytic framework arguably differs. Finally, stand-alone registries usually have less onerous requirements than child and sex offender registries and thus far often have not been coupled with community notification, which is of critical importance.

Nonetheless, stand-alone registries will very likely continue to grow in scope and number, for much the same reasons that sex and child offender registries have, and in time regularly include trappings such as community notification. Whether targeting persons convicted of drug crimes, arson, domestic abuse, homicide, or any of the numerous other crimes now befitting registries, as well as others certain to arise, they will prove politically popular. These other subgroups, as well, have criminal histories that justify ongoing government-imposed burdens and public disclosure of their identities and whereabouts. Indeed, to the extent that other offenders are recognized as having comparably higher rates of recidivism, one can expect even more interest in subjecting them to registration and notification. To an unforgiving public that feels a moral entitlement to information, such registries, like those relating to child and sex offenders, are "costless."

Looming on the horizon, however, is the intriguing issue of whether registration and notification will expand beyond convicted criminal offenders. Already, in Ohio persons found only by a preponderance of the evidence (a civil standard) to have engaged in child abuse (Chapter 3) are subject to registration and notification. If we are to take the judiciary at its word, registries are merely benign regulatory efforts that assemble and make available already public information. If so, there might be no objection to disseminating such information on a broader (nonconvict) swath of the population. Such an expansion, however, would not be "costless"—either to legislators or to their constituents.[69] Indeed, an incident recently occurred that calls into question the verity of the "just information" rationale so often used to justify the laws.

The incident occurred in Roanoke, Virginia, where as part of "Sunshine Week," celebrating the "public's right to know," a local newspaper published an Internet link to a Virginia database containing the names and addresses of persons lawfully permitted to carry a concealed weapon. A supporting editorial appearing in the newspaper asserted:

> A state that eagerly puts sex offender data online complete with an interactive map could easily do the same with gun permits, but it does not ... As a Sunshine Week gift, the *Roanoke Times* has placed the entire database, mistakes and all,

online . . . You can search to find out if neighbors, carpool partners, elected officials or anyone else has permission to carry a gun.

In the wake of the gun registry's publication, after the newspaper was deluged by irate complaints, and the editorialist received numerous threats and had his own home address listed online, the newspaper quickly removed the registry link.[70]

The uproar inspired in Virginia was not unprecedented. Previously, websites disclosing names and addresses of police officers[71] and police informants,[72] also posting assembled publicly available information, triggered vociferous resistance. Similarly, physicians providing abortions have successfully sued to enjoin posting of their names, photos, and addresses—all "public" information—by antiabortion activists.[73]

Such an adverse reaction is entirely understandable. Persons holding lawful gun permits, for example, are not enamored of being publicly exposed, with the attendant risk of violence or harassment.[74] However, the Virginia gun registry episode and others like it highlight the speciousness of the "just information" premise. No one, including lawful gun permit holders and criminal convicts, favors being singled out for public attention, let alone being branded a "predator." Disclosure of even neutral, publicly obtainable information does indeed come at a "cost," and when the gamut of those bearing the cost is expanded to include noncriminal populations, protests will likely occur and prevail.

However, it is worthwhile to keep in mind that identification technologies, including registration and notification, have shown a powerful capacity to expand their reach. Government efforts to achieve universal fingerprinting, as discussed earlier, foundered for decades, yet fingerprinting today figures centrally in the modern administrative state. The evolution of DNA technology shows signs of following a similar course. While initially targeting only convicted sex offenders, DNA samples soon were taken from other criminal subpopulations, and today all kinds of felons and many misdemeanants must provide DNA. Predictably, of late efforts have been undertaken to require DNA samples of arrestees (not merely convicted persons). In the face of this evolution, two commentators recently advocated that samples be taken of the entire population, noting that "[a] DNA database cannot deter or lead to apprehension before a profile is included in the database," and that in principle, "it is not at all clear why the obligation to provide personally identifying information should be restricted to those swept into the criminal justice system."[75]

While to date universal registration of the nonconvict population has been resisted, the foregoing precedents give greater hope than ever before that it will take root. After all, much of our identifying information is "public" and susceptible to collection. Indeed, it is far less "personal" than fingerprints and genetic samples. The government merely needs to assemble the data, which it can do quite cheaply,[76] and in doing so, it can be asserted, public safety can be enhanced vis-à-vis the entire population. Just as many Americans condoned post-9/11 data mining and surveillance efforts by the U.S. government with the view that "I've got nothing to hide,"[77] the public's privacy-security value calculus provides a fertile environment for broader future use of registration and notification.

Finally, the future of registration and notification, whether or not extended to other populations, must be conceived in conjunction with the ever-growing popularity of similar "techno-correction" strategies. Of particular note, the increasing use of global positioning systems, which permit continuous, real-time depictions of individuals' locations has obvious complementary social control benefits.[78] Not only will website registries be able to provide information on where registrants live and work, as they do today, but they will also be able to provide real-time location information.[79] The future might also hold complementary use of subdermal implants ("chips") that use radio frequencies to identify and ascertain the location of registrants, a strategy already advocated by state legislators.[80]

## AMERICAN EXCEPTIONALISM

Before concluding, mention must be made of how exceptional the nation's modern embrace of registration and community notification has been. American exceptionalism, of course, is well-known today, certainly relative to criminal justice matters, with the nation's resort to the death penalty coming immediately to mind. Registration and notification provide another compelling example.

While registration has enjoyed some acceptance internationally, American-style community notification has not. Notably, each of the other nations with national sex offender registration systems—including Australia, Canada, France, Ireland, Japan, and the United Kingdom—have not wholeheartedly embraced notification. The experience of the United Kingdom, which shares many legal and cultural traditions with the United States, highlights this distinctiveness.

The UK's sex offender registry, which is nonretroactive in scope, originated in 1997, and eschewed notification from the outset. A major campaign to adopt broad notification occurred in July 2000, however, when the kidnapping, sexual assault, and murder of 8-year-old Sarah Payne prompted *News of the World*, a British tabloid, to initiate a sustained "name and shame" campaign intended to change government policy. The campaign, which lasted several weeks and published the photos and names of convicted sex offenders (how the information was obtained remains unknown), resulted in numerous acts of vigilantism.[81] For several years thereafter, the government considered general notification, but in April 2007 rejected the policy, citing U.S. experience with vigilantism and concern that disclosure would drive registrants underground. In lieu thereof, the government focused on sexual abuse of children in the home, for instance by expanding the access of select individuals such as care providers to registry information.[82]

Today, other than the United States, only South Korea and a handful of Canadian provinces[83] permit notification of some kind. In both latter contexts, however, disclosure is quite limited compared to the United States. For instance, since 2000 Korea has disclosed the identities of individuals convicted of a few specified child sex offenses (in September 2002, numbering only 671 individuals).[84] Eligible individuals remain registered for a period of five years, and their identifying information remains posted on a government website for six months and on government bulletin boards for one month.[85] While Korean law initially made registry information available only to victims, their parents, and youth-related educational institutions, and residence information reflected only a general geographic area (the equivalent of U.S. counties), since 2006 the public at large has had access to address-specific registrant information by means of the website and bulletin boards for the limited periods specified above.[86]

## CONCLUSION

The goal here, in this last chapter, has been to provide a sense of where registration and notification laws might he headed. For students of law, social control, and politics in particular, the future promises to be highly interesting. As the laws continue to evolve and mature, they will, as they have over the past two decades, both reflect and influence changes in American society. Whether the next twenty years of this history is as active and transformative as the past twenty years, of course, remains to be seen. What one can be confident of, however, is that registration and notification, in some form and to some extent, will endure. The need to know about others in an ever more anonymous society, and the felt sense of power that attends such knowledge, is such that the future cannot be otherwise.

# CONCLUSION

THE DISCUSSION HERE BEGAN by noting the enduring psychic anxiety bred by social anonymity, a condition evinced in philosopher Jeremy Bentham's plaintive plea in 1843: "Who are you, with whom I have to deal?"[1] Over time, as societies became ever more mobile and populous, this anxiety only increased, especially relative to criminal offenders. Criminal registration, among other technologies, emerged as a means to allay concern over individual criminal risk. However, registration afforded important advantages over technologies such as anthropometry and fingerprint analysis, which, while having similar comparative superior data management features, merely served as static repositories of information. With registration, government, by compelling information from registrants themselves, could at once monitor individuals and instill in them a sense of being watched.

The story of American use of registration is one of fits and starts. While antebellum governments required African American freedmen to register, and registration was employed with other select subgroups in the early twentieth century (such as German Americans amid World War I), registration did not really catch on until the 1930s. Then, local governments, concerned about an influx of itinerant "gangsters," gravitated to registration, and in ensuing years states as well created registries. Overall, however, use of registration was uneven and sporadic, and the laws fell into disuse. This disinterest quickly vanished in the 1990s, however, when the nation became transfixed by the appeal of registering criminals—child kidnappers and sex offenders in particular. As a result of funding pressure from the federal government starting in 1994, registration laws were soon enacted nationwide, creating an interconnected registry of unprecedented complexity and scope, today containing information on over 600,000 individuals. Moreover, recently states have targeted other criminal subpopulations with registration, highlighting its flexibility and appeal.

Yet this dramatic change is only part of the story. Since the 1990s, American registration laws have been complemented by community notification. No longer is registry information monopolized by police; rather, it is provided to community members as well, who are expected to use it to protect themselves and others from recidivist predation. With the advent of Internet website registries, the capacity for such disclosures has expanded exponentially. While the nation has belatedly embraced registration—compared to nineteenth-century Europe, where the technique enjoyed use—when it did, it did so with notable zeal and entirely transformed the practice by empowering not only police with registry information, but communities and the world at large as well.

Whether modern-era laws actually achieve their avowed public safety goals, or actually make communities less safe, remains unclear. What is clear, however, is that registration and community notification have already had major influence on American society. Although born of a "panic" in the early 1990s, the laws have become entrenched and institutionalized. Panic, as sociologist Stanley Cohen once observed, can have residual effects, serving to change "the way [a] society conceives itself."[2] This is manifestly the case with registration and notification.

For the first time, American governments have assembled and publicly disseminated identifying information on ex-offenders, compelling their ongoing surveillance, under threat of punishment, very possibly for their lifetimes. In the past, in the shadow of revelations of similar tactics by totalitarian governments, even limited use of registration alone was condemned as "un-American" and contrary to the precept that ex-offenders deserve a "second chance." Over the course of a few decades, however, this resistance has disappeared, highlighting the nation's increasingly unforgiving sensibility and anxiety over criminal offenders.

Likewise, while the "psychic effect" of providing registry information only to police before provoked significant concern, today broad dissemination of much more detailed information is considered a matter of public entitlement. To proponents, registry data is "just information," gathered from otherwise disparate publicly available sources; in truth, however, the information is highly stigmatizing and intrusive and is backed by pejorative labels such as "predator," concerning individuals, the vast majority of whom are law-abiding. American society and the judiciary, however, have remained unperturbed, with important ramifications for the nation's legal traditions and understandings of informational privacy.

At the same time, registration and notification have transformed methods of governance, in two major respects. Today, no longer is public safety regarded solely as a governmental function and responsibility. With the nationwide advent of registration and notification, government has become an information broker and ceded responsibility for public protection against potential recidivists to communities themselves. In the process, traditional relations have been recast between governments and those they govern, especially those subject to registration. For registrants, the deprivation of physical liberty associated with prison or jail is only the initial—and very often the least personally significant—consequence flowing from a criminal conviction. Registration and notification impose long-term (perhaps lifetime) requirements, limits, and burdens, designed to ensure continued surveillance by ex-offenders' fellow community members and government.

Second, the recent political history of registration and notification has had major impact on the historic relationship between states and the federal government. By threatening states with loss of allocated funds, Congress and the president have recast registration and notification in accord with federal preferences, giving rise to an unprecedented nationwide criminal justice policy and national police apparatus. As a consequence, state-federal relations have been remolded, and long-held values regarding the benefits of federalism have been discounted.

The account provided here is of necessity incomplete, as registration and community notification continue to rapidly evolve. While data storage and access capabilities have improved dramatically over the decades, the core difficulty, dating back to nascent registration efforts in the eighteenth and nineteenth centuries, remains: the need to rely on criminally recalcitrant individuals to affirmatively provide information for use in their ongoing community control and stigmatization. The deficiencies resulting from this Achilles' heel played a significant role in registration's resulting dormancy through the late 1980s.

Registration, however, never died; it sprang forth anew Phoenix-like in the 1990s, complemented by community notification, enjoying nationwide use by the decade's end. For reasons discussed, there is every reason to expect that interest in registration and notification laws will remain robust in coming years, spreading as they have already, to other subpopulations. Moreover, as other information-based social control technologies such as global positioning systems and even subdermal "chipping" develop, we should expect synergies, with registration and notification affording both an administrative infrastructure and receptive sensibility necessary for the occurrence.

It remains to be seen whether American-style registration and community notification will catch on elsewhere. To date, registration has been adopted in only a few other nations, in comparatively limited form, and broad community notification has been resisted. Yet anxiety over and disdain for criminal offenders, including but certainly not exclusively sex and child offenders, will not likely diminish any time soon. Nor will we likely see diminution in what has been termed the global, post-9/11 "new terrorized political culture,"[3] such as manifest in proposals in the United Kingdom for a "terrorist registry."[4] As the world becomes increasingly borderless and fearful, in short, circumstances will remain ripe for more widespread adoption of registration and community notification. Only time will tell whether America's unique approach to registration and notification will become yet another of the nation's exports to the world at large.

# NOTES

## Introduction

1. Jeremy Bentham, "Principles of Penal Law," in *Works of Jeremy Bentham*, vol. 1, ed. John Bowring (Edinburgh: William Tait, 1843), 557.

2. Michel Foucault, *Discipline and Punish: The Birth of the Prison*, trans. Alan Sheridan (London: Penguin Books, 1977), 185.

3. Cass R. Sunstein, *Laws of Fear: Beyond the Precautionary Principle* (New York: Cambridge University Press, 2005), 208.

## Chapter 1

1. See Mauri Nieminen, "250 Years of Population Statistics in Finland," Statistics Finland, Population Statistics, http://stat.fi/isi99/proceedings/arkisto/varasto/niem1020.pdf (Finland); Peter Skold, "The Birth of Population Statistics in Sweden," *History of the Family* 9 (2004): 7–9 (Sweden).

2. Ian Hacking, *The Taming of Chance: Ideas in Context* (Cambridge: Cambridge University Press, 1990), 18.

3. James Scott, *Seeing Like a State: How Certain Schemes to Improve the Human Condition Have Failed* (New Haven, CT: Yale University Press, 1998), 65.

4. Hacking, *Taming of Chance*, 18.

5. Ibid., 105.

6. Ibid.

7. Ibid.

8. Valentin Groebner, "Describing the Person, Reading the Signs in Late Medieval and Renaissance Europe: Identity Papers, Vested Figures, and the Limits of Identification, 1400–1600," in *Documenting Individual Identity: The Development of State Prac-*

*tices in the Modern World*, ed. Jane Caplan and John Torpey (Princeton, NJ: Princeton University Press, 2001), 25–26.

9. Leon Radzinowicz, *A History of English Criminal Law and Its Administration from 1750*, vol. 8 (London: Stevens and Sons, 1956), 46–47. Shortly thereafter, coordination and communication was enhanced by a Police Gazette, disseminated throughout the country on a quarterly and weekly basis, which contained information on offenders at large and their crimes. Ibid., 47–54.

10. Simon A. Cole, *Suspect Identities: A History of Fingerprinting and Criminal Identification* (Cambridge, MA: Harvard University Press, 2001), 15.

11. John Pratt, *Governing the Dangerous: Dangerousness, the Law and Social Change* (Annandale, Australia: Federation Press, 1997), 13, 17. For an overview of the increasing interest in criminal statistics during this era, including in the United States, see Scott Decker, "The Evolution of Crime Statistics as a Police Problem," *Journal of Police Science & Administration* 6 (1978): 67.

12. See Note, "Selective Incapacitation: Reducing Crime Through Predictions of Recidivism," *Harvard Law Review* 96 (1982): 511.

13. See Pamela Sankar, "State Power and Record-Keeping: The History of Individualized Surveillance in the United States, 1790–1935" (PhD diss., University of Pennsylvania, 1992).

14. Ibid., 84.

15. Ibid., 85

16. Ibid., 86.

17. Ibid., 103–5.

18. Michael Ignatieff, "State, Civil Society and Total Institutions: A Critique of Recent Social Histories of Punishment," in *Social Control of the State: Historical and Comparative Essays*, ed. Stanley Cohen and Martin Scull (Oxford: Martin Robertson, 1983), 87.

19. Gustave de Beaumont and Alexis de Tocqueville, *The Penitentiary System in the United States and Its Application in France* (Carbondale: Southern Illinois University Press, 1964), 101. Tocqueville's observation no doubt stemmed in significant part from the vast differences between the highly migratory U.S. population and the sedentary French population, as well as the fact that French prisoners were required to return to their village of origin until allowed by police to relocate. Ibid., 131.

20. As Peter Spierenburg has observed, "branding was a preindustrial method for identifying recidivists." Peter Spierenburg, "The Body and the State: Early Modern Europe," in *Oxford History of the Prison: The Practice of Punishment in Western Society*, ed. Norval Morris and David J. Rothman (New York: Oxford University Press, 1998), 48.

21. On this transformation of U.S. policing, especially in the nation's urban areas, see Lawrence W. Friedman, *Crime and Punishment in American History* (New York:

Basic Books, 1993), 27–30, 66–68; Kermit Hall, *The Magic Mirror: Law in American History* (New York: Oxford University Press, 1989), 578–90.

22. Peter Becker, "The Standardized Gaze: The Standardization of the Search Warrant in Nineteenth-Century Germany," in Caplan and Torpey, *Documenting Individual Identity*, 155.

23. Ibid., 145.

24. Sankar, *State Power*, 139–40.

25. Previously, in 1819, Germany and France experimented with more primitive technologies: in Germany, portraits, and in France, use of the "physionotrace," a device that permitted a person's bodily shadow to be projected onto paper in silhouette form when the person was placed between the device and a light. Becker, "Standardized Gaze," in Caplan and Torpey, *Documenting Individual Identity*, 154–56. Portraits, however, had the drawback of reflecting the subjective interpretative impression of the artist and required a talented artist to be available. Silhouettes, while more mechanical and not dependent on artisan skill, lacked sufficient detail to permit identification. Ibid., 156.

26. Cole, *Suspect Identities*, 20.

27. Donald Dilworth, ed., *Identification Wanted: Development of the American Criminal Identification System, 1893–1943* (Gaithersburg, MD: International Association of Chiefs of Police, 1977), 71; Howard O. Sprogle, *The Philadelphia Police: Past and Present* (Philadelphia, 1887), 117–18, 275.

28. Photos, of course, then as now remained a staple in the police armature. In 1936, for instance, concerned that an influx of anonymous criminals might prey on visitors to the Democratic Party Convention, Philadelphia police amassed photographs of some ten thousand pickpockets, hotel thieves, swindlers, and ex-convicts, along with their Bertillon measurements, and shared information on the "undesirables" with hotel detectives and floor managers. "Philadelphia Dons Convention Dress," *New York Times*, June 19, 1936; "Photos of 10,000 Crooks Gathered for Convention," *New York Times*, June 17, 1936.

29. *Twenty-Fourth Annual Report of the Executive Committee of the Prison Association of New York and Accompanying Documents for 1868* (Albany, NY: The Argus Co., 1869), 546, 551.

30. Ibid., 553.

31. Ibid.

32. M. Bonneville de Marsangy, "Criminal Registers Considered as a Means of Knowing the Antecedents (Criminal Biography) of Persons Charged with Crime or Trespass," in *Transactions of the National Congress on Penitentiary and Reformatory Discipline*, ed. E. C. Wines (Albany, NY: The Argus Co., 1871), 239–40.

33. Raymond D. Fosdick, *European Police Systems* (New York: The Century Co., 1915), 354–55.

34. Ibid., 353. The address information was accessible to members of the public for a small fee, but criminal records were "closely guarded." Ibid., 353, 355*n*1.

35. Ibid., 353–54.

36. Ibid., 356.

37. Ibid., 357–58.

38. Mathieu Deflem, "Surveillance and Criminal Statistics," in *Studies in Law, Politics and Society*, vol. 17, ed. Austin Sarat and Patricia Ewick (Greenwich, CT: JAI Press, 1997), 149, 161.

39. Fosdick, *European Police Systems*, 358.

40. Ibid., 358–59. Fosdick also noted that the system was of no utility with respect to "unknown criminals" or those known only by description, and of little utility with foreign criminals or Germans with criminal records in foreign states. "Its chief utility centers around the advantage which it affords the police of knowing where each citizen in a community can be found and what his past history has been." Ibid., 360.

41. Leon Radzinowicz and Roger Hood, "Incapacitating the Habitual Criminal: The English Experience," *Michigan Law Review* 78 (1980): 1308. As in the United States, discussed later in the context of its own criminal registration laws, the statistical data supporting this perceived fear of criminal engulfment were lacking in merit, later to be deemed inflated and unreliable. Ibid., 1309–13.

42. Ibid., 1336–38.

43. Ibid., 1341.

44. Ibid., 1342–43. During 1869–70, for instance, 35,633 individuals were registered and similar proportions were added annually thereafter. Ibid. 1347. According to one account, however, in 1870 there had not been a single police inquiry of the main registry from major cities such as Liverpool, Manchester, Birmingham, or Bristol. Ibid., 1348. By 1875, 150,000 persons were on the national registry, but only 1,000 identifications had been made. Leon Radzinowicz and Roger Hood, *A History of English Criminal Law and Its Administration from 1750*, vol. 5 (London: Stevens and Sons, 1986), 262. According to Metropolitan Police, however, 373 instances of detection occurred as a result of identification of photos registered in the Habitual Criminals Office. Radzinowicz and Hood, "Incapacitating the Habitual Criminal," 1348*n*94.

45. Ibid., 1345–46.

46. Ibid., 1347 (quoting 1896 newspaper report of quote attributed to Frazer).

47. Ibid., 1348.

48. Ibid., 1349.

49. Havelock Ellis, *The Criminal* (London: Walter Scott, 1895), 23.

50. In addition, at the time the Convict Supervision Office at Scotland Yard maintained records on ex-convicts, including photographs, a register of tattoos, and an index of modus operandi. Radzinowicz and Hood, *Criminal Law*, vol. 5, 261.

51. Ibid.

52. Anand A. Yang, "Dangerous Castes and Tribes: The Criminal Tribes Act and the Magahiya Doms of Northeast India," in *Crime and Criminality in British India*, ed. Anand A. Yang (Tucson: University of Arizona Press, 1985), 109.

53. Bengal authorities included in their list of potential groups: *Sunnyassees*, "religious mendicants who wander about the country . . . live by begging, cheating, and pilfering"; *Nutts*, "professional jugglers of gipsy habits, and sometimes given to pilfering"; *Rajwars*, "thievish, neglected, half-starved, and utterly degraded set of beings"; *Banjors*, "workers in bamboo . . . cheats and thieves"; and *Sowakhyas or Kowakyas*, "gipsy origin . . . snare and eat crow." Ibid., 113–14.

54. Ibid., 109–10. While groups had no judicial recourse to their designation, individuals had the right to lodge a protest. Ibid., 109. The Act remained in force until 1952. Ibid., 110.

55. Sankar, *State Power*, 145–46.

56. Ibid., 153–54; Cole, *Suspect Identities*, 54.

57. Sankar, *State Power*, 154.

58. Ibid., 155.

59. Alphonse Bertillon, *Instructions for Taking Descriptives for the Identification of Criminals and Others by the Means of Anthropometric Indications*, trans. Gallus Muller (New York: AMS Press, 1977).

60. Cole, *Suspect Identities*, 37.

61. Ibid., 45.

62. Martha Merrill Umphrey, "'The Sun Has Been Too Quick for Them': Criminal Portraiture and the Police in the Late Nineteenth Century," *Studies of Law, Politics, & Society* 16 (1997): 139.

63. Charles Colbert, *A Measure of Perfection: Phrenology and the Fine Arts in America* (Chapel Hill: University of North Carolina Press, 1997); John Davies, *Phrenology: Fad and Science—A 19th Century American Crusade* (New Haven, CT: Yale University Press, 1955).

64. For more on this receptivity, and the reasons for it, see Nicole Hahn Rafter, "Criminal Anthropology: Its Reception in the United States and the Nature of Its Appeal," in *Criminals and Their Scientists: The History of Criminology in International Perspective*, ed. Peter Becker and Richard F. Wetzell (New York: Cambridge University Press, 2006), 159–81. The intricate bodily measurements of Bertillonism fit nicely with contemporary efforts by criminal anthropologists, most notably Italian Cesare Lombroso, who sought to chronicle the physical manifestations of criminality, recording skull size and shapes, tattoos, and the like. For his part, however, Bertillon was leery of using anthropometry for any purpose other than subsequently identifying persons previously convicted of crimes. Cole, *Suspect Identities*, 58.

65. Sankar, *State Power*, 196–97.

66. Ibid., 197.

67. "Prison Reform—V: The Incorrigible Criminal," *Ft. Wayne News* (Indiana), December 30, 1896.

68. "Prison Reform—VI: Criminal Registration," *Ft. Wayne News* (Indiana), January 6, 1897.

69. Dilworth, *Identification Wanted*, 28–29.

70. R. W. McClaughry, "Introduction," in Alphonse Bertillon, *Signaletic Instructions, Including the Theory and Practice of Anthropometrical Identification*, ed. R. W. McClaughry (Chicago: Werner Co., 1896).

71. Cole, *Suspect Identities*, 147–49.

72. Sankar, *State Power*, 199.

73. Ibid., 199.

74. Ibid., 201.

75. Ibid., 202.

76. Ibid., 203–4.

77. Ibid., 205–6.

78. Ibid., 207.

79. Cole, *Suspect Identities*, 65, 73. Herschel used "sign-manuals" to identify prisoners, while Faulds suggested in a letter in the journal *Nature* that "finger-marks" might be used to identify criminal suspects. Simon Cole notes that use of prints might be said to have originated even earlier, in the United States, as the result of the investigative work of Albany, New York, detective John Malloy, in the late 1850s. Ibid., 120. He also notes that Thomas Taylor, a scientist who founded the division of microscopy at the U.S. Department of Agriculture, encouraged use of palm and finger marks as a means to identify criminal suspects during a lecture in 1877, but his suggestion was not followed up on. Ibid., 120–21. Another history places Herschel's discovery at an even earlier date—July 1858, when serving as chief magistrate in Jungipoor, India, he took the palm and fingerprints of local merchants to enhance the enforceability of contracts. See Michael Harling, *Origins of the New York State Bureau of Investigation* (Albany: New York State Division of Criminal Justice Services, 1996).

80. Faulds, the British surgeon-superintendent at a hospital in Tokyo, began a study of "skin-furrows" after noticing finger marks on ancient pottery. He forwarded his system of classification system and a sample of his forms for recording impressions to Charles Darwin, who passed the material on to his cousin Sir Francis Galton. Harling, *Origins*.

81. Cole, *Suspect Identities*, 137–38.

82. A prime reason for the appeal of fingerprinting stemmed from the work of Briton E. R. Henry, who built upon Galton's research and in 1900 published his seminal *Classification and Uses of Fingerprints*, which advanced a standardized order for the taking and storage of prints. Sankar, *State Power*, 225–26.

83. Cole, *Suspect Identities*, 152.

84. Sankar, *State Power*, 213–14.

85. According to Simon Cole, the widespread adoption of fingerprinting was gradual and not due alone to the commonly recounted 1903 saga of Will West, which Cole debunks as apocryphal. According to the story, West, an African American man newly imprisoned at the U.S. penitentiary at Leavenworth, Kansas, was, based on his anthropometric measurements, mistaken for a William West, already imprisoned at the facility. According to lore, fingerprints of the two men revealed their distinct identities. Cole highlights a variety of factual and logical inconsistencies in the story, attributing its emergence and durability to the later success of federal authorities in creating "a tidy, appealing creation story for what was by then [the 1930s] the FBI's prized, unrivaled identification technique"—fingerprints. Cole, *Suspect Identities*, 143. See also David L. Grieve, "The Identification Process: Traditions in Training," *Journal of Forensic Identification* 40 (1990): 195 (providing a similar debunking of the Will West scenario). A similar confabulation stirred concern in England, in 1897, with the wrongful identification and imprisonment of Adolph Beck, who was exonerated because he, unlike the individual with whom he was confused, was not circumcised. Radzinowicz and Hood, *Criminal Law*, vol. 5, 765–66.

86. Cole, *Suspect Identities*, 165.

87. Ibid., 52.

88. "Federal Crime Registry Results in 236 Arrests," *Los Angeles Times*, September 12, 1932. By mid-1956, the FBI had well over 142 million fingerprints on file. Don White-head, *The FBI Story: A Report to the People* (New York: Random House, 1956), 139.

89. Sankar, *State Power*, 262.

90. Ibid., 264.

91. Ibid., 262.

92. Cole, *Suspect Identities*, 135. For other early references, see *New York Times*, October 25, 1913; *Journal of Criminal Law & Criminology* 4, no. 3 (September 1913).

93. Simon A. Cole, "Lessons from the Past for the Genetic Future," *Brooklyn Law Review* 67 (2001): 109.

94. See, e.g., J. Edgar Hoover, "Fingerprinting School Children," *School Life* 21 (1935): 2.

95. Dilworth, *Identification Wanted*, 215. Amnesia was of apparently grave concern during the era; according to a newspaper report, "modern speed of living is result-ing in increase of amnesia—loss of memory." Ibid., 218. In 1937, FBI Director Hoover evinced a similar understanding of the plight, noting that with a "professor or a doc-tor" it might be that "excessive work and mental strain" could trigger an amnesia attack and prompt such a person to "wander away." J. Edgar Hoover, "Fingerprint Everybody? Yes," *The Rotarian*, January 1937, 17.

96. United News, "May Check Crime by Registrations," *Dallas Morning News*, January 3, 1921.

97. Jon Agar, "Modern Horrors: British Identity and Identity Cards," in Caplan and Torpey, *Documenting Individual Identity*, 104. Later, Britain enacted the Prevention of Violence (Temporary Provisions) Act of 1939, which targeted the Irish Republican Army for registration. Under the act, if the secretary of state was "reasonably satisfied" that an individual was involved in the preparation or instigation of acts of violence or was harboring such a person, the individual was required to provide personal identifying information to police, to be photographed and measured, and to report to police regularly. *Prevention of Violence (Temporary Provisions) Act*, 1939, c. 50, § 1(3); see also Clive Walker, *The Prevention of Terrorism in British Law*, 2nd ed. (Manchester, NY: Manchester University Press, 1992), 31–46.

98. See, e.g., *Bulletin of the Pan American Union* 75 (1941): 374; John White, "Indexed Fingers," *The Inter-American* 2, December 1943, 27; Robert Kempner, "The German National Registration System as Means of Police Control of Population," *Journal of Criminal Law & Criminology* 36 (1946): 362.

99. "Forced Registration of All in Nation Urged in State Chamber Report to Curb Crime," *New York Times*, January 1934.

100. Current Note, "Universal Registration," *Journal of Criminal Law & Criminology* 25 (1934–35): 650–51.

101. Dilworth, *Identification Wanted*, 215.

102. Ibid., 218.

103. Hoover, "Fingerprint Everybody?" 16.

104. E.R.A. Seligman and A. Johnson, eds., *Encyclopedia of the Social Sciences* (New York: The Macmillan Company, 1932).

105. Dilworth, *Identification Wanted*, 223.

106. Ibid., 110.

107. Maxwell Lehman, *Thumbs Down! The Fingerprint Menace to Civil Liberties* (New York: American Civil Liberties Union), 12–19. The *New Republic* shared this view, referring derisively in an editorial to the "Berkeley fingerprinting jamboree," and calling the various arguments advanced in support "specious." "Fingerprints of Fascism," *New Republic*, June 10, 1936, 118.

108. Dilworth, *Identification Wanted*, 228.

109. Cole, *Suspect Identities*, 247.

110. Athan Theoharis et al., *The FBI: A Comprehensive Reference Guide* (Phoenix, AZ: Oryx Press, 1999), 221.

111. Federal Alien Registration Act of 1940; *Fiswick v. United States*, 329 U.S. 211 (1946); *Hines v. Davidowitz*, 312 U.S. 52 (1941).

112. Cole, *Suspect Identities*, 247.

113. See *The Subversive Activities Control Act of 1950*, 50 U.S.C. § 786 (1964). For a survey of Communist registration laws, enacted both federally and by the states dur-

ing the late 1940–early 1950s, see Robert J. Goldstein, *Political Repression in America: From 1870 to the Present* (Boston: G.K. Hall, 1978), 285–396.

114. See 26 U.S.C. § 4412; *Marchetti v. United States*, 390 U.S. 39 (1968) (invalidating conviction for failing to register as violative of privilege against compelled self-incrimination).

115. Acts of Tennessee, 1806, chap. 32, § 1. See also Edgar F. Love et al., "Registration of Free Blacks in Ohio: The Slaves of George C. Mendenhall," *Journal of Negro History* 69 (1984): 38 (surveying use of freedman registration laws in Ohio as part of a broader effort to discourage emigration into the state, which "exhibited an intense and persistent hostility toward the presence of free blacks within its borders").

116. See, e.g., *City of Manchester v. Leiby*, 117 F.2d 661 (1st Cir.), cert. denied, 313 U.S. 562 (1941).

117. See, e.g., *Walton v. City of Atlanta*, 181 F.3d 693 (5th Cir. 1950).

118. See, e.g., *Itzkowitz & Sons, Inc. v. Geraghty*, 247 N.Y.S. 703 (N.Y. Sup. Ct. 1931).

119. See, e.g., *Norman v. Las Vegas*, 177 P.2d 442 (Nev. 1947). In Miami Beach, the law was enacted to limit the ability of "casual employees" to target the "sun-seeking wealthy," and required that workers provide fingerprints and photos, which were compared to files maintained by the FBI. Workers were also required to carry an identification card. According to the chief of police, registration had a significant crime-fighting benefit: "We instituted this procedure as an aid to eliminating crime, and it certainly has done that. And it's been the reason we've picked up plenty of criminals wanted in states all over the country for crimes ranging from murder on down." "Employees Must Register: Miami Beach Seeks to Trip Up the Dishonest," *Lincoln Evening Journal* (Nebraska), November 5, 1936.

120. Acts of Tennessee, 1806, chap. 32, § 1. See also Hurd, *The Law of Freedom* (surveying similar state laws, including those in Delaware, Georgia, Indiana, Louisiana, Michigan, Ohio, and Virginia).

121. John Hope Franklin, *The Free Negro in North Carolina: 1790–1869* (Chapel Hill: University of North Carolina Press, 1943).

122. Walter Clark, ed., *State Records of North Carolina*, vol. 24, *Laws 1777–1788* (Raleigh, NC: C.M. Uzzell, 1905), 727–28.

123. *Slavery Code of the District of Columbia* 26, 32, §§ 1, 11 (1827).

124. Ibid., 36, § 29 (1848).

125. Letitia Woods Brown, *Free Negroes in the District of Columbia 1790–1846* (New York: Oxford University Press, 1972), 56.

126. Love et al., "Registration of Free Blacks in Ohio," 38.

127. Martine Kaluszynski, "Republican Identity: Bertillonage as Government Technique," in Caplan and Torpey, *Documenting Individual Identity*, 131–37.

128. Ibid., 137. In addition, in another parallel to modern U.S. criminal registra-

tion efforts (see Chapter 5), the onerous requirements of the law actually enhanced the mobility of Gypsies. Ibid.

129. See generally Raul Hilberg, *Destruction of the European Jews*, rev. and definitive ed. (New York: Holmes and Meier, 1985).

130. Robert M.W. Kempner, "The German National Registration System as Means of Police Control of Population," *Journal of Criminal Law & Criminology* 36 (1945): 366.

131. Ibid., 378–81.

132. Ibid., 383.

133. See generally Amy W. Knight, *The KGB: Police and Politics in the Soviet Union*, rev. ed. (Boston: Unwin Hyman, 1990).

134. See generally Roger Omond, *The Apartheid Handbook*, 2nd ed. (New York: Penguin Books, 1986).

## Chapter 2

1. See Jerome Michael and Mortimer J. Adler, *Crime, Law and Social Science* (Montclair, NJ: Patterson Smith, 1971), 268 (citing reports in Cleveland, Ohio and elsewhere).

2. See, e.g., U.S. National Commission on Law Observance and Enforcement, *Report on Crime and the Foreign Born* (Washington, DC: U.S. Government Printing Office, 1931); U.S. National Commission on Law Observance & Enforcement, *Report on Lawlessness in Law Enforcement* (Washington, DC: U.S. Government Printing Office, 1931).

3. See E. R. Cass, "National Crime Commission Conference," *Journal of the American Institute of Criminal Law & Criminology* 18 (1928): 497.

4. Senate Committee on Commerce, *Hearings before the Senate Subcommittee of the Committee on Commerce*, 73rd Cong., 2d sess., 1933.

5. *Cong. Rec.* 78 (1934): S 449 (statement of Sen. Royal S. Ferguson).

6. Carl V. Eimbeck, "Some Recent Methods of Harassing the Habitual Criminal," *St. Louis Law Review* 16 (1930–31): 148–49 ("Particularly shocking is the condition of which has existed and does exist at this time in certain cities where organized gangsters, racketeers, extortionists, and hoodlums of all sorts have ushered in an era of lawlessness and violence without parallel in history.").

7. See, e.g., Edwin H. Sutherland, *Principles of Criminology*, 4th ed. (Chicago: Lippincott, 1947), 33 (citing report reflecting data from 1930–33 in support of the view that the data "show a slight upward trend during this period, with no sudden surge that could be called a crime wave"); "Experts Discover No 'Wave' of Crime: Hoover Research Group Finds No Gain Since 1925 in Minor and Many Major Categories," *New York Times*, February 27, 1933.

8. See Oscar Hallam, "Dealing with Crime—Some Urgent Needs, in Modern Crime, Its Prevention and Punishment," *Annals of the American Academy of Political and Social Science*, May 1926, 126 ("We talk and write endlessly and criticize volubly, knowing all the time that we have not adequate information as to facts to show us the places where criticism should fall."); Frank O. Lowden, "Criminal Statistics and Identification of Criminals," *Journal of the American Institute of Criminal Law & Criminology* 19 (1928–29): 36 (citing National Crime Commission report bemoaning the "woeful lack of criminal statistics" during the time). National estimates for offense rates were not available until 1933. President's Commission on Law Enforcement and Administration of Justice, *The Challenge of Crime in a Free Society: A Report* (Washington, DC: U.S. Government Printing Office, 1967), 24. Moreover, crime data from rural areas were not accurately collected until 1958, further undercutting the accuracy of national crime rates. Ibid.

9. "Life Terms to End Crime Advocated," *Oakland Tribune*, September 28, 1925. Registration was one of four recommendations, "based on plain common sense and scientific knowledge," intended to target recidivists, the other three being extended prison terms for recidivists, segregation of offenders according to type, and diversified prison programs for different types of offenders. Ibid.

10. Current Note, "Universal Registration," *Journal of the American Institute of Criminal Law and Criminology* 25 (1934–35): 650–51.

11. Donald Dilworth, ed., *Identification Wanted: Development of the American Criminal Identification System, 1893–1943* (Gaithersburg, MD: International Association of Chiefs of Police, 1977), 214.

12. Ibid., 215.

13. See Wayne A. Logan, "Civil and Criminal Recidivists: Extraterritoriality in Tort and Crime," *University of Cincinnati Law Review* 73 (2005): 1618–19.

14. Forrest W. Lacey, "Vagrancy and Other Crimes of Personal Condition," *Harvard Law Review* 66 (1953): 1203; Note, "Use of Vagrancy-Type Laws for Arrest and Detention of Suspicious Persons," *Yale Law Journal* 50 (1950): 1351.

15. See, e.g., *Lanzetta v. New Jersey*, 306 U.S. 451 (1939) (invalidating New Jersey law making it a crime to be a "gangster"); *Illinois v. Belecastro*, 190 N.E. 301 (Ill. 1934) (invalidating Illinois law making it a crime to be a "habitual" criminal); *People v. Licavoli*, 250 N.W. 520 (Mich. 1933) (invalidating Michigan's "public enemy" law). But see *People v. Pieri*, 199 N.E. 495 (N.Y. 1936) (upholding New York's law targeting any person "[w]ho bears an evil reputation and with unlawful purpose consorts with thieves and criminals").

16. See, e.g., *People v. Baum*, 231 N.W. 95, 96 (Mich. 1930) (concluding that banishment "tends to incite dissension, provoke retaliation, and disturb that fundamental equality of political rights among the several states which is the basis of the Union itself"); see also *In re Scarborough*, 173 P.2d 825, 827 (Cal. 1946) (the "[s]ame principle

which prohibits the banishment of a criminal from a state . . . applies with equal force to a county or city"). Despite this principle, as discussed later, banishment came to be employed in tandem with violations of registration laws, with localities conditioning suspension of prosecution on the promise that violators leave town.

17. "How Can We Halt the Rising Flood of Crime Here?" *Los Angeles Times*, January 18, 1931.

18. "Gangsters to Be Fought with Registration Law," *Los Angeles Times*, September 23, 1931. Fitts himself, in a separate letter to the Board, elaborated on the perceived inadequacy of available laws:

> The present state of the law does not enable the peace officers to cope with the class of persons who come to this county and engage in criminal activities and in various unlawful enterprises. The only available statute would be the vagrancy law and the persons who would fall within the scope of this ordinance are immune from prosecution under the vagrancy law. They are well supplied with funds and are always able to defeat any efforts to proceed against them under such law. If the peace officers of this county are acquainted with the whereabouts of the persons contemplated by the provisions of the proposed ordinance, it will be an effectual deterrent to [registrants'] criminal activities and will go to great lengths in diminishing crime in Los Angeles county.

"Felon Registry Law Softened," *Los Angeles Times*, September 26, 1931.

19. Ibid.

20. "Delay on Crime Edict Probable," *Los Angeles Times*, September 27, 1931.

21. "Board Delays Gang Check," *Los Angeles Times*, September 29, 1931.

22. "Anti-Gangster Action Delayed," *Los Angeles Times*, October 15, 1931.

23. Ibid.

24. Ibid.

25. "Gangster Law Threshed Out," *Los Angeles Times*, October 28, 1931.

26. "Anti-gangster Plan Adopted," *Los Angeles Times*, December 2, 1931.

27. "Gang-Check Move Again Under Way," *Los Angeles Times*, January 7, 1932.

28. Associated Press, "Los Angeles County Registers Felons in a Drastic Move to Wipe Out Gangs," *New York Times*, September 13, 1933.

29. Consistent with voiced concern posed by migratory criminals, correspondence from the Board urging the City to adopt the County's ordinance suggested a belief that the provision required registration of "all convicts who have been convicted of a felony outside of the State of California," not also persons who had been convicted in California. Letter from Arthur G. Baraw, secretary of Los Angeles Board of Police Commissioners to the Los Angeles City Council, September 11, 1933. A letter from the City of Los Angeles chief of police urging that the Board adopt the ordinance mirrored this understanding. Letter from James E. Davis, City of Los Angeles Chief of Police to the City Board of Police Commissioners, September 11, 1933.

30. City of Los Angeles ordinance no. 73013, adopted September 12, 1933.

31. Los Angeles County ordinance no. 2339, § 8, adopted September 11, 1933.

32. Ibid., § 1. The ten-year retroactive frame of reference exceeded that proposed in the ordinance initially considered by the County two years earlier. In 1931, the backers of the law proposed a seven-year period, noting:

> We feel that the seven-year clause will be sufficient to take care of the situation for which the ordinance is proposed. It is not the purpose of the measure to harass or intimidate upright citizens who might have been convicted of one of the crimes set out, and have subsequently been living honorable and upright lives. The seven-year period is based on the statistical cycle of crime and the ordinance so amended will take care of that class of gangsters and racketeers for which it is designed.

Ibid. The provision originally also did not require that registrants update their location information in the event of a move. Until the adopted provision, as discussed, residence changes had to be reported within twenty-four hours. "Criminal-Registry Law Passed by Supervisors," *Los Angeles Times*, September 12, 1933.

33. Los Angeles County ordinance no. 2339, § 6, adopted September 11, 1933.

34. Ibid., § 1.

35. Ibid., § 3.

36. Ibid., § 7. Each day in violation of the law was deemed a "separate violation" warranting separate punishment. Ibid.

37. Letter, "Mr. Rogers Recommends a New Anti-Crime Move," *New York Times*, September 14, 1933. Rogers elaborated that "[i]t looks like every time a man commits a crime and is caught his prison record reads like he had been a tourist inmate of every prison worth attending. There hasn't been an amateur crook caught in years."

38. The Miami Beach City Council declared that registration was needed

> by reason of the fact that many of the crimes enumerated are of great danger to this community and have been and are being committed by habitual and dangerous criminals traveling from place to place throughout the United States and the State of Florida, and because there is no means whereby the peace officers of the City of Miami Beach, Florida, may be apprized of the arrival into said city or the presence in said city of such criminals until a crime shall have been committed by them, and because the undisclosed presence of such criminals within the City of Miami Beach, Florida, will constitute a serious menace to the safety and welfare of the citizens of said city.

39. City of Miami Beach Ordinance no. 332, § 1 (1933).

40. L.A. Municipal Code § 52.38.

41. L.A. Municipal Code § 52.40(a), (b) (1936). Convicted persons in the city when the law went into effect had five days to register. Ibid., § 52.39. Any change of residence

or stopping place was to be reported within forty-eight hours of its occurrence. Ibid., § 52.40(c).

42. L.A. Municipal Code § 52.38(e).

43. L.A. Municipal Code § 52.42.

44. On this era, and the public concern over the Mafia generated by well-publicized Special Senate Committee hearings under the leadership of Tennessee Senator Ernest Kefauver, see President's Commission, *Challenge of Crime*, 192–98.

45. Based on the author's survey of newspaper reports from 1900 to 1990, only a handful of political defeats were discovered: in Lima, Ohio (1962) and Middletown, New Jersey (1965). See "Other Men's Views," *Manitowoc Herald-Times* (Wisconsin), January 30, 1965; Stan Wyman, "Police Losers on Felon Law," *Lima News* (Ohio), May 15, 1962. Also, in 1949, in Helena, Montana, an ordinance apparently was defeated after the mayor opposed a proposal out of concern that it would not be effective or enforceable. See "Murray and Tripp Appear Against Proposed Ordinance," *Independent Record* (Helena, Montana), May 9, 1949. Minneapolis, Minnesota, also apparently rejected an ordinance on an unknown date. See Note, "Criminal Registration Ordinances: Police Control over Potential Recidivists," *University of Pennsylvania Law Review* 103 (1954): 65n26.

46. Robert H. Dreher and Linda Kammler, *Criminal Registration Statutes and Ordinances in the United States; a Compilation* (Carbondale: Center for the Study of Crime, Delinquency, and Corrections, Southern Illinois University, 1969), 32. The number is based on a national survey of 384 localities and excludes ten California localities where local laws were invalidated on preemption grounds by the California Supreme Court in 1960 (discussed later herein). Ibid., 34.

47. Ibid., 33.

48. In 1935, however, New York's police commissioner ordered that detectives create and maintain a record of ex-felons and persons convicted of specified crimes (e.g., drug possession or weapons possession). The commissioner "made it clear that the order did not contemplate the registration of criminals by having them appear at the detective bureaus." Rather, detectives were to survey their precincts to know where such individuals "are living and what they are doing." Such information was to be kept current and photographs of all registrants were to be filed. The commissioner also ordered that "in addition to the recording of all local criminals, the records of out-of-town criminals shall be sent to their home towns for the information of police in those localities." "Watch on 55,000 Known Criminals Ordered by Valentine in City-Wide Police Check-up," *New York Times*, July 13, 1935. Also, Phillip Jenkins has written of "sex bureau registries for keeping track of sex offenders against children" being operated in New York and Chicago in 1937, but fails to provide authority for the assertion. Phillip Jenkins, *Moral Panic: Changing Concepts of the Child Molester in Modern America* (New Haven, CT: Yale University Press, 1999), 80.

49. See *Abbott v. City of Los Angeles*, 349 P.2d 974, 977n4 (Cal. 1960) (noting that in California seven of ten localities with registration laws were clustered in the Los Angeles area), "Criminal Registration Ordinances," *University of Pennsylvania Law Review*, 65 (noting that 80% of localities with laws were clustered in five geographic regions).

50. Dreher and Kammler, *Criminal Registration Statutes*, 34n3.

51. This wariness is evidenced today as localities, domino-style, have enacted laws preventing registered sex offenders from living in specified areas, functionally serving to banish them. For discussion of this phenomenon, see Wayne A. Logan, "Constitutional Collectivism and Ex-Offender Residence Exclusion Laws," *Iowa Law Review* 92 (2006): 1.

52. See, e.g., Jerome Michael and Mortimer J. Adler, *Crime, Law and Social Science* (Montclair, NJ: Patterson Smith, 1933): 178 (noting nascent efforts in this regard).

53. See Dreher and Kammler, *Criminal Registration Statutes*, 42 (identifying the sole exceptions as Covington, Kentucky; Cincinnati, Columbus, and Parma, Ohio; as well as the State of Ohio itself). Of note, Illinois in 1986 enacted a "Habitual Child Sex Offender Registration Act," triggered by a second conviction of one of four enumerated serious sexual offenses against victims less than 18 years of age. See Public Act no. 84-1279, art. I, § 2, 1986 Ill. Laws 1467. However, the law was soon amended to require registration upon a single conviction of a broadened array of registerable offenses.

54. The Supreme Court's decision in *Loving v. Virginia*, 388 U.S. 1 (1967) invalidated miscegenation laws on constitutional grounds. However, two years later, in 1969, the ordinances remained in effect in several Florida towns. Dreher and Kammler, *Criminal Registration Statutes*, 42.

55. See, e.g., Paul W. Tappan, *The Habitual Sex Offender: Report and Recommendations of the Commission on the Habitual Sex Offender, New Jersey State Legislature* (Trenton, N.J., 1950), 14 ("[S]ex offenders have one of the lowest rates as 'repeaters' of all types of crime. . . . Among serious crimes homicide alone has a lower rate of recidivism."). In addition, registering convicted sex offenders distracts from the empirical reality that most sex offenses are committed by first-time offenders. As one study of New York City concluded: "First offenders commit most sex crimes . . . Where sex offenders do have prior criminal records, it is usually for non-sexual crimes . . . Police department fingerprint records disclose that only 7% of the persons convicted of sex crimes in 1930 were arrested on charges of sex crime during the period 1930–1941." Sol Rubin, *The Law of Criminal Correction* (St. Paul, MN: West Publishing, 1963), 412–13. See also *Report of Mayor's Committee for Study of Sex Offenses* (New York, 1943), 11.

56. Dreher and Kammler, *Criminal Registration Statutes*, 51. For other similar instances see Dick Case, "Readers Write of Brides, Veterans, Landlords, Criminals," *Herald-Journal* (Syracuse, New York), December 19, 1981 (noting that Sherburne, New York, posts a sign at the village's boundary warning of a registration requirement);

Lilla Hill, "Traveling Correspondent," *Mountain Democrat Times* (Placerville, California), November 28, 1968 (noting that the State of New Jersey posted a "Criminal Registration Required" sign).

57. Dreher and Kammler, *Criminal Registration Statutes*, 47.

58. In 1952, Congress required aliens over 18 years of age to carry a card. See *Immigration and Naturalization Act of 1952*, 8 U.S.C. § 1304 (Supp. 1952).

59. Dreher and Kammler, *Criminal Registration Statutes*, 48. The cards were often put to other uses. For instance, registrants employed cards as a means of identification to perpetrate check fraud. See, e.g., "Check Cashed by Con's Card," *Union-Bulletin* (Walla-Walla, Washington), September 18, 1957 (Seattle); "Ex-convict Card Gets Check Cashed," *Abilene Reporter-News* (Texas), July 17, 1954 (Long Beach, California). Police also were able to use cards, when on the body of an otherwise unidentified decedent, to make a physical identification. See, e.g., "Suspect Gang in Camden Slaying," *Chester Times* (Pennsylvania), December 31, 1946 (Camden, New Jersey); "Body of Underworld Character Found," *New Castle News* (Pennsylvania), July 21, 1941 (Cape May, New Jersey).

60. "Criminal Registration Ordinances," *University of Pennsylvania Law Review*, 72.

61. Dreher and Kammler, *Criminal Registration Statutes*, 45–46.

62. Ch. 18107, Laws of Fla. 1937, § 2. In 1953, the legislature extended the requirement to counties with a population of 450,000 or more, serving to single out Dade County. Chap. 28470, Laws of Fla., 1953. Why the legislature did so remains a curiosity given that at the time major municipalities in Dade under both the 1937 and 1953 circa laws had registration ordinances in effect. It might be that by imposing a countywide requirement the legislature shifted the job of registration to county sheriffs and state constitutional officers, with consequent resource savings for local police. However, the countywide effect also served to impose registration requirements in smaller locales, presumably not so beleaguered by concerns over ex-convicts. At any rate, in 1957 the legislature saw fit to impose the registration requirement, which since 1953 had targeted felons more generally, to the state as a whole. Chap. 57-19, Laws of Fla., 1957.

63. Cal. Penal Code § 290 (1947).

64. Ariz. Code § 43-6117 (Cum. Supp. 1951).

65. N.J. Stat. § Ann. 2A; 169A-1 (1953).

66. Ill. Ann. Stat. chap. 38 § 192.29 (1953).

67. Nev. Rev. Stat. §§ 207.080–.150 (1961).

68. Ohio Rev. Code §§ 2950.01–.99 (Anderson Supp. 1972).

69. 1967 Ala. acts 506, at 1220, codified at Ala. Code § 15-20-1 to -5 (1967).

70. 1987 Ark. Sess. Laws ch. 587 (April 4, 1987).

71. 1987 Utah Sess. Laws ch. 156 (March 16, 1987).

72. 1989 Mont. Sess. Laws ch. 293 (March 24, 1989).

73. 1989 Okla. Sess. Laws ch. 212 (May 9, 1989).

74. Persons were required to register in a "registration book kept by the sheriff." The moral turpitude category cast a broad net, including homicides, robberies, rape, arson, mayhem, uttering, treason, kidnapping, and wire tapping. Ch. 18107, Laws of Fla. 1937, § 2. In 1953, the Florida Legislature excised the moral turpitude criterion, requiring registration of persons convicted of felonies more generally. See Ch. 28470, Laws of Fla. 1953, § 1. The 1953 amendment also required that registrants provide residence address information for the preceding twenty years. The requirement was absent from the 1957 amendment.

75. Chap. 28470, Laws of Fla., 1953.

76. Letter from Alameda County District Attorney Ralph E. Hoyt to Governor Earl Warren, July 2, 1947. In January 1947, the Los Angeles County Board of Supervisors considered a sex offender–specific registration law, prompted by what the local prosecutor called "the increasing number of cases involving crimes of violence and murder which . . . undoubtedly arise because of the activities of morally unsound persons." "Law Urged to Compel Sex Offenders' Roster," *Los Angeles Times*, January 21, 1947.

77. Memorandum from Legislative Secretary Beach Vasey to Governor Earl Warren, July 3, 1947.

78. Ibid.

79. Ariz. Rev. Stat. Ann. §§ 13-1271 to -1274 (1951).

80. See, e.g., *Voelker v. Tyndall*, 75 N.E.2d 548 (Ind. 1947).

81. Two years later, the law was amended to include misdemeanor lewd vagrancy, Cal. Penal Code, § 290 (West 1970) (Historical Note) (citing 1949 Cal. Stat. ch. 13, § 1, at 27), which California law at the time deemed any person "who loiters in or about public toilets." Cal. Penal Code § 647(5) (1959). The goal, according to the California Legislature, was to "provide local authorities with knowledge of the whereabouts of habitual sex offenders and sex deviates." E. A. Riddle, "Compulsory Registration: A Vehicle of Mercy Discarded," *California Western Law Review* 3 (1967): 199.

82. Cal. Penal Code § 290 (1947).

83. From July 1952 to December 1961, 2,509 individuals registered, with the highest volume (381) registering in 1953 and the lowest volume (172) registering in 1955. New Jersey Commission on Narcotic Control, *Seventh Report of Study and Recommendations* (Trenton, N.J., 1962), 25, 29. Demographic data were as follows: 87% male; 87% between 20 and 40 years of age (4% under age 19); 76% nonwhite; 62% had lived in their present residence for more than 10 years (22% less than one year); 67% used heroin (12% marijuana); 51% had not been convicted of a crime prior to their registerable offense (of those with convictions, 4% committed an offense against a person); and of those receiving a prior conviction, 36% had only one conviction. Ibid., 29–41. The report concluded that while most registrants had prior criminal histories, drug violations were not the driving force: "Surprisingly enough, most of the narcotic reg-

istrants were convicted of a single narcotic violation. Only 43 per cent of them were repeaters and the largest category of recidivists [was] involved in two violations while 8 percent were found in the 5 violations and over category." Ibid., at 41. In 1958, the following "cases" were filed in municipal court: 27, failure to register; 44, failure to notify of change of address; and 32, failure to have registration card in possession. New Jersey Commission on Narcotic Control, *Fifth Report of Study and Recommendations* (Trenton, N.J., 1959), 60.

84. N.J. Stat. 2A:169A-1 and -2.

85. N.J. Stat. 2A:169A-3 and -4.

86. N.J. Stat. 2A:169A-5.

87. N.J. Stat. 2A:169A-8.

88. Ill. Stat. ch. 38 § 192.29 (1953).

89. Cal. Health and Safety Code § 11850 (1961).

90. Ibid. § 11853.

91. *Stats.* 1972, c. 1407.

92. Cal. Health and Safety Code § 11850.1 (year). The U.S. Government, from 1956 to 1970, required that a drug "user" or convict register with customs before entering or leaving the country. Individuals were required to provide their name; social security number; address; status as a "user" or convict; conviction-related information; expected port, date, and means of return; signature; and date of registration. Upon registering individuals were provided with a certificate that they were required to show upon reentry. Violation was punished as a felony. See 18 U.S.C. §§ 1401 to 1407 (1956).

93. Cal. Penal Code § 457.1 (1984).

94. "Criminal Registration Ordinances," *University of Pennsylvania Law Review* 64*n*24.

95. "Felon Listing Starting Today," *Los Angeles Times*, September 13, 1933.

96. "Gang Suspects Quitting City," *Los Angeles Times*, September 18, 1933.

97. Lawrence Davies, "Camden No Longer Criminals' Haven: New Jersey City Expects Its Registration Rule to Curb the Lawless," *New York Times*, July 15, 1934. See also "Chief Wants Ex-Convicts to Register," *Mansfield News-Journal* (Ohio), July 5, 1953 (reporting that local police chief backed registration because it "would keep undesirable persons out of the city and could prove valuable in criminal investigations").

98. "Birmingham Police to Register All Ex-Felons in the City," *New York Times*, July 4, 1935.

99. *The Literary Digest*, September 30, 1933, 39.

100. "Criminal Registration Ordinances," *University of Pennsylvania Law Review*, 86.

101. "Two Laws Provide Invisible Weapons Against Crime in Minnesota City," *Albuquerque Journal*, May 31, 1955.

102. Ibid. According to L.A. Angeles District Attorney Burton Fitts, a main pro-

ponent of the city's ordinance, registration "was indeed effective. It consists of secret information and establishes a file of great use to law enforcement agencies without harm to the individual in view of its secrecy." "Criminal Registration Ordinances," *University of Pennsylvania Law Review,* 60n5.

103. "Sheriffs Say Bill Not Designed to Harass Ex-felons," *Gastonia Gazette* (North Carolina), February 26, 1937.

104. See "Felon Registry Law Softened," *Los Angeles Times,* September 26, 1931 (noting that vagrancy charges were often easily defeated by suspected gangsters).

105. See, e.g., Davies, "Camden No Longer Criminals' Haven." In resort locations, with both "casual employee" and criminal registration provisions, the laws acted synergistically. As the Reno, Nevada, chief of police said of its employee law: "It aids us in picking up ex-felony convicts who fail to register under the ex-convict registration law and keep the standards of employees in gambling and liquor dispensing establishments at a high level, protecting both the employer and the public." "Fingerprint Law Called Civil Abuse," *Nevada State Journal,* October 4, 1945.

106. "'Ignorance of the Law' a Defense to Conviction Under Criminal Registration Ordinance," *Utah Law Review* 6 (1958): 125 (citing *Literary Digest,* September 30, 1933, at 39).

107. See, e.g., Ernest Jerome Hopkins, *Our Lawless Police* (New York: Viking Press, 1931).

108. "Called No.1 Hood—Cohen Released," *San Antonio Light,* October 22, 1958.

109. "Cohen Arrested as Gambler," *Bridgeport Post,* October 22, 1958.

110. "Criminal Registration Ordinances," *University of Pennsylvania Law Review,* 93.

111. Ibid., 87, 91.

112. Jon J. Gallo et al., "The Consenting Adult Homosexual and the Law: An Empirical Study of Enforcement and Administration in Los Angeles County," *UCLA Law Review* 13 (1966): 737–38.

113. See, e.g., *Lustig v. United States,* 338 U.S. 74 (1949) (noting room search by Camden, New Jersey, police predicated on arrest warrant for violation of city's "known criminal" registration law); *Eagleston v. United States,* 448 F.2d 1389 (10th Cir. 1971) (addressing search based on arrest warrant for violation of Tulsa felon registration law); *People v. Chilton,* 48 Cal. Rptr. 212 (Cal. Ct. App. 1966) (upholding in-home arrest and search based on arrest warrant for failure to register as drug offender). For examples of registration-based arrests deemed invalid, resulting in exclusion of evidence found, see *O'Neil v. State,* 194 So.2d 40 (Fla. App. 1967) (invalidating arrest based on City of Miami felon registration law); *State v. Orr,* 225 A.2d 157 (N.J. 1967) (invalidating arrest and resulting search based on New Jersey's narcotic offender registration law). For more on the historic power of police to search incident to arrest, see Wayne A. Logan,

"An Exception Swallows a Rule: Police Authority to Search Incident to Arrest," *Yale Law & Policy Review* 19 (2001): 381.

114. Riddle, "Compulsory Registration," 199.

115. Ibid., 199–200.

116. Gallo, "Consenting Adult Homosexual," 772.

117. "Criminal Registration Ordinances," *University of Pennsylvania Law Review*, Appendix C, 109. Similar data were reported by the *Ulesky* court in the mid-1960s: Under the Borough of Belmar, New Jersey, law challenged there, no registrations were on record in 1965, four in 1966, four in 1967, and none in 1968. *State v. Ulesky*, 252 A.2d 720, 723n1 (N.J. 1969). See also "Ex-Criminals Register," *New York Times*, May 17, 1952 (noting that in Jersey City, New Jersey, 121 persons, mostly waterfront workers, registered within two weeks of the registration law's adoption, which compared favorably to the city's Communist registration ordinance enacted a year before, which had been ignored).

Indeed, this obliviousness was highlighted by a scenario played out in Paducah, Kentucky, where local leaders in the 1960s enacted a registration law targeting felons and narcotics law violators only to discover that a registration requirement had already been in effect since the 1950s. Linda Kammler, "Criminal Registration Statutes and Ordinances in the United States: A Survey" (M.A. Thesis, Southern Illinois University, Department of Government, May 1969), 36–37.

118. "Criminal Registration Ordinances," *University of Pennsylvania Law Review*, 85.

119. Ibid., 88.

120. Ibid., 103.

121. Ibid., 88.

122. Ibid., 103.

123. Ibid. Moreover, the study found a number of instances in Philadelphia (and other cities) of there being palpable evidence of a registration violation but that a charge was not brought. Ibid., 89.

124. Ibid., 92. For similar examples of de facto banishment, with individuals told to register or leave town, see "Suspect Banished by Atlantic City," *Chester Times* (Pennsylvania), January 24, 1936; "Must Quit Miami: Two New Yorkers Given 12-Hour Notice by City," *Anniston Star* (Alabama), November 22, 1935.

125. "Criminal Registration Ordinances," *University of Pennsylvania Law Review*, Appendix D, 110–11.

126. Ibid., 90. In the 24 cases resulting in dismissal, "the fact that the individuals involved had not violated the ordinance would have been obvious to the officers making the charges if they had known the details of the ordinance or made necessary inquiries." Ibid.

127. Ibid., 89.

128. Ibid., 95.

129. Ibid.

130. Ibid., 86.

131. Supplemental Brief of Appellee, *Lambert v. California*, September 27, 1957, Appendix B, 7–8 (reporting data provided by the Los Angeles Public Information Division).

132. Howard Jay Whitman, *Terror in the Streets* (New York: Dial Press, 1951), 383–84. The laws were criticized by academic commentators as well. See, e.g., "Criminal Registration Ordinances," *University of Pennsylvania Law Review*, 60; "Criminal Registration Law," *Journal of the American Institute of Criminal Law and Criminology* 27 (1936–37): 295.

133. Memorandum from State of California Director of Corrections Richard A. McGee to Governor Earl Warren, July 2, 1947.

134. W. Keith Wilson et al., "Are Criminal Registration Laws Sound?" *National Probation and Parole Journal* 4 (1958): 272 (citing Opinion of the Utah State Attorney General to W. Keith Wilson, compact administrator, Utah Department of Probation and Parole, December 6, 1956).

135. "Criminal Registration Ordinances," *University of Pennsylvania Law Review*, 61*n*5.

136. Ibid., 86.

137. Ibid.

138. Ibid.

139. Wilson et al., "Are Criminal Registration Laws Sound?" 271–74.

140. Ibid., 274.

141. Ibid., 271.

142. "Criminal Registration Law," *Journal of the American Institute of Criminal Law & Criminology*, 295–96.

143. 278 U.S. 63, 65 (1928).

144. 312 U.S. 52 (1941).

145. In addition, under the state law, registration occurred at police stations, while under the federal law it occurred at post offices, presumably a less stigmatizing venue. Ibid., 57, 73.

146. See *United States v. Harris*, 347 U.S. 612 (1954) (lobbyists); *United States v. Kahiger*, 345 U.S. 22 (1953) (gamblers). See also, e.g., *Norman v. City of Las Vegas*, 177 P.2d 442 (Nev. 1947) (upholding a Las Vegas ordinance requiring employees in establishments selling liquor to register with police and submit to photographing and fingerprinting).

147. *Walton v. City of Atlanta*, 181 F.2d 693 (5th Cir. 1950) (taxi and bus drivers); *City of Manchester v. Leiby*, 117 F.2d 661 (1st Cir. 1941) (bootblacks and sellers of literature

on the streets); *United States v. Pease Information Center*, 97 F. Supp. 255 (D.D.C. 1951) (foreign agents).

148. See, e.g., *Allutson v. Mallard*, 106 F. Supp. 635 (E.D. Mich. 1952) (upholding Michigan statute requiring Communists to register with state police).

149. See, e.g., *Sterling v. City of Oakland*, 24 Cal. Rptr. 696 (Cal. Ct. App. 1962); *Kolb v. O'Connor*, 142 N.E.2d 818 (Ill. Ct. App. 1957); *Mavity v. Tyndall*, 74 N.E.2d 916 (Ind. 1947).

150. *Mavity v. Tyndall*, 66 N.E.2d 755, 762 (Ind. 1946).

151. *Itzovitch v. Whitaker*, 42 So.2d 228, 229 (1906). See also *State v. Harris*, 153 S.W.2d 834, 837 (Mo. 1941) (prohibiting circulation of prints and photo of alleged traffic law violator); *Schulman v. Whitaker*, 42 So.2d 227, 227 (La. 1906) (condemning the "extreme measures" of photographing and posting pictures of persons not convicted of crime, noting that it "may prove useful in some cases, but it may lead to abuses and injustice in others").

152. "Ex-convict Registration Invalid," *Reno Evening Gazette* (Nevada), December 17, 1957.

153. 355 U.S. 225 (1958).

154. Appellant's Opening Brief, *Lambert v. California*, February 23, 1957, 4–5.

155. Ibid., 6–7.

156. Lambert's cause was backed by an amicus brief by Warren Christopher, a former law clerk to Justice William O. Douglas, the author of *Lambert*, and later to serve as secretary of state in the Carter administration, but then in private practice in Los Angeles. Christopher's brief was praised by Professor Herbert Packer as "one of those rare performances that must gladden the hearts of justices." Herbert L. Packer, "Mens Rea and the Supreme Court," *Supreme Court Review 1962* (1962): 128. The matter was restored to the Court's docket after an initial and presumably insufficient initial submission to the Court during the prior term. See *Lambert v. California*, 354 U.S. 936 (1957).

157. Supplemental Brief of Appellee, *Lambert v. California*, September 27, 1957, 1–2.

158. Ibid., 6.

159. According to the counsel for the City:

In years gone by when communities were small and the population thereof remained the same, the police were well aware of the presence of persons within their community who were potentially criminally inclined, or who suffered prior conviction, but that situation no longer exists. With the great influx of persons to the larger cities and the rapid means of transportation, it is not now possible to be aware of the presence of all persons deemed to be a potential threat to the community . . . [The City] had a reasonable basis for enacting this ordinance in an effort to add a needed protection to the health, morals, welfare and safety of the public.

Ibid.

160. *Lambert*, 355 U.S. at 229.
161. Ibid.
162. Ibid.
163. Ibid., 229–30.
164. 349 P.2d 974 (Cal. 1960).
165. 252 A.2d 720 (N.J. 1969).
166. Ibid., 721.
167. Ibid., 722
168. Ibid., 723.
169. Ibid.
170. Ibid., 722–23.
171. 515 P.2d 12 (Cal. 1973).
172. Ibid., 16–17.
173. 663 P.2d 216 (Cal. 1983).
174. Ibid., 222.
175. 204 Cal. Rptr. 39 (Cal. Ct. App. 1984) (invalidating registration for indecent exposure). California appellate courts, however, upheld registration for more serious offenses. See *People v. Monroe*, 215 Cal. Rptr. 51 (Cal. Ct. App. 1985) (upholding registration for child annoyance and molestation); *People v. Mills* 146 Cal. Rptr. 411 (1978) (upholding registration for lewd and lascivious behavior on a child under age 14).
176. See *Atteberry v. State*, 438 P.2d 789 (Nev. 1968). The court distinguished two prior U.S. Supreme Court decisions (neither of which cited *Lambert*) finding that required registration of Communist Party members and gamblers violated the Fifth Amendment's privilege against compelled self-incrimination. See *Marchetti v. United States*, 390 U.S. 39 (1968) (gamblers); *Albertson v. SACB*, 382 U.S. 70 (1965) (Communist Party members). A few years later, in *Eagleston v. United States*, 448 F.2d 1389, 1390 (10th Cir. 1971), the Tenth Circuit denied a self-incrimination challenge against a criminal registration law in particular, stating that "[r]egistration by felons is not self-incriminating. The disclosure is of a condition resulting from past actions and, if made, no jeopardy attaches."
177. *Atteberry*, 438 P.2d at 791–92.
178. Ibid., 791.
179. "Sinatra Reportedly Hosts Patty Hearst," *Times-Standard* (Eureka, California), November 9, 1977.
180. 146 Cal. Rptr. 411 (Cal. Ct. App. 1978).
181. Ibid., 417.
182. Ibid., 416. The court also concluded that subjecting Mills to lifetime registration was not cruel and/or unusual punishment under the California or U.S. Constitutions. Emphasizing that Mills had been convicted of child molestation, the court stated: "If there be an ignominious badge imposed it would appear deserved." Ibid.

183. See, e.g., *Eagleston*, 448 F.2d at 139 (noting same with respect to Tulsa, Oklahoma, ordinance).

184. See *Abbott*, 349 P.2d at 680 (noting that in *Lambert* the Court "refused to pass upon the constitutionality of [registration] per se"). This lack of principled objection was also manifest in the backing by federal courts of a federal law requiring registration of U.S. citizens addicted to drugs or convicted of a drug offense when entering or leaving the country. The law was justified by the reality that "most of the narcotic drugs used by citizens of the United States come from other countries, and there is great public danger of attempts to smuggle such drugs into the county every time an addict or user crosses the boundary line." *United States v. Bologna*, 181 F. Supp. 706, 708 (S.D. Cal. 1960). See also *United States v. Eramdjian*, 155 F. Supp. 914 (S.D. Cal. 1957).

185. See, e.g., *Ulesky*, 252 A.2d at 721 (registration held promise because police would "benefit by an awareness of individuals whose prior offenses reveal an added risk").

186. Scott Matson and Roxanne Lieb, *Sex Offender Registration: A Review of State Laws* (Olympia: Washington Institute for Public Policy, 1995), 5. In 1977, the Virginia Legislature considered a sex offender registry, advocated by the mother of a 13-year-old Fairfax County girl who was raped and murdered, but the bill apparently died in committee. Athelia Knight, "Virginia Considering 69 Crime Bills," *Washington Post*, January 27, 1977.

187. 730 Ill. Comp. Stat. Ann. 150/1–150/10 (West 1983) (citing 1986 Ill. Laws 84-1279).

188. Ark. Code Ann. § 12-12-901 to -909 (1993) (citing 1987 Ark. Acts 585).

189. Ariz. Code Ann. § 13-3821 to -3824 (1983).

190. In Florida, it was reported that Chicago underworld figures wintering in Miami Beach ignored the registration requirement with impunity. According to a news report: "The Chicago gangsters generally behave themselves here, usually registering [in hotels] under assumed names" to avoid having to register. Robert Wiedrich, "Chicago Hoodlums Prefer Florida Heat," *Chicago Tribune*, January 21, 1968.

191. "Howser Demands Strict Enforcement of Act," *Los Angeles Times*, November 17, 1949. In 1961, consideration briefly was given to rescinding the state's drug offender registration law. The California Assembly rejected the effort by a vote of 34-28, despite contentions that the law was "'silly,' costly and unworkable." "Bill to Kill Registration of Drug Offenders Fails," *Fresno Bee*, May 2, 1961.

192. *In re Reed*, 663 P.2d 216, 219n7 (Cal. 1983).

193. Kenneth Reich, "Many Simply Ignore Law; Sex Offender Registration Not Working, Experts Say," *Los Angeles Times*, August 8, 1986.

194. Ibid.

195. Ibid.

196. Ibid.

197. Roy Lewis, *Effectiveness of Statutory Requirements for the Registration of Sex Offenders* (Sacramento: California Dept. of Justice, 1988), 6.

198. Ibid., 1. Testament to this concern, in 1988 California lawmakers considered adopting a proposal that would provide citizens with monetary rewards if they helped in identifying and reporting noncompliant registrants. "Offender 'Surveillance,'" *Los Angeles Times*, April 27, 1988.

199. Simon A. Cole, *Suspect Identities: A History of Fingerprinting and Criminal Identification* (Cambridge, MA: Harvard University Press, 2001), 163–64.

## Chapter 3

1. While in prison, Shriner apparently told cellmates that when released he would get a van, furnish it with chains and cages, and use it to capture, sexually abuse, and kill children. Jerry Sepder, "Official Defends Not Committing Child Molester," *Washington Times*, July 24, 1989.

2. For a comprehensive chronological discussion of the events leading to the creation of Washington's law, by one of its chief architects, see David Boerner, "Confronting Violence: In the Act and in the Word," *University of Puget Sound Law Review* 15 (1992): 525.

3. In the wake of the tragedy, Ms. Harlow became a well-known public advocate for the overhaul of Washington's sex offender laws, yet her son's name remains unknown because he does not share her surname. Ms. Harlow later became the object of public scorn, when some members of the public felt that she failed to expend the donated money in the best interests of her son. Ann Japenga, "Solace with Strings," *Los Angeles Times*, January 7, 1990.

4. The Brigade was jointly formed by Ms. Harlow and Ida Ballasiotes, mother of Diane Ballasiotes, who in September 1988 had been raped and killed by a convicted sex offender in the community on a work-release program. Ballasiotes, who had tried without success to toughen sex offender–related laws in the wake of her daughter's death, figured prominently in the movement and eventually was elected to the Washington Legislature. "The Revolving Door: When Sex Offenders Go Free," *Turning Point*, ABC, September 23, 1994.

5. Shriner's crime was the latest in a series of child and adult sexual victimizations by ex-convicts. As noted above, in September 1988, Diane Ballasiotes was raped and murdered by Gene Raymond Kane. In December 1988, Gary Minnix, who had been found incompetent to stand trial for four rape charges, raped and stabbed another adult female victim (his sixth) while in the community on furlough. Barry Siegel, "Locking Up 'Sexual Predators': A Public Outcry in Washington State Targeted Repeat Violent Sex Criminals," *Los Angeles Times*, May 10, 1990. In September 1989, two brothers, ages 10 and 11, were murdered in Vancouver, Washington, and only two weeks later a 4-year-old boy was kidnapped from a school yard, raped, and killed. Soon thereafter,

Westley Dodd was arrested for abducting a 6-year-old boy from a movie theater bath-room. Dodd was subsequently charged with all four murders amid reports that he had a lengthy history of child abduction and molestation. "Dodd Changes Plea to Guilty—Jury to Decide Death Penalty in Rapes, Killings," *Seattle Times*, June 12, 1990.

6. Boerner, "Confronting Violence," 541.

7. See Eric S. Janus and Wayne A. Logan, "Substantive Due Process and the In-voluntary Confinement of Sexually Violent Predators," *Connecticut Law Review* 35 (2003): 319.

8. Before 1990, the term *sexual predator* was typically found "in the literature of crime fiction and true crime, where it appeared extensively in book titles and blurbs, alongside phrases implying primitivism, animal savagery, and hunting." Phillip Jen-kins, *Moral Panic: Changing Concepts of the Child Molester in Modern America* (New Haven, CT: Yale University Press, 1999), 193–94.

9. See, e.g., Ariz. Stat. § 13-1273 ("No statement, photograph or fingerprint . . . shall be made available to any person other than a duly elected or appointed law enforce-ment officer"); Cal. Penal Code § 290 (registrant information collected "shall not be open to inspection by the public").

10. The community notification provision was included after the Task Force pub-lished its final report, based on the recommendation of Mountlake Terrace Police Chief John Turner, who had approached Task Force leaders with the idea. In late July, only two months after Shriner's May 20 attack, Turner was alarmed that an 18-year-old believed to pose a high risk for molesting children was to reside in his community, and released his physical description to the public and school authorities. The indi-vidual's name and address, however, were not disclosed. Ron Judd and Ignacio Lobos, "'We're Just Waiting for Someone to Ruin Lives': School Officials Told of Release of Man with 'Predatory' Nature," *Seattle Times*, July 21, 1989.

11. Joe Cantlupe, "Sex Offender Registration Is Questioned," *San Diego Union-Tribune*, June 7, 1987.

12. Wash. Rev. Code § 71.05.440.

13. Ibid., § 71.05.670.

14. Ibid., §§ 9A.144.030(5); 9.94A.030(29).

15. In 1991, the legislature significantly shortened the period of time permitted for registration, requiring for instance that those newly released from prison register within 24 hours of entering the community. Ibid., § 9A.44.130(3) (1991).

16. Washington State Institute for Public Policy, "Washington State's Community Notification Law: 15 Years of Change," February 2006, 1; Jolayne Houtz, "When Do You Unmask a Sexual Predator?" *Seattle Times*, August 30, 1990.

17. See Mary Anne Kircher, "Registration of Sexual Offenders: Would Washing-ton's Scarlet Letter Approach Benefit Minnesota?" *Hamline Journal of Public Law & Policy* 13 (1992): 171–73. Local departments also varied in terms of the kinds of informa-

tion they publicly disclosed, e.g., actual versus approximate registrant addresses, work addresses, and vehicle identification information. See Sheila Donnelly and Roxanne Lieb, *Washington's Community Notification Law: A Survey of Law Enforcement* (Olympia: Washington State Institute for Public Policy, 1993), 5.

18. The following offenses triggered registration: kidnapping of a minor; criminal sexual conduct toward a minor; solicitation of a minor to engage in sexual conduct; use of a minor in a sexual performance; or solicitation of a minor to engage in prostitution. The law made no mention of out-of-state convicted offenders relocating to Minnesota but specified that eligible offenders already in the community had fourteen days to register.

19. See Wayne A. Logan, "Jacob's Legacy: Sex Offender Registration and Community Notification Laws, Practice, and Procedure in Minnesota," *William Mitchell Law Review* 29 (2003): 1290–94.

20. "Girl's Slaying Adds Momentum to Plans to Track Sex Offenders," *San Francisco Chronicle*, August 8, 1994.

21. 1991 La. Sess. L. Act no. 338, S.B. no. 1111 (June 18, 1992).

22. Margaret Litvin, "Metairie Parents Alarmed by Paroled Sex Offender," *Times Picayune* (New Orleans), October 19, 1995.

23. Ed Anderson, "'Scarlet Letter' Bill Signed by Edwards," *Times Picayune* (New Orleans), July 14, 1992.

24. Susan Schramm, "Tape Played in Molester's Slaying Trial; Detective Says Man Denied Seeing Boy Day He Vanished, Then He Said He Had," *Indianapolis Star*, February 7, 1995.

25. Diane Jennings, "It Was that Kind of Year," *Dallas Morning News*, December 26, 1996.

26. Richard C. Padock, "Parolee Says He Killed Girl After Deputies Left," *Los Angeles Times*, December 7, 1993.

27. Michelle Ruess, "A Mother's Plea: Pass Megan's Bill," *Record* (Bergen, New Jersey), September 27, 1994. See also Deborah Privitera, "Helping Children Be Aware," *Record* (Hackensack, New Jersey), May 19, 1995, A1 (quoting Maureen Kanka: "Had I known that there were three pedophiles living across the street from my home, I never would have allowed Megan to walk out of the door of my house alone. I guarantee she would be alive today.").

28. Douglas A. Campbell, "'Megan's Law': Is There Really a Right to Know?" *Philadelphia Inquirer*, August 7, 1994.

29. Jan Hoffman, "New Law Is Urged on Freed Sex Offenders," *New York Times*, August 4, 1994.

30. Michelle Ruess, "Megan's Law Moving Fast in Assembly Crackdown on Sex Offenders," *New Jersey Record*, August 16, 1994. In response to criticism that the bill was being expedited, Speaker Haytaian responded "I do not think you can ever move

quickly enough when it comes to the safety of our children." "Megan's Law Signed by Governor," *Record* (Hackensack, New Jersey), November 1, 1994.

31. As with Earl Shriner in Washington State, Timmendequas' brutal act was not without recent precedent, and did not act as the sole catalyst for change. On March 6, 1994, roughly four months before Megan's murder, 6-year-old Amanda Wengert of Manalapan Township was abducted and murdered by a neighbor with a history of sexual offenses against children. Ivette Mendez, "Megan's Law: 10 Sex Offender Bills Clear the Senate," *Star-Ledger* (Newark, New Jersey), October 4, 1994.

32. Unlike in Washington and New Jersey, where brutal child victimizations served as legislative catalysts, community notification laws in Alaska and Tennessee seemingly stemmed from more generalized interest and concern. Peter Finn, *Sex Offender Community Notification* (Washington, DC: National Institute of Justice, 1997), 3.

33. For discussion of the law's particular provisions, along with details of its swift legislative adoption, see Robert J. Martin, "Pursuing Public Protection Through Mandatory Community Notification of Convicted Sex Offenders: The Trials and Tribulations of Megan's Law," *Boston University Public Interest Law Journal* 6 (1996), 33–36.

34. *Doe v. Poritz*, 662 A.2d 367, 422 (N.J. 1995) (noting same).

35. Ibid., 372–73.

36. Associated Press, "Jacob's Parents Urge Support for Abuser Bill," *Star Tribune* (Minneapolis), May 26, 1991 (noting and discussing Senate Bill 1170). A year earlier, Senator Durenberger, with Patty Wetterling and her husband Trevor in the public gallery, spoke to his colleagues of Jacob's abduction and called for "more study and resources into reducing" child abductions. He also entered into the record a Department of Justice report and newspaper stories on the issue, as well as information on the Wetterling Foundation. *Cong. Rec.* 136 (May 7, 1990): S 5761. For a fuller description of federal efforts relative to registration and notification, see Wayne A. Logan, "Criminal Justice Federalism and National Sex Offender Policy," *Ohio State Journal of Criminal Law* 6 (2008): 51.

37. *Cong. Rec.* 137 (May 23, 1991): S 6703 (statement of Sen. Durenberger).

38. Ibid. (referring to S. 1170).

39. *Cong. Rec.* 137 (July 10, 1991): H 5339-02 (citing H.R. 2862).

40. See *Cong. Rec.* 140 (March 10, 1994): S 2825 (statement of Sen. Durenberger recounting legislative history).

41. See *Cong. Rec.* 137 (July 11, 1991): S 9822 (statement of Sen. Durenberger).

42. See *Cong. Rec.* 139 (November 20, 1993): H 10321 (statement of Rep. Ramstad: "We know that child sex offenders are repeat offenders. Child sex offenders repeat their crimes again and again to the point of compulsion."); see also, e.g., ibid., H 10321, H 10322 (statement of Rep. Grams: "[S]tudies have shown that child sex offenders are some of the most notorious repeat offenders . . . this bill gives society the right to know where these convicted offenders reside.").

43. See, e.g., *Cong. Rec.* 139 (November 20, 1993): H 10310 (statement of Rep. Ramstad); ibid.: H 10319, H 10320 (statement of Rep. Sensenbrenner).

44. See *Cong. Rec.* 139 (November 20, 1993): H 10321 (statement of Rep. Ramstad).

45. *Cong. Rec.* 139 (November 20, 1993): H 10320 (statement of Rep. Sensenbrenner).

46. *Cong. Rec.* 139 (November 20, 1993): H 10321 (statement of Rep. Ramstad).

47. See *Cong. Rec.* 137 (May 23, 1991): S 6655-01; *Cong. Rec.* 139 (November 20, 1993): H 10320.

48. Robert T. Nelson, "Gorton, Dunn, Oppose Crime Bill," *Seattle Times*, August 24, 1994.

49. Ibid.

50. *Cong. Rec.* 140 (July 13, 1994): H 5612 (statement of Rep. Dunn).

51. See *Cong. Rec.* 140 (July 13, 1994): H 5612, H 5613 (statement of Rep. Nadler raising concern over possible vigilantism and banishment of registrants).

52. Nelson, "Oppose Crime Bill," *Seattle Times*.

53. *Cong. Rec.* 140 (August 4, 1994): S 10631-04 (statement of Sen. Gorton).

54. *Cong. Rec.* 140 (August 11, 1994): H 7934-01 (statement of Rep. Dunn).

55. *Cong. Rec.* 140 (August 11, 1994): H 7934-01 (statement of Rep. Smith). See also Fred Bayles, "Murder Renews Calls for Sex Crime Registry," *Chicago Sun-Times*, August 8, 1994.

56. See *Cong. Rec.* 140 (August 16, 1994): S 11889-01 (statement of Sen. Lautenberg, recounting that the president had called him twice urging that a notification provision be included); Joseph F. Sullivan, "Whitman Approves Stringent Restrictions on Sex Criminals," *New York Times*, November 1, 1994 ("When President Clinton lobbied for the Federal crime bill last summer, he mentioned Megan and the need for a community-notification provision. That provision is now part of federal law."). Clinton, as part of his "new Democrat" orientation, and anxious over Republican assertions that his policy of permitting gays to remain in the military amounted to condoning sexual perversion, and public criticism that his Justice Department was lax in prosecuting child pornography, quickly backed the legislation. Soon thereafter, following substantial electoral gains by Republicans in the 1994 elections, Clinton, wishing to avoid being outflanked by Republicans' "family values" mantra, became a staunch supporter of the legislation. Jenkins, *Moral Panic*, 198–99.

57. Jennifer Bucksbaum, "NJ Victims' Parents See Crime Bill Signed," *New Jersey Record*, September 14, 1994.

58. *Violent Crime Control and Law Enforcement Act of 1994*, Public Law 103-322, § 17010(b)(3), *Stat.* (1994): 1796, 2038 (codified at 42 U.S.C. § 17010). The expansive law contained thirty-two separate titles, ranging from community policing, violence against women, the death penalty, mandatory minimum sentences for federal crimi-

nal offenders, and "truth-in-sentencing" provisions that provided "incentive grants" to states to ensure that state violent offenders serve at least 85% of their terms.

59. *Cong. Rec.* 140 (August 18, 1994): S 12530 (statement of Sen. Gorton).

60. 42 U.S.C. § 14071(f)(2) (1994). According to a U.S. Government website, the Byrne Grant Program:

> is a partnership among federal, state, and local governments intended to create safer communities and improve criminal justice systems. [It] is authorized to award grants to states for use by states and units of local government to improve the criminal justice system, with emphasis on violent crime and serious offenders, and to enforce state and local laws that establish offenses similar to those in the federal Controlled Substances Act. Grants may be used to provide personnel, equipment, training, technical assistance, and information systems for widespread apprehension, prosecution, adjudication, detention, and rehabilitation of offenders who violate state and local laws. Grants may also be used to provide assistance (other than compensation) to crime victims.

Http://www.ncjrs.gov/html/bja/edbyrne/bja2.html.

The 1991 circa version of the bill, introduced as amended by Senator Durenberger, specified that noncompliant states would be totally ineligible for funds under the Victims of Crime Act (42 U.S.C. § 10603), and later threatened a 25% reduction under the Byrne Act. See *Cong. Rec.* 137 (May 23, 1991): S 6704 (reprinting S. 1170); *Cong. Rec.* 137 (June 27, 1991): S 8914; H.R. 324, 103d Cong., 1st Sess. (1993); S. 8, 103d Cong., 1st Sess. (1993).

61. 42 U.S.C. § 14071(f).

62. *Cong. Rec.* 137 (May 23, 1991): S 6704 (containing S. 1170).

63. Such an offense was defined as:

any criminal offense in a range of offenses specified by State law which is comparable to or which exceeds the following range of offenses:

> (i) kidnapping of a minor except by a parent;
> (ii) false imprisonment of a minor, except by a parent;
> (iii) criminal sexual conduct toward a minor;
> (iv) solicitation of a minor to engage in sexual conduct;
> (v) use of a minor in a sexual performance;
> (vi) solicitation of a minor to engage in prostitution;
> (vii) any conduct that by its nature is a sexual offense against a minor;
> (viii) any attempt [to commit one of the aforementioned offenses].

For purposes of this subparagraph conduct which is criminal only because of the age of the victim shall not be considered a criminal offense if the perpetrator is 18 years of age or younger.

64. Defined to include "any criminal offense that consists of aggravated sexual

abuse or sexual abuse" (as defined by federal law) or "an offense that has as its elements engaging in physical contact with another person with intent to commit aggravated sexual abuse or sexual abuse" (as defined by federal law). 42 U.S.C. § 14071(a)(3)(B).

65. Defined as "a person who has been convicted of a sexually violent offense and who suffers from a mental abnormality or personality disorder that makes the person likely to engage in predatory sexually violent offenses." 42 U.S.C. § 14071(a)(1)(C). See also ibid., § 14071(a)(1)(D)(E) (providing definitions for "mental abnormality" and "predatory").

66. "Final Guidelines for the Jacob Wetterling Crimes Against Children and Sexually Violent Offender Registration Act," *Federal Register* 61 (April 4, 1996): 15100 [hereinafter "Wetterling Guidelines"].

67. Standards and requirements described in the text are set forth in the "Wetterling Guidelines," ibid., 1511–17.

68. See *Cong. Rec.* 142 (May 7, 1996): H 4453 (statement of Rep. Zimmer). See also House Committee on the Judiciary, *House Report no. 104-555*, 104th Cong., 2d sess., May 6, 1996, 2 ("It has been brought to the attention of the Committee . . . that notwithstanding the clear intent of Congress that relevant information about these offenders be released to the public . . . some law enforcement agencies are still reluctant to do so.").

69. See *Cong. Rec.* 142 (May 7, 1996): H 4452 (statement of Rep. McCollum).

70. House Subcommittee on Crime of the Committee on the Judiciary *Minor and Miscellaneous Bills (Part 2)*, 104th Cong., 2nd sess., March 7, 1996, 98 (statement of Rep. Dick Zimmer).

71. The unanimous vote was specifically sought by floor leaders and occurred after a handful of initially dissenting House members changed their votes. For fuller discussion of this evolution, see Lord Windlesham, *Politics, Punishment, and Populism* (New York: Oxford University Press, 1998), 179–80.

72. Megan's Law, Public Law 104–45, *Stat.* 110 (1996): 1345 (amending 42 U.S.C. § 14071(d) (1994)).

73. Bill Clinton, "Remarks on Signing Megan's Law and an Exchange with Reporters," in *Public Papers of the Presidents of the United States, William J. Clinton* (Washington, DC: Government Printing Office, 1996), 763–64.

74. "President Clinton's Weekly Radio Address," *CNN.com*, June 22, 1996, http://www.cnn.com/US/9602/22Clinton.radio/transcript.html.

75. See *Cong. Rec.* 140 (August 21, 1994): H 8963 (statement of Rep. Edwards).

76. 42 U.S.C. § 14071(d) (1996).

77. "Final Guidelines for Megan's Law and the Jacob Wetterling Crimes Against Children and Sexually Violent Offender Registration Act," *Federal Register* 69 (July 21, 1997): 39019.

78. Ibid.

79. *Pam Lychner Sexual Offender Tracking and Identification Act of 1996*, Public Law 104-236, *Stat.* 110 (1996): 3093 (codified at 42 U.S.C. § 14072).

80. Lychner and her two daughters were killed in the explosion of TWA flight 800 off the coast of Long Island in 1996. Later that year Congress passed the Lychner Act in her memory.

81. 42 U.S.C. § 14072(d)(2). "Aggravated sexual abuse" included among other things sexual acts accompanied by force or threats, as well as any sexual act with a minor under the age of 12. 18 U.S.C. § 2241.

82. *Jacob Wetterling Crimes Against Children and Sexually Violent Offenders Registration Improvements Act of 1997*, Public Law 105-119 (1997).

83. *General Provisions of Title I of the Departments of Commerce, Justice, and State, the Judiciary, and Related Agencies Appropriations Act*, Public Law 105-119, *Stat.* 11 (1998): 2461; Public Law 105-277, Title XIII, § 123 (October 21, 1998).

84. *Campus Sex Crimes Prevention Act*, Public Law 106–386, § 1601(b) & (c), *Stat.* 114 (2000): 1538 (codified at 20 U.S.C. § 1092(f)(1) and 42 U.S.C. § 14071(j)).

85. *The Prosecutorial Remedies and Other Tools to End the Exploitation of Children Today (PROTECT) Act*, Public Law 108-21, *Stat.* 117 (2003): 650.

86. Dru's Law, S 792, 109th Cong., 1st sess, *Cong. Rec.* 151 (April 15, 2005): S 3731 (directing the attorney general to make available a national registry via the Internet). The site address is http://www.nsopr.gov.

87. Public Law 109-248, *Stat.* 120 (2006): 587 (codified at 42 U.S.C. § 16901 et seq.).

88. Public Law 109-248, § 2, *Stat.* 120 (2006): 590.

89. 42 U.S.C. § 16902.

90. See, e.g., 42 U.S.C. § 16920 (establishing "Dru Sjodin National Sex Offender Public Website"); 42 U.S.C. § 16988 (establishing "Jessica Lunsford Address Verification Grant Program"); 42 U.S.C. § 16911(5)(A) ("Amie Zyla Expansion of Sex Offense Definition").

91. Public Law 109-248, § 129, *Stat.* 120 (2006): 587, 600–601.

92. 42 U.S.C. § 16901 ("Declaration of Purpose").

93. In addition to the references above, see, e.g., *Cong. Rec.* 142 (May 7, 1996): H 4452, H 4453 (statement of Rep. Zimmer urging adoption of the Megan's Law "so that all 50 states [would] be held to a common standard of community notification").

94. See, e.g., House Committee on the Judiciary, *Report on Children's Safety Act of 2005*, 109th Cong., 1st sess., September 9, 2005, 23–24; *Cong. Rec.* 151 (September 14, 2005): H 7889 (statement of Rep. Green); *Cong. Rec.* 152 (July 20, 2006): S 8018 (statement of Sen. George Allen), S 8022 (statement of Sen. DeWine), S 8030 (statement of Sen. Frist).

95. *Cong. Rec.* 152 (July 20, 2006), S 8012, S 8013 (statement of Sen. Hatch).

96. The AWA excludes from coverage any offense involving "consensual sexual conduct"—if the victim was an adult, "unless the adult was under the custodial au-

thority of the offender at the time of the offense, or if the victim was at least 13 years old and the offender was not more than 4 years older than the victim." 42 U.S.C. § 16911(5)(C).

97. Ibid., § 16911(5)(A)(i).

98. Ibid., § 16911(7).

99. The scope of retroactive application is reflected in guidelines issued by the attorney general. See U.S. Dept. of Justice, "Final Guidelines for Title I of the Adam Walsh Child Protection and Safety Act of 2006, the Sex Offender Registration and Notification Act (SORNA)," http://www.ojp.usdoj.gov/smart/guidelines_final.htm [hereinafter "AWA Guidelines"].

100. Ibid., 16. "Sexual act" includes genital and oral penetration as well as oral-genital and anal contact. Ibid.

101. The foreign conviction does not compel registration if it was "not obtained with sufficient safeguards for fundamental fairness and due process for the accused." Ibid., § 16911(5)(B). The Guidelines specify that convictions secured in Canada, the United Kingdom, Australia, and New Zealand qualify, as do convictions in jurisdictions with justice systems with safeguards deemed sufficient by the U.S. Department of State. "AWA Guidelines," 16–17.

102. See 42 U.S.C. § 16927. On the history of registration in Indian Country more generally, see Timothy J. Droske, "The New Battleground for Public Law 280 Jurisdiction: Sex Offender Registration in Indian Country," *Northwestern Law Review* 101 (2007): 897.

103. 42 U.S.C. § 16911(1)-(4).

104. 42 U.S.C. § 16915 (duration), 16916 (verification intervals). The AWA specifies, however, that certain individuals can have their registration periods reduced: (i) Tier I registrants, reduced by five years if they have a "clean record" for 10 years (i.e., 10-year total duration) and (ii) Tier III registrants who are juveniles, reduced to 25 years if "clean" for 25 years (e.g., 25-year total duration). Ibid., § 16915(b)(2),(3). For a definition of "clean record," see ibid., § 16915(b)(1).

105. 42 U.S.C. § 16913(c).

106. 42 U.S.C. § 16918(a). The AWA provides that jurisdictions may exempt from disclosure "any information about a [T]ier I sex offender convicted of an offense other than a specified offense against a minor"; the name (but not location) of a registrant's employer; the name of the institution where a registrant is a student; and any other information the attorney general deems appropriate. Ibid., § 16918(c).

107. 42 U.S.C. § 16921(b).

108. 18 U.S.C. § 2250. In addition, individuals who commit a "crime of violence" under federal law, the law of the District of Columbia, tribal law, or the law of any U.S. territory of possession, while unregistered, face a minimum of five years and a maximum of thirty years. Ibid., § 2250(c).

109. 42 U.S.C. § 16941(a).

110. See U.S. Marshals, "Operation FALCON," http://www.usdoj.gov/marshals/falcon/index.html. The acronym represents "Federal and Local Cops Organized Nationally."

111. 42 U.S.C. § 16926(c). The effort was not unprecedented: in March 1998 the Bureau of Justice Statistics, part of the U.S. Department of Justice, created the National Sex Offender Registry Assistance Program, intended to assist states in satisfying federal directives, starting with *Wetterling* in 1994. See Devon B. Adams, *Summary of State Sex Offender Registries, 2001* (Washington, DC: Bureau of Justice Statistics, Dept. of Justice, 2002), 1.

112. 42 U.S.C. § 16926.

113. Public Law 109-248, §§ 634–37, *Stat.* 120 (2006): 5877, 645–46.

114. 42 U.S.C. § 16924. Alternatively, jurisdictions have one year after the attorney general makes available computer software for the establishment and operation of "uniform sex offender registries and Internet sites," if the software is available later than July 2009. Ibid., § 16918(a)(2). The attorney general is also authorized to permit two one-year extensions of the deadline. Ibid., § 16924(b).

115. Doris Sue Wong, "Weld Signs Bill Creating Sex-Offender Registry—Those Convicted Have to Register," *Boston Globe*, August 15, 1996.

116. "Roundhouse Roundup," *Albuquerque Tribune*, March 13, 1999, D5.

117. See Wayne A. Logan, "Criminal Justice Federalism and National Sex Offender Policy," *Ohio State Journal of Criminal Law* 6 (2008): 51.

118. James Popkin and John Simons, "Natural Born Predators," *U.S. News & World Report*, September 1994, 64. Perhaps due to its more controversial nature, notification has been more visibly affected by federal influence. In 1995, before *Megan's Law* pressured states to adopt notification, only five states authorized it: Alaska, Louisiana, New Jersey, Tennessee, and Washington. See Michelle Pia Jerusalem, "A Framework for Post-Sentence Sex Offender Legislation: Perspectives on Prevention, Registration, and the Public's 'Right to Know,'" *Vanderbilt Law Review* 48 (1995): 240–41.

119. See *State v. Chun*, 76 P.3d 935, 940 (Haw. 2003) (citing language in Hawaii legislative debates).

120. See, e.g., Kirk Mitchell and Sean Kelly, "Predator or Just an Offender? A Colorado Law Is Supposed to Inform Neighbors When High-Risk Offenders Move Nearby. But It's Been Used Rarely and Works Poorly, Some Say by Design," *Denver Post*, May 29, 2005, A1 (noting relative laxness of Colorado's law and quoting a state official as saying that the state adopted community notification only under federal pressure).

121. *New State Ice Co. v. Liebmann*, 285 U.S. 262, 311 (1932) (Brandeis, J., dissenting).

122. For instance, in California as of mid-2008, over 169 offenses triggered regis-

tration. See California Dept. of Justice, "California's Megan's Law," http://www.meganslaw.ca.gov/registration/offenses.aspx.

123. By way of example, as of late November 2003, of the over 18,000 registrants in Illinois, 78% were convicted of aggravated criminal sexual abuse, aggravated criminal sexual assault, or criminal sexual assault. Illinois State Police, *Sex Offender Registration in Illinois* (February 2004), 5, http://www.isp.state.il.us.media/docdetails.cfm?docID=551.

124. See, e.g., Roberto Suro, "Town Faults Law," *Washington Post*, May 11, 1997 (discussing the case of an 18-year-old Wisconsin boy forced to register as a result of having consensual sex with his 15-year-old girlfriend). For a discussion of statutory rape as a basis for registration, including the twenty-eight jurisdictions allowing registration to stem from strict liability-based convictions, see Catherine L. Carpenter, "The Constitutionality of Strict Liability in Sex Offender Registration Laws," *Boston University Law Review* 86 (2006): 325.

125. Associated Press, "Sheep Abuser Must Register as a Sex Offender," *News Channel 3* (Hampton Roads, Virginia), February 15, 2006.

126. L. L. Brasier, "Judges: Sheep Sex Doesn't Make Man a Sex Offender," *Detroit Free Press*, September 25, 2008.

127. "Offender Told to Register for Assaulting Dog," *Journal-World* (Lawrence, Kansas), March 21, 2008.

128. "Creek County Ex-Judge Registers as Sex Offender," *Tulsa World*, May 8, 2008.

129. See Ala. Code § 13A-11-200 (1994); Idaho Code § 18-8304(1)(a) (Supp. 1998); La. Rev. Stat. § 15:542(E) (Supp. 1988); Miss. Code § 45-33-1(4) (Supp. 1997); Mo. Stat. §§ 589.400-1(4), 566.010–.141 (Supp. 1998); S.C. Code § 23-3-430(C) (Supp. 1997). In mid-2000, before *Lawrence*, in New Orleans an estimated 44% of registrants had been convicted of sodomy, an offense typically used to target male and female prostitutes. Pamela Coyle, "400 Sex Offenders in Region," *Times-Picayune* (New Orleans), May 2, 2000.

130. Kan. Stat. § 22-4902(b)(12) (defined as meaning that "one of the purposes for which the defendant committed the crime was for the purpose of the defendant's sexual gratification").

131. See *State v. Patterson*, 963 P.2d 436 (Kan. Ct. App. 1998) (upholding registration requirement). The court noted that it had "some concern over the possibility that this statute could be extended beyond reason. For instance, would a defendant fall under the provisions of the [Act] if he or she stole contraceptives or engaged in disorderly conduct by shouting sexually explicit words?" Ibid., 440. In Arizona, where registration can be imposed upon a finding of "sexual motivation," the court of appeals expressed concern that it could be required for "such situational and often victimless

misdemeanors as adultery, sodomy, lewd and lascivious acts, and open and notorious cohabitation." *Arizona v. Noble*, 808 P.2d 325, 329 (Ariz. Ct. App. 1990).

132. Cal. Penal Code § 290(a)(2)(E); Wash. Rev. Code §§ 9A.44.130, 9.94A.127 (1997). See also *State v. Halstien*, 857 P.2d 270, 282 (Wash. 1993) (requiring registration of a juvenile paperboy who broke into a woman's house and stole a box of condoms and a sex toy).

133. Ind. Code § 5-2-12-4(1)(E).

134. S.C. Code § 23-4-430(D).

135. Minn. Stat. § 242.166 subd. 1(a)(1).

136. *State v. Newell*, no. C1-02-310, 2002 WL 31253657 * 2 (Minn. Ct. App. 2002). See also *Gunderson v. Hvass*, 339 F.3d 639 (8th Cir. 2003) (upholding Minnesota registration provision in a federal habeas corpus proceeding while noting that provision might lead to "unfair results in some cases," for instance when a jury acquits defendant of an enumerated offense and convicts of a nonenumerated offense).

137. For a full discussion of this phenomenon and its consequences, see Wayne A. Logan, "Horizontal Federalism in an Age of Criminal Justice Interconnectedness," *University of Pennsylvania Law Review* 154 (2006): 257.

138. California has codified an exception to this blanket importation, specifying that certain foreign convictions (e.g., indecent exposure and incest) triggering registration elsewhere will not require registration in California. See Cal. Penal Code § 290(a)(2)(D).

139. Ohio Rev. Code § 2721.21. The provision was apparently inspired by a desire to avoid an alternative proposal to suspend the civil statute of limitations for claims stemming from the Catholic church clergy child sex abuse scandal. Jim Provance, "Sex-Offender Registry Takes Shape: Ohio Online Program a First for Any State," *Blade* (Toledo, Ohio), July 1, 2006.

140. Ohio Rev. Code § 2721.21(D).

141. For instance, they must annually verify their registration information, Ohio Rev. Stat. § 3707.04; have their information disseminated to all residential units within one thousand feet of their residence, Ohio Rev. Stat. § 3797.06; and not live within one thousand feet of a school premises, Ohio Rev. Stat. § 3797.11

142. See Mass. Gen. Laws, Ch. 6, 178K(2)(d); Massachusetts Sex Offender Registry Board Regulations 1.06, 1.07, 1.22.

143. Idaho Code § 18-8304(4).

144. See Wayne A. Logan, "A Study in 'Actuarial Justice': Sex Classification Practice and Procedure," *Buffalo Criminal Law Review* 3 (2000): 626–33.

145. See, e.g., Ark. Code § 12-12-906 (Supp. 1993); W. Va. Code § 61-8F-4 (Supp. 1993).

146. See, e.g., Colo. Rev. Stat. § 18-3-412.5 (West Supp. 1993) (twenty, ten, or five

years); N.H. Rev. Stat. § 632-A:16 (Supp. 1993) (life or ten years); N.D. Cent. Code § 12.1-32-15 (Supp. 1993) (five or ten years).

147. Michele L. Earl-Hubbard, "The Child Sex Offender Registration Laws: The Punishment, Liberty Deprivation, and Unintended Results Associated with the Scarlet Letter Laws of the 1990s," *Northwestern University Law Review* (1996): 805*n*111.

148. Scott Matson and Roxanne Lieb, *Sex Offender Registration: A Review of State Laws*, rev. ed. (Olympia: Washington Institute for Public Policy, 1996), 6.

149. Earl-Hubbard, "The Child Sex Offender," 805–6.

150. Karen J. Terry, *Sexual Offenses and Offenders: Theory, Practice, and Policy* (Belmont, CA: Thomson Learning/Wadsworth, 2006): 185–88.

151. See, e.g., Ky. Rev. Stat. § 17.510 (1996) (14 days); N.M. Stat. § 29–11A-4 (1996) (15 days for new arrivals but 30 days for persons released from in-state facilities). See generally Staci Thomas and Roxanne Lieb, *Sex Offender Registration: A Review of State Laws* (Olympia: Washington Institute for Public Policy, 1995), 18–25, tbl. 2.

152. Matson and Lieb, *Sex Offender Registration*, 21–30.

153. Earl-Hubbard, "Child Sex Offender," 805*n*111.

154. Terry, *Sexual Offenses and Offenders*, 184–88.

155. See, e.g., *People v. Molnar*, 857 N.E.2d 209 (Ill. 2006).

156. Alabama, for instance, criminalized unintentional registration violations. Ala. Code §. 15-20-23(a). Prior law, by contrast, required that violations be intentional. See Ala. Code § 15-20-23(a) (Supp. 2004).

157. See, e.g., R.I. Gen. Laws § 11-37-16 (Supp. 1993) (90 days in jail and one year probation).

158. Earl-Hubbard, "Child Sex Offender," 812–13. Ten states treated subsequent violations as felonies. Ibid.

159. Lara Farley, "The Adam Walsh Act: The Scarlet Letter of the Twentieth-First Century," *Washburn Law Journal* 47 (2008): 477.

160. See, e.g., *People v. Carmony*, 92 P.3d 369, 371 (Cal. 2004). But see Bradshaw v. State, 671 S.E.2d 485 (Ga. 2008) (invalidating on Eighth Amendment grounds law that imposed mandatory life term based on second conviction for registration violation).

161. Steve Quinn, "Legislature Approves Crime Bills," *Associated Press*, April 13, 2008.

162. "Sex-offender Registry Update Signed into Law," *Telegraph* (Nashua, New Hampshire), July 9, 2008.

163. Retroactivity can also reactivate dated social morays. A foremost example of this persisted in California, where until being amended in the late 1990s the state's registration law, retroactive to 1944, swept up hundreds of gay men previously convicted of offenses involving adult consensual sex. See Jeff Leeds, "Megan's Law Calling up Old, Minor Offenses," *Los Angeles Times*, February 24, 1997 (describing experiences of

Korean- and World War II–era veterans who were forced to register based on decades-old convictions for sexual improprieties).

164. Robert L. Jacobson, "Megan's Laws: Reinforcing Old Patterns of Anti-Gay Police Harassment," *Georgetown Law Journal* 87 (1999): 2467.

165. Between 1992 and 1995, for instance, 40 U.S. jurisdictions made it easier to prosecute juveniles as adults in criminal court, and 47 singled out serious juvenile offenders for harsher treatment. Patricia Torbet et al., *State Responses to Serious and Violent Juvenile Crime* (Washington, DC: U.S. Dept. of Justice, Office of Justice Programs, Office of Juvenile Justice and Delinquency Prevention, 1996), 3, 59.

166. Matson and Lieb, *Sex Offender Registration*, 9.

167. Andy Newman, "New Jersey Court Says 12-Year-Old Must Register as a Sexual Offender," *New York Times*, April 12, 1996.

168. Angela Rozas, "Do Young Sex Offenders Belong on Adult Register?" *Chicago Tribune*, January 16, 2007.

179. Franklin E. Zimring, *An American Travesty: Legal Responses to Adolescent Sexual Offending* (Chicago: University of Chicago Press, 2004), 148.

170. For an overview of these variations, see Elizabeth Garfinkle, "Coming of Age in America: The Misapplication of Sex-Offender Registration and Community-Notification Laws to Juveniles," *California Law Review* 91 (2003): 179–82.

171. See, e.g., "'Romeos' Can Avoid Sex Offender Status," *St. Petersburg Times* (Florida), May 3, 2007 (discussing Florida law exempting juvenile offenders who are no more than four years older than their sexual partner, when the partner is at least 14 years old, and when a court determines that the encounter was consensual).

172. See Maggie Jones, "How Can You Distinguish a Budding Pedophile from a Kid with Real Boundary Problems?" *New York Times Magazine*, July 22, 2007, 33, 35–36.

173. See Fla. Stat. § 775.13 (2007). The law applies to persons convicted of felonies by Florida courts, as well as courts outside the state if the crime would be a felony if committed in Florida. See ibid. § 775.13(2), (3). Felons must register within 48 hours of entering Florida, be fingerprinted and photographed, and provide the following information: crime of conviction, place of conviction, sentence imposed, name, aliases, address, and occupation. Ibid. § 775.13(2), (3). While the law does not specify, it appears that the registration requirement applies for five years. E-mail correspondence to author from Jim Martin, General Counsel of the Florida Department of Law Enforcement, July 12, 2007.

174. Fla. Stat. § 775.261. Such persons can petition for relief from registration after 20 years yet must register within 24 hours of release and must provide a greater amount of information than convicted felons. Unlike felons, they must also register at the Motor Vehicles Department, acknowledge their status as a career offender, show proof of registration, and secure a driver's license or identification card. The sheriff is

to verify the accuracy the registration information of career offenders on an annual basis.

175. See Fla. Stat. § 943.0435.

176. See ibid. § 775.21.

177. Miss. Code § 97-35-27.

178. Nev. Code § 179C.090.

179. Ala. Code § 13A-11-181

180. Jocelyn Black, "Illinois House and Senate Agree to Send 'Sex Offender Only' Bill," *Medill News Service*, April 6, 2006; Brian Mackey, "New Registry Proposed for Convicts," *Chicago Daily Law Bulletin*, January 18, 2006, 1.

181. 730 Ill. Code § 154/1 et seq. The Act covers persons convicted of kidnapping, aggravated kidnapping, unlawful restraint, aggravated unlawful restraint, first-degree murder, child abduction, and forcible detention when the victim is less than 18 years of age. 730 Ill. Code § 154/5(b). At sentencing, courts must verify in writing that the offense was not sexually motivated, which would require that the individual be listed on the sex offender registry. 730 Ill. Code 154/85. The law is coupled with the "Child Murderer and Violent Offender Against Youth Community Notification Law." See 730 Ill. Code § 154/75 et seq.

182. 730 Ill. Code § 150/1 et seq. The law is coupled with the "Sex Offender Community Notification Law." See 730 Ill. Code § 152/120 et seq.

183. Haw. Rev. Stat. § 846E-2.

184. See Okla. Stat. tit. 57 § 591.

185. Cal. Penal Code § 457.1.

186. See, e.g., Ga. Stat. § 35-3-50; 730 Ill. Comp. 180/10; Okla. tit. 74 § 150.12C; W. Va. Code § 60A-10-1.

187. See Tenn. Code § 39-17-436; Tennessee Bureau of Investigation, "Tennessee Meth Offender Registry Database," http://www.tennesseeanytime.org/methor/.

188. Editorial, "New Branding Campaign: Latest Criminal Registry Idea Wrong-headed," *Sacramento Bee*, January 24, 2007.

189. Cal. Penal Code § 457.1.

190. 730 Ill. Code § 148/10.

191. Cal. Penal Code § 186.30.

192. See Tennessee Dept. of Health, "Abuse Registry," http://health.state.tn.us/abuseregistry.

193. La. Rev. Stat. § 15:643.

194. Penn. H.B. 561, S.B. 756 (2009–2010 Gen. Assem. Reg. Sess.).

195. "Robin's Law: A Statewide, Violent Offenders' Database Would Help to Avoid Domestic Dangers," *Morning Call* (Allentown, Pennsylvania), May 21, 2007.

196. Andrea Siegel, "Officials Target Hate Crimes: Sentencing Renews Attention to Issue of Race Relations," *Baltimore Sun*, February 15, 2006.

197. Teri Burton, "Legislation Calls for Animal Abusers to Be Nationally Registered," *Tennessean.com*, September 9, 2007.

198. George Graham, "Senator Seeks Dangerous Dog Registry," *Republican* (Springfield, Massachusetts), August 29, 2007.

199. See Inhumane.org, "Through Their Eyes, The National Animal Abuse Registry," http://www.inhumane.org.

200. See John Fritze, "Tenant, Gun Bills Signed into Law," *Baltimore Sun*, October 2, 2007.

201. Oklahoma's violent crime offender registry is an exception: registrants are subject to Internet notification, and habitual violent-crime offenders are subject to active community notification.

202. This is the case with Tennessee's meth registry, for instance.

203. Like criminal registries, child abuse registries originated in cities, were later adopted by states, and fostered by federal legislation. See Maryann Zavez, "Child Abuse Registries and Juveniles: An Overview and Suggestions for Change in Legislative and Agency Direction," *Seton Hall Legislative Journal* 22 (1998): 409–10.

204. See *Artway v. Attorney General*, 876 F. Supp. 666, 689 (D. N.J. 1995) ("Megan's Law goes well beyond all previous provisions for public access to an individual's criminal history."); *Doe v. Poritz*, 662 A.2d 367, 429 (N.J. 1995) (Stein, J., dissenting) ("[Other states] either do not require law enforcement to notify the public, or authorize far more limited public notification than that mandated by New Jersey's statute.").

205. See 42 U.S.C. § 16925(b).

206. See, e.g., *Doe v. Attorney General*, 686 N.E.2d 1007, 1013 (Mass. 1997).

207. For an overview of notification methods employed in the mid-late 1990s, see Peter Finn, *Sex Offender Community Notification* (Washington, DC: U.S. Dept. of Justice, Office of Justice Programs, National Institute of Justice, 1997).

208. As of 1999, California, Florida, New York, and Wisconsin were the only states to have hotlines. California alone made registrant information available by CD-ROM. Devon B. Adams, *Summary of State Sex Offender Registry Dissemination Procedures* (Washington, D.C.: Bureau of Justice Statistics, U.S. Dept. of Justice, 1999), 1. In California, the attorney general authorized viewing of the CD-ROM, containing information on 64,000 registrants organized by zip code, at county fairs, and viewing booths were very popular. William Claiborne, "At the Los Angeles County Fair, 'Outing' Sex Offenders," *Washington Post*, September 20, 1997.

209. Devon B. Adams, *Summary of State Sex Offender Registries, 2001* (Washington, DC: Bureau of Justice Statistics, U.S. Dept. of Justice, 2002), 8–12.

210. The telephone service had a less than propitious start, when due to a malfunction some callers were wrongly directed to a phone-sex service. James P. Sweeney, "Child-Molester Hotline Can't Be Called a Ringing Success," *San Diego Tribune*, August 9, 1995.

211. According to a U.S. government study, 6 states had websites in 1998; 15 states had sites in 1999; and 29 states and the District of Columbia had sites by early 2001, with at least 6 more developing or planning sites. Adams, *Summary*, 3.

212. See Christina Locke and Bill F. Chamberlin, "Safe from Sex Offenders? Legislating Internet Publication of Sex Offender Registries," *Urban Lawyer* 39 (2007): 11.

213. California State Attorney General, *California Sex Offender Information: Megan's Law* (June 2008).

214. See Office of the California the Attorney General, http://www.ag.ca.gov/megan/pdf/july2001.pdf. During the year there were also 616,702 mail-in requests. Ibid.

215. Melissa Moore, "New Sex Offender Site Can't Tell Entire Story," *Advocate* (Baton Rouge, Louisiana), May 10, 2000. See also, e.g., "Governor Rell Announces $1 Million to Improve Megan's Law Database in Next Bond Package," *States News Service*, September 5, 2007 (noting that Connecticut's website receives more than 1.3 million hits a year).

216. Regina B. Schofield, "National Sex Offender Public Registry," *Public Management* 35, no. 1 (January 1, 2006).

217. As of summer 2007, only two states—New York and Vermont—required that site viewers provide their names and addresses. See Human Rights Watch, *No Easy Answers: Sex Offender Laws in the US* (New York: Human Rights Watch, 2007), 55–56.

218. This frustration manifested itself in the mid-late 1990s when private sites were created by individuals with access to registrants' information. One such website was operated by Michigan State Representative Dave Jaye who posted information on Macon County registrants so that parents would know "if a perv lives in [their] neighborhood." Logan, "Federal Habeas," 200*n*247. See also Logan, "Jacob's Legacy," 1300 (discussing publication in 1995 of Minnesota newsletter prior to state's adoption of community notification law).

219. Jane Small, Note, "Who Are the People in Your Neighborhood? Due Process, Public Protection, and Sex Offender Notification Laws," *New York University Law Review* 74 (1999): 1465*n*81.

220. Human Rights Watch, *No Easy Answers*, 56–58.

221. Ibid., 92, 94. The Adam Walsh Act, however, prescribes that state registries contain such a warning, and states wishing to receive Byrne Program funds presumably will be obliged to do so.

222. See, e.g., Kansas Bureau of Investigation, "KBI Registered Offender Website," http://www.accesskansas.org/kbi/ro.shtml (Kansas).

223. See, e.g., Texas Dept. of Public Safety, "TxDPS Sex Offender Registry," https://records.txdps.state.tx.us/DPS_WEB/SorNew/PublicSite/index.aspx?SearchType =Name ("[I]t is your responsibility to make sure the records you access through this site pertain to the person about whom you are seeking information. Extreme care

should be exercised in using any information obtained from this Web site.") (accessed September 7, 2008).

224. This approach, as noted later, is consistent with the Supreme Court's holding in *Connecticut Dept. of Public Safety v. Doe*, 538 U.S. 1, 4 (2003).

225. Ala. Code § 15-20-21(3).

226. Ala. Code § 15-20-25(a)(1)-(3).

227. Tex. Code of Crim. Proc. § 62.056.

228. La. Rev. Stat. § 15: 542.

229. See, e.g., North Carolina State Bureau of Investigation, "North Carolina Offender Registry," http://ncfindoffender.com/default.aspx (North Carolina); North Dakota Office of the Attorney General, "North Dakota Sex Offender Web Site," http://www.sexoffender.nd.gov (North Dakota).

230. See, e.g., FamilyWatchdog, http://www.familywatchdog.com. With profits to be made, the technology has been used by the unscrupulous to alarm communities about the presence of registrants and then charge a fee to reveal information on their identity and location. See "Police Say Business Has Caused Panic, Flooded Phone Lines," *9News.com*, July 10, 2007, http://www.9news.com/news/article.aspx?storyid=73479. Police in Broomfield, Colorado, where the flyers were distributed, were overwhelmed by calls from anxious residents, causing concern that emergency-related service calls could not be handled properly. Ibid.

231. See "Parents for Megan's Law," http://www.parentsformeganslaw.com.

232. As of fall 2007, Alabama, Delaware, Florida, Louisiana, Mississippi, Oklahoma, and West Virginia required that registrants have a recognizable notation on their licenses indicating their status. Alabama required that persons subject to twice-convicted felon registration law also carry an identification card. See Ala. Code § 13A-11-182. By contrast, Nevada's general felon registration law expressly stated that registrants shall not be required to carry a card. See Nev. Code § 179C.100.

233. See John Hill, "Bill Would Mark Licenses of Sex Offenders," *Times* (Shreveport, Louisiana), May 19, 2006 (noting that the law passed the State Senate unanimously and would generate an estimated $116,000 in annual renewal fees).

234. See, e.g., Dave Wedge, "IMAPERV Plate Proposed," *Boston Herald*, May 3, 2005; "Lawmakers Want Pink Plates Put on Cars of Sex Offenders," *Columbus Dispatch*, May 3, 2005.

235. See Wayne A. Logan, "Constitutional Collectivism and Ex-Offender Residence Exclusion Laws," *Iowa Law Review* 92 (2006): 1.

236. Ibid., 9.

237. See, e.g., La. Rev. Stat. § 29:726; Jacksonville, Fla. Code § 674.501.

238. Logan, "Constitutional Collectivism," 7. Congress in 1999 rejected an effort to bar registrants from national parks. Introduced by Representative Mark Green (R-

WI), H.R. 1925, the Safe Park Act of 1999, would have subjected registrants who knowingly enter parks to a fine and/or imprisonment for a maximum of three years.

239. See Karen Salvemini, "Sex Offender Parents: Megan's Law and Schools' Legal Options," *Widener Law Journal* 17 (2008): 1031.

240. See, e.g., Mich. Comp. Laws §§. 28.734(1)(a); 28.733(f); Okla. Stat. Ann. tit. 57, § 589(A).

241. See, e.g., Idaho Code § 18-8327(2).

242. See, e.g., Ind. Code § 5-2-12-12; Okla. Stat. Ann. tit. 57, § 584(F).

243. See, e.g., Cal. Civ. Proc. Code § 1279.5 (no change unless "it is in the best interest of justice to grant [the change] and that doing so will not adversely affect the public safety); 730 Ill. Comp. Stat. § 5/21-101 (no change for duration of registration period); N.H. Rev. Stat. § 547:3-I (allowed only if registrant "makes a compelling show that a name change is necessary").

244. See *Smith v. Doe*, 538 U.S. 84, 101–2 (2003) (discussing requirement in Alaska).

245. Scott Ehlers, "State Legislative Affairs Update," *Champion*, July 2007, 59.

246. Ed Johnson, "Laws Tighten Reins on Sex Offenders; Job Checks, Tracking, Driver's Licenses Part of New Effort," *News-Press* (Fort Myers, Florida), June 28, 2007.

247. See Human Rights Watch, *No Easy Answers*, 48–49 (noting enactments in Florida, Illinois, Virginia, and Washington).

248. See Cal. Penal Code § 290 (historical notes).

249. While typically expansion has resulted from legislative involvement, in 2000 New Jersey residents themselves got directly involved. By an overwhelming margin, voters backed a proposed state constitutional amendment allowing for increased Internet-based community notification. As a result, rather than information on Tier II and III registrants being disseminated to persons they were "likely to encounter," as under prior law, such information could be made available to all persons with computer access. *A.A. v. State*, 895A.2d 453, 459 (N.J. Sup. Ct. 2006) (citing N.J. Const. at. IV, § 7, para. 12). As a technical matter the amendment only authorized the legislature to adopt a law permitting Internet notification; however, such a law was adopted several months later. Ibid., 455.

250. Associated Press, "Furor in Montana: Anti-Gay Section of Sex-Offender Bill Cut," *Atlanta Constitution*, March 24, 1995.

251. Peter Freiberg, "'Megan's Laws' Bode Ill for Some Gay People," *Washington Blade*, April 4, 1997. Congress, meanwhile, resisted an effort in 1997 to prevent adult consensual sodomy from being a registerable offense. Representative Chuck Schumer (D-NY) offered an amendment to *Wetterling* that would have barred states requiring registration on this basis from receiving Byrne Grant funds. By a party-line vote, the amendment was rejected by the House Judiciary Committee, with the majority justifying its position on the ground that the federal government should not intrude

upon state prerogative. Eleven dissenters to the Committee Report (all Democrats) branded the position as "specious," noting that the "Act already imposes a multitude of requirements on states. The Act contains four full pages of dense statutory text telling states how their sex offender registration programs must operate." House Committee on the Judiciary, *Jacob Wetterling Crimes against Children and Sexually Violent Offenders Registration Improvements Act of 1997*, H.R. Report no. 105-256, 105th Cong., 1st sess., 1997, 41–42.

252. See Cal. Penal Code § 290 (West Supp. 1999) (historical and statutory notes).

253. Until the 1960s, when the judiciary prohibited the practice, it was customary for gay men to plead guilty to offenses not requiring registration. E.A. Riddle, "Compulsory Registration: A Vehicle of Mercy Discarded," *California Western Law Review* 3 (1967): 195. California eventually deleted entries for over 8,000 individuals, either because they were dead or their offenses no longer required registration. Jacobson, "Reinforcing Old Patterns," 2460–61.

254. Adams, *Summary*, 6 app. 2. The report notes that for 2001 data from Massachusetts were not included, although Massachusetts reported that 17,000 individuals were registration-eligible. Also, 1998 data from Connecticut were omitted. Ibid., 2.

255. The figures cited in the text result from data cited in Adams, *Summary*, ibid., and the "Parents for Megan's Law" website; see Parents for Megan's Law, "Nationwide Registries & Links," http://www.parentsformeganslaw.com/html/links.lasso.

256. The surge in judicial caseload had several explanations. First, with laws in effect nationwide by the mid-1990s registration could no longer be avoided. Second, unlike in the past, when registration was enforced unevenly at best and maintenance of registries ranked as a low priority, in the modern era registration figured much more prominently. Third, and critically important, in the 1990s the laws became far more onerous, including expansion in offense eligibility, requiring far more identifying information (e.g., workplace and vehicles), stepped-up verification intervals, and enhanced penalties. And perhaps most important, modern laws also entailed community notification, with its manifold negative consequences for individuals.

257. 538 U.S. 84 (2003). The implications of both decisions are discussed at length in Chapter 6.

258. 538 U.S. 1 (2003).

259. Ibid., 7 (quoting from website).

260. Ibid., 4.

261. Ibid., 7.

262. Ibid.

263. See, e.g., *Fullmer v. Michigan Dept. of State Police*, 360 F.3d 579 (6th Cir. 2004) (upholding Michigan law).

264. Ron Fournier, "Clinton Signs Law on Sex Offenders," *Chicago Sun-Times*, May 18, 1996.

Chapter 4

1. Jerry Gray, "Sex Offender Legislation Passes in the Senate," *New York Times*, October 4, 1994.

2. Ivette Mendez, "Megan's Law: 10 Sex Offender Bills Clear the Senate," *Star-Ledger* (Newark, NJ), October 4, 1994.

3. Data from 1985–95 highlight this remarkable surge. As of November 1995, 46 states had registration laws, with 42 laws being adopted since 1985, and 28 since 1991. G. Scott Rafshoon, Comment, "Community Notification of Sex Offenders," *Emory Law Journal* 44 (1995): 1637–38.

4. See, e.g., *Random House Webster's College Dictionary*, 2nd rev. and updated ed. (New York: Random House, 2000), 826.

5. Edwin H. Sutherland, "The Diffusion of Sexual Psychopath Laws," *American Journal of Sociology* 56 (1950): 146–47.

6. Stanley Cohen, *Folk Devils and Moral Panics: The Creation of the Mods and Rockers*, 3rd ed. (New York: Routledge, 2002), 1.

7. Phillip Jenkins, *Moral Panic: Changing Concepts of the Child Molester in Modern America* (New Haven, CT: Yale University Press, 1998).

8. J. Edgar Hoover, "War on the Sex Criminal," *New York Herald Tribune*, September 26, 1937.

9. J. Edgar Hoover, "How Safe Is Your Daughter?" *American Magazine*, July 1947, 32.

10. Ibid.

11. Jenkins, *Moral Panic*, 72.

12. Deborah W. Denno, "Life Before the Modern Sex Offender Statutes," *Northwestern University Law Review* 92 (1998): 1351.

13. See Newton Minon, "The Illinois Proposal to Confine Sexually Dangerous Persons," *Journal of Criminal Law and Criminology* 40 (1949): 196 ("[T]he sex offender is a special type of criminal, demanding special consideration and attention. Sexual psychopaths are invariably recidivists who habitually fail to learn from experience. Statistics of sex crimes have reached appalling totals . . . The realization has deepened that sex crimes are not ordinary crimes, and that sex offenders are not ordinary criminals with ordinary motives.").

14. Denno, "Life Before," 1374n276 and 1379n290

15. See Jenkins, *Moral Panic*, 85–88; see also James Hughes, "The Minnesota Sexual Irresponsibles Law," *Mental Hygiene* 25 (1941): 80 (urging that the law be used against "homosexuals and those liable to attack children").

16. Paul W. Tappan, *The Habitual Sex Offender: Report and Recommendations of the Commission on the Habitual Sex Offender, New Jersey State Legislature* (Trenton, N.J., 1950), 13–14.

17. Ibid., 14; see also Sol Rubin, *The Law of Criminal Correction* (St. Paul, MN: West Publishing, 1963), 412–13.

18. *Report of Mayor's Committee for the Study of Sex Offenses* (New York, 1943), 11.

19. Simon A. Cole, "From the Sexual Psychopath Statute to 'Megan's Law': Psychiatric Knowledge in the Diagnosis, Treatment, and Adjudication of Sex Criminals in New Jersey, 1949–1999," *Journal of the History of Medicine and Allied Sciences* 55 (2000): 297.

20. Jenkins, *Moral Panic*, 72–73.

21. Denno, "Life Before," 1385.

22. Jenkins, *Moral Panic*, 93.

23. Sandy Rovner, "Hot Line of Hope After 'Adam,' Three Children Are Found," *Washington Post*, May 1, 1985.

24. Tom Shales, "Something Good Comes of TV-Film," *San Diego Tribune*, April 20, 1984.

25. As Phillip Jenkins points out, public anxiety spiked in the early 1930s, when news stories on the child sexual depravations of Albert Fish combined with the Lindbergh baby kidnapping by Bruno Hauptmann, causing readers "to see the generalized danger to children in sexually explicit terms." Jenkins, *Moral Panic*, 50.

26. John Gill, "Missing-Kids' Groups Foster Fear Rather than Facts," *Newsday* (Long Island, NY), April 11, 1989.

27. Diana Griego and Louis Kilzer, "The Truth About Missing Children: Exaggerated Statistics Stir National Paranoia," *Denver Post*, May 12, 1985.

28. Gill, "Foster Fear Rather than Facts."

29. David Finkelhor et al., *Missing, Abducted, Runaway, and Throwaway Children in America, First Report: Numbers and Characteristics* (Washington, DC: U.S. Dept. of Justice, 1990), v–xv. Testament to the difficulty of specifying the extent of the problem, the FBI reported that 50–70 children were abducted by strangers in 1988. Brian E. Albrecht, "What's Happened to the Missing Kids?" *Plain Dealer* (Cleveland, Ohio), March 4, 1990. A report issued in 1996 places the estimate of childhood abductions in the 50–155 range. Stephen R. Donziger, *The Real War on Crime: The Report of the National Criminal Justice Commission* (New York: Harper Perennial 1996), 67.

30. Albrecht, "What's Happened to the Missing Kids?"

31. "Moral panic," while useful as an analytic framework suggestive of the tenor of the times, implies that the underlying concern is somehow not worthy of concern. While perhaps accurate relative to the teenage "Mods and Rockers," of concern to Cohen, in a crucial respect the notion is inapt here: sexual abuse of children and adults alike, no matter what its actual extent, surely warrants major concern.

32. John Pratt, *Governing the Dangerous: Dangerousness, Law and Social Change* (Sydney: Federation Press, 1997), 70 (noting trend starting in the 1930s of the "'sexualization' of crime risks").

33. See Michael Tonry, "Rethinking Unthinkable Punishment Policies in America," *UCLA Law Review* 46 (1999): 1752 (referring to "a repressive era when punishment policies that would have been unthinkable in other times and places are not only commonplace but also . . . enthusiastically supported by public officials, policy intellectuals, and much of the general public").

34. Bert Useem et al., "Popular Support for the Prison Build-Up," *Punishment and Society* 5 (2003): 10–11.

35. *Sourcebook of Criminal Justice Statistics*, 31st ed. (Washington, DC: Bureau of Justice Statistics, 2005), tbl. 6.1.

36. Lauren E. Glaze and Thomas P. Bonczar, *U.S. Bureau of Justice Statistics, Probation and Parole in the United States, 2005* (Washington, DC: Bureau of Justice Statistics, 2006).

37. Kevin R. Reitz, "Don't Blame Determinacy: U.S. Incarceration Growth Has Been Driven by Other Forces," *Texas Law Review* 84 (2006): 1789–90.

38. Wayne A. Logan, "Casting New Light on an Old Subject: Death Penalty Abolitionism for a New Millennium," *Michigan Law Review* 100 (2002): 1337.

39. Patricia Torbet and Linda Szymanski, *State Legislative Responses to Violent Juvenile Crime: 1996–1997 Update* (Washington, DC: Office of Juvenile Justice and Delinquency Prevention, 1998).

40. One of the first modern instances occurred in 1987 when an Oregon judge required that a paroled child molester place a sign in front of his home proclaiming "Dangerous Sex Offender—No Children Allowed." For discussion of this and other similar instances during the era, see John Larrabee, "Fighting Crime with a Dose of Shame," *USA Today*, June 19, 1995; Henry Reske, "Scarlet Letter Sentences," *A.B.A. J.*, January 1996.

41. See Janice Morse, Note, "Les Miserables: Chain Gangs and the Cruel and Unusual Punishments Clause," *Southern California Law Review* 70 (1997): 1459.

42. Franklin E. Zimring et al., *Punishment and Democracy: Three Strikes and You're Out in California* (New York: Oxford University Press, 2001). As the victimizations of Jacob Wetterling (1989) and Megan Kanka (1994) triggered interest in registration and notification, the October 1993 kidnapping and murder of 12-year-old Polly Klaas in California by a recently paroled, twice-convicted violent offender propelled adoption of "three strikes" in California and elsewhere starting in 1994.

43. See Clayton Ettinger, *The Problem of Crime* (New York: R. Long & R. R. Smith, 1932), 303 (referring to laws as a "legislative thunderbolt," being responsible for major drops in crime and the departure of many criminals from states). Habitual felon laws were not actually creations of the 1930s, but rather dated back centuries, even to the Massachusetts Bay Colony. See Wayne A. Logan, "Civil and Criminal Recidivists: Extraterritoriality in Tort and Crime," *University of Cincinnati Law Review* 73 (2005): 1618.

44. V. F. Nourse, "Rethinking Crime Legislation: History and Harshness," *Tulsa Law Review* 39 (2004): 930 (noting that laws were passed or operative in over twenty states between 1920 and 1945 but thereafter enjoyed less use).

45. For discussion of the deeper sociological reasons explaining why sex offenders, in particular, have been the subject of such notably harsh treatment, see James F. Quinn et al., "Societal Reaction to Sex Offenders: A Review of the Origins and Results of the Myths Surrounding Their Crimes and Treatment Amenability," *Deviant Behavior* 25 (2004): 215. According to the authors, initial harshness stemmed from religious bans on the "joys of the flesh" and valuation of female virginity, giving way over time to concern for the unique vulnerability of victims (most often women and children), sacred taboos such as against incest, and the view that sex offenders are irredeemably prone to recidivate.

46. See Nora V. Demleitner, "First Peoples, First Principles: The Sentencing Commission's Obligation to Reject False Images of Criminal Offenders," *Iowa Law Review* 87 (2002): 571–74.

47. See Lawrence Greenfeld, *Sex Offenses and Offenders: An Analysis of Data on Rape and Sexual Assault* (Washington, DC: Office of Justice Programs, 1997), 17 (noting that from 1980 to 1997, while state prison populations increased 220%, the number of convicted sex offenders rose 330%).

48. In 1996, for instance, California required chemical castration for repeat sex offenders. Drummond Ayres, "California Bill Would Require 'Chemical Castration' for Repeat Sex Offenders," *New York Times*, August 27, 1996.

49. See generally Eric S. Janus and Wayne A. Logan, "Substantive Due Process and the Involuntary Commitment of Sexually Violent Predators," *Connecticut Law Review* 35 (2003): 323.

50. See Jonathan Simon, *Governing Through Crime: How the War on Crime Transformed American Democracy and Created a Culture of Fear* (New York: Oxford University Press, 2007).

51. See David Garland, *The Culture of Control: Crime and Social Order in Contemporary Society* (Chicago: University of Chicago Press, 2001).

52. See Anthony E. Bottoms, "The Philosophy and Politics of Punishment and Sentencing," in *The Politics of Sentencing Reform*, ed. Rod Morgan and Chris Clarkson (New York: Oxford University Press, 1995), 17.

53. See Katherine Beckett, *Making Crime Pay: Law and Order in Contemporary American Politics* (New York: Oxford University Press, 1997); Sara Sun Beale, "The New Media's Influence on Criminal Justice Policy: How Market-Driven News Promotes Punitiveness," *William & Mary Law Review* 48 (2006): 397. As Senator Joe Biden quipped in 1994, after passage of a massive federal crime bill, including the *Wetterling Act*, along with significant additions to the scope of the federal death penalty, the creation of over one hundred new offenses, and major new limits to the availability of

federal habeas corpus: "If someone proposed barb wiring the ankles of anyone who jaywalks, I think it would pass." Helen Dewar, "New Penalties' Scope Would Be Limited: Few Violent Crimes Go to Federal Court," *Washington Post*, November 10, 1993.

Whether in fact the public is as harshly punitive as the laws would suggest remains debatable. According to some scholars, citizens favor not only tougher punishments but also education, training, and employment of inmates. See Donald Braman, "Punishment and Accountability: Understanding and Reforming Criminal Sanctions in America," *UCLA Law Review* 53 (2007): 1185–86 (citing studies). Political leaders, however, as a rule hear and respond only to the punitive refrain, resulting in the shift discussed in the text. At the same time, synergistically, political rhetoric exaggerating crime risks and backing draconian sanctions has fueled a harshening of public sentiment. See Beckett, *Making Crime Pay*, 8.

54. Zimring, *Punishment and Democracy*, 178.

55. As one editorial writer surmised in 1934: "Time was when a murder in another locality did not strike home." Editorial, "A Change Toward Criminals," *Muskogee Daily Phoenix* (Oklahoma), May 4, 1934. See also Edwin F. Sutherland, "The Diffusion of Sexual Psychopath Laws," *American Journal of Society* 56 (1950): 144 (noting that "fear is produced more readily in the modern community than it was earlier in our history because of increasing publicity").

56. See Nourse, "Rethinking Crime Legislation," 925 (noting parallels between crime-fighting legislation in the 1920s and 1930s with the 1980s and 1990s).

57. See James Q. Whitman, *Harsh Justice: Criminal Punishment and the Widening Divide Between America and Europe* (New York: Oxford University Press, 2003). See also Braman, "Punishment and Accountability," 1192 (citing studies over the past thirty years consistently showing that a large majority of Americans believe that punishments are not harsh enough).

58. Garland, *Culture of Control*, 10.

59. See generally Elizabeth M. Schneider, *Battered Women and Feminist Lawmaking* (New Haven, CT: Yale University Press, 2000), 20–34.

60. See Shirley S. Abrahamson, "Redefining Roles: The Victims' Rights Movement," *Utah Law Review*, no. 3 (1985): 528 ("[S]upporters were reacting to the Warren Court's expansion of defendants' rights.").

61. See Markus Dubber, *Victims in the War on Crime: The Use and Abuse of Victims' Rights* (New York: New York University Press, 2002).

62. See Joel Best, *Threatened Children: Rhetoric and Concern About Child Victims* (Chicago: University of Chicago Press, 1990): 46–50, 71.

63. *Cong. Rec.* 142 (May 7, 1996): H 4452 (statement of Rep. Zimmer).

64. Ibid., H 4454 (statement of Rep. Jackson-Lee).

65. In New York, for instance, legislators made recurrent reference to Sherry Lindsay, of Binghamton, described by one speaker as being "lured into the house of a con-

victed sex offender while . . . trying to make a little extra money. She was held in the basement for three days before he finally killed her." See, e.g., *New York State Senate Minutes of SB-11-B* (May 24, 1995): 6620 (statement of Sen. Skelos).

66. Daniel M. Filler, "Making a Case for Megan's Law: A Study in Legislative Rhetoric," *Indiana Law Journal* 76 (2001): 346.

67. *Cong. Rec.* 137 (May 23, 1991): S 6703 (statement of Sen. Durenberger). The absolutist tenor of the statement was echoed in other sentiments expressed during the era with respect to criminal justice initiatives. For instance, in 1994, in urging adoption of his proposed bill, LIFER ("Life Imprisonment for Egregious Recidivists"), Representative Bob Livingston (R-LA) urged that "[a]s far as I am concerned, even one crime averted, one life saved, is worth the effort. In the end, crime is not about statistics, it is not about numbers—it is about people's lives and the quality of those lives." Subcommittee on Crime and Criminal Justice of the House Committee on the Judiciary, *Correcting Revolving Door Justice*, 103rd Cong., 2d sess., 1994, 14 (statement of Rep. Livingston).

68. See, e.g., *Cong. Rec.* 142 (May 7, 1996): H 4457 (statement of Rep. Molinari: "For those of you who oppose this bill, I ask you to envision the loss of your child."). An even more vivid example is found in 1994, when Representative Jennifer Dunn (R-WA) castigated her colleagues' initial refusal to include a community notification provision in the Wetterling Act, ominously asserting that

> Conferees who worked to protect the rights of sexual predators should understand this: The next little girl killed by a released sexual predator will haunt them . . . It is outrageous that this bill effectively denies notification to the next Megan Kanka or the next Polly Klaas, or to your mother or sister or daughter. And it is outrageous that we would place the rights of criminals over the rights of victims.

*Cong. Rec.* 140 (August 11, 1994): H 7934-01 (statement of Rep. Dunn).

69. *Cong. Rec.* 142 (May 8, 1996) E 732 (statement of Rep. Martini).

70. *Cong. Rec.* 142 (May 7, 1996): H 4453 (statement of Rep. Zimmer).

71. Filler, "Making a Case," 351. In Washington State, where legislation was not personalized by name, political pressure was brought to bear by activist Ida Ballasiotes, whose daughter had been murdered by a released recidivist, who threatened to publicize the names of any legislator who voted against the Community Protection Act of 1990. Stuart A. Scheingold et al., "Sexual Violence, Victim Advocacy, and Republican Criminology: Washington State's Community Protection Act," *Law & Society Review* 28 (1994): 729. David Boerner, a law professor who figured centrally in drafting the legislation, would later write that the involvement of Ballasiotes and others who lost family members "made it impossible to view these issues as abstract legal issues . . . [T]heir presence made us constantly aware that whatever we did, or chose not to do, would have a direct, tangible impact on individuals." David Boerner,

"Confronting Violence: In the Act and in the Word," *University of Puget Sound Law Review* 15 (1992): 576.

72. See Sutherland, "Diffusion of Sexual Psychopath Laws."

73. 42 U.S.C. § 16901 (emphasis added). In support of the bill, Wisconsin Representative James Sensenbrenner (R-WI) offered, after naming the seven individuals: "Their names comprise a roll call of insufferable loss and a call to national action— the injustice of each assault compounded by the cruel recognition that it might have been prevented. The continued vulnerability of America's children to sexual predators is a national tragedy demanding strong congressional action." *Cong. Rec.* 152 (July 25, 2006): H 5722 (statement of Rep. Sensenbrenner).

74. 42 U.S.C. § 16902.

75. In 2005 alone, for instance, almost one-half of the roughly 1,400 murder victims under age 18 were nonwhite and almost 45% of the roughly 59,300 victims of sexual abuse were nonwhite. See U.S. Dept. of Health and Human Services, Administration for Children and Families, "Child Maltreatment 2005," tbl. 3-12, http://www.acf. hhs.gov/programs/cb/pubs/cm05/table3_12.htm (sexual abuse); Federal Bureau of Investigation, "Crime in the United States 2005," tbl. 2, http://www.fbi.gov/ucr/05cius/ data/table_02.html (murder).

Moreover, it should not escape attention that all of the defendants in the Walsh Act "roll call" for whom a racial background was able to be determined were white. This demographic distinction is notable, given the common view that "get-tough" criminal justice policies are most often promoted by animus against African Americans, the infamous disparity in punishment of crack and powder cocaine being perhaps the most notable example. More research needs to be done, however, on whether registration laws, in actual effect, have a racially disproportionate impact on nonwhites. According to one study, such an effect is in evidence. See Daniel M. Filler, "Silence and the Racial Dimension of Megan's Law," *Iowa Law Review* 89 (2004): 1535. According to two Australian researchers, registration and community notification are justified by the need of white Americans to be able to single out potentially dangerous white offenders—who otherwise would remain anonymous and not trigger concern. "'Stranger danger' is therefore of a *white stranger,* upsetting the racial schema that white people, including children and their parents, may use in negotiating safety and danger in their neighborhoods." Lyn Hinds and Kathleen Daly, "The War on Sex Offenders: Community Notification in Perspective," *Australian and New Zealand Journal of Criminology* 34 (2001): 256.

76. Alan H. Swanson, "Sexual Psychopath Statutes: Summary and Analysis," *Journal of Criminal Law, Criminology, and Police Science* 51 (1960): 216.

77. Or. Rev. Stat. § 181.586 (1999). Contrast also the manner in which Canada, which also has registration laws, refers to registrants; there, notwithstanding similar

inflammatory rhetoric by the media, initiatives focus on "high-risk offenders." Michael Petrunik, "The Hare and the Tortoise: Dangerousness and Sex Offender Policy in the United States and Canada," *Canadian Journal of Criminology & Criminal Justice* 45 (2003): 57.

78. *Cong. Rec.* 140 ( August 11, 1994): S 11301 (statement of Sen. Dole).

79. *Cong. Rec.* 142 (May 7, 1996): H 4452, H 4457 (statement of Rep. Molinari).

80. *Cong. Rec.* 142 (July 24, 1996): S 8639 (statement of Sen. Hutchison).

81. Subcommittee on Crime, Terrorism, and Homeland Security, *House Bills on Sexual Crimes Against Children: Hearing on H.R. 764,* 109th Cong., 1st sess., 2005, 7 (statement of Rep. Foley).

82. *Doe v. Pataki,* 940 F. Supp. 603, 621–22 (S.D.N.Y. 1996), aff'd in part rev'd in part, 120 F.3d 1263 (2d Cir. 1997).

83. See, e.g., David Gergen, "Taming Teenage Wolfpacks," *U.S. News & World Report,* March 25, 1996, 68.

84. Mary Douglas, *Purity and Danger: An Analysis of the Concepts of Pollution and Taboo* (London: Ark, 1966).

85. William Ian Miller, *The Anatomy of Disgust* (Cambridge, MA: Harvard University Press, 1997), 8–9.

86. Joseph Kennedy, "Monstrous Offenders and the Search for Solidarity through Modern Punishment," *Hastings Law Journal* 51 (2000): 829.

87. Cass R. Sunstein, "On the Divergent American Reactions to Terrorism and Climate Change," *Columbia Law Review* 107 (2007): 542–43.

88. Jeremy Bentham, "Principles of Penal Law," pt. II, bk. 1, ch. 6, in *The Works of Jeremy Bentham,* ed. John Bowring (New York: Russell & Russell, 1962), 401.

89. *Cong. Rec.* 142 (1996): 10314 (statement of Rep. Cunningham).

90. Anthony Giddens, *Modernity and Self-Identity: Self and Society in the Late Modern Age* (Stanford, CA: Stanford University Press, 1991), 3, 28.

91. Cass R. Sunstein, *Laws of Fear: Beyond the Precautionary Principle* (New York: Cambridge University Press, 2005), 4.

92. Malcolm Feeley and Jonathan Simon, "The New Penology," *Criminology* 30 (1992): 452 (emphasis added). To David Garland, in the past crime was viewed "retrospectively and individually, in order to individualize wrongdoing and allocate punishment and treatment. The new criminologies tend to view crime *prospectively* and in *aggregate* terms, for the purpose of calculating risks and shaping preventive measures." Garland, *Culture of Control,* 128.

93. *Cong. Rec.* 137 (June 27, 1991): S 8914.

94. See, e.g., *Cong. Rec.* 152 (July 20, 2006): S 8017, S 8018 (statement of Sen. Allen asserting that "the highest recidivist rate . . . of any crime—even higher than murderers, even higher than robbers—is sex offenders").

95. See, e.g., Ark. Code Ann. § 12-12-902 (1999) ("The General Assembly finds that

sex offenders pose a high risk of reoffending after release from custody"); Fla. Stat. Ann § 775 21(3)(a) (1999) ("Sexual offenders are extremely likely to use physical violence and repeat their offenses."); Neb. Rev. Stat. § 29-4002 (1999) ("The Legislature finds that sex offenders present a high risk to commit repeat offenses."); S.C. Code § 23-3-400 (1999) ("Statistics show that sex offenders pose a high risk of reoffending.").

96. See, e.g., David van Biema, "Burn Thy Neighbor," *Time*, July 26, 1993, 58 (referring to sex offenders as "irredeemable monsters"); David A. Kaplan et al., "The Incorrigibles," *Newsweek*, January 18, 1993, 48 (emphasizing that recidivism rates for sex offenders are higher than other offender subpopulations); Lorraine Woellert, "Virginia Bill Proposes Registry for Sex Offenders," *Washington Times*, January 27, 1994 (registration of sex offenders is justified "because they have the highest rate of recidivism").

97. See, e.g., Jill S. Levenson et al., "Public Perceptions About Sex Offenders and Community Protection Policies," *Analyses of Social Issues and Public Policy* 7 (2007): 17 (reporting survey data from a Florida community reflecting that considerable majorities believe in extremely high sex offender recidivism rates, homogeneity of sex offender population, and extent of sexual abuse committed by strangers). In assessing such findings, it is important to note that social scientists are reluctant to infer a causal influence by the media on the public's fear of crime. David Law Altheide, *Creating Fear: News and the Construction of Crisis* (New York: Aldine de Gruyter, 2002), 24.

98. For further discussion of how the public and the media rely upon legislators as "official sources," see Beckett, *Making Crime Pay*, 24–25, 77.

99. See David Finkelhor and Lisa M. Jones, *Explanations for the Decline in Child Sexual Abuse Cases* (Washington, DC: Office of Juvenile Justice and Delinquency Prevention, 2004) (noting decrease in child sexual abuse of 50% during 1991–2004). The authors, researchers at the University of New Hampshire, attribute the decline to numerous factors, especially prevention and treatment.

100. See U.S. Dept. of Justice, Federal Bureau of Investigation, "Crime in the United States 2006," *Uniform Crime Reports*, 2007; Shannon Catalano, *2005 National Crime Victimization Survey* (Washington, DC: Bureau of Justice Statistics, 2006).

101. See Robert Anglen, "Arrests for Sex Crimes Falling," *Arizona Republic*, November 23, 2007. Cf. Denno, "Life Before," 1345, 1359 (noting that sexual psychopath laws also originated and grew amid falling rates).

102. For elaboration on the points made here, see Wayne A. Logan, "A Study in 'Actuarial Justice': Sex Offender Practice and Procedure," *Buffalo Criminal Law Review 3* (2000): 593.

103. On this shift more generally, see Bernard E. Harcourt, *Against Prediction: Profiling, Policing, and Punishment in an Actuarial Age* (Chicago: University of Chicago Press, 2007), 174–92. For discussion of the highly ordered penal classification re-

gimes of the era, see Stanley Cohen, *Visions of Social Control: Crime, Punishment and Classification* (New York: Blackwell, 1985), 192–93.

104. Patrick A. Langan et al., *Recidivism of Sex Offenders Released from Prison in 1994* (Washington, DC: Bureau of Justice Statistics, 2003), 24; R. Karl Hanson and Kelly Morton-Bourgon, "The Characteristics of Persistent Sexual Offenders: A Meta-Analysis of Recidivism Studies," *Journal of Consulting and Clinical Psychology* 73 (2005): 1154; R. Karl Hanson and Kelly Morton-Bourgon, *Predictors of Sexual Recidivism: An Updated Meta-Analysis* (Ottawa: Public Safety and Emergency Preparedness Canada, 2004), 8.

105. Andrew J. Harris and R. Karl Hanson, *Sex Offender Recidivism: A Simple Question* (Ottawa: Public Safety and Emergency Preparedness Canada, 2004), 11.

106. Langan et al., *Recidivism of Sex Offenders*, 14. See also E. Drake and R. Barnoski, *Sex Offenders in Washington State: Key Findings and Trends* (Olympia: Washington State Institute for Public Policy, 2006), 12 (noting that felony sex offenders in Washington State had the lowest rates of felony reoffense (13% versus over 30%)). As with other studies, the Washington data reflect that sex offenders who do recidivate by committing felonies commit sex-related crimes at a higher rate than other criminal subgroups: 2.7% versus less than 1%. Ibid.

107. Timothy S. Bynum, *Recidivism of Sex Offenders* (Silver Spring, MD: Center for Sex Offender Management, 2001), 3.

108. Lisa L. Sample and Timothy M. Bray, "Are Sex Offenders Different? An Examination of Rearrest Patterns," *Criminal Justice Policy Review* 17 (2006): 86–87.

109. See James F. Quinn et al., "Societal Reaction to Sex Offenders: A Review of the Origins and Results of the Myths Surrounding Their Crimes and Treatment Amenability," *Deviant Behavior* 25 (2004): 222.

110. The tendency was also manifest in the profusion of "sexual psychopath" commitment laws, popular from the late 1930s to the 1960s, which swept up many nondangerous offenders, in particular gay men engaging in consensual sex acts and African Americans (for the "following of a white female," for example). See Denno, "Life Before," 1344*n*127, 1352, 1385*n*327. In the 1990s, perhaps the most vivid manifestation of this bias at the federal level came from California Representative Robert Dornan, who in advocating adoption of the federal Megan's Law, characterized child sexual molestation as "basically a male homosexual problem." *Cong. Rec.* 142 (1996): 17,114 (statement of Rep. Dornan).

111. Howard N. Snyder, *Sexual Assault of Young Children as Reported to Law Enforcement: Victim, Incident, and Offender Characteristics* (Annapolis Junction, MD: Bureau of Justice Statistics Clearinghouse, 2000), 10.

112. Ibid.

113. Tara Bahrampour, "Discovering a World Beyond the Front Yard," *Washington*

*Post*, August 27, 2006 (citing data from the National Center for Missing and Exploited Children).

114. See, e.g., Jeffrey T. Walker and Gwen Ervin-McLarty, *Sex Offenders in Arkansas: Characteristics of Offenders and Enforcement of Sex Offender Laws* (Little Rock: Arkansas Crime Information Center, 2000), 18 (73% of sex offenders in registry sample surveyed were first-time offenders).

115. The reasons behind the skewed emphasis on "stranger danger" are complex and intriguing. As good an analysis as any was offered by Phillip Jenkins, who observed that it is easier to impose harsh restrictions on strangers, and in an even deeper psychological sense, to conceive of sexual abuse as an outgrowth of individual pathology rather than an endemic social problem. Jenkins, *Moral Panic*, 236. Joel Best adds that studies of public response to crime elide the "texture of our fears," in particular the anxiety prompted by "the strangers who attack without warning or provocation." Joel Best, *Random Violence: How We Talk about New Crimes and New Victims* (Berkeley: University of California Press, 1999), xi.

116. Testament to this tendency, one sees states parroting one another's "legislative findings" on risk as justifications for their own laws, notwithstanding the significant variations of state registration and notification regimes, including with respect to specific criminal subpopulations targeted.

117. As Phillip Jenkins explains: "Statistics and research findings gain credibility to the extent they fit public expectations . . . After a few years, the perception of a problem becomes so well entrenched that its reality and significance seem not to brook questioning." Jenkins, *Moral Panic*, 220.

118. See, e.g., James Popkin and John Simons, "Natural Born Predators," *U.S. News & World Report*, November 19, 1994, 64 (cover story noting inter alia that registration laws are overinclusive and that laws wrongly emphasize "stranger danger").

119. In this respect, the evolution of registration and notification parallels the broader political disinterest in empiricism evident in the 1990s. As Franklin Zimring has observed, "[t]he public believes that analytic and statistical implications of policy choices in criminal justice are unimportant." Franklin E. Zimring, "Populism, Democratic Government, and the Decline of Expert Authority," *Pacific Law Journal* 28 (1996): 254. See also Samuel H. Pillsbury, "Why Are We Ignored? The Peculiar Place of Experts in the Current Debate About Crime and Justice," *Criminal Law Bulletin* 31 (1995): 305.

A contemporaneous example is found in the 1994 decision by Congress to overhaul the Federal Rules of Evidence to permit introduction of highly prejudicial evidence of prior sexual misconduct, including but not limited to convictions, representing a sharp break with past prohibitions on "character evidence." Advocates frequently resorted to personalized accounts of victims and offenders, as in registration-related debates, and the proposals themselves, while vigorously opposed by the bench and bar, were also ultimately successful. See Michael S. Ellis, "The Politics Behind Federal Rules of Evidence 413, 414, and 415," *Santa Clara Law Review* 38 (1998): 961.

120. This misconception was commonly reflected in the press as well. See, e.g., Jack Sullivan, "Net Gives Parents Info. in Many States," *Boston Herald*, December 12, 1999 (referring to Jacob Wetterling as "a slain Minnesota boy who was the victim of a convicted child molester"). As history would have it, the 1938 abduction of a St. Paul girl, also a case in which no suspect was apprehended and the child was never located, was likewise attributed without basis to a sex offender; it triggered enactment of Minnesota's "sexual psychopath" law that same year. Britt Robson, "A Prison by Any Other Name," *City Pages* (Minneapolis), June 18, 1989, http://www.citypages.com/databank/18/863/print3579.asp.

121. See Filler, "Making the Case," 351 (citing news accounts based on interviews with neighbors).

122. Nathaniel J. Pallone, "Without Plea-Bargaining, Megan Kanka Would Be Alive Today," *Criminology and Public Policy* 3 (2003): 83. Similarly, Leroy Hendricks, a chronic recidivist sex offender who motivated the State of Kansas to adopt its "sexual psychopath" involuntary commitment law in the early 1990s, which the U.S. Supreme Court upheld in *Kansas v. Hendricks* (1997), was eligible for life imprisonment but cut a deal permitting his release. See Wayne A. Logan, "The Ex Post Facto Clause and the Jurisprudence of Punishment," *American Criminal Law Review* 35 (1998): 1261.

123. Jonathan Simon, "Positively Punitive," *Texas Law Review* 84 (2006): 2172.

124. KOMO Staff and News Service, "Task Force Debates Sex Offender-Free Zones," *KOMONews.com*, September 26, 2005, http://www.komonews.com/news/archive/4165286.html. "Statistics," as Joseph Kennedy has observed, can thus be perceived as a "denial of the sacred," used by opponents of anticrime measures to treat victims as "dispensable people." "In rejecting statistics," Kenney writes, "the American public is essentially rejecting information about the criminal justice system." Kennedy, "Monstrous Offenders," 895–96. Cf. Phoebe Ellsworth and Lee Ross, "Public Opinion and Capital Punishment: A Close Examination of the Views of Abolitionists and Retentionists," *Crime & Delinquency* 29 (1983): 162 (noting that most of the respondents in the study "willingly admitted that their attitude [toward the death penalty] would remain the same even if it turned out that they were mistaken about deterrence").

125. See generally, Ortwin Renn and Bernd Rohrmann, eds., *Cross-Cultural Risk Perception: A Survey of Empirical Studies* (Boston: Kluwer, 2000); Paul Slovic, "Perception of Risk," in *The Perception of Risk*, ed. Paul Slovic (Sterling, VA: Earthscan Publications, 2000), 220.

126. See Baruch Fischhoff et al., "How Safe Is Safe Enough? A Psychometric Study of Attitudes Toward Technological Risks and Benefits," in *Perception of Risk*, ed. Slovic, 80, 99.

127. For an insightful discussion of why the war on terror has been mounted, yet

similar efforts to combat climate change have not, despite the latter being far more statistically likely to cause human harm, see Sunstein, "On the Divergent American Reactions," 503.

128. Ibid., 524.

129. Sunstein, *Laws of Fear*, 35–41.

130. Sunstein, "On the Divergent American Reactions," 535 (quoting Amos Tversky and Daniel Kahneman, "Judgment Under Uncertainty: Heuristics and Biases," in *Judgment Under Uncertainty: Heuristics and Biases*, ed. Daniel Kahneman et al. (New York: Cambridge University Press, 1982), 3, 11.

131. Sunstein, *Laws of Fear*, 222.

132. Cf. Roger G. Noll and James E. Krier, "Some Implications of Cognitive Psychology for Risk Regulation," *Journal of Legal Studies* 19 (1990): 771–79 (asserting that political actors have strong incentive to impose harsh sentences based on constituents' cognitive miscalculations).

133. Full discussion of the complex psychological reasons motivating this failure (or refusal) to recognize known risk, in the context of sexual victimization, is not possible here. However, it should be noted that the phenomenon more generally is not uncommon. Americans fret incessantly over remote harms, such as bird flu and mad cow disease, yet fail to recognize the much greater mortal risks that pervade everyday life, such as heart attacks and obesity-related sicknesses. For more on this irrational tendency, see Barry Glassner, *The Culture of Fear: Why Americans Are Afraid of the Wrong Things* (New York: Basic Books, 1999); Jeffrey Kluger, "How Americans Are Living Dangerously," *Time Magazine*, November 26, 2006.

134. On this lower prioritization and why criminal victimization by familiars can actually be more harmful than by strangers, see Carissa Hessick, "Violence Between Lovers, Strangers, and Friends," *Washington University Law Review* 85 (2007): 343.

135. Testimony of Maureen Kanka, House of Representatives Judiciary Subcommittee on Crime, Federal Document Clearing House Congressional Testimony (March 7, 1996), 1996 WL 17175.

136. See Megan Nicole Kanka Foundation, "Megan Nicole Kanka Foundation-Mission," http://www.megannicolekankafoundation.org/mission.htm.

137. Idaho Code Ann. § 18-8301.

138. Margaret Canovan, *Nationhood and Political Theory* (Brookfield, Vt.: Edward Elgar, 1996), 80. See also, e.g., Phillip Bobbitt, *The Shield of Achilles: War, Peace and the Course of History* (New York: Knopf, 2002), chap. 10.

139. See Wash. Code Ann. § 4.24.550 (1990) ("[R]elease of information about sexual predators . . . will further the governmental interests of public safety and public scrutiny of the criminal and mental health systems.").

140. The sustained interest in registration and notification thus differs in an important way from the political dynamic Professor Franklin Zimring has observed rel-

ative to modern criminal justice policy more generally. To Zimring, modern policy is marked by a "paradoxical politics of government distrust," consisting of lower public confidence in government, which itself results in greater government involvement in the form of harsher criminal justice policies. Franklin Zimring, *An American Travesty: Legal Responses to Adolescent Sexual Offending* (Chicago: University of Chicago Press, 2004), 147. Registration and notification laws, while clearly stemming from low public confidence in the capacity of government to ensure public safety, seek to empower communities—rather than the government. No paradox thus per se exists; increased use of registration and notification is entirely consistent with increasing distrust of government.

141. See, e.g., *Cong. Rec.* 144 (October 1, 1998): H 9203 (statement of Rep. Dunn advocating notification because it would allow citizens "to take the necessary precautions to ensure that there are not the second, third, or fourth victims").

142. See, e.g., Ohio Rev. Code § 2950.02(A)(1) ("If the public is provided adequate notice and information . . . members of the public and communities can develop constructive plans to prepare themselves and their children."); Tenn. Code Ann. § 40-39-101(b)(6) ("To protect the safety and general welfare of the people of this state, it is necessary to provide for continued registration of sexual offenders and for the public release of specified information regarding sexual offenders.").

143. See, e.g., Arizona Dept. of Public Safety, "Welcome to Arizona's Sex Offender Information Center," https://az.gov/webapp/offender/main.do ("Furnishing the public with information regarding convicted sex offenders is a critical step toward encouraging the public to protect themselves from potential future attacks.").

144. Alabama Dept. of Public Safety, "Community Information Center," http://community.dps.alabama.gov.

145. See, e.g., Colo. Rev. Stat. § 18-3-412(6.5)(a) (1999) ("The general assembly finds that persons convicted of an offense involving unlawful sexual behavior have a reduced expectation of privacy because of the public's interest in public safety."); Tenn. Code § 40-39-101(b)(3) ("[P]ersons convicted of these sexual offenses have a reduced expectation of privacy because of the public's interest in public safety . . . . In balancing the offender's due process and other rights against the interest of public security, the general assembly finds that releasing information about sexual offenders . . . will further the primary governmental interest of protecting vulnerable populations from harm.").

146. Garland, *Culture of Control*, 181. Franklin Zimring has a similar understanding, regarding community notification as part of a "zero-sum fallacy" whereby it is believed that policies harming criminal offenders by definition benefit crime victims. To Zimring, "[t]he further punishment of sex offenders was attractive for its own sake for those who resented sex offenders, and it also promised results to those who believed that anything that created substantial disadvantage to offenders must also

help their potential victims." Zimring, *An American Travesty*, 147. While surely true to some degree, I see the calculus as being more victim-centered: the value of informational empowerment is foremost, with negative effects (e.g., stigmatization) on registrants constituting a secondary benefit.

147. See, e.g., *United States v. Morrison*, 529 U.S. 598, 618 (2000) (emphasizing that that crime control "has always been the province of the states"); *Screws v. United States*, 325 U.S. 91, 109 (1945) ("Our national government is one of delegated powers alone. Under our federal system the administration of criminal justice rests with the States except as Congress, acting within the scope of those delegated powers, has created offenses against the United States.").

148. See *United States v. Lopez*, 514 U.S. 549, 566 (1995) ("The Constitution . . . withhold[s] from Congress a plenary police power."). See also Phillip B. Heyman and Mark H. Moore, "The Federal Role in Dealing with Violent Street Crime: Principles, Questions, and Cautions," *Annals of the American Academy of Political and Social Science* 543 (1996): 108 (noting historic fear of a national police force).

149. *Lopez*, 514 U.S. at 552. The U.S. Constitution itself cedes only limited direct criminal lawmaking authority to the federal government. Article I, section 8, for instance, granted Congress the authority to punish counterfeiting, piracies, and offenses committed on federal property, and Article III, section 3 empowered Congress to punish treason.

150. Lawrence M. Friedman, *Crime and Punishment in American History* (New York: Basic Books, 1993), 209, 263. See also *Jerome v. United States*, 318 U.S. 101, 102 (1943) (noting that "[b]y 1934, great concern had been expressed over interstate operations by gangsters against banks—activities with which local authorities were frequently unable to cope," and noting new federal legislation to address the concern); *Cong. Rec.* 75 (June 17, 1932): H 13282, H 13289 (statement of Rep. LaGuardia in support of the Lindbergh Act, asserting that the nation had passed the era when "crime was localized and escape was slow").

151. Friedman, *Crime and Punishment*, 273.

152. "President Demands War on Gangsters; Puts Duty on States: Calls for 'Awakening to Failure of Some Local Governments to Protect Their Citizens,'" *New York Times*, November 26, 1930.

153. Richard Powers, *Secrecy and Power: The Life of J. Edgar Hoover* (New York: Free Press, 1987), 175. See also Horace L. Bomar, Jr., "The Lindbergh Law," *Law & Contemporary Problems* 1 (1934): 436 ("Public sentiment having been aroused by this atrocious deed, there was an instant demand that Congress 'do something' about it.").

154. See *Cong. Rec.* 75 (1932): H 13283 (statement of Rep. Michener: "[T]his must not become a precedent for more legislation giving the Federal Government concurrent authority with the States in enforcing police regulations and laws dealing with the matter in which the States are primarily interested, and which can be properly

dealt with by State action."); James D. Calder, *The Origins and Development of Federal Crime Control Policy: Herbert Hoover's Initiatives* (Westport, CT: Praeger, 1993): 201 (quoting President Hoover as stating with regard to the Lindbergh kidnapping that his administration "was not in favor of using the case as an excuse for extending Federal authority in the area of law enforcement").

155. For discussion of this national political shift, see Ted Gest, *Crime and Politics: Big Government's Erratic Campaign for Law and Order* (New York: Oxford University Press, 2001); Nancy E. Marion, *A History of Federal Crime Control Initiatives, 1960–1993* (Westport, CT: Praeger, 1994).

156. One commentator explained the silence as a result of a "complex of political cross-currents":

> No interest group—liberal or conservative—is prepared to argue against federalization on grounds of the state interest in criminal law. Liberals, who generally oppose federalization because of its threat to civil rights and harsher federal criminal penalties, distrust arguments supporting states' rights. Such arguments, which are ultimately based on federalism concerns, are reminiscent of anti-civil rights efforts. Conservatives, who historically distrust federal government initiatives, generally endorse law and order measures and so, therefore, do not oppose the federalization of criminal law. Moreover, the states are loath to complain about federal encroachment because federal law enforcement efforts supplement state efforts to control crime.

Geraldine Moohr, "The Federal Interest in Criminal Law," *Syracuse Law Review* 47 (1997): 1130.

157. Sara Sun Beale, "The Many Faces of Overcriminalization: From Morals and Mattress Tags to Overfederalization," *American University Law Review* 54 (2005): 753.

158. U.S. Const. art. I, § 8, cl. 3.

159. See Brannon Denning and Glenn Reynolds, "Rulings and Resistance: The New Commerce Clause Jurisprudence Encounters the Lower Courts," *Arkansas Law Review* 55 (2003): 1253.

160. See, e.g., William H. Rehnquist, "The 1998 Year-End Report of the Federal Judiciary," reprinted in *Federal Sentencing Report* 11 (1998): 135 (quoting Chief Justice William Rehnquist, in a 1998 Report to Congress: "The pressure in Congress to appear responsive to every highly publicized social ill or sensational crime needs to be balanced with an inquiry into . . . whether we want most legal relationships decided at the national rather than the local level.").

161. For overviews of these and other principal objections to federalization, see Steven D. Clymer, "Unequal Justice: The Federalization of Criminal Law," *Southern California Law Review* 70 (1997): 643; Michael A. Simons, "Prosecutorial Discretion and Prosecution Guidelines: A Case Study in Controlling Federalization," *New York University Law Review* 75 (2000): 907–19.

162. U.S. Const. art. I, § 8, cl. 1.

163. *Pennhurst State School Hosp. v. Halderman*, 451 U.S. 1, 17 (1981); see also *Barnes v. Gorman*, 536 U.S. 181, 186 (2002) ("We have repeatedly characterized . . . Spending Clause legislation as 'much in the nature of a contract'") (citation omitted).

164. *South Dakota v. Dole*, 483 U.S. 203, 212 (1987).

165. Richard W. Garnett, "The New Federalism, the Spending Power, and Federal Criminal Law," *Cornell Law Review* 89 (2003): 25, 33. See also Lynn A. Baker and Mitchell N. Berman, "Getting Off the Dole: Why the Court Should Abandon Its Spending Doctrine, and How a Too-Clever Congress Could Provoke It to Do So," *Indiana Law Journal* 78 (2003): 461 (referring to current Supreme Court oversight as "toothless").

166. As noted in Chapter 3, in the *Adam Walsh Act* Congress created a new federal failure-to-register offense, enacted pursuant to its Commerce Clause authority.

167. *Lopez*, 514 U.S. at 561n3 (citation omitted).

168. A narrow exception arises in the relatively uncommon instance when the federal government criminalizes a behavior that a state decides does not warrant criminalization, such as addressed in *Gonzales v. Raich* (noted in the text). For more on this phenomenon, see Susan R. Klein, "Independent-Norm Federalism in Criminal Law," *California Law Review* 90 (2002): 1541.

169. *Davis v. Monroe County Board of Education*, 526 U.S. 629, 654–55 (1999) (Kennedy, J., dissenting). See also Thomas R. McKoy and Barry Friedman, "Conditional Spending: Federalism's Trojan Horse," *Supreme Court Review* (1988): 116 ("[A]ny time that Congress finds itself limited by . . . delegated regulatory powers, . . . [it] need only attach a condition on a federal spending grant that achieves the same (otherwise invalid) regulatory objective.").

170. For more on the history of federal involvement, see Wayne A. Logan, "Criminal Justice Federalism and National Sex Offender Policy," *Ohio State Journal of Criminal Law* 6 (2008): 51.

171. See, e.g., "Idaho Law Doesn't Mandate Public Disclosure of Registry," *Lewiston Morning Tribune* (Idaho), December 5, 1993 (noting concern among Idaho lawmakers).

172. In Canada, the political dynamic was exactly the opposite. There, the provinces during the 1990s unsuccessfully pressured the federal government to enact a national registry, which it ultimately did in 2004. See Michael Petrunik et al., "American and Canadian Approaches to Sex Offenders: A Study of the Politics of Dangerousness," *Federal Sentencing Reporter* 21 (2008): 111, 119. Canada's approach is also quite muted compared to that of the United States; for instance, while several provinces allow for some form of community notification, Canadian federal law does not, and the federal government makes registry information available only to law enforcement. Also, unlike in the United States, the federal registry is not retroactive in effect, and only contains individuals whose recidivist risk is thought to warrant registration. Ibid.

According to commentators, the varied federal responses in the two nations is attributable to the reign of a Liberal Party government in Canada for the past twenty years, which resisted public and interest group pressure for tougher provisions, in part out of concern for privacy rights ensured by the Charter of Rights and Freedoms. Petrunik, "Hare and Tortoise," 56; Petrunik et al., "American and Canadian Approaches," 119.

173. See Rachel E. Barkow, "Federalism and the Politics of Sentencing," *Columbia Law Review* 105 (2005): 1303 (noting the tendency of Congress to enact laws of "the 'feel-good, do-something' variety rather than to seek out the most cost-effective way to address a particular problem"); David Boerner and Roxanne Lieb, "Sentencing Reform in the Other Washington," *Crime & Justice* 28 (2001): 121–22 (observing that the political symbolism of crime "is much easier when it is disconnected from the reality of managing scarce resources").

174. For analysis of the political dynamic typically driving contemporary criminal justice policy, see William J. Stuntz, "The Pathological Politics of the Criminal Law," *Michigan Law Review* 100 (2001): 505.

175. See, e.g., Benjamin M. Friedman, *The Moral Consequences of Economic Growth* (New York: Knopf, 2005). The premise also betrays the collective wisdom of Montesquieu, Tocqueville, and Durkheim. See William Bradford, *An Enquiry How Far the Punishment of Death Is Necessary in Pennsylvania* (Philadelphia: Printed by T. Dobson, 1793), 20 (quoting Montesquieu to the effect that "as freedom advances, the severity of the penal law decreases"); Emile Durkheim, *The Division of Labor in Society,* trans. W.D. Halls (New York: Free Press, 1984), 44 (asserting that as human relations become increasingly "contractualized" penalization would diminish); Alexis de Tocqueville, *Democracy in America* (New York: Library of America), 655 (contending that social "mores become milder as conditions become more equal").

## Chapter 5

1. Roxanne Lieb and Corey Nunlist, *Community Notification as Viewed by Washington's Citizens: A 10-Year Follow-Up* (Olympia: Washington State Institute for Public Policy, March 2008), 4; Dretha M. Phillips, *Community Notification as Viewed by Washington's Citizens* (Olympia: Washington State Institute for Public Policy, March 1998), 4.

2. J. O. Hansen, "Sexual Predators: Why Megan's Law Is Not Enough," *Atlanta Journal-Constitution,* June 10, 1997.

3. See, e.g., Jeff Tuttle, "A Perception of Security," *Bangor Daily News* (Maine), April 22, 2006; "Va. Unveils Enhanced Sex-Offender Registry," *Richmond Times-Dispatch* (Virginia), June 13, 2006.

4. Note, "Criminal Registration Law," *Journal of the American Institute of Criminal Law & Criminology* 27 (1936–37): 295–96.

5. Don Martinez, "Sex Offenders Swamp State," *San Francisco Examiner*, January 16, 1994.

6. Kirk Mitchell, "Assault Threat in Our Midst," *Denver Post*, April 16, 2007.

7. The figure also figured prominently in congressional concern motivating toughened provisions in the *Adam Walsh Act*, including provision of federal marshals to capture itinerant registration scofflaws and the enactment, for the first time, of a federal law making failure to register (after crossing state lines) a federal crime. See Wayne A. Logan, "Criminal Justice Federalism and National Sex Offender Policy," *Ohio State Journal of Criminal Law* 6 (2008): 51.

8. Kim Curis, "Survey: States Have Lost Track of Thousands of Sex Offenders," *Associated Press*, February 6, 2003.

9. See, e.g., Charles Sheehan, "Sex Offenders Slip Away," *Chicago Tribune*, March 31, 2006 (in Chicago, more than 75% of addresses provided by a randomized sample of registrants were invalid; either the registrant did not reside at the address provided or the address was for an abandoned building or empty lot); Richard Tewksbury, "Validity and Utility of the Kentucky Sex Offender Registry," *Federal Probation* 66 (June 2002): 21 (in Kentucky, 26% of urban registrants listed an address that could not have constituted an actual residence, and more than 50% of registrants overall lacked a photograph on the state-run website);, "Attorney General Kline Releases Results of Kansas Offender Registry Audit," *U.S. Federal News*, August 16, 2006 (in Kansas, a random sample of the state's registrants revealed the following deficiencies: 21% for home addresses; 29% for current employment information; and 24% for current vehicle identification information).

10. In 1997, for instance, California deleted from its registry eight thousand individuals either who were dead or whose crime no longer required registration. Nicholas Riccardi and Jeff Leeds, "Megan's Law Calling Up Old, Minor Offenses," *Los Angeles Times*, February 24, 1997.

11. Associated Press, "Survey Finds States Have Lost Track of Thousands of Sex Offenders," *St. Petersburg Times* (Florida), February 7, 2003, http://www.sptimes.com/2003/02/07/Worldandnation/Florida_among_best_on.shtml.

12. See North Dakota Attorney General, "Sex Offender Laws," http://www.ag.state.nd.us/Brochures/FactSheet/SexOffenders.pdf (accessed October 31, 2007).

13. See Top Ten Reviews, "Sex Offender Registry Review," http://sex-offender-registry-review.toptenreviews.com (accessed September 7, 2008).

14. James Carlson, "Ghosts in the Machine: Are Dead Sex Offenders Really Dangerous?" *Orlando Weekly*, November 24, 2005. Another survey indicated that over 50% of Florida registrants reported registry inaccuracies, although it was unclear what information was thought invalid. Jill Levenson and Leo Cotter, "The Effect of Megan's Law on Sex Offender Reintegration," *Journal of Contemporary Criminal Justice* 21 (2005): 49.

15. See James Fuller, "Sex Offenders at Large? Police Struggle to Keep Track of Them," *Chicago Daily Herald*, September 17, 2007 (noting that GPS monitoring costs $7 to $10 a day per offender).

16. See Isaac Rosenberg, "Involuntary Endogenous RFID Compliance Monitoring," *Yale Journal of Law & Technology* 10 (2008): 331.

17. U.S. Government Accounting Office, *National Sex Offender Registry: New Hires Data Has Potential for Updating Addresses of Convicted Sex Offenders: Report to Congressional Requesters* (Washington, DC: U.S. GAO, 2006).

18. Alexis Simendinger, "Tracking Sex Offenders," *National Journal*, September 15, 2007.

19. As one Missouri sheriff put it: "our records now are only as accurate as the sex offenders tell us. It's kind of an honor system, unless we get a tip or there's some contradiction." Amos Bridges, "Registry for Sex Crimes Lagging," *Springfield News-Leader* (Missouri), April 30, 2007. The Greene County Sheriff's Department, responsible for registering individuals and updating information on the registry (with over five hundred registrants), dedicates one full-time employee to the job. Ibid.

20. It bears mention that in the United Kingdom, a 97% compliance rate was announced in 2002. See Kristy Hudson, *Offending Identities: Sex Offenders' Perspectives of Their Treatment and Management* (Portland, OR: Willan, 2005), 163. The impressive rate would appear to provide support for the government's decision in 2007 to eschew broad community notification out of fear that it would drive registrants "underground." However, as in the United States, it is difficult to assess the accuracy of the compliance figure in the absence of a rigorous verification regime.

21. Ellen Perlman, "Where Will Sex Offenders Live?" *Governing Magazine*, June 2006, 54.

22. U.S. Government Accountability Office, *Long-Term Care Facilities: Information on Residents Who Are Registered Sex Offenders or Are Paroled for Other Crimes: Report to Congressional Requesters* (Washington, DC: U.S. GAO, 2006). The report, which was commissioned to study the extent of registrants working in long-term care facilities and only incidentally discovered the shortcomings of the NSOR, speculated that the discrepancy was attributable to a lack of state resources or an inability to comply with FBI reporting requirements. Ibid., 4.

23. See U.S. Dept. of Justice, "Review of the Department of Justice's Implementation of the Sex Offender Registration and Notification Act," v–vi (December 2008).

24. Stan Diel, "Sex Offender List Out of Date; State Backlog Creates Raft of Inconsistencies in Local, State Data," *Birmingham News*, May 30, 2007.

25. Concern remains in some quarters, however, that individuals will "shop" among states for more lenient registration regimes. To date, however, only anecdotal evidence exists in support of this occurrence. The prospect of migration, however, has

been of concern to Congress, prompting inter alia Megan's Law in 1996, justified by worry that not all states engaged in community notification. See Chapter 3.

26. Donna Schram and Cheryl Milloy, *Community Notification: A Study of Of- fender Characteristics and Recidivism* (Seattle: Urban Policy Research, 1995).

27. Scott Matson and Roxanne Lieb, *Community Notification in Washington State: 1996 Survey of Law Enforcement* (Olympia: Washington State Institute for Public Pol- icy, 1996).

28. Donna Schram and Cheryl Milloy, *A Study of the Characteristics and Recidi- vism of Sex Offenders Considered for Civil Commitment But for Whom Proceedings Were Declined* (Olympia: Washington State Institute for Public Policy, 1998).

29. Geneva Adkins et al., *The Iowa Sex Offender Registry and Recidivism* (Des Moines, IA: Criminal and Juvenile Justice Planning, 2000).

30. Richard G. Zevitz, "Sex Offender Community Notification: Its Role in Recidi- vism and Offender Reintegration," *Criminal Justice Studies* 19 (2006): 193.

31. Bob Edward Vasquez et al., "The Influence of Sex Offender Registration and Notification Laws in the United States," *Crime & Delinquency* 54 (2008): 175.

32. Kristen Zgoba et al., New Jersey Dept. of Corrections, "Megan's Law: Assess- ing the Practical and Monetary Efficacy" (Washington, DC: U.S. Dept. of Justice, De- cember 2008), 2.

33. J. J. Prescott and Jonah E. Rockoff, *Do Sex Offender Registration and Notifica- tion Laws Affect Criminal Behavior?* (Cambridge, MA: National Bureau of Economic Research, 2008), http://www.nber.org/papers/w13803.

34. Grant Duwe and William Donnay, "The Impact of Megan's Law on Sex Of- fender Recidivism: The Minnesota Experience," *Criminology* 46 (2008): 411.

35. Nationally, for instance, sex offenses against children fell 49% between 1990 and 2004. See David Finkelhor and Lisa Jones, "Why Have Child Maltreatment and Child Victimization Declined?" *Journal of Social Issues* 62 (2006): 685.

36. Sam Wood, "N.J. Study Scrutinizes Megan's Law Effect," *Philadelphia Inquir- er*, May 6, 2007.

37. Robert Barnoski, *Sex Offender Sentencing in Washington State: Has Commu- nity Notification Reduced Recidivism?* (Olympia: Washington State Institute for Public Policy, 2005).

38. Minnesota Dept. of Corrections, *Sex Offender Recidivism in Minnesota* (St. Paul: Minnesota Department of Corrections, 2007), 33–35.

39. Unfortunately, the ongoing efforts of Congress to make state laws more uni- form limits the opportunity for such comparative work. Despite the abiding uncer- tainty over the benefits of registration and notification, and the superiority of any one approach over another, Congress has imposed requirements on states. This effort recently reached its zenith with the Adam Walsh Act (2006), in which Congress inter alia required that all states to adopt a conviction-based classification method.

40. See, e.g., Idaho Code § 18-8302 ("[E]fforts of law enforcement agencies to protect their communities, conduct investigations and quickly apprehend offenders who commit sexual offenses are impaired by the lack of current information available about individuals who have been convicted of sexual offenses.").

41. Jeffrey T. Walker and Gwen Ervin-McLarty, *Sex Offenders in Arkansas: Characteristics of Offenders and Enforcement of Sex Offender Laws* (Little Rock: Arkansas Crime Information Center, 1999), 47.

42. Richard G. Zevitz and Mary Ann Farkas, "Sex Offender Community Notification: Assessing the Impact in Wisconsin," *NIJ Research in Brief* (National Institute of Justice, December 2000), 6.

43. See, e.g., Rick Hampson, "What's Gone Wrong with Megan's Law?" *USA Today*, May 14, 1997 (noting incident in West Chicago, Illinois, in which police saw a boy entering a registrant's apartment and learned that the registrant had been molesting the boy).

Research done in Britain suggests police preemptive use of registry information. One study indicated that British police use registry information to intervene in high-risk situations and to prevent misconduct. The same study, however, concluded that registry information played only a limited role after the criminal misconduct had occurred—in investigations and prosecutions. Joyce Plotnikoff and Richard Woolfson, *British Home Office, Where Are They Now? An Evaluation of Sex Offender Registration in England and Wales* (London: Policing and Reducing Crime Unit, Research, Development and Statistics Directorate, 2000).

44. As noted by one San Francisco–area police spokesperson in 1994, police departments "have historically enforced [registration] with the same vigor as they do 'bicycle registrations.'" Aurelio Rojas and Thaai Walker, "Sex Offender Registration System Failing: Police Say It's Outdated, Ignored—and Little Hindrance to New Crimes," *San Francisco Chronicle*, April 4, 1994.

45. California Dept. of Justice, Criminal Justice Statistics Center's Offender-based Transaction Statistics System, 2006 (provided to author by Special Request Unit on September 17, 2007). The data, the Department warns, might understate the true extent of violations, both because of underreporting and because with persons arrested or convicted of more than one offense only the most serious offense is counted.

46. Katherine Rosenberg, "No Compliance, No Problem for Sex Offenders," *Daily Press—Victoriaville* (California), June 10, 2007.

47. Mac Daniel, "Audit Identifies Registry Delays," *Boston Globe*, June 6, 2006.

48. Robert P. Barnoski, *Sex Offender Sentencing in Washington State: Failure to Register as a Sex Offender*, rev. ed. (Olympia: Washington State Institute for Public Policy, 2006). Convictions for failure to register occurred throughout the five-year tracking period and were not concentrated during the first few months after commu-

nity entry. Nor did registrants' demographic background or offending history play a predictive role with respect to failure-to-register convictions.

49. See, e.g., Vicki Torres, "Sex Offender Arrested in Two Girls' Abductions," *Los Angeles Times*, June 20, 1992. In what surely is an overstatement, a 1988 report by the California Department of Justice reported that registration "assisted in the investigation of thousands of cases." The report does list, however, the "cracking" of two major Orange County cases: "Freeway Killer" William Bonin, convicted of killing 14 people, who was identified as a result of his registrant status, and Robert Jackson Thompson, convicted of killing a twelve-year-old boy, in which "the registration process aided" his capture. Roy Lewis, *Effectiveness of Statutory Requirements for the Registration of Sex Offenders: Report to the California Legislature* (Sacramento, CA: Bureau of Criminal Statistics and Special Services, 1988), 4.

50. See, e.g., Don Martinez, "Sex Offenders Swamp State," *San Francisco Examiner*, January 16, 1994 (instances in Alameda County and Sacramento in which the registry should have been helpful but was not); Josh Meyer and Geoffrey Mohan, "Flawed System Hampers Valley Molester Search," *Los Angeles Times*, December 15, 1993 (inadequacy of registry in San Fernando Valley cases).

51. Schram and Milloy, *Community Notification*.

52. Ibid., 19.

53. Richard G. Zevitz, "Sex Offender Community Notification: Its Role in Recidivism and Offender Reintegration," *Criminal Justice Studies* 19 (2006): 193.

54. See, e.g., Robert Barnoski, *Sex Offenders in Washington State: Key Findings and Trends* (Olympia: Washington State Institute for Public Policy, 2006), 11 (61% of sex offenders committed to the department of corrections were first-time commitments, compared with 44% of violent offenders and 41% of other felony offenders); Walker and Ervin-McLarty, *Sex Offenders in Arkansas*, 18 (73% of sex offenders in registry sample surveyed were first-time offenders).

55. Such was the case with Richard Alton Davis, convicted of murdering Polly Klaas: his long history of sexually abusive behavior resulted in pleas to lesser offenses not the subject of California's sex offender registration law. See Mia Jerusalem, "A Framework for Post-Sentence Sex Offender Legislation: Perspectives on Prevention, Registration and the Public's Right to Know," *Vanderbilt Law Review* 48 (1995): 221n8. The approach taken in a few states, such as Minnesota where registration is triggered if a registerable offense is charged and a conviction results in "another offense arising out of the same set of circumstances," provides a possible solution. Minn. Stat. § 243.166(1)(a)(1).

56. Victoria S. Beck and Lawrence F. Travis III, "Sex Offender Notification: A Cross-State Comparison," *Police Practice and Research* 7 (2006): 293.

57. Victoria S. Beck and Lawrence F. Travis, "Sex Offender Notification and Pro-

tective Behavior," *Violence and Victims* 19 (2004): 289. The researchers confirmed these results in another 2004 study of the same Ohio jurisdiction. Victoria S. Beck et al., "Community Response to Sex Offenders," *Journal of Psychiatry & Law* 32 (2004): 141. See also Victoria S. Beck and Lawrence F. Travis, "Sex Offender Notification: An Exploratory Assessment of State Variation in Notification Processes," *Journal of Criminal Justice* 34 (2006): 54 (reporting similar results from Ohio and Kentucky).

58. Alicia A. Caputo and Stanley L. Brodsky, "Citizen Coping with Community Notification of Released Sex Offenders," *Behavioral Sciences & the Law* 22 (2004): 239. The study's authors noted, however, that their findings were limited by the lack of a nonnotified control group to gain insight into whether notification had any effect at all on such measures, i.e., whether residents in general are resistant to taking protective measures.

59. Phillips, *Washington's Citizens*.

60. Amy L. Anderson and Lisa L. Sample, "Public Awareness and Action Resulting from Sex Offender Community Notification Laws," *Criminal Justice Policy Review* 19 (2008): 371.

61. A 2008 Washington State study reflected similar sentiments: 70% of respondents reported feeling safer knowing of registrants' whereabouts, and 88–91% reported being more aware of their surroundings or safety conscious. Also, 90% reported being more likely to notify police of suspicious behavior, yet less than 3% actually contacted police with respect to a registrant. Lieb and Nunlist, *10-Year Follow-Up*, 3–4.

62. Robert E. Freeman-Longo, *Myths and Facts about Sex Offenders* (Silver Spring, MD: Center for Sex Offender Management, 2002), 1. See also Richard G. Zevitz, "Sex Offender Community Notification: Its Role in Recidivism and Offender Reintegration," *Criminal Justice Studies* 19 (2006): 205 (among high-risk Wisconsin registrants who sexually recidivated and were subject to community notification, none of the victims were strangers). In this sense, concern over registration and notification is akin to that raised relative to current efforts requiring ex-offenders to wear global positioning satellite (GPS) tracking devices—the devices reveal only the whereabouts of individuals, which is of no public safety benefit if sexual victimizations occur in locations where they are permitted to be (such as their home).

63. See Timothy S. Bynum, *Recidivism of Sex Offenders* (Silver Spring, MD: Center for Sex Offender Management, 2001), 3; David Lisak and Paul Miller, "Repeat Rape and Multiple Offending among Undetected Rapists," *Violence and Victims* 17 (2002): 73.

64. Anthony J. Petrosino and Carolyn Petrosino, "The Public Safety Potential of Megan's Law in Massachusetts: An Assessment from a Sample of Criminal Sexual Psychopaths," *Crime & Delinquency* 45 (1999): 140.

65. See, e.g., Grant Duwe et al., "Does Residential Proximity Matter? A Geographic Analysis of Sex Offense Recidivism," *Criminal Justice & Behavior* 35 (2008): 484.

66. Petrosino and Petrosino, "Public Safety Potential," 152.

67. See Minnesota Dept. of Corrections, *Residential Proximity & Sex Offense Recidivism in Minnesota* (St. Paul: Minnesota Dept. of Corrections, 2007); Minnesota Dept. of Corrections, *Level Three Sex Offenders Residential Placement Issues: 2003 Report to the Legislature* (St. Paul: Minnesota Dept. of Corrections, 2003).

68. Colorado Sex Offender Management Board, *Report on Safety Issues Raised By Living Arrangements for and Location of Sex Offenders in the Community* (Denver: Sex Offender Management Board, 2004).

69. See Prescott and Rockoff, *Affect Criminal Behavior.*

70. See Wayne A. Logan, "Constitutional Collectivism and Ex-Offender Residence Exclusion Laws," *Iowa Law Review* 92 (2006): 1. Aside from efficacy concerns, the failure of policy makers to target other offenders with similar provisions highlights the illogic of the initiatives more generally. As one registrant lamented: "[They] don't make drunk drivers live 2,000 feet from the nearest bar. Shoplifters are not forced to live 2,000 feet from the nearest mall." Stephanie Simon, "Ex-cons Exiled to Outskirts, Iowa Sex Offenders Forbidden to Live Within 2,000 Feet of School and Child Care Centers," *Los Angeles Times*, December 5, 2002.

71. See Suzanna Hartzell-Baird, "When Sex Doesn't Sell: Mitigating the Damaging Effect of Megan's Law on Property Values," *Real Estate Law Journal* 35 (2006): 353; Leigh Linden and Jonah Rockoff, "Estimate of the Impact of Crime Risk on Property Values from Megan's Laws," *American Economic Review* 98 (2008): 1103.

72. According to a committee convened by the Vermont Legislature to examine the utility of Internet-based registries:

Currently, there is insufficient evidence to determine whether posting information about registered sex offenders on the Internet is a valuable and effective public policy tool. However, the general assembly determined . . . that the majority of the public feels that the Internet registry provides important information that can be used to protect families and expects such information to be a mater of public record.

Vermont Legislative Council, *Sex Offender Supervision and Community Notification* (Montpelier: Vermont Legislative Council, 2005), 11, http://www.leg.state.vt.us/reports/05SexOffender/report.pdf.

73. Sarah W. Craun, "Evaluating Awareness of Registered Sex Offenders in the Neighborhood," *Crime & Delinquency* (in press).

74. Andrea Sedlak et al., *Third National Incidence Study on Child Abuse and Neglect: Final Report* (Washington, DC: National Center on Child Abuse and Neglect, 1996) (children living below poverty line are 18 times as likely to be sexually abused as children living at or above national median income).

75. Human Rights Watch, *No Easy Answers: Sex Offender Laws in the US* (New York: Human Rights Watch, 2007), 58.

76. Ibid. By contrast, while not noted by the report, New Jersey's law provides the risk level of the registrant (high or moderate), and relates the gender of the victim, whether the victim was a child or an adult, and even brief details on the offense (e.g., that the registrant was a care provider or a stranger). See New Jersey State Police, "NJ Sex Offender Internet Registry," https://www6.state.nj.us/LPS_spoff/SetSession.

77. Current Note, "Criminal Registration Law," *Journal of the American Institute of Criminal Law & Criminology* 27 (1936–37): 295–96.

78. See, e.g., Karl Hanson and Kelly Morton-Bourgon, "The Characteristics of Persistent Sexual Offenders: A Meta-Analysis of Recidivism Studies," *Journal of Consulting and Clinical Psychology* 73 (2005): 1154; Candace Kruttschnitt et al., "Predictors of Desistance among Sex Offenders: The Interaction of Formal and Informal Social Controls," *Justice Quarterly* 17 (2000): 80.

79. Richard G. Zevitz and Mary Ann Farkas, "Sex Offender Community Notification: Managing High Risk Criminals or Exacting Further Vengeance?" *Behavioral Sciences & the Law* 18 (2000): 388.

80. See, e.g., *Doe v. Pataki*, 940 F. Supp. 603, 609 (S.D.N.Y. 1996); Steven Amick, "Protestors Win, Sex Offender Will Move," *Oregonian* (Portland), July 30, 1996; David Chanen, "Threats Lead to Eviction of St. Paul Sex Offender," *Star-Tribune* (Minneapolis), February 26, 1998; John T. McQuiston, "Sex Offender Is Suing His Neighbors over Protests," *New York Times*, June 20, 1997.

81. See, e.g., David Abel, "Many Sex Offenders End Up at Shelters," *Boston Globe*, June 18, 2007 (reporting that 65% of recently released Tier II registrants were living in homeless shelters).

82. Katherine Long, "Gas Station Picketed over Ex-Con's Hiring: Boss Stands By Choice," *Seattle Times*, February 2, 1995.

83. Cynthia Mercado et al., "The Impact of Specialized Sex Offender Legislation on Community Reentry," *Sexual Abuse: A Journal of Research & Treatment* 20 (2008): 194. See also, e.g., Jan Hollingsworth, "Protesters Hound Owner of Pet Shop," *Tampa Tribune*, January 27, 2008 (community protests that forced registrant to close his business); Emily Ramshaw, "'Sex Offender' Label Makes No Distinction," *Dallas Morning News*, October 2, 2006 (registrant who lost multiple jobs after employers learned he was on registry).

84. Richard Tewksbury, "Collateral Consequences of Sex Offender Registration," *Journal of Contemporary Criminal Justice* 21 (2005): 67 (16% among Kentucky registrants).

85. Judy Harrison, "Deaths of Gunman, Sex Offenders Probed," *Bangor Daily News* (Maine), April 19, 2006.

86. "Man Anticipates Support, Not Jail, for Attacking Pedophiles," *Portsmouth Herald* (New Hampshire), May 6, 2005.

87. Kira Millage, "Suspect Sought after Double Homicide in City," *Bellingham Herald* (Washington), August 28, 2005.

88. A study of Kentucky registrants, for instance, indicated that 47% experienced harassment in person, 28% received harassing or threatening phone calls, and just under 25% received harassing or threatening mail. See Tewksbury, "Collateral Consequences."

89. Jan Hoffman, "New Law Is Urged on Freed Sex Offenders," *New York Times*, August 4, 1994.

90. See, e.g., Robert Hanley, "Neighbor Accused of Firing at House of Paroled Rapist," *New York Times*, July 1, 1998; Paul Zielbauer, "Posting of Sex Offender Registries on Web Sets off Both Praise and Criticism," *New York Times*, May 22, 2000.

91. See, e.g., Jill S. Levenson et al., "Megan's Law and Its Impact on Community Re-entry for Sex Offenders," *Behavioral Sciences & the Law* 25 (2007): 594 (Connecticut and Indiana registrants); Jill S. Levenson and Leo P. Cotter, "The Effect of Megan's Law on Sex Offender Registration," *Journal of Contemporary Criminal Justice* 21 (2005): 58 (Florida registrants). See also Steven Amick, "Vandals Attack Ex-Convict's Home," *Oregonian* (Portland), July 27, 1996; David Ammons, "Released Sex Offender Hounded in Northwest," *Los Angeles Times*, August 1, 1993; Kathryn Wexler and Sarah Schweitzer, "Fears Build into Second Arson of Predator's Home," *St. Petersburg Times* (Fla.), November 24, 1999; Joshua W. Shank, "Do Megan's Laws Make a Difference?" *U.S. News & World Report*, March 9, 1998, 27; Carolyne Zinko, "Flyers Falsely Call Artist a Molester," *San Francisco Chronicle*, July 14, 1997.

92. See, e.g., Todd S. Purdum, "Death of Sex Offender is Tied to Megan's Law," *New York Times*, July 9, 1998.

93. Jill S. Levenson and Leo P. Cotter, "Megan's Law and Its Impact on Community Re-entry for Sex Offenders," *Journal Contemporary Criminal Justice* 21 (2005): 52. Indeed, the self-fulfilling outcome evokes Nathaniel Hawthorne's view of the scarlet letter affixed to Hester Prynne as a result of her commission of adultery: "No man, for any considerable period can wear one face to himself, and another to the multitude, without finally getting bewildered as to which may be true." Nathaniel Hawthorne, *The Scarlet Letter* (New York: Bantam Books, 1986): 197.

94. Richard Tewksbury and Matthew Lees, "Perceptions of Sex Offender Registration: Collateral Consequences and Community Experiences," *Sociological Spectrum* 26 (2006): 309; see also Tewksbury, "Collateral Consequences," 67 (Kentucky registrants).

95. Richard Tewksbury, "Experiences and Attitudes of Registered Female Sex Offenders," *Federal Probation* 68 (2004): 301.

96. Jill S. Levenson and Leo P. Cotter, "The Effect of Megan's Law on Sex Offender Registration," *Journal of Contemporary Criminal Justice* 21 (2005): 49.

97. Levenson et al., "Impact on Community Re-entry," 587.

98. See, e.g., Allen G. Breed, "Paroled Sex Offender Tests Couple's Faith," *Dallas Morning News*, September 2, 1999; Zevitz and Farkas, "Sex Offender Community Notification," 382–84.

99. See, e.g., Gene Warner, "2 Sex Offenders Say They Don't Deserve Harsh Label," *Buffalo News*, December 27, 1999.

100. See, e.g., Frederick Kunkle, "Caught in a Neighborhood Web: Innocent Man Mistaken for Registered Offender," *Washington Post*, May 13, 2006 (individual mistakenly targeted by neighborhoodwide e-mail notification, when his license plate was traced by a neighbor to a home address once used by a registrant); Connie Piloto, "Retarded Man's Beating Spreads Fear," *Dallas Morning News*, October 16, 1999 (beating of a mentally disabled Texas man whom the assailant mistook for a registrant who formerly lived at the man's address); "Man Mistakenly Branded as Sex Offender by Officials," *Des Moines Register*, May 4, 1997 (Kansas family with two children whose trailer was mistakenly assailed by rocks thrown by vigilantes).

101. In Iowa, for instance, in the wake of the state's implementation of exclusion zones, the number of noncompliant registrants doubled. Perlman, "Where Will Sex Offenders Live?" 54.

102. Indeed, courts have reversed convictions for failing to register because individuals, lacking a residence to register, were unable to file a change of residence notice. See, e.g., *Twine v. State*, 901 A.2d 1132 (Md. Ct. App. 2006); *State v. Iverson*, 664 N.W.2d 346 (Minn. 2003); *State v. Pickett*, 975 P.2d 584 (Wash. 1999). As of late 2007 two-thirds of the states allowed registrants to specify that they live in a homeless shelter or an inexact location, and registries in at least a dozen states list hundreds of registrants as "transient" and without specific addresses. Wendy Koch, "More Sex Offenders Transient, Elusive," *USA Today*, November 19, 2007.

103. Lorine Hughes and Colleen Kadleck, "Sex Offender Notification and Community Stratification," *Justice Quarterly* 25 (2008): 469.

104. See, e.g., Elizabeth E. Mustaine et al., "Social Disorganization and Residential Locations of Registered Sex Offenders: Is This a Collateral Consequence?" *Deviant Behavior* 27 (2006): 329; Richard Tewksbury and Elizabeth Mustaine, "Where to Find Sex Offenders: An Examination of Residential Locations and Neighborhood Conditions," *Criminal Justice Studies* 19 (2006): 61; Richard G. Zevitz, "Sex Offender Community Notification and Its Impact on Neighborhood Life," *Crime Prevention and Community Safety: An International Journal* 5 (2006): 41.

105. To proponents, the traditional desire to keep juvenile records confidential and the asserted lessened culpability of youths are trumped by the need for police and communities to have ready access to information on sex offenders, no matter how young. According to a House Judiciary Committee Report:

All too often, juvenile sex offenders have exploited current limitations that permit them to escape notification requirements to commit sexual offenses. While the Committee recognizes that States typically protect the identity of a juvenile who commits criminal acts, in the case of sexual offenses, the balance needs to change; no longer should the rights of the juvenile offender outweigh the rights of the community and victims to be free from additional sexual crimes. For victims, whether the offender is an adult or a juvenile has no bearing on the impact of that sexual offense on the life of the victim. [The AWA] strikes the balance in favor of protecting victims, rather than protecting the identity of juvenile sex offenders.

House Committee on the Judiciary, *Report on Children's Safety Act of 2005*, 109th Cong., 1st sess., September 9, 2005, 25.

106. Franklin E. Zimring, *An American Travesty: Legal Responses to Adolescent Sexual Offending* (Chicago: University of Chicago Press, 2004), 147–59; Michael F. Caldwell, "Sexual Offense Adjudication and Sexual Recidivism among Juvenile Offenders," *Sexual Abuse: A Journal of Research & Treatment* 19 (2007): 107; Donna Vandiver, "A Prospective Analysis of Juvenile Male Sex Offenders: Characteristics and Recidivism Rates as Adults," *Journal of Interpersonal Violence* 21 (2006): 673. The one-size-fits-all approach is reflected in state legislative findings, which almost universally fail to note the distinct risks posed by juveniles, as opposed to adult offenders. In Idaho, for instance, where separate publicly available registries are maintained for adult and juvenile offenders, language in the findings sections of both authorizing statutes is the same except that with the latter the term "juvenile" is inserted in each instance reference is made to the asserted high-risk posed by sex offenders. Elizabeth Garfinkle, "Coming of Age in America: The Misapplication of Sex-Offender Registration and Community-Notification Laws to Juveniles," *California Law Review* 91 (2003): 182.

107. For anecdotal evidence of the difficulties faced by juvenile registrants, see Maggie Jones, "How Can You Distinguish a Budding Pedophile from a Kid with Real Boundary Problems?" *New York Times Magazine*, July 22, 2007, 33.

108. Ibid., 58.

109. Franklin E. Zimring et al., "Sexual Delinquency in Racine, Wisconsin: Does Early Sex Offending Predict Later Sex Offending in Youth and Youth Adulthood?," *Criminal & Public Policy* 6 (2007): 527; see also Franklin E. Zimring et al., "The Predictive Power of Juvenile Sex Offending: Evidence from the Second Philadelphia Birth Cohort Study," *Justice Quarterly* (in press), http://works.bepress.com/franklin_zimring/4.

110. See Richard Tewksbury and Matthew Lees, "Perceptions of Punishment: How Registered Sex Offenders View Registries," *Crime & Delinquency* 53 (2007): 394; Tewksbury, "Female Sex Offenders," 32.

111. See Tewksbury, "Female Sex Offenders," 32; Richard Tewksbury, "Collateral Consequences," 77. Survey work done in Britain, where notification is used only in isolated instances, shows similar principled support for registration. Registrants in-

terviewed generally agreed that registration could assist police investigation and act as a deterrent to individuals inclined to recidivate. Sentiment on the possible use of community notification, on the other hand, was decidedly more negative. See Hudson, *Offending Identities*, 161–68.

112. See Levenson et al., "Megan's Law and Its Impact," 595.

113. Tewksbury, "Female Sex Offenders," 32. The view is shared by "Jake Goldenflame," a registered sex offender who frequently appears on the Internet, an outspoken advocate of registration and community notification. See Candis McLean, "'People Like Us': Only a Public Registry Will Work," *28 Report NewsMagazine* (Canada), August 20, 2001, 41.

114. Zevitz and Farkas, "Sex Offender Community Notification," 389; see also Tewksbury and Lees, "Perceptions of Punishment," 393 (a minority of registrants thought the laws would deter reoffense).

115. Mercado et al., "Impact of Specialized Sex Offender Legislation," 196.

116. Alvin Malesky and Jeanmarie Keim, "Mental Health Professionals' Perspectives on Sex Offender Registry Web Sites," *Sexual Abuse: A Journal of Research & Treatment* 13 (2001): 53 (over 80% of such professionals believe registration and notification will not decrease rates of child sexual abuse).

117. Yolanda Brannon et al., "Attitudes About Community Notification: A Comparison of Sexual Offenders and the Non-offending Public," *Sexual Abuse: A Journal of Research & Treatment* 19 (2007): 374; Levenson and Cotter, "Effect of Megan's Law," 57.

118. Tewksbury, "Collateral Consequences," 77.

119. Pamela D. Schultz, "Treatment for Sex Offenders Can Protect the Community," *Newsday* (New York), December 3, 2006.

120. Mercado et al., "Impact of Specialized Sex Offender Legislation," 197.

121. See Levenson et al., "Megan's Law and Its Impact," 596 (Kentucky and Indiana); Levenson and Cotter, "Effect of Megan's Law," 58 (Florida); Tewksbury and Lees, "Perceptions of Punishment," 398 (Kentucky).

122. Levenson et al., "Megan's Law and Its Impact," 596; Levenson and Cotter, "Effect of Megan's Law," 58–59.

123. Oregon Dept. of Corrections, *Sex Offender Community Notification in Oregon* (Salem: Oregon Dept. of Corrections, 1995), 15.

124. See, e.g., Toni Makkai and John Braithwaite, "Criminological Theories and Regulatory Compliance," *Criminology* 29 (1991): 191; Joan Petersilia and Elizabeth Deschenes, "What Punishes? Inmates Rank the Severity of Prison vs. Intermediate Sanctions," *Federal Probation* 58 (1994): 3; Tom R. Tyler, "Trust and Law-Abidingness: A Proactive Model of Social Regulation," *Boston University Law Review* 81 (2001): 361.

125. See, e.g., Eric B. Elbogen et al., "The Impact of Community Notification Laws on Sex Offender Treatment Attitudes," *International Journal of Law & Psychiatry* 26

(2003): 209 (getting individuals involved in risk assessments has therapeutic benefits including treatment compliance).

126. Kay Lazar, "States Lack Money, Manpower to Do the Job," *Boston Herald*, July 19, 1988.

127. "California: Police Need $20M to Enforce Megan's Law," *Crime Control Digest*, January 17, 2003, 6.

128. Joseph Turner, "State Will Help Track Sex Offenders," *News Tribune* (Tacoma, Washington), October 18, 2007.

129. Christy Scatterella, "Release of Sex-Offender Data Varies by Jurisdiction," *Seattle Times*, February 20, 1991.

130. In states requiring risk assessments, the judicial and administrative processes are costly, requiring experts and possibly the provision of defense counsel. Whether states will continue to pursue the approach after the Adam Walsh Act mandate of a conviction-based regime remains unclear. However, to date funding shortages have resulted in significant backlogs in registrant risk evaluations. In Nevada, for instance, which from 1998–2004 experienced an 82% increase in registrants, community notification on potentially eligible registrants was delayed three months or longer. Allison Bath, "Workload Means Delay in Processing Registrations, Community Notification," *Reno Gazette-Journal* (Nevada), September 24, 2004.

131. Mary A. Farkas and Richard G. Zevitz, "The Law Enforcement Role in Sex Offender Community Notification: A Research Note," *Journal of Crime & Justice* 23 (2000): 134.

132. See U.S. Bureau of Justice Assistance, *Managing Sex Offenders: Citizens Supporting Law Enforcement* (Alexandria, VA: International Association of Chiefs of Police, 2007), 11–32.

133. As Phillip Jenkins has noted, the modern wave of registration laws has served to "foreclose discussion of other possible avenues of approach to child abuse. In the mid-1990s, the federal lawmakers most enthusiastic for predator statutes and Internet regulation showed themselves equally determined to cut social welfare programs .... After all, had Congress not already dealt with the problem of 'real' child abuse?" Phillip Jenkins, *Moral Panic: Changing Concepts of the Child Molester in Modern America* (New Haven, CT: Yale University Press, 1998), 238.

134. See, e.g., Amos Bridges, "Registry for Sex Crimes Lagging," *Springfield News-Leader* (Missouri), April 30, 2007; Brian Evans, "Putnam Sheriff Airs Concerns About Unfunded Mandates," *Lima News* (Ohio), July 20, 2007. It bears mention that because the laws are implemented at the local level, without adequate financial assistance from states, bigger and more affluent localities naturally have greater opportunity to fund such matters as registration compliance checks by police, leading in effect to different registries in a given state. See, e.g., James Macpherson, "'Monsters in Our Closets'—

Officials: Tracking Sex Offenders with Surprise Visits Spotty in Most Cities," *Grand Forks Herald* (North Dakota), April 9, 2007.

135. See, e.g., News Service, "Compliance Money Sought," *Seattle Times*, January 10, 1999 (county obtains reimbursement from state for money spent as a result of state-mandated registration compliance measures).

136. See Allison Bath, "Workload Means Delay in Processing Registrations, Community Notification," *Reno Gazette-Journal* (Nevada), September 24, 2004 (noting concern among Nevada authorities that fee "would send more offenders underground").

137. *Fushek v. State*, 183 P.3d 536, 543–44 (Az. 2008).

138. See, e.g., Alison Bass, "Suspects Battle to Stay Off Sex Offender Registry," *Boston Globe*, August 16, 1999. See also *In re Reed*, 663 P.2d 216, 219n7 (Cal. 1983) (noting belief of Los Angeles city attorney that mandatory registration "leads defendants to claim their right to a jury trial rather than plead guilty, even when the evidence of guilt is overwhelming").

139. See, e.g., Mo. Stat. § 589.400(1); S.C. Code § 23-3-430(C). Mississippi requires registration only for convictions relating to carnal knowledge of nonbiologically related children. See Miss. Code § 45-33-23(g).

140. See, e.g., Sarah Glazer, "Punishing Sex Offenders," *CQ Researcher*, Jan. 12, 1996, 30 (New Jersey incest victims resisted reporting because they feared public identification); Jones, "How Can You Distinguish," 58 (mother who regretted informing son's therapist of sexual misconduct between the son and his sister because of son's resulting inclusion on public registry).

141. See National Center for Prosecution of Child Abuse, *Investigation and Prosecution of Child Abuse* (3d ed. 2004), 94 (noting pressures brought to bear by nonoffending parents on abused children); Julie Ortiz y Pino and Jean Goodwin, "What Families Say: The Dialogue of Incest," in *Sexual Abuse: Incest Victims and Their Families*, ed. Jean Goodwin (Boston: J. Wright, 1982), 73 (noting hesitance of incest victims to report their abuse for fear of negative repercussions to offenders). For a powerful anecdotal exposé on the strong intrafamilial pressures placed on children to remain silent in the face of sexual abuse by a relative, see Diane Jennings and Darlean Spangenberger, "Do Tough Sex Laws Help or Hurt?" *Dallas Morning News*, October 21, 2007.

142. See Tim Collie, "New Fla. Law Will Brand Teens as Sex Offenders for Life," *South Florida Sun-Sentinel*, August 9, 2007.

143. See, e.g., Nancy G. Calley, "Juvenile Sex Offenders and Sex Offender Legislation: Unintended Consequences," *Federal Probation* 72 (2008): 37; Elizabeth J. Letourneau et al., "Effects of Sex Offender Registration Policies on Juvenile Justice Decision Making," *Sexual Abuse: A Journal of Research and Treatment* (in press).

Chapter 6

1. *Hines v. Davidowitz*, 312 U.S. 52, 70–71 (1941).

2. 355 U.S. 225 (1958).

3. See *Abbott v. Los Angeles*, 349 P.2d 974 (Cal. 1973); *State v. Ulesky*, 252 A.2d 720 (N.J. 1969).

4. See *In re Reed*, 663 P.2d 216 (Cal. 1983) (lewd conduct); *In re King*, 204 Cal. Rptr. 39 (Cal. Ct. App. 1984) (indecent exposure).

5. *In re Birch*, 515 P.2d 12, 17 (Cal. 1973).

6. See, e.g., *People v. Mills*, 146 Cal. Rptr. 411, 414 (Cal. Ct. App. 1978) ("[It] cannot be doubted" that registration "has de facto punitive aspects": registrants suffer "a multitud[e] of disabilities" and registration "severely limits a person's freedom of movement, and places him under continuous police surveillance.").

7. 538 U.S. 84 (2003).

8. 538 U.S. 1 (2003).

9. The Clause prohibits laws that "make more burdensome the punishment for a crime, after its commission." *Beazell v. Ohio*, 269 U.S. 167, 169–70 (1925).

10. *People v. Alva*, 92 P.3d 311, 317 (Cal. 2004).

11. 530 U.S. 466 (2000).

12. See, e.g., *People v. Golba*, 729 N.W.2d 916 (Mich. Ct. App. 2007); *Young v. State*, 806 A.2d 233 (Md. 2002).

13. See *Kennedy v. Mendoza-Martinez*, 372 U.S. 144 (1963).

14. *Smith*, 538 U.S. at 108–9 (Souter, J., concurring).

15. Gary T. Marx, *Undercover: Police Surveillance in America* (Berkeley: University of California Press, 1988), 220.

16. *Smith*, 538 U.S. at 114 (Ginsburg, J., dissenting).

17. Ibid., 110 (Stevens, J., dissenting).

18. *State v. Taylor*, 835 P.2d 245, 250 (Wash. Ct. App. 1992) (Agid., J., dissenting).

19. See *ACLU v. City of Albuquerque*, 137 P.2d 1215, 1225 (N.M. Ct. App. 2006) ("looking at each provision in isolation tends to artificially dilute the overall impact of the [registration and notification] ordinance").

20. See Joan Petersilia, *Community Corrections: Probation, Parole and Intermediate Sanctions* (St. Paul: West Publishing, 1998), 1, 19–24 (noting that because actual supervision of parolees and probationers is modest due to high officer caseloads, registrant restrictions "may actually exceed those of probationers and parolees").

21. Cf. *Anti-Fascist Refugee Committee v. McGrath*, 341 U.S. 123, 175 (1951) (Douglas, J., concurring) (characterizing the government's classification of organizations as Communist or subversive as a stigmatizing "determination of status").

22. *Doe v. Pryor*, 61 F. Supp. 2d 1224, 1231 (M.D. Ala. 1999). See also *E.B. v. Vernierno*, 119 F.3d 1077, 1125 (3d Cir. 1997) (Becker, C. J., concurring) ("The burden imposed by

the collective weight of all these effects is borne by the offender in all aspects of his life .... The effects of notification permeate his entire existence."). For the classic discussion of the disabling effects of social stigma, see Erving Goffman, *Stigma: Notes on the Management of Spoiled Identity* (Englewood Cliffs, NJ: Prentice-Hall, 1963). As Goffman observed: "We believe the person with the stigma is not quite human. On this assumption, we reduce his chances." Ibid., 5.

23. *People v. David W.*, 733 N.E.2d 206, 210 (N.Y. 2000) (citation omitted). As Professor Seth Kreimer has observed: "No one doubts that Hester Prynne's scarlet letter provided more than neutral information, or that the effort of Senator Joseph McCarthy to 'expose' the background of his political opponents was not simply public education." Seth Kreimer, "Sunlight, Secrets, and Scarlet Letters: The Tension Between Privacy and Disclosure in Constitutional Law," *University of Pennsylvania Law Review* 140 (1991): 7.

24. Jean-Paul Sartre, *Being and Nothingness: An Essay on Phenomenological Ontology*, trans. Hazel E. Barnes (New York: Philosophical Library, 1956), 222.

25. Note, "Criminal Registration Ordinances: Police Control over Potential Recidivists," *University of Pennsylvania Law Review* 103 (1954): 60, 64n24.

26. Richard G. Zevitz and Mary Ann Farkas, "Sex Offender Community Notification: Managing High Risk Criminals or Exacting Further Vengeance?" *Behavioral Sciences & the Law* 18 (2000): 375, 382–83.

27. Jeremy Bentham, *The Panopticon Writings*, ed. Miran Bozovic (New York: Verso, 1995)

28. Michel Foucault, *Discipline and Punish: The Birth of the Prison*, trans. Alan Sheridan (Harmondsworth: Penguin Books, 1979), 201.

29. Thomas Mathiesen, "The Viewer Society: Michel Foucault's 'Panopticon' Revisited," *Theoretical Criminology* 1 (1997): 217.

30. Stanley Cohen, *Visions of Social Control: Crime, Punishment and Classification* (New York: Blackwell, 1985), 71.

31. See Foucault, *Discipline and Punish*, 203, 207.

32. *State v. Taylor*, 835 P.2d 245, 250 (Wash. Ct. App. 1992) (Agid, J., dissenting).

33. Ron Fournier, "Clinton Signs Law on Sex Offenders," *Chicago Sun-Times*, May 18, 1996.

34. John C. Hamilton, *History of the Republic of the United States as Traced in the Writings of Alexander Hamilton and His Contemporaries* (New York: D. Appleton & Co., 1859), 34 (quoting Alexander Hamilton).

35. *Fletcher v. Peck*, 10 U.S. (6 Cranch) 87, 137–38 (1810) (emphasis added).

36. See Wayne A. Logan, "The Ex Post Facto Clause and the Jurisprudence of Punishment," *American Criminal Law Review* 35 (1998): 1275.

37. *United States v. Brown*, 381 U.S. 437, 442 (1965).

38. *DeVeau v. Braisted*, 363 U.S. 144, 147 (1960).

39. See, e.g., *Doe v. Miller*, 405 F.3d 700 (8th Cir. 2005) (upholding Iowa law); *Lee v. State*, 895 So. 2d 1038 (Ala. 2004); *Mann v. State*, 603 S.E.2d 283 (Ga. 2004).

40. *Smith*, 538 U.S. at 108.

41. *CDPS*, 538 U.S. at 8.

42. The *CDPS* Court stressed that the website made clear that registration is triggered by "an offender's conviction alone—a fact that a convicted offender has already had a procedurally safeguarded opportunity to contest." *CDPS*, 538 U.S. at 7. It then added: "Indeed, the disclaimer on the Website explicitly states that the respondent's alleged nondangerousness simply does not matter." Ibid.

43. See *Milks v. State*, 894 So. 2d 924 (Fla. 2005); *Doe v. O'Connor*, 790 N.E.2d 985 (Ind. 2003).

44. *Marshall v. Jerrico*, 446 U.S. 238, 242 (1980).

45. Indeed, the Connecticut Legislature signaled its recognition of this reality by allowing for discretionary judicial exemption of certain youthful sex offenders when registration was not required by public safety. See *CDPS*, 538 U.S. at 9 (Souter, J., concurring) (citing Conn. Stat. § 54-251 (2000)).

46. As the Wyoming Supreme Court earlier observed: "If the statutory classification system is to have any integrity, the State must prove more than the mere commission of the original offense, especially where the offender has been out and about in society in the interim without further offense." *Avery v. State*, 47 P.3d 973, 978 (Wyo. 2002); see also *State v. Bani*, 36 P.3d 1255, 1267 (Haw. 2001) (without risk evaluations, persons "who do not pose a significant danger to the community are at substantial risk of being erroneously deprived of their liberty interests").

47. *Russell v. Gregoire*, 124 F.3d 1079, 1094 (9th Cir. 1997).

48. *Doe v. Kelly*, 961 F. Supp. 1105, 1112 (W.D. Mich. 1997).

49. See, e.g., *People v. Logan*, 705 N.E.2d 152, 160–61 (Ill. Ct. App. 1998) (the Illinois "Registration Act merely compiles truthful, public information, and the Notification Law makes this information more readily available").

50. See, e.g., *Akella v. Michigan Dept. of State Police*, 67 F. Supp. 2d 716, 729 (E.D. Mich. 1999) ("[P]laintiffs have cited no authority for the proposition that the magnitude of dissemination, in and of itself, is sufficient to trigger a deprivation of a liberty interest.").

51. *United States Dept. of Justice v. Reporters' Comm. for Freedom of the Press*, 489 U.S. 749, 763 (1989).

52. Ibid., 763, 770.

53. *Doe v. Poritz*, 662 A.2d 367, 411 (N.J. 1995).

54. Ibid.

55. *Artway v. N.J. Attorney General*, 876 F. Supp. 666, 689 (D. N.J. 1995). See also *Boutin v. LaFleur*, 591 N.W.2d 711, 718 (Minn. Ct. App. 1999) ("[T]here is a distinct dif-

ference between the mere presence of such information in court documents and the active dissemination of such information.").

56. *United States Dept. of Defense v. Federal Labor Relations Authority*, 51 U.S. 487, 500 (1994).

57. Ibid., 501.

58. See *Poritz*, 662 A.2d at 409 ("[W]here as a result of the information disclosed under the Notification Law, plaintiff may be exposed to uninvited harassment, we conclude that disclosure of plaintiff's home address . . . implicates a liberty interest.").

59. 67 F. Supp. 2d 716, 731–32 (E.D. Mich. 1999).

60. 400 U.S. 433 (1971).

61. Ibid., 437.

62. 424 U.S. 693 (1976).

63. Ibid., 701.

64. Ibid., 708.

65. Henry P. Monaghan, "Of 'Liberty' and 'Property,'" *Cornell Law Review* 62 (1977): 426.

66. See, e.g., *Doe v. Phillips*, 194 S.W.3d 833, 844 (Mo. 2006) (stigma from "listing on the registry comes not from [the fact that petitioners] are listed, but from their convictions of the offenses that led to their listing"); *Welvaert v. Nebraska State Patrol*, 683 N.W.2d 357, 366 (Neb. 2004) (stigma flows not from the laws "but from the fact of conviction, already a matter of public record").

67. See, e.g., *Meinders v. Weber*, 604 N.W.2d 248, 257 (S.D. 2000) ("The information contained in the sex offender registry is almost the same information available as a public record in the courthouse where the conviction occurred.").

68. According to the Florida Supreme Court the term "predator" is permissible because the only fact material to such a designation is a prior conviction, even if from the distant past. See *Milks v. State*, 894 So. 2d 924 (Fla. 2005). Justice Anstead, in an opinion with which two other members of the court joined, distinguished the Connecticut regime approved in *CDPS*, stating:

> It is one thing to provide the public with public information about sexual offenders, but quite another to tell the public that the State has determined that certain persons are "sexual predators." It is pure sophistry to suggest that these actions are the same . . . Common sense tells us that there is a clear inference between an "offender" and a "predator."

Ibid., 929–30 (Anstead, J., concurring and dissenting in part). The "predator" designation "may or may not be warranted, depending on the circumstances of each designation." Ibid., 933.

69. *Noble v. Board of Parole and Post-Prison Supervision*, 964 P.2d 990, 995 (Or. 1998).

70. *Cutshall v. Sundquist*, 193 F.3d 466, 479 & 480 (6th Cir. 1999).

71. Ibid., 481.

72. *Doe v. Kelly*, 961 F. Supp. 1105, 1112 (W.D. Mich. 1997).

73. See *Doe v. Pryor*, 61 F. Supp. 2d 1224, 1231 (M.D. Ala. 1999); *Roe v. Farwell*, 999 F. Supp. 174, 196–97 (D. Mass. 1998); *Doe v. Pataki*, 662 A.2d 367, 419 (N.J. 1995).

74. *Pryor*, 61 F. Supp. 2d at 1232.

75. See, e.g., *In re C.M.*, 578 N.W.2d 391, 397 (Minn. Ct. App. 1998) (finding "plus" based on Remedies Clause of Minnesota Constitution). It warrants mention that courts have readily found the stigma-plus test satisfied in challenges to child abuse registries. See, e.g., *Valmonte v. Bane*, 18 F.3d 992 (2d Cir. 1994); *Bohn v. City of Dakota*, 772 F.2d 1433 (8th Cir. 1985). Placement on a registry, based on a prior conviction, is seen as an independent act of government, warranting additional due process. See *State v. Jackson*, 496 S.E.2d 912, 915 (Ga. 1998).

76. See, e.g., *Ewing v. California*, 538 U.S. 11 (2003).

77. *United States v. Rabinowitz*, 339 U.S. 56, 69 (1950) (Frankfurter, J., dissenting).

78. Carol S. Steiker, "Supreme Court Review Foreword: The Limits of the Preventive State," *Journal of Criminal Law & Criminology* 88 (1998): 774.

79. 521 U.S. 346 (1997).

80. 60 U.S. 393, 404–5 (1856).

81. Eric S. Janus, *Failure to Protect: America's Sexual Predator Laws and the Rise of the Preventive State* (Ithaca, NY: Cornell University Press, 2006), 94.

82. Ibid., 106. The exceptionalism discussed here has obvious parallel to the application of decisions justifying the diminished (or nonexistent) constitutional protections of noncitizens. As Professor David Cole has observed, the government can quite readily "cross the citizen–non-citizen divide" and justify rights-stripping of certain citizens based on dangerousness deriving from their race (e.g., the internment of Japanese Americans in the 1940s) or political affiliation (e.g., McCarthyism in the 1950s). See David Cole, *Enemy Aliens: Double Standards and Constitutional Freedoms in the War on Terrorism* (New York: New Press, 2003): 85–87.

83. Sex offenders would appear to readily implicate what Professors Farber and Sherry have called the "pariah principle," which "forbids the government from designating social groups as untouchable." Constitutional concern over the designation, however, is "at its strongest when the individuals so targeted are not responsible for their status." Daniel Farber and Suzanna Sherry, "The Pariah Principle," *Constitutional Commentary* 13 (1996): 266–68. Persons who voluntarily engage in sexual misconduct and other crimes would appear poor candidates for such heightened concern.

84. See, e.g., *People v. Pieri*, 199 N.E. 495, 499 (N.Y. 1936) (Cardozo, J.) (ex-convicts are "not outcasts and are not to be treated as such").

85. See, e.g., *Cummings v. Missouri*, 71 U.S. (4 Wall.) 277 (1867) (invalidating on ex post facto grounds a state law targeting Confederate sympathizers for criminal liability).

86. See Transcript of Oral Argument, *Smith v. Doe*, 538 U.S. 84 (2003), http://www.oyez.org/cases/2000-2009/2002/2002_01_729/argument, 22.

87. See, e.g., Ala. Code § 15-20-20.1 ("[Registrants] have a reduced expectation of privacy because of the public's interest in safety and in the effective operation of government."); Colo. Rev. Stat. § 18-3-412.5(6.5) ("The general assembly finds that the persons convicted of offenses involving unlawful sexual behavior have a reduced expectation of privacy because of the public's interest in public safety.").

88. N.J. Const. art. IV, § 7, para. 12 (adopted November 7, 2000).

89. Benjamin N. Cardozo, *The Nature of the Judicial Process* (New Haven, CT: Yale University Press, 1921), 83.

90. *Trop v. Dulles*, 356 U.S. 86, 103–4 (1958). The judiciary, as Alexander Hamilton long ago wrote, ideally serves as an "intermediate body" between legislatures and citizens, whose liberties can be jeopardized by legislative decisions. Alexander Hamilton, "The Federalist No. 78," in *The Federalist Papers*, ed. Isaac Kranmick (Harmondsworth: Penguin, 1987), 438.

91. *Marbury v. Madison*, 5 U.S. 137, 178 (1803).

92. *Northern Securities Co. v. United States*, 193 U.S. 197, 400–401 (1904) (Holmes, J., dissenting).

93. See *Doe v. Pataki*, 940 F. Supp. 603, 622n15 (S.D.N.Y. 1996), rev'd, 120 F.3d 1263 (2d Cir. 1997), cert. denied, 522 U.S. 1122 (1998).

94. Rick Hampson, "What's Gone Wrong With Megan's Law?" *USA Today*, May 14, 1997.

95. Fla. Stat. Ann. § 775.24(1).

96. *Kansas v. Hendricks*, 521 U.S. 346, 396 (1997) (Breyer, J., dissenting).

97. See generally Paul Finkelman, "The Second Casualty of War: Civil Liberties and the War on Drugs," *Southern California Law Review* 66 (1993): 1389.

98. Simson Garfinkel, *Database Nation: The Death of Privacy in the 21st Century* (Cambridge, MA: O'reilly, 2000).

99. Rick Weiss, "Vast DNA Bank Pits Policing vs. Privacy," *Washington Post*, June 3, 2006.

100. Ellen Nakashima, "FBI Prepares Vast Biometrics Database," *Washington Post*, December 27, 2007.

101. 355 U.S. 225, 229 (1957).

102. "Informational" privacy is to be distinguished from "decisional" privacy. The latter has been defined as the "freedom to make decisions about one's body and family," and involves "matters such as contraception, procreation, abortion, and child rearing," figuring centrally in the Supreme Court's jurisprudence on what has been

known as the right to privacy. Daniel J. Solove et al., *Information Privacy Law*, 2d ed. (New York: Aspen, 2005), 1,

103. Ruth Gavison, "Privacy and the Limits of the Law," *Yale Law Journal* 89 (1980): 428.

104. Charles Fried, "Privacy [A Moral Analysis]," in *Philosophical Dimensions of Privacy: An Anthology*, ed. Ferdinand David Schoeman (New York: Cambridge University Press, 1984), 218.

105. Ibid., 210 (noting that privacy in its "dimension of control over information is an aspect of personal liberty"); see also John A. Hall, *Liberalism: Politics, Ideology and the Market* (Chapel Hill: University of North Carolina Press, 1988), 86–87 ("[T]wo facts give the individual a meaningful sense of human freedom: his ability to control information about himself and his right to choose separate the audiences before whom he can play separate roles.").

106. See Goffman, *Stigma*, 41–72 (discussing the ways in which uncontrolled informational disclosure disempowers personal identity).

107. Jeffrey H. Reiman, "Driving to the Panopticon: A Philosophical Exploration of the Risks to Privacy Posed by the Highway Technology of the Future," *Santa Clara Computer & High Technology Law Journal* 11 (1995): 39.

108. *Briscoe v. Reader's Digest Ass'n*, 483 P.2d 34, 37 (Cal. 1971), rev'd, 101 P.3d 552 (Cal. 2004).

109. See Jeffrey Rosen, *The Unwanted Gaze: The Destruction of Privacy in America* (New York: Random House, 2000), 10. See also Helen Merrell Lynd, *On Shame and the Search for Identity* (New York: Harcourt, Brace, 1958), 50 ("The thing that has been exposed is what I am.").

110. Cf. Charles J. Sykes, *The End of Privacy* (New York: St. Martin's Press, 1999), 101 ("Data is like a prostitute; once it is on the street, everybody has access to it.").

111. In this sense, the privacy intrusion here is unlike that currently raising concern in the commercial context, such as when during the course of transactions consumers provide information to merchants and this information is then sold. In such situations the individual, albeit implicitly, is willingly providing personal information to the other party, as part of the transaction (e.g., by means of use of a credit card); he or she is not forced to do so.

112. Fried, "Privacy," 214–15.

113. See James B. Jacobs, "Mass Incarceration and the Proliferation of Criminal Records," *University of St. Thomas Law Journal* 3 (2006): 399–400.

114. See, e.g., Peter B. Edelman, "Free Press v. Privacy: Haunted by the Ghost of Justice Black," *Texas Law Review* 68 (1990): 1224 ("[T]he immense value of truth will always outweigh the countervailing interest of an individual in nondisclosure of private information.").

115. Diane L. Zimmerman, "Requiem for a Heavyweight: A Farewell to Warren

and Brandeis's Privacy Tort," *Cornell Law Review* 68 (1983): 341. See also, e.g., Kreimer, "Sunlight," 72 ("[I]nformation is a prerequisite to the effective exercise of choice. As knowledge increases so does societal and individual freedom . . . Those who suppress information may be seeking to manipulate an audience's choices.").

116. See, e.g., Richard Posner, *Economic Analysis of Law*, 5th ed. (New York: Aspen Law & Business, 1998), 46, 660–63. According to Richard Epstein, "the plea for privacy is often a plea for the right to misrepresent one's self to the rest of the world." Richard A. Epstein, "The Legal Regulation of Genetic Discrimination: Old Responses to New Technology," *Boston University Law Review* 74 (1994): 12.

117. See Lior Strahilevitz, "Privacy versus Antidiscrimination," *University of Chicago Law Review* 75 (2008): 363, 365–66.

118. Ibid., 380.

119. Daniel J. Solove, "The Virtues of Knowing Less: Justifying Privacy Protections Against Disclosure," *Duke Law Journal* 53 (2003): 1033, 1035.

120. Ibid., 1035.

121. Rosen, *Unwanted Gaze*.

122. While myriad examples exist of this mentality, the recent decision of a federal appeals court approving a Michigan provision requiring registration of persons whose convictions have been "set aside"—dictating that the individuals "shall be considered not to have been previously convicted"—is especially telling. *Does v. Munoz*, 507 F.3d 961, 963 (6th Cir. 2007).

123. John W. Porter, "How Should We Treat Sex Offenders?" *Portland Press Herald* (Maine), September 10, 2006.

124. Maggie Jones, "How Can You Distinguish a Budding Pedophile from a Kid with Real Boundary Problems?" *New York Times Magazine*, July 22, 2007, 58.

125. See, e.g., Ala. Code § 13A-11-200 (1994); Idaho Code § 18-8304(a)(1) (Supp. 2002); Kan. Stat. Ann. § 22-4902(a)(5)(B) (Supp. 2003); La. Rev. Stat. § 15:541(14.1) (2003).

126. The experience of California in 1997 provides perhaps the most vivid example in this regard, when the expansive retroactive reach of the State's law (to 1944) required elderly men, with decades-old convictions for such offenses as lewd conduct and public indecency, to register, even though many such convictions likely resulted from police entrapment and antigay animus. See Robert Jacobson, Note, "'Megan's Law': Reinforcing Old Patterns of Anti-Gay Harassment," *Georgetown Law Journal* 87 (1999): 2460. More recently, in Indiana, where in 2007 the legislature for the first time required violent offenders to register, with full retroactive reach, officers were required to track down individuals who were convicted decades ago and have since lived lawfully. See "14 News Investigates: Violent Offender Registry," http://www.14wfie.com/global/story.asp?s=7303381.

127. As commented by Professor George Fletcher in "Disenfranchisement as

Punishment: Reflections on the Racial Use of Infamia," *UCLA Law Review* 46 (1999): 1907:

> Punishment as an imperative of justice hardly makes sense if the program of punishment fails to include an opportunity for the offender's reintegration into society. There is no point to the metaphor of paying one's debt to society unless the serving of punishment actually cancels out the fact of having committed the crime. The idea that you pay the debt and be treated as a debtor (felon) forever verges on the macabre.

128. *Briscoe v. Reader's Digest Ass'n*, 483 P.2d 34, 41–42 (Cal. 1971). Forty years before, the same court avowed that "we, as right-thinking members of society, should permit [the law abiding ex-offender] to continue in the path of rectitude rather than throw him back into a life of shame or crime." *Melvin v. Reed*, 297 P.2d 91, 93 (Cal. 1931).

129. David Garland, *Culture of Control: Crime and Social Order in Contemporary Society* (Chicago: University of Chicago Press, 2001): 135–36. See also Nora V. Demleitner, "Preventing Internal Exile: The Need for Restrictions on Collateral Sentencing Consequences," *Stanford Law & Policy Review* 11 (1999): 153 (drawing parallels between noncitizens and registrants).

130. See generally Robert Putnam, *Bowling Alone: The Collapse and Revival of American Community* (New York: Simon & Schuster, 2000). The essential interrelatedness of social life was noted by John Dewey over a century ago: "We cannot think of ourselves save as to some extent *social* beings. Hence we cannot separate the idea of ourselves and our own good from our idea of others and of their good." John Dewey, "Ethics (1908)," in *The Middle Works: 1899–1924*, vol. 5, ed. Jo Ann Boydston (Carbondale: Southern Illinois University Press, 1978), 268.

131. The predictive value of prior convictions, including aged ones, for future crime has always been accepted as an article of faith. Research has shown, however, that recidivism risk declines quickly over time, such that after six or seven years the risk of new offense among ex-offenders resembles offense commission among nonoffenders. See Megan Kurlychek et al., "Scarlet Letters and Recidivism: Does an Old Criminal Record Predict Future Offending?" *Criminology & Public Policy* 5 (2006): 483.

132. As Director of the California Department of Corrections, Richard McGee stated in a 1947 memorandum to Governor Earl Warren, noting his concern over California's proposed sex offender registration law: "It has never been the practice in America to require citizens to register with the police, except while actually serving a sentence under the Probation or Parole Laws." Inter-Office Memorandum from Richard A. McGee to the Honorable Earl Warren, Regarding AB 2097, July 2, 1947.

133. See *Doe v. Attorney General*, 686 N.E.2d 1007, 1015–16 (Mass. 1997) (Fried, J., concurring) ("To require registration of persons not in connection with any particu-

lar activity asserts a relationship between government and the individual that is in principle quite alien to our traditions, a relationship which when generalized has been the hallmark of totalitarian government.").

134. Jonathan Simon, "Managing the Monstrous: Sex Offenders and the New Penology," *Psychology, Public Policy & Law* 4 (1998): 460.

135. In this sense, notification is consistent with community policing initiatives surfacing in the 1980s and 1990s. See Roy Roberg et al., *Police & Society*, 3d. ed. (Cary, NC: Roxbury, 2005), 88 (noting that community policing sought to "encourage individual citizens and community groups to shoulder some responsibility" for community safety). Parallel can also be seen in the advent of the private security industry, which has similarly diffused policing responsibility. See Les Johnston and Clifford D. Shearing, *Governing Security: Explorations in Policing and Justice* (New York: Routledge, 2003).

136. Indeed, the individual identified as having conceived of community notification, Mountlake Terrace, Washington Police Chief John Turner, unabashedly acknowledged in 1990 that the policy sought to absolve government of responsibility. Jolayne Houtz, "When Do You Unmask a Sexual Predator?" *Seattle Times*, August 30, 1990.

137. As one New Jersey resident commented in 1995: "The state says 'We think he's a danger, a threat, a time bomb waiting to go off and we thought you'd like to know.' But if the state couldn't deal with him, what can I do?" Shankar Vedantam, "Sex Offender Notification Law Questioned by Experts: Offenders' Civil Rights One Issue," *Times-Picayune* (New Orleans), September 17, 1995.

138. Jonathan Simon, "Megan's Law: Crime and Democracy in Late Modern America," *Law & Social Inquiry* 25 (2000): 1142.

139. *NAACP v. Alabama ex rel. v. Patterson*, 357 U.S. 449, 463 (1958).

140. *Brown v. Socialist Workers '74 Campaign Comm.*, 459 U.S. 87, 93 (1982).

141. See *DeShaney v. Winnebago City Dept. of Social Services*, 489 U.S. 189, 197 (1989).

142. Ibid.

143. James Q. Whitman, "What Is Wrong with Shame Sanctions?" *Yale Law Journal* 107 (1998): 1059.

144. Ibid., 1088.

145. Richard Zevitz, "Sex Offender Placement and Neighborhood Social Integration: The Making of a Scarlet Letter Community," *Criminal Justice Studies* 17 (2004): 212. Another survey of Wisconsin residents attending a community notification meeting revealed that 38% were more concerned, 27% were unchanged, and 35% were less concerned than before. Richard G. Zevitz and Mary Ann Farkas, *Sex Offender Community Notification: Assessing the Impact in Wisconsin* (Washington, DC: National Institute of Justice, 2000), 3. Question also exists over whether the anxiety inspired has

beneficial effect. In Ohio, for instance, researchers were unable to conclude whether the "fear created by notification resulted in healthy community outcomes." Victoria S. Beck and Lawrence F. Travis III, "Sex Offender Notification and Fear of Victimization," *Journal of Criminal Justice* 32 (2004): 461.

146. See Alicia Caputo and Stanley L. Brodsky, "Citizen Coping with Community Notification of Released Sex Offenders," *Behavioral Sciences & the Law* 22 (2004): 239 (noting that anxiety is especially likely if, as is typically the case today, notification is not accompanied by information on how recipients can take protective action).

147. *McCulloch v. Maryland*, 17 U.S. (4 Wheat) 316, 405 (1819) (Marshall, C. J.). The Constitution expressly grants the federal government criminal police power in only five specific areas: counterfeiting, piracy, military crimes, crimes against the law of nations, and treason. See U.S. Const. art. I §§ 3, 8.

148. See U.S. Const. amend. X ("The powers not delegated to the United States by the Constitution, nor prohibited to it by the States, are reserved to the States respectively, or to the people.").

149. See *New York v. United States*, 505 U.S. 144, 181 (1992); see also James Madison, "The Federalist No. 51," in Kranmick, *Federalist Papers*, 323 ("In the compound republic of America . . . a double security arises to the rights of the people. The different governments will control each other, at the same time that each will be controlled by itself.").

150. See *Gregory v. Ashcroft*, 501 U.S. 452, 458 (1991); see also David L. Shapiro, *Federalism: A Dialogue* (Evanston, IL: Northwestern University Press, 1995), 91–92.

151. See, e.g., *United States v. Morrison*, 529 U.S. 598, 618 (2000) ("the Founders denied the National Government [the police power] and reposed [it] in the States).

152. U.S. Const. art. I, § 8, cl. 3.

153. See *United States v. Morrison*, 529 U.S. 598 (2000) (invalidating federal law permitting a civil remedy for persons victimized by gender-motivated violent crime); *United States v. Lopez*, 514 U.S. 549 (1995) (invalidating federal law making it a crime to carry a firearm within 1,000 feet of a school). The Court's more recent decision in *Gonzales v. Raich*, 545 U.S. 1 (2005), upholding a federal law criminalizing marijuana in the face of a California law permitting its medicinal use, seemingly marks a retrenchment. See Symposium, "Federalism after *Gonzales v. Raich*," *Lewis & Clark Law Review* 9 (2005): 743.

154. U.S. Const. art. I, § 8, cl. 1.

155. See *South Dakota v. Dole*, 483 U.S. 203, 206 (1987) (Congress can "further [its] broad regulatory objectives by conditioning receipt of federal moneys upon compliance by the recipient with federal statutory and administrative directives.").

156. See, e.g., Sara Sun Beale, "Too Many and Yet Too Few: New Principles to Define the Proper Limits for Federal Criminal Jurisdiction," *Hastings Law Journal* 46 (1995): 1009 ("Conditioning federal aid upon acceptance of federal standards formally

observes the bounds of federalism while, as a practical matter, moving the federal system toward uniform standards.").

157. See *David v. Monroe City Board of Education*, 526 U.S. 629, 654 (1999) (Kennedy, J., dissenting) ("Congress can use its Spending Clause power to pursue objective outside of its [delegated powers] by attaching conditions to the grant of federal funds.").

158. *U.S. Term Limits, Inc. v. Thornton*, 514 U.S. 779, 838 (1995) (Kennedy, J., concurring).

159. See Brannon P. Denning and Glenn H. Reynolds, "Rulings and Resistance: The New Commerce Clause Jurisprudence Encounters the Lower Courts," *Arkansas Law Review* 55 (2003): 1253.

160. Activities Report of the Committee of the Judiciary, S. Rep. No. 109–369, at 16 (2006).

161. 42 U.S.C. § 16901 (2006). The shift in degree was plainly not lost on Congress itself, which emphasized that the AWA's provisions "constitute, in relation to States, only conditions required to avoid the reduction of Federal funding," 42 U.S.C. § 16925(d), a clear nod to concern that its extensive prescriptions might violate the Tenth Amendment's anticommandeering prohibition. See *Printz v. United States*, 521 U.S. 898, 935 (1997).

162. *Addington v. Texas*, 441 U.S. 418, 431 (1979).

163. *New State Ice Co. v. Liebmann*, 285 U.S. 262, 311 (1932) (Brandeis, J., dissenting).

164. See James Madison, "The Federalist No. 10," in Kranmick, *Federalist Papers*, 83–84 (positing that national leaders will likely have "enlightened views and virtuous sentiments [that] render them superior to local prejudices and schemes of injustice.").

165. Rachel E. Barkow, "Federalism and the Politics of Sentencing," *Columbia Law Review* 105 (2005): 1310.

166. See Beale, "Too Many," 1295 ("Many of the most promising trends in criminal law enforcement began at the state and local level, including specialized drug courts, community policing . . . and sentencing guidelines."). Ironically, while intended to satisfy the get-tough appetite of Congress, the federal mandate of a conviction-based regime might have the opposite result. Such is the case, for example, when in a risk-based classification system an individual pleads guilty to a lesser offense. In such an instance, evaluators can impose more onerous conditions on the individual than the plea basis itself would warrant, because an individualized risk assessment is undertaken. See, e.g., Ark. Code Ann. 12-12-917.

167. *Lopez*, 514 U.S. at 561n3 (quoting *United States v. Bass*, 404 U.S. 336, 349 (1971)).

168. See, e.g., *Cong. Rec.* 142 (May 7, 1996): H 4451, H 4456 (statement of Rep. Watt); *Cong. Rec.* 140 (July 13, 1994): H 5612, H 5613 (statement of Rep. Nadler).

169. Such was the case in Ohio, for instance, where the state rushed to adopt the

AWA, only to discover that federal bonuses for such early-bird compliance were not available. Worse yet, the state carried out its overhaul before the U.S. attorney general issued final guidelines on implementation, themselves of critical importance. See Margo Pierce, "Next Comes Burning at the Stake: Is Ohio Getting Too Tough on Sex Offenders?" *City Beat* (Cincinnati), August 15, 2007.

170. David E. Engdahl, "The Spending Power," *Duke Law Journal* 44 (1994): 92. Notably, the Wetterling Act and successor laws are not subject to the limitations imposed by the Unfunded Mandate Reform Act. See Unfunded Mandate Reform Act of 1995 § 421, 2 U.S.C. § 658(5)(A) (1995) (excluding from coverage duties that are imposed as a condition of receiving federal assistance).

## Chapter 7

1. See also John Braithwaite, *Crime, Shame and Reintegration* (New York: Cambridge University Press, 1989), 60. In 1870s Colonial India, as well, the British discontinued registration of "criminal tribes" due to concern that its stigmatizing effects would self-fulfill future criminality. See Amanda A. Yang, *Crime and Criminality in British India* (Tucson: University of Arizona Press 1985), 116.

2. Michael Tonry, *Thinking About Crime: Sense and Sensibility in American Penal Culture* (New York: Oxford University Press, 2004), 15.

3. A related example is found in the recent experience of Iowa with its residence exclusion law. State legislators there rejected a proposal by law enforcement associations to modify the law, based on its detrimental effects. Editorial, "Who Will Stand Up for Making Kids Safer?" *Telegraph Herald* (Dubuque, Iowa), December 14, 2007. See also Jill Y. Miller, "Keeping Sex Offenders Away from . . . Schools/Playgrounds/ Bus Stops/Churches—Is It as Practical as It Sounds?" *Atlanta Journal-Constitution*, March 17, 2006 (noting lobbying effort by Georgia Sheriff's Association seeking to modify exclusion zone provision relating to school bus stops due to enforcement difficulties and quoting one sheriff as saying: "We're kind of against the wall on this one because if you don't support it [the bill] you're seen as soft on crime.").

4. For instance, the group Parents for Megan's Law maintains on its website results from annual surveys, with states receiving grades of A–F. See http://www.parentsformeganslaw.com/html/links.lasso.

5. For instance, after O'Reilly categorized Alabama among the "states that don't seem to care about this issue at all," the Alabama Legislature convened a special session to consider tougher registration and community notification requirements. After the requirements were enacted, the governor echoed the sentiments of a state senator that "no one can say that Alabama is 'soft' on sex offenders." Recent Legislation, "Criminal Law—Sex Offender Notification Statute—Alabama Strengthens Restrictions on Sex Offenders," *Harvard Law Review* 119 (2006): 942.

6. See Wayne A. Logan, "'Democratic Despotism' and Constitutional Constraint: An Empirical Analysis of Ex Post Facto Claims in State Courts," *William & Mary Bill of Rights Journal* 12 (2003): 468, 495 (surveying extensive public choice literature noting the political impotence of ex-offenders).

7. A prime example of this disdain recently arose in California, where a couple sued the seller of a home they purchased claiming that he should have disclosed his sex offender registrant status. Eric Louie, "Seller's Sex-Offender Status Angers Alamo Home Buyers," *Contra Costa Times*, May 29, 2007. On the issue of modern disdain for sex offenders more generally, see Eric S. Janus and Wayne A. Logan, "Substantive Due Process and the Involuntary Commitment of Sexually Violent Predators," *Connecticut Law Review* 35 (2003): 320–21.

8. 42 U.S.C. § 16902.

9. Franklin E. Zimring et al., *Punishment and Democracy: Three Strikes and You're Out in California* (New York: Oxford University Press, 2001), 221–23.

10. 42 U.S.C.S. § 16991 (2007).

11. The Institute is to assess the new law's effectiveness in (1) increasing compliance with registration and notification requirements, (2) enhancing public safety, and (3) optimizing public dissemination of registrants' information on the Internet. Ibid., § 16990(a)(b). The AWA also requires assessment of associated "costs and burdens" and recommendations for increasing the effectiveness of registration. Ibid.

12. Angela Rozas, "Report Hits Laws Aimed at Sex Offenders," *Chicago Tribune*, September 12, 2007.

13. Sam Wood, "N.J. Study Scrutinizes Megan's Law Effect," *Philadelphia Inquirer*, May 6, 2007.

14. See Christine Jolls et al., "A Behavioral Approach to Law and Economics," *Stanford Law Review* 50 (1998): 1477.

15. See Cass R. Sunstein, "Probability Neglect: Emotions, Worst Cases, and Law," *Yale Law Journal* 112 (2002): 61.

16. See Raymond Nickerson, "Confirmation Bias: A Ubiquitous Phenomenon in Many Guises," *Review of General Psychology* 2 (1998): 175–76 (describing confirmation bias as "the inappropriate bolstering of hypotheses or beliefs whose truth is in question" and a "one-sided case-building process").

17. "The Greatest Fear," *Economist*, August 26, 2006, 25 (reporting results of Gallup poll).

18. Testament to this, according to one recent study, 73% of residents in a Florida locality stated that they would support registration and notification laws even if they were shown to have no crime reduction benefit. Jill Levenson et al., "Public Perceptions About Sex Offenders and Community Protection Policies," *Analyses of Social Issues and Public Policy*, 7 (2007): 1, 14.

19. Cass R. Sunstein, *Laws of Fear: Beyond the Precautionary Principle* (New York: Cambridge University Press, 2005), 208.

20. Over the last decade or so, legal scholars have attached increasing significance to expressive theories of criminal justice interventions, focusing on the social and political messages sent by particular sanctions themselves. See, e.g., Dan M. Kahan, "What Do Alternative Sanctions Mean?" *University of Chicago Law Review* 63 (1996): 631–35 (asserting that shaming sanctions are likely to enjoy political favor because the public will regard them as vivid expressions of condemnation, compared to other alternative sanctions such as fines and community service).

21. *New York Times v. Sullivan*, 403 U.S. 713, 729 (1971) (Stewart, J. concurring). Cf. William Blake, "Annotations to Sir Joshua Reynolds Discourses," in *The Complete Writings of William Blake: With All the Variant Readings*, ed. Geoffrey Keynes (London: Nonesuch Press, 1957), 451 (averring that "to generalize is to be an idiot. To particularize is the Alone Distinction of Merit.").

22. See *In re Registrant E.I.* 693, A.2d 505, 508 (N.J. Super. Ct App. Div 1997) ("[I]f Megan's Law is applied literally and mechanically to virtually all sexual offenders, the beneficial purpose of this law will be impeded."). Cf. *Thompson v. County of Alameda*, 614 P.2d 728, 735 (Cal. 1980) (holding that notifying communities of released prisoners "would, in our view, produce a cacophony of warnings that by reason of their sheer volume would add little to the effective protection of the public"); *VanLuchene v. State*, 797 P.2d 932, 936 (Mont. 1990) (noting that the state "legislature recognized the futility of issuing a public warning regarding the release of every potentially violent offender").

23. See Dan Gunderson, "Sex Offender Laws Have Unintended Consequences," *National Public Radio*, June 18, 2007, http://minnesota.publicradio.org/display/web/2007/06/11/sexoffender1/.

24. Indeed, the skewed public fear over strangers is in some sense justified by evidence suggesting that as a class stranger-assailants cause more severe physical harm and death to their victims than nonstrangers. Michele L. Meloy, *Sex Offenses and the Men Who Commit Them* (Boston: Northeastern University Press, 2006), 22. Other research, however, points to the especially harmful effects of violent victimization by familiars. See Carissa Hessick, "Violence Between Lovers, Strangers, and Friends," *Washington University Law Review* 85 (2007): 343.

25. Phillip Jenkins, *Moral Panic: Changing Concepts of the Child Molester in Modern America* (New Haven, CT: Yale University Press, 1998), 232–33.

26. *Hines v. Davidowitz*, 312 U.S. 52, 70–71 (1941).

27. This sensibility was evidenced in 1942, when amid early reports of Nazi medical atrocities and genocide, the Supreme Court in *Skinner v. Oklahoma*, 316 U.S. 535 (1942) invalidated an Oklahoma law authorizing sterilization of recidivist criminal offenders, marking a sharp contrast with the Court's decision in *Buck v. Bell*, 274 U.S.

200 (1927), which upheld (Justice Holmes writing for the Court) Virginia's involuntary sterilization law for "imbeciles."

28. Editorial, "Fine-Tuning Megan's Laws," *New York Times*, July 30, 2008.

29. *Doe v. Dept. of Public Safety*, 92 P.3d 398, 409 (Alaska 2004).

30. See, e.g., *State v. Robinson*, 873 So. 2d 1205 (Fla. 2004); *ACLU v. City of Albuquerque*, 137 P.3d 1215 (N.M. Ct. App. 2006); *People v. Moi*, 801 N.Y.S.2d 780 (N.Y. Sup. Ct. 2005).

31. See, e.g., *People v. Johnson*, 870 N.E.2d 415 (Ill. 2007); *People v. Cintron*, 827 N.Y.S.2d 445 (N.Y. Sup. Ct. 2006).

32. *People v. Taylor*, 835 N.Y.S.2d 241, 246 (N.Y. App. 2d Div. 2007).

33. 662 A.2d 367, 411 (N.J. 1995).

34. Ibid., 412.

35. *State v. Druktenis*, 86 P.3d 1050, 1071 & 1082 (N.M. Ct. App. 2004).

36. *FCC v. Beach Communications*, 508 U.S. 307, 315 (1993).

37. See, e.g., City of Cleburne v. Cleburne Living Center, 473 U.S. 432 (1985) (invalidating zoning law allowing exclusion of persons with mental disabilities); Lawrence Tribe, "Lawrence v. Texas: The 'Fundamental Right' That Dare Not Speak Its Name," *Harvard Law Review* 117 (2004): 1893, 1902–3.

38. See *Conn. Dept. of Pub. Safety v. Doe*, 538 U.S. 1, 10 (2003) (Souter, J., concurring) (noting that the case did not involve an equal protection claim and provided no "occasion to speak [to] . . . the standard of scrutiny that might be in order" vis-à-vis law's allowance for some statutorily eligible registrants to be exempted while others were not).

39. For an effort to make the contrary case that ex-offenders constitute an immutable suspect class, although not specifying what level of heightened scrutiny would be warranted, see Ben Geiger, Comment, "The Case for Ex-offenders as a Suspect Class," *California Law Review* 94 (2006): 1191.

40. *Does v. Munoz*, 462 F. Supp. 2d 787, 799n6 (E.D. Mich. 2006), aff'd, 490 F.3d 491 (6th Cir. 2007). Cf. *State v. Douglas*, 586 N.E.2d 1096, 1099 (Ohio Ct. App. 1989) (rejecting Eighth Amendment challenge to registration alone, noting its "efficacy" was "doubtful" and it posed "considerable" risk of harassment, because laws should not be invalidated because they are "silly or undesirable").

41. *Does v. Munoz*, 490 F.3d 491 (6th Cir. 2007).

42. *Aquirre v. Philips*, 127 S.W.3d 883, 887–88 (Tex. Ct. Crim. App. 2004).

43. *Cutshall v. Sundquist*, 193 F.3d 466, 482–83 (6th Cir. 1999).

44. *Doe v. Moore*, 410 F.3d 1337, 1346–48 (11th Cir. 2005).

45. On a handful of occasions, however, the courts have granted relief relative to specific classification decisions. For instance, in 2006, the California Supreme Court invalidated the state's decision (since 1947) to impose a mandatory lifetime registration requirement on adults convicted of voluntary oral copulation with a minor, yet

allow discretion on whether adults convicted of voluntary sexual intercourse with minors must register. The court found no "plausible reason, based on reasonably conceivable facts" to justify the distinction. The remedy for the equal protection violation, however, was something less than individuals such as the litigant might have desired. The California Legislature remained free, the court held, to "requir[e] lifetime registration both for persons convicted of voluntary oral copulation *and* for those convicted of voluntary sexual intercourse, thus treating both groups the same." *People v. Hofsheier*, 129 P.3d 29, 42 (Cal. 2006). See also *State v. Limon*, 122 P.3d 22 (Kan. 2005) (invalidating on equal protection grounds distinction between homosexual and heterosexual sodomy with a minor, with the former resulting in an enhanced registration requirement); *In the Interest of Z.B.*, 757 N.W.2d 595 (Utah 2008) (invalidating on equal protection grounds law allowing adult but not juvenile registrants to seek registry removal based on certain preconditions).

46. 932 A.2d 552 (Me. 2007).

47. See, e.g., *Fullmer v. Michigan Dept. of State Police*, 360 F.3d 579 (6th Cir. 2004) (upholding Michigan law).

48. The presumptive strength of this disclaimer is such that registration is permitted even when a conviction has been lawfully set aside. See *Does v. Munoz*, 462 F. Supp. 2d 787, 794 (E.D. Mich. 2006) ("[E]ven if Plaintiffs claim a liberty interest in 'not being falsely designated as currently dangerous sex offenders,' Michigan's [public registry] does not designate individuals listed on the registry as currently dangerous.").

Moreover, there is room in *CDPS* itself to infer that a disclaimer is not needed, that a lawful conviction alone suffices. This is a position adopted by at least two courts. See *Milks v. State*, 894 So. 2d 924, 928 (Fla. 2005) ("The only material fact under Florida's statutory scheme, just as under Connecticut's, is the fact of a previous conviction—all of the burdens of the Act . . . [flow] from the fact of a previous conviction."); *Doe v. O'Connor*, 790 N.E.2d 985, 989 (Ind. 2003) ("To paraphrase the Supreme Court, even if Doe could prove that he is not likely to be currently dangerous, the Legislature has decided that the registry information of all sex offenders—currently dangerous or not—must be publicly disclosed."). The *CDPS* Court stressed that the website made clear that registration is triggered by "an offender's conviction alone—a fact that a convicted offender has already had a procedurally safeguarded opportunity to contest." *CDPS*, 538 U.S. at 7. It then added: "Indeed, the disclaimer on the Website explicitly states that the respondent's alleged nondangerousness simply does not matter." Ibid.

49. 199 P.3d 935, 945 (Utah 2008).

50. Ibid., 947.

51. Similarly, the Idaho Supreme Court recently invalidated the state's "violent sexual offender" designation, which relegated individuals to a particular website link and more onerous registration requirements, without affording any due process protection. See *Smith v. State*, 203 P.3d 1221 (Idaho 2009).

52. 339 F.3d 639 (8th Cir. 2003).

53. See *Boutin v. LaFleur*, 591 N.W.2d 711 (Minn. 1999); *In re Risk Level Determination of C.M.*, 578 N.W.2d 391 (Minn. Ct. App. 1998). But see *In re Risk Level Determination of E.M.N.*, 2006 WL 2053034 (Minn. Ct. App. 2006) (holding that due to statutory changes notification was permissible).

54. Case law upholding similar provisions in other states, where registration leads automatically to community notification, will serve as precedent to help reject due process challenges to such broad provisions. See, e.g., *People v. Meidinger*, 987 P.2d 937, 938 (Colo. Ct. App. 1999); *State v. Patterson*, 963 P.2d 436, 437 (Kan. Ct. App. 1998); *State v. Halstien*, 857 P.2d 270, 282 (Wash. 1993).

55. *Ark. Department of Corrections v. Bailey*, 247 S.W.2d 851 (Ark. 2007).

56. William J. Brennan, Jr., "State Constitutions and the Protection of Individual Rights," *Harvard Law Review* 90 (1977): 491.

57. See, e.g., Ala. Const. art. I, § 13 ("[E]very person, for any injury done him, in his . . . persons, or reputation . . . shall have a remedy by due process of law."); Conn. Const. art. I, § 10 ("All courts shall be open, and every person, for an injury done to him in his person, property or reputation, shall have the remedy by due course of law.").

58. See, e.g., Mont. Const. art. II, § 10 ("The right of individual privacy is essential to the well-being of a free society.").

59. See, e.g., N.M. Const. art. II, § 4 (recognizing fundamental right of "seeking and obtaining health and happiness"). See also *State v. Yoskowitz*, 563 A.2d 1, 13–15 (N.J. 1989) (discussing State's "fairness and rightness" doctrine).

60. See Ellen A. Peters, "Capacity and Respect: A Perspective on the Historic Role of the State Courts in the Federal System," *New York University Law Review* 73 (1998): 1065.

61. It bears mention that petitioners can also, depending on their crime of conviction and the statutory criteria used in a given jurisdiction, seek to challenge registration eligibility on statutory grounds. To date, such offense-specific challenges have achieved a measure of success. See, e.g., *State v. Chun*, 76 P.3d 942 (Haw. 2003) (invalidating registration requirement because indecent exposure did not constitute an offense entailing "criminal sexual conduct"); *State v. Andrews*, 40 P.3d 708 (Wyo. 2002) (invalidating registration requirement because burglary conviction did not qualify as a "sex offense").

62. *Doe v. Poritz*, 662 A.2d 367, 419 (N.J. 1995).

63. *Doe v. Attorney General*, 686 N.E.2d 1007, 1012, 1013 (Mass. 1997). Two years later, the court emphasized that registration alone represented "a continuing, intrusive, and humiliating regulation of the person himself." *Doe v. Attorney General*, 715 N.E.2d 37, 43 (Mass. 1999).

64. *State v. Bani*, 36 P.3d 1255, 1264 (Haw. 2001).

65. *State v. Guidry*, 96 P.3d 242, 249, 251 (Haw. 2004). Federal courts in New Jersey and Massachusetts have also looked to state constitutions and found the lack of due process afforded by state legislatures problematic. See *E.B. v. Verniero*, 119 F.3d 1077, 1105 (3d Cir. 1997); *Roe v. Farwell*, 999 F. Supp. 174, 196 (D. Mass. 1998).

66. *Doe v. State*, 189 P.3d 999 (Ak. 2008). State courts have also invoked state constitutional provisions barring "retroactive" burdens as a basis for relief. See, e.g., *Doe v. Phillips*, 194 S.W.3d 833 (Mo. 2006).

67. See James N. G. Cauthen, "Expanding Rights Under State Constitutions: A Quantitative Appraisal," *Albany Law Review* 63 (2000): 1202.

68. See, e.g., *Helman v. State*, 784 A.2d 1058 (Del. 2001) (concluding that state constitution's protected right to "reputation" and "open courts" provisions were not violated by conviction-based scheme); *Doe v. O'Connor*, 790 N.E.2d 985 (Ind. 2003) (concluding that the state constitution's protected rights to "reputation" and right to "remedy by due course of law" were not violated, citing *CDPS* in support).

69. Employing similar logic, John Hart Ely long ago recognized that the political process is dominated by a "we-they" divide: the greater the gulf between the negative effects of a law and the lives of legislators or their supporters, the more likely a law is to be enacted, and vice versa. John H. Ely, "The Constitutionality of Reverse Discrimination," *University of Chicago Law Review* 41 (1973): 723.

It warrants mention that the "they" increasingly may be less different than the "we." In 2006, an estimated forty-eight million persons in the United States (one of every six residents) had a criminal history of some kind. U.S. Dept. of Justice, *The Attorney General's Report on Criminal History Background Checks* (Washington, DC: Office of the Attorney General, 2006). While it remains the case that persons with criminal histories often hail from lower socioeconomic circumstances, and hence are less likely to enjoy political influence, the sheer magnitude of imprisonment rates might well have influence in jurisdictions. Cf. Eric Rasmusen, "Stigma and Self-Fulfilling Expectations of Criminality," *Journal of Law & Economics* 39 (1996): 541 ("[I]f crime is sufficiently prevalent, a criminal record loses its informativeness and thus its stigmatizing effect.").

70. Dave Russell, "Too Much 'Sunshine' on Gun Issue," *Asheville Citizen-Times* (North Carolina), March 21, 2007.

71. Adam Liptak, "A Web Site Causes Unease in Police," *New York Times*, July 12, 2003.

72. Adam Liptak, "Web Sites Listing Informants Concern Justice Dept.," *New York Times*, May 22, 2007.

73. *Planned Parenthood v. American Coalition of Life Activists*, 290 F.3d 1058, 1065 (9th Cir. 2002) (en banc).

74. One irate local resident, for instance, wrote the newspaper to relate that she

had fled an abusive domestic relationship and, as a result of having her address listed, was forced to move for a third time. Russell, "Too Much Sunshine."

75. D. H. Kaye and Michael E. Smith, "DNA Identification Databases: Legality, Legitimacy, and the Case for Population-Wide Coverage," *Wisconsin Law Review* (2003): 413, 459.

76. See Ronald Corbett and Gary T. Marx, "Critique: No Soul in the New Machine: Technofallacies in the Electronic Monitoring Movement," *Justice Quarterly* 8 (1991): 400 ("[T]echnical developments drastically alter the economics of surveillance such that it becomes much less expensive per unit watched.").

77. See Daniel J. Solove, "'I've Got Nothing to Hide' and Other Misunderstandings of Privacy," *San Diego Law Review* 44 (2007): 745.

78. See generally Ellen Perlman, "Where Are They Now? States and Localities are Using GPS to Put Moving Targets on the Map," *Governing.com*, October, 2005, http://governing.com/articles/10gps.htm. See also Wendy Koch, "More Sex Offenders Tracked by Satellite," *USA Today*, June 7, 2006 ("If the offender enters a restricted area, such as a playground, the receiver immediately alerts a data center, which notifies officials.").

79. The Adam Walsh Act, in addition to creating a national database of registrants, authorizes money for state GPS tracking systems. See Public Law 109-248, 120 *Stat.* 587.

80. See Isaac Rosenberg, "Involuntary Endogenous RFID Compliance Monitoring," *Yale Journal of Law & Technology* 10 (2008): 331. Today, RFID can only monitor individuals physically situated within several feet of radio receivers, and can merely note their presence in a specified location. But as the technology becomes more sophisticated, its appeal will doubtless grow. Registrants themselves might see its appeal, as compared to GPS monitoring, which is visually and physically more obtrusive.

81. Terry Thomas, "When Public Protection Becomes Punishment? The UK Use of Civil Measures to Contain Sex Offenders," *European Journal on Criminal Policy and Research* 10 (2005): 337, 341.

82. Nigel Morris, "Ministers Rule Out Emulating America's Hardline 'Megan's Law,'" *Independent* (London), April 11, 2007; Alex Young, "UK 'Megan's Law' Plans Restricted," Birmingham (UK) Post, April 11, 2007.

83. At time of this writing, the following provinces permit public access to government-run Web registries: Alberta, British Columbia, Manitoba, Newfoundland, Ontario, and Saskatchewan. Quebec, for its part, rejected a proposal to make its registry public, citing concerns of vigilantism. According the province's public security minister: "There is a great risk as we saw in the US that people would take justice into their own hands . . . we don't want that kind of society." Kristy Rich, "Sex Offender Registry Won't Be Made Public," *CJAD.com*, November 21, 2007, http://www.cjad.com/news/565/625125.

84. "List of 671 Sex Criminals Made Public," *Korea Times*, September 25, 2002. Eligible offenses include: child prostitution, trafficking of minors, production or distribution of child pornography, and rape or sexual assault of minors. Junseob Shin and Young-Boon Lee, "Korean Version of the Notification Policy on Sexual Offenders: Did It Enhance Public Awareness of Sexual Crimes Against Minors?" *International Journal of Offender Therapy & Comparative Criminology* 49 (2005): 378–79.

85. Dong Keun Lee, "Country Report-Korea," in *Annual Report for 2006* (Tokyo: UNAFEI, August 2007), 113–14.

86. Chung Ah-young, "Sex Offenders Face Tougher Penalties," *Korea Times* (April 6, 2006).

## Conclusion

1. Jeremy Bentham, "Principles of Penal Law," in *Works of Jeremy Bentham*, vol. 1, ed. John Bowring (Edinburgh: William Tait, 1843), 557.

2. Stanley Cohen, *Folk Devils and Moral Panics: The Creation of Mods and Rockers*, 3rd ed. (New York: Routledge, 2002), 1.

3. Ian Loader and Neil Walker, *Civilizing Security* (Cambridge: Cambridge University Press, 2007), 234.

4. Richard Ford, "Reid Proposes Register for Terror Offenders," *Times* (London), June 7, 2007.

# INDEX

Critical Perspectives on Crime and Law

**Edited by Markus D. Dubber**

**Vera Bergelson**, *Victims' Rights and Victims' Wrongs: Comparative Liability in Criminal Law*
2009

**Markus D. Dubber and Mariana Valverde, editors**, *Police and the Liberal State*
2008

**David Alan Sklansky**, *Democracy and the Police*
2007

**Markus D. Dubber and Lindsay Farmer, editors**, *Modern Histories of Crime and Punishment*
2007

**Markus D. Dubber and Mariana Valverde, editors**, *The New Police Science: The Police Power in Domestic and International Governance*
2006